A Valuable Property

THE LIFE STORY OF MICHAEL TODD

Michael Todd, Jr.
and Susan McCarthy Todd

PaperJacks LTD.

Markham, Ontario, Canada

PaperJacks

One of a series of books
published by PaperJacks Ltd.

A VALUABLE PROPERTY: The Life Story of Michael Todd

Published by arrangement with Arbor House Publishing Company.

Arbor House edition published 1983

PaperJacks edition published July 1984

ISBN 0-7701-0299-9

Acknowledgments

To all the people I have quoted who were so generous with their time. (Some of these quotes were taken from filmed interviews that were part of a television program I did about my father in 1968.)

And to Dick Williams, who took many of the photos included in this book.

My special thanks to my friend, James Odell, for his encouragement and editorial advice.

Foreword

The Michael Todd in this book is the man I knew and loved. He was unique and he gave me the most precious gift I have ever received—his love.

His devotion was total, and because of his pride and confidence in me I gained an inner strength that has never deserted me, although at the time of his death I thought I could never go on without him.

Mike created excitement wherever he went and his enthusiasm for life gave an extra dimension to even the quiet and peaceful times we spent together.

As detailed in this book, there was much of Mike's earlier life that I neither knew about nor of course shared. But I knew, because Mike told me so and because I could sense and feel it, our time together was the beginning of his achieving his life's ambitions.

In this book Michael Jr. gives a loving account of Mike's amazing life, and I'm pleased that others can now share in some measure the joyful experience of knowing Michael Todd.

—Elizabeth Taylor

Introduction

My father, Michael Todd, had a long and flamboyant theatrical career. It alternated between spectacular successes and extended periods of failure. He always surmounted the failures to achieve even greater successes.

He was married three times: twenty-three years to my mother, then to Joan Blondell and finally to Elizabeth Taylor.

It is a quarter of a century since his death, and his fame and accomplishments have faded in the memory of those over thirty-five and are unknown to those who have yet to reach middle age. The people who knew him spark with enthusiasm when they speak of him today. He was exciting and amusing, likable and forceful.

In the spring of 1957, nine months before he was killed in the crash of his private plane, my father and I flew back together from the Boston premiere of his film *Around the World in 80 Days*. We were circling to come in for a landing at La Guardia when he turned to me out of the blue and said, "Whatever else you do, hold on to the story of my life. It's colorful, dramatic and covers an era. It will be a valuable property."

There is nothing I've ever had a share in that has been of greater value to me.

—Michael Todd, Jr.

CHAPTER 1

THE EVENTS OF my father's early life read like a Jewish Horatio Alger story. He was born on or about June 22, 1907, in Minneapolis, the seventh of eight children of Chaim and Sophia Hellerman Goldbogen—recent immigrants from Poland—and their first child to be born in the United States. Before he was ten there were weeks that he made more money than his father. At thirteen he was the youngest person in the history of the state of Illinois to be granted an assistant pharmaceutical license. At fifteen he was a college president—a self-proclaimed president of a bricklayer's college. Four months short of age sixteen he was married. By the time he was nineteen he had made and lost a million dollars in the construction business in Chicago. He moved to California when he was twenty and landed contracts to build some of the first sound stages used for the "talkies." This launched his second successful career as a general contractor, but it soon collapsed with the onset of the Great Depression. At an age when most young men are just beginning their first business career, he had had dramatic ups and downs in over half a dozen.

He was born at home but his birth was never registered. His parents spoke and thought in Yiddish and marked time by the Hebrew calendar. His birth was remembered only as coming so many days after a minor Jewish holy day, and with the Jewish holy days falling on different dates from year to year, the exact date of his birth could never be verified.

During his marriage to Joan Blondell, he returned from a trip to Minneapolis with a birth certificate that gave the year of his birth as 1909. He and Joan were the guests of honor at the Aquatennial, an annual civic festival, and he became a close friend of Hubert Humphrey, who was then the mayor of Minneapolis. On his last visit to Minneapolis, for the opening of *Around the World in 80 Days* in 1957, when he was newly married to Elizabeth Taylor, he obtained a birth certificate giving the year of his birth as 1911. I'm sure his continued friendship with Senator Humphrey helped.

If Humphrey had become President, my father would have wound up younger than I.

Dad's father and grandfather were both Orthodox rabbis. My father had no interest in religion—he was guided by his belief in himself and his admiration and respect for his father. He meant it when he said, "My father was my college."

Chaim Goldbogen was the gentle, studious son of a highly respected rabbi, Moishe Goldbogen. When Chaim was sixteen, a marriage was arranged for him with the nineteen-year-old daughter of the Hellermans, the wealthiest Jewish family in Drubnin, Poland. With the support of the Hellermans, Chaim became a rabbi and raised a family. Persecuted and ruined financially during the pogroms in the first decade of the century, Chaim Goldbogen brought his wife and children to Minneapolis, where a brother-in-law had earlier settled. The small Jewish community there did not require a second rabbi. Chaim had no experience or ability in business, and a series of small enterprises and jobs ended in failure. The three eldest sons— Joe, Frank and Carl—all left home in their mid-teens and supported themselves. Chaim moved the family to nearby Bloomington, where he was able to make a marginal living operating a general store. He never gave up his hope of finding a congregation, and during his stay in Minnesota he maintained a position in the Orthodox community by doing the prescribed form of slaughtering required for kosher meats. This provided him with a steady, if small, supplement to his meager income. In 1918 his ambitions were realized when he was offered a congregation on the Near Northwest side of Chicago.

My mother's father, David Freshman, who also immigrated to the United States in 1903, soon became very prosperous. By the end of World War I, he was the owner of a successful tavern and retail liquor outlet in Boston. When Prohibition wiped out this enterprise, he moved to Chicago and within a couple of years had a thriving wholesale grocery business.

The Freshman family dismissed Chaim Goldbogen's inadequacy as a breadwinner because of their reverence for his character. I never heard my Grandmother Freshman speak so highly of anyone as she did of my father's father. She would glowingly describe him as a truly wise and gentle man, with great dignity and wit, and even taciturn Grandfather Freshman would grudgingly nod his concurrence.

My father's most often used conversational preamble was "As my father used to say . . ." While this was a fixed cliché with him, there was always a discernible note of respect in his voice that indicated a measure of his feeling for his father. As did his older brothers, Dad realized early on that he would have to rely on his own abilities for his economic welfare, but his father's personal and moral values set an example to emulate for life.

As a youngster my father was called Toaty or Toady. There are two versions of how he acquired his nickname. His older brothers and sisters maintained that even at the earliest age he was always running out of the house, busy with his elaborate schemes. The coatrack was above his reach, and not able to properly pronounce the word, he was always screaming for someone to "Gimme my toat!"

My father's version is that at the age of four he became friends with the local garbage man, whose nickname was Toady, helping him collect trash. Dad soon got Toady to let him accompany him on his route. Toady would often let him sit on his lap and hold the horses' reins. They spent so much time together that Dad's family and friends started calling *him* Toady. Later this became corrupted and shortened to Todd.

My father named me Michael as an anglicized version of Moishe, in memory of his grandfather. Several years after my birth, when my father got into show business and decided the name Avrom Goldbogen—or as he was commonly called, *Abe* Goldbogen—did not have a theatrical ring to it, he legally changed it to Michael Todd. Michael, because he liked the name he had given me. I called him Daddy Todd until I was six or seven. Until he was in his twenties, family and friends most often called him Todd. Later he was usually called Mike by those closest to him.

As with most of Todd's enterprises, his association with Toady, the garbage man, had an extra kicker. He was able to accumulate all kinds of interesting pieces of junk. Either through barter or direct sale he converted his collection of odds and ends into cash.

Like other poor kids, Todd took up shining shoes. As he told the story, there was a brothel in his Minneapolis neighborhood that attracted his attention because of the volume of well-dressed men who frequented the establishment. In addition to the greater number of shoeshining jobs he could get outside the brothel, Todd enjoyed listening to the piano music he heard coming from the front parlor of the house. The madam, however, often had the janitor shoo Todd away, because she didn't want a pesky kid soliciting her customers on her doorstep. This particular kid was not easily shooed away and was occasionally used for running an errand. The madam finally thought of a way to get Todd off her doorstep. She gave him a handful of calling cards and told him that if he took his shoeshine box and himself to Hennepin Avenue and gave a card to each customer when he finished the shine, he could come back to the house at the end of his working hours and collect a quarter for each card returned to her and get a fresh supply.

Soon after learning to read, Todd became intrigued by the Boys Wanted ads he saw in newspapers and magazines. They held out the promise, extravagantly illustrated, that a valuable gift would be given to any enterprising boy who could sell a boxload of the advertiser's product. Todd's initial venture in this field required him to sell a gross lot of blueing at a nickel a throw; in return, he was to be rewarded with a magnificent banjo. Even with his diligence, it was not easy to get rid of 144 boxes of blueing. The sixteen-inch toy banjo he received in return for the seven dollars plus proceeds of his sales was clearly an insult to his intelligence. For several years Todd answered every one of these ads, but now the proceeds went directly into his own pocket.

Todd talked about his first regular job:

> I worked for a pitchman in Minneapolis . . . and I had a
> knife through my neck. I was known as the shill to get the
> tip . . . the tip means the "crowd". . . . Now this pitchman,
> Doc Benton, was probably the guy who started me in show
> business and I was about seven years old.

His younger brother Dave described one of Todd's next ventures:

> Attracted on Saturdays by such stirring serials as *Stingeree*, he began hanging around the Zone Picture Palace in our neighborhood. By helping to set up the folding chairs and cleaning up after the shows, he so ingratiated himself with the manager that he landed himself a job. Among his other duties he was stationed at the side door to make sure no kids could sneak in. Todd drew fifteen cents a week for his work, but he soon found a way to supplement this salary when, during the First World War, an amusement tax skyrocketed the admission to six cents. Todd dropped the word around the neighborhood that if you came to the side door, not only could you have the benefit of the original five cents admission, but two could come in for that price. Todd was doing great until one day a couple of kids went up to the box office and demanded the two-for-five-cents admission, whereupon the manager booted out his side-door partner.

Early in life Todd developed the ability to turn adversities into assets. When his tonsils were removed at the age of nine, he made his way back to school the next day and charged each classmate two cents to look at his tonsil-less throat.

In one of his noncommercial childhood activities, Todd picked up a rudimentary knowledge of music that was useful to him throughout the rest of his life. During his childhood a municipal benefactor founded an institution called the Minneapolis Working Boys Marching Band. There is only one word that could adequately describe the uniforms of that band—splendiferous. Todd had to have one. The catch was that aside from being able to march, you had to be able to make a reasonable pretense at playing an instrument. Anything Todd did was all out. He saved up from his various commercial enterprises and bought a cornet from a hock shop. He quickly learned to play a few Sousa tunes. He got his uniform. When his father moved the family to Bloomington, Todd was devastated. Not only would his business ventures be curtailed by living in such a small village, but he would have to resign from the Minneapolis Working Boys Marching Band and return his uniform.

Living in the country—and Bloomington, Minnesota, in those days was very much in the country—held little interest for Todd. He claimed that he commuted almost daily to Minneapolis, not only for the commercial opportunities it offered, but for the cultural ones as well.

Even as a kid he was a big spender—no piggy banks for Todd. He left judiciously small amounts of cash at home to help out the family, and with the balance of his earnings he indulged himself in Minneapolis with food and entertainment. He often described as the most enjoyable meals of his life those he had at the Baltimore Dairy Lunch, where for a quarter you could get a Minneapolis version of a Delmonico feast. His other indulgence was second balcony seats for touring theatrical companies and the occasional opera.

When the family moved to Chicago as the war was ending in 1918, the big city offered Todd's enterprising nature a wider scope, and his projects took a more deliberate turn. Todd's formal education ended in the sixth grade. He was kicked out of school when he was caught running a crap game in the school yard. A younger schoolmate and neighborhood chum, the comedian Jack E. Leonard (né Fats Libitsky), said:

Mike Todd arrived from a small town in Minnesota called Bloomington and moved into our neighborhood, called the Wicker Park area. His father was assigned to a synagogue in our neighborhood. His father was a very wonderfully educated-type man. He was a rabbi and Mike was a pretty sharp little kid. I'll never forget, he was here only about three or four days when he decided to form a fraternal club. He charged us about three-cents-a-month dues, which he of course put in his own pocket. He also promoted a man called Mr. Moore, who owned a boiler factory in our poor neighborhood, to give us a shed for a clubhouse. He also talked this Mr. Moore into giving us a pool table.

You see, Mike became the head man in the crap game in the school yard and I was to get ten cents to be the lookout. I was to watch out for the cops. Incidentally, Mike never paid me.

Soon after his arrival in Chicago, Todd got the better of a con game operator. Hanging around a neighborhood street carnival, he became fascinated with the improbability of the action at one of the booths. The game seemed simple enough. A player would pay ten cents to try to toss three balls into a wooden bucket, tilted on a board at the back of the booth. If all three of the balls stayed inside the bucket, the player would win a live duck. While Todd was watching, some players were able to get two balls in and win a junk prize, but nobody was able to get three balls to remain in the bucket. During the course of a long evening, drifting away and then back to the booth, he became convinced that there was something more than met the eye going on, as the original contingent of ducks was still intact.

Todd hung around until the carnival closed for the night. He saw a kid his own age crawling out from the canvas under the platform, and from the way the kid was stretching and rubbing himself, it was clear he had spent a long time in a cramped position. Coming closer, Todd overheard the kid complain that a whole night lying underneath the bucket was worth more than thirty-five cents. The pitchman was deaf to the kid's arguments.

When the grumbling kid departed, Todd said he would work the next night for two bits. His offer was accepted. He was to lie under the tilted board and pull a spring attached to the bottom of the bucket that would bounce one ball out when the pitchman gave Todd his cue by shouting, "Pitch 'til you win!"

Todd and a neighborhood pal decided they would bag a collection of ducks. When the boss yelled, "Pitch 'til you win!" Todd's friend would shout out his reply, "I will, mister!" as the signal for Todd not to pull the spring. By the time his friend had won the fourth duck, Todd could hear the pitchman's shout of "Pitch 'til you win!" from the corner a block away, where he had arranged to meet his accomplice to divvy the spoils.

When he left school in the sixth grade, Todd got his first full-time job at a drugstore on the corner of Division and Wood. He began as the errand boy and was so conscientious that he was soon made a soda jerk. He liked to recall that at the end of his first day's work in the store he found a five-dollar bill lying under the counter, close to the cash register. Suspecting a plant, Todd immediately picked up the bill and ran it over to his boss, who was behind the drug counter. The boss was delighted with his newly promoted soda jerk. When Todd indicated he wanted to take up the study of pharmacy, his employer gave him enthusiastic encouragement and guidance. In less than a year, while attending to his regular duties, he took the state pharmaceutical exam. At thirteen, he was the youngest person to win an assistant pharmaceutical license in Illinois.

As a qualified pharmacist working behind a drugstore counter, his wages were increased. Todd's income was further supplemented. This was Prohibition, and a palatable form of alcohol could be dispensed for a variety of medicinal purposes under a doctor's prescription. Customers were grateful when Todd indicated he had given them extra measure on their prescriptions, and his generosity was always rewarded with a nice tip.

He was now making a great deal more money than his father and could afford to indulge his taste for fine food, clothes and entertainment. His mother knew his stipulated wage and was delighted when he contributed almost all of it to the family budget. He was making more from tips than his wages and could easily afford to rent an inexpensive apartment, where he kept a wardrobe of flashy clothes to wear on evenings out. He could now buy lavish meals and orchestra seats at the theater. "From when I was a kid," Todd said, "I could be out three days at a time, and they didn't know I was gone." So the family had no suspicions about the double life he was leading.

In the Roaring Twenties, Todd's older sister Shirley was a flapper deluxe, married to a prosperous contractor, Philip Maas, who gave her jewels, a fashionable wardrobe and a Pierce-Arrow. Maas taught Todd how to drive the car and took him along as chauffeur on weekend trips that he and Shirley made to the tony resorts of Wisconsin and Michigan. Maas loved opera and Shirley didn't, so Todd got to see a lot of operas. Maas liked poetry and read highbrow literature. To keep up his end of their conversations, Todd did a crash course in the classics.

He tried to learn as much as he could about the construction business from his brother-in-law, thinking he could follow in Maas's footsteps and make his own fortune. Maas, although glad to share his avocations with Todd, was not interested in giving Todd a business education. Although he was making good money, Todd felt that working behind a pharmacy counter was leading him nowhere.

He got a job as a salesman in a Florsheim shoe store. Customers were waited on in rotation. If a salesman was unable to make a sale after showing a customer several pairs of shoes, or if he simply was irritated by the customer, he could go into the stockroom and pass on the difficult customer to another salesman. If the second salesman was able to consummate a sale with the rejected customer, his commission was higher than if it were a first-time sale. Although he was the youngest salesman in the store, Todd soon became the master of the second sale and was

earning more than any other salesman. He was made the assistant sales manager.

His success went to his head. The Florsheim brothers had a
suggestion box in each of their stores. From day one of his
employment Todd had been stuffing the box with instructions
on how to improve the operation of the business. No acknowledgment or recognition was ever given to his brainstorms. Soon
after his appointment as assistant manager, Todd felt he had to
take matters into his own hands.

After several urgent requests, he secured an appointment
with Irving Florsheim. Mr. Florsheim, thinking that he was
about to be informed about shrinkage in the inventory or some
other form of theft, was totally taken aback by Todd's nonstop
barrage on how to completely overhaul the operation of the
Florsheim shoe company. Todd was fired on the spot.

As Irving and Harold Florsheim told Todd many years later,
they did not feel quite ready, back in 1922, to take in a third
partner, especially a fifteen-year-old one.

With no capital and no particular scheme in mind to promote,
Todd looked for another job after the Florsheim experience,
determined to get out on his own as soon as possible. With
ill-defined prospects, but with the notion it would lead to something else, he took a job trimming windows. He soon proved to
his employer that he was capable of handling his work without
supervision. He won a small prize from a drug firm for the best
display of its products in the Chicago area when he created a
twenty-foot replica of their toothpaste tube as a window center-
piece.

With some money saved, he went into business for himself.
He concentrated on special sales promotions for small-store
owners. Recalling his window-trimming career, Todd said: "To
get the curtain up, I'd plaster the storefronts with posters in
huge red letters, announcing: 'FINAL LIQUIDATION,' 'DRAS-
TIC PRICE CUTS,' 'ALL GOODS MUST GO,' 'LEASE END-
ING,' and for a few days you'd have to fight off the customers.
But it was a tough act to follow."

Working part time in his brother-in-law's construction business, Todd learned that there was a big shortage of bricklayers
in Chicago. A building boom was under way and union bricklayers were earning big money, fifteen dollars a day. Todd established the American College of Bricklaying in a rented hall on
the Near North Side. He borrowed bricks, sand and mortar from

his brother-in-law and bought secondhand trowels. His faculty consisted of one retired bricklayer. The largest part of his investment was dedicated to classified ads: "EARN FIFTEEN DOLLARS A DAY—BECOME A BRICKLAYER!" More than one hundred students enrolled at twenty-five dollars a head for tuition. No cement was used in the mortar. At the end of the day the students were required to wash off the bricks so that they could be used again in the next day's classes. It was a two-week course, and after expenses Todd cleared almost two thousand dollars. However, when the first class graduated and discovered that their diploma from the American College of Bricklaying did not gain them entry into the union, as had been clearly implied but not stated by Todd in his ads and welcoming speech, Todd's career as a college president was at an end.

With his profits from the bricklaying school, Todd got together with his older brother Frank, and they helped their father buy and renovate the house at 2034 West LeMoyne Avenue, which the family had been renting since their arrival from Bloomington.

Frank had enlisted in the navy at the age of fourteen and served on a gunboat in China before World War I. Including his service during the war, Frank had been on overseas duty for almost ten years and had returned to Chicago with a substantial savings. He was now a chief warrant officer assigned to the Ninth Naval District Intelligence Office, which was located in the Loop.

As the family's house was being renovated, Todd and Frank became frustrated by the fact that for each part of the job they had to deal with a different contractor—electrical, plastering, plumbing. The contractors were either getting in each other's way, or would not start their work until one of the other contractors had finished his work.

This gave Todd the idea of forming a general contracting firm, which would have various specialists as subcontractors, and would assume complete responsibility for an entire renovation. General home repair contracting, a new thing in the Chicago building trade at that time, would make financing easier for the customer. Todd talked his brother Frank into joining him. Frank's naval duties were minimal and since he was over twenty-one he could legally sign contracts.

Borrowing the name of the grocery chain, they formed the Atlantic and Pacific Construction Company. They opened an office on LaSalle Street, in the same building where Frank was stationed, so that he could slip away from the Intelligence Office to mind the store while Todd was out hustling customers. Again, the major initial investment was newspaper ads:

DON'T WAIT—YOU TOO CAN BE A HAPPY HOMEOWNER

Be the First One on Your Block to Modernize Your Home
Call Today

THE ATLANTIC AND PACIFIC CONSTRUCTION COMPANY

Todd—barely fifteen—was an enthusiastic and effective salesman. He left the callers with wondrous visions of the home improvements the Atlantic and Pacific Construction Company could provide. The fact was, a real service was performed—the work was coordinated and professionally done. Another fact was that this kind of work qualified for mechanic's liens, if this proved necessary, ensuring that these payments came before all other obligations on the property, including a first mortgage, so that there were no risks involved once a contract was signed, other than performing the work specified—at a profit. The business flourished.

Although he had been dating for a few years, Todd's contacts with girls had been infrequent and uncomplicated. As a prosperous businessman he now felt ready for a more serious involvement. He became interested in a young beauty named Leah Comroe. He had a snappy red roadster, lots of spending money and he was good company. Leah could take that much seriously, but when after a few months Todd pressed his attentions Leah would not go along.

To put Leah in her place, Todd started dating one of her best friends, Bertha Freshman. Bertha liked Todd and felt she could handle him. Before moving to Chicago she had been admitted to the Boston Latin School, a notable academic accomplishment. She was an honor student in Chicago. She was the eldest of seven surviving Freshman children, and having helped her mother for years manage the younger children, she was poised and self-confident. She was also very attractive. When Todd pressed his attentions he was not rebuffed, but was put off and pointed toward marriage. On Valentine's Day, 1923, they eloped and were married by a justice of the peace in Crown Point, Indiana.

With the experience and profits made from the remodeling business, it was an ambitious but logical step to go on to contracting for the construction of a complete home. After making money building half a dozen, Todd and Frank took the even bolder step of bidding on a larger construction job. With the low bid and some fast talk from Todd they won the contract to build an apartment house. Frank handled the business end, providing the credit and credibility for the bridging loans to cover their construction costs. Several years' work and all their accumulated capital would evaporate if they mismanaged this job.

From hanging around his brother-in-law Philip Maas, and from the day-to-day experience gained during the growth of the Atlantic and Pacific Construction Company, Todd had picked up firsthand knowledge of almost every aspect of the building trades. With the help of Frank, who now stole even more time from the navy, Todd personally superintended every step of the construction of the five-story apartment building their future depended on. It came in on time, on budget, and fully up to specifications. The client was pleased, and the bonding house with which Frank had arranged the financing was satisfied.

Todd and Frank were now in the construction business in a big way. They built apartment buildings all over the North Side of Chicago. They built a housing development in the suburbs. They were subcontractors of a large portion of the construction of a block-square water pumping station. At the age of eighteen, Todd had assets in excess of a million dollars—on paper. He had plenty of folding money as well. He built a small town house for Bertha and himself on Goethe Street near the lake, one of the most fashionable neighborhoods in the city.

An early taste of luxuries had whetted Todd's appetite; he was now fully able to indulge himself. He and Bertha bought all the clothes they desired. Although they took only the occasional trip out of the city, he bought a car to rival that of Philip Maas. He and Frank paid off the mortgage on their parents' house and fully furnished it.

In lieu of full payment of the construction costs on some of the apartment buildings, they held second mortgages and operated the buildings in partnership with their clients. My Uncle Frank told me that as hard and capable a businessman as my father was, he was a soft touch with tenants who were delinquent with their rent in the buildings they controlled. So soft that he not only carried their arrears; but if a convincingly sad story went with it, he was good for a loan out of his own pocket. He was in need of one himself after a couple of years at the top.

The Atlantic and Pacific Construction Company's bonding house folded and Todd went broke. He was unable to meet the mortgage payments on his own house.

Frank was in much better shape. He was single, still drawing pay from the navy and had been investing his profits from the business in the rapidly rising stock market. Before the dust had settled on the collapse of Todd's first construction empire, the design for his second was formulated.

With the success of *The Jazz Singer,* it occurred to Todd that the film studios would need to adapt their stages for the recording of sound. One of the selling points for the homes and apartments built by the Atlantic and Pacific Construction Company was how quiet they were. This was made possible by the innovation of applying Celotex tiles to the ceilings as an effective soundproofing device. Todd had been using Celotex tiles for years and considered himself an expert in soundproofing.

He received a loan from Frank and went to the coast to sell his expertise to the film studios. Talking fast as his money was short, Todd won a contract to soundproof Columbia's film stages.

This gave him a new start, but things were still a bit tight, and he devised an ingenious scheme for getting himself a home in California. Bids were invited to demolish three houses that stood on the site of an intended office building. Todd submitted the low bid. He wrecked two of the houses and moved the third one to a vacant lot that he had bought a block and a half away. He had a new home and had made a slight profit in the process of acquiring it.

Todd's new construction business began to thrive. He built office buildings and developed a successful subdivision. He repaid the loan to Frank and persuaded Philip Maas, whose building business in Chicago had failed, to come out to the coast to assist him. On his twenty-first birthday, in 1928, Todd was well on his way to making his second million.

He had always been a gambler, and with his renewed prosperity he had sizable sums to wager. He developed a weakness for betting on horses. He began associating with people in the film business and other free spenders who introduced him to golf. When he began to feel that he could play the game, he wagered on this as well.

The rules of golf permit you to carry up to fourteen clubs in your bag. Todd started out with an incomplete set, and as his interest and ability developed he began trying different clubs. He picked up an oddball club called a chipper—a slightly elongated, lofted and heavier putter, designed to be used from just off the surface of the green to run the ball up to the pin. Todd became handy with this club.

One day, to liven up a match, he made a big bet with an opponent, who was proudly displaying an expensive new set of clubs, that he could beat him playing with only his chipper. The opponent had a caddy to carry his full set of golf clubs. Todd, not to be outdone, hired a caddy to carry his chipper and the three cigars he smoked during a round of golf. Todd won, and for the rest of his life played golf using only that chipper.

I played with him only three or four times, and it was demoralizing to be struggling with a full set of clubs as he blithely made use of one simple stick throughout the entire round. Because the shaft of the chipper was short, he would stand only a few inches away from the ball. With his arms stretched straight down he took a big pendulumlike swing and, to my irritation, drove the ball about 180 yards straight down the middle of the fairway. His scores were always in the mid eighties.

He made one of his first substantial betting coups during the late twenties while attending a Hollywood Angels baseball game. The crowd he went with didn't just bet on the outcome of the game; there was a continual series of wagers being made— pitch by pitch, inning by inning. Todd had bet on the Hollywood Angels against the San Francisco Seals, and in the top of the sixth the Seals scored five to stretch their lead over the Angels to eight runs. Angel backers in his section started to leave the stadium in disgust. Todd collared as many as he could and offered to buy their bets for ten cents on the dollar. By the top of the ninth, with the score still the same, he was buying Angel bets for a couple of cents on the dollar and had bought close to five thousand dollars in bets for a little more than two hundred dollars. In the bottom of the ninth, the Angels scored nine runs to win the game.

At the end of 1929, Todd's second successful construction business folded. This time his brother Frank was unable to extend him a loan for a fresh start. Less than a year before, Frank had resigned from the navy, with only a year and a half to go before he could take his twenty-year retirement, which would have entitled him to half pay for the rest of his life. He had made a fortune in the market, and many weeks the rise in the value of his stocks greatly exceeded a year's navy retirement pay— why stick it out?

As Frank tells it, on Thursday, October 24, 1929, he skipped breakfast to get in early to his stockbroker's office, as the market had been jittery and he was apprehensive about the recent downward fluctuations. He was greatly relieved when the market opened strong; and when a friend suggested they go out for a cup of coffee he was glad to join him. Frank said, "I was very hungry and had a ham sandwich. We got to talking and had several cups of coffee. When I got back to the broker's office, the panic was on. Like a lot of guys, I sat there paralyzed, not believing what I was seeing on the board and thinking the market would bounce back any minute. At the end of the trading day, I counted up my losses and figured out that the ham sandwich had cost me $650,000."

Todd was struggling on the coast, not too successfully, to keep a remnant of his construction business going, when he got a wire from Frank, on September 30, 1931, telling him that their father had died from a massive hemorrhage of a duodenal ulcer.

In the Orthodox Jewish religion, the dead are buried within twenty-four hours, unless the Sabbath or a holy day intervenes. Todd had to be there. He wired Frank to delay the funeral one day. It took three days to get to Chicago by train. Todd made arrangements to fly with the mail in an open two-seater biplane. When he arrived at his family's house he was arrested. The check he had written to pay for the flight home had bounced. Frank, with the Freshman family's assistance, got him out on bail so that he could attend the funeral.

My grandfather's body was brought to the cemetery in a handsome wooden casket. In accordance with Hebrew law, his body was removed from the casket and buried face down in the grave, in a shroud. At the end of the service, the undertakers started to carry away the casket. In Orthodox funerals, the family pays for the casket, and the undertakers continue to use it. Todd found a strange way to give vent to the sorrow and frustration he felt at his father's death. Grabbing his brothers Dave and Frank, he told the undertakers to put the coffin on the ground. He and his brothers pulled the coffin off to one side. Trying to maintain their dignity, the undertakers protested. Todd lit a piece of newspaper and threw it into the coffin. As the undertakers tried to save it, Todd shouted that he and his brothers had paid for the coffin and this was what they chose to do with it. The three brothers silently stood guard until the coffin was a pile of smoldering ashes.

This act so struck a responsive note in my uncles that I heard them retell the story many times.

A short time after my grandfather died Todd moved back to Chicago. Bertha's family loaned him the money to square his debts on the coast. For a year or so her family provided enough money to keep us going and put Todd on the dole of a dollar a day for pocket money. He got involved with various friends in a variety of unsuccessful gambling schemes, from punchboards to bookmaking.

Whippet racing, making use of the diminutive breed of greyhounds, had been a big thing in the twenties. Todd and an old neighborhood pal, Joe Bigelow, got the idea of training white mice to run around a miniature track. They clipped their tails with the notion that they would call this new sport "Clippet Racing." To give the promotion a dash of panache, Todd claimed to have imported a special breed of white mice from South America. That was the only dash in the scheme, as they could never train the mice to race.

Todd had made and lost two fortunes by his early twenties. Now, like the rest of the country, he was trying to struggle his way out of the depths of the Great Depression. Imagination and experience were all he had to work with. Show business was a field where imagination was almost everything. He spent the remainder of his life in show business.

CHAPTER 2

WALTER MATTHAU, AFTER long years of receiving outstanding reviews in many minor and several starring roles on the stage and in the movies, finally achieved national prominence and stardom in the stage production of *The Odd Couple*. He said at the time, "All you need to become an overnight success in show business is twenty-two good breaks."

It was Todd's ambition to become the next Florenz Ziegfeld. He spent five years struggling in Chicago to launch his career on Broadway. His first attempt was with a comedy he coauthored about a producer who had the same ambition as Todd—*Call Me Ziggy*. It was a fiasco. A year later he produced a play that almost made it. His third production, *The Hot Mikado*, received fabulous notices. Business was good for the first few weeks of its run, but an unusual set of circumstances made it a certainty that the show would never earn back its investment. Here was where the "boy genius"—as he was to be labeled in the New York press a few years later—was separated from the boys, when his quick thinking and action turned a sure loser into his first big show business bonanza.

His ambition to be a top producer forced him to create a variety of projects that were often on the outer fringes of show business. His total commitment to his career and the necessity to put some bread on the table made him less than the stereotyped ideal father during the early years of my childhood. There was a considerable strain on my mother, who didn't want to undermine his ambitions but greatly desired the security and stability offered by a steady job, which was always available through her family. She stood by him when he began to have even modest successes, but her innate uneasiness about show business was a San Andreas Fault beneath their marriage. Her jealous nature was fueled by his close proximity to beautiful show girls and justifiably inflamed by his attachment to one in particular. By the time his success in show business as a Broadway producer was of a quality and degree that satisfied her, they were a world apart.

Shortly before I got married, I asked my father what he thought of my fiancée. He said, "She's a really wonderful girl . . . for a civilian." Anyone not involved in show business was, in my father's lexicon, a civilian. Much more than anything else, the fatal flaw in my parents' marriage was that Bertha was a civilian. After Bertha he had no serious romantic involvements with anyone outside show business.

It was a frantic scramble for Todd during the thirties to become a master showman. But there was no need to transform his personality—since his youth he had been a showman disguised in civvies. Paper, pencil and persistence provided him with an entry into the theatrical world.

Talking pictures had accelerated the death of vaudeville, but a modified form hung on as a supplement to the movies. Every large city had a few so-called presentation houses where an abbreviated live stage show shared the bill with a feature film. There were several in Chicago, and the comedy acts were always in search of fresh material.

The show business publication *Variety*, in addition to carrying all theatrical news, including listings of all touring stage shows, was an effective go-between for acts needing material and writers trying to sell it. A cross section of theatrical people— press agents, performers, promoters—crowded into the tiny *Variety* office in Chicago, exchanging news and gossip, with the hope that ideas and leads for work might develop.

The Chicago *Variety* correspondent was Danny Goldberg, a quiet man with a wry sense of humor. In order to get on with his own work, he had to turn a deaf ear to the continual barrage of improbable schemes and publicist hyperbole that was directed at him. Being a kindly soul, he kept an appreciative smile and an attentive look on his face, while he typed away or worked on the phone.

Todd, trying to sell jokes and sketches he had written, romanced Danny as much as any woman he ever went after in his life. Goldberg was amused by Todd, and in an effort to get rid of him told him where and how he might be able to sell his material. Todd sold some gags to local radio and skits to touring acts and helped Goldberg write a humorous column for *Variety*.

Todd got permission from Harold Costello, the owner of the Oriental Theatre Building, to improvise an office of sorts for himself. Jule Styne, the Broadway composer and producer who later wrote the music for such shows as *High Button Shoes, Gentlemen Prefer Blondes, Bells Are Ringing, Gypsy* and *Funny Girl*, described this setup:

> I grew up with Mike in Chicago. He was one of the greatest salesmen and hustlers I ever met in my life and I used to pal around with him. He used to come out to my house. He loved cold fried fish. My mother would fry it up the night before and put it in the icebox. Mike could eat that cold fried fish till it came out of his ears. I wasn't a songwriter then, I was just another piano player around Chicago. Mike liked me. He said, "You aren't going to be just a piano player all your life, you're going to be a big songwriter." He always borrowed money from me—a dollar a day.
>
> Mike opened an office and I was his partner. It was on the eighteenth floor of the Oriental Theatre Building, but the eighteenth floor was a Masonic Hall where the Masons met once a week. So we took an anteroom, and we'd drag in pulpits—Mike's desk was two of those high pulpits pushed together. He did all his work standing up. We put a long cord on a telephone that was there for the Masons and pulled it into our office. We had our own little sign outside the door, saying "Mike Todd Productions." Every night we'd hide the sign and push the pulpits back into the hall.
>
> One day Mike came to me and said, "I got this idea for a production number for the Chicago Theatre." He told me the idea. The number was to be called "The Moth and the Flame."
>
> "You are out of your mind," I said.
>
> "I want you to write the tune," Mike insisted.
>
> "Who's going to write the lyrics?"
>
> "What do you mean, 'Who's going to write the lyrics?' *I* am."
>
> "What are the lyrics about, Mike?"
>
> "You know . . . the moth and the flame and you are to blame."
>
> "Oooh nooo . . ." I said.

"Just write it. You do the tune. I'll have the words. I'm going out to sell it."

He came back in about an hour and said, "I sold it." And he gave me two hundred dollars.

"You're going to write the lyrics, Mike? Where are they?"

"Here are the lyrics." He gave them to me, and they were ghastly. But what did I care. I had two hundred dollars, a fortune in those days . . . and just for writing a tune on a piece of paper.

"You must have gotten four hundred dollars for selling the song. Is that right, Mike?"

"No," he said, "I got five hundred dollars. I took three. I think I'm entitled to a hundred for selling it."

Now, with his foot in the door, Todd hung around the *Variety* office even more, sounding out his increasingly ambitious plans. He bullied Goldberg into an association that lasted through the thirties. Goldberg became Todd's advisor, confidant, collaborator and sometime partner. Two more contrasting personalities can hardly be imagined. They had a warm and friendly appreciation of each other but in later years, after Todd became prominent, they both made light of their early days together. For his part, Todd didn't want to acknowledge that he had required assistance to get his career launched. He cultivated the image that Mike Todd was wholly a creation of his own imagination. True enough, but Danny Goldberg was the collaborator who helped Todd gain the experience and confidence that enabled him to get going. Goldberg enjoyed his privacy and wanted no part in claiming the credit or bearing the responsibility for creating Mike Todd.

Their first moneymaking endeavor was providing the main attraction for the French Village during the second year of the 1933–34 Chicago World's Fair, the Century of Progress Exposition. The first year of the fair, Sally Rand and her fan dance had been the star act at the French Village and by far the biggest money-maker on the midway. Some very influential citizens, the kind Chicago became famous for during the twenties, had induced Sally Rand to move, in the second year of the fair, to a location they controlled, leaving the French Village looking for a crowd getter. As Goldberg recalled: "Todd said to me: 'It behooves us to get an attraction for the French Village.' And we decided it should be a girl who would take off her clothes in some spectacular manner."

Todd devised a flamboyant way to strip a girl. The act was called "The Flame Dance," whose motif was the biological phenomenon of a moth's attraction to light. A girl wearing gauzy wings does an artistic dance around a huge candle (a singular bit of phallic symbolism) and at a point short of tiring the customers not interested in artistic dances, the girl gets her wings too close to the flame and her costume burns off, leaving a seemingly naked girl to flutter offstage. The girl wore a form-fitting, flesh-colored asbestos undergarment. It was a technically tricky bit of business. Todd said, "I burned up four girls before I got it right."

To play the moth he hired a tall gorgeous redhead named Shannon Dean. Shannon got singed a couple of times while the mechanics of the act were being perfected, and although she was a real knockout, her dancing left something to be desired. Todd later used Miss Dean as a lead show girl in his touring shows during the thirties and then in some of his Broadway musicals.

Shannon Dean's replacement was small, dark and beautiful and had professional ballet training. An integral part of Todd's overall concept was that this was not just another striptease, but a dance with artistic merit, featuring a delicate and refined creature who, in an exciting manner, just so happens to wind up starkers at the end of the number.

While playing Pygmalion, Todd changed Shannon Dean's replacement's perfectly acceptable name of Eva Gardiner to what he considered the much tonier one of Muriel Page. This was early 1934, and intermittently during the next seven years she continued to do the Flame Dance. During the earlier years it was an economic necessity, since the act was successful and was the nucleus of various touring road shows Todd put together. Later it was a means of prolonging a relationship that had developed between them.

This was the first of the two extended extramarital affairs he had in his life. In my early childhood I remember hearing muffled explosions of fury that my mother directed at my father behind their closed bedroom door. Undoubtedly his affair with Muriel Page was the major or even sole cause of these tirades. My father's guilt explained his taking the abuse silently, then and in later years, when my mother made no effort to conceal her anger. Muriel Page who must have been totally devoted to my father, having literally walked through fire for him.

Danny Goldberg described the further mileage he and Todd got out of their novelty striptease act:

> When the World's Fair was over, we decided to capitalize on the big success of the Flame Dance, and we put Muriel Page in a presentation unit. You needed a lot of costumes and girls and acts to fill up the huge stages of those movie palaces. This unit that Todd and I produced was called *Bring on the Dames*, with Muriel Page as a star, but just almost the star, because the other star that competed for billing and attention was Pete the Personality Penguin. This is because Admiral Byrd was in the news at this time for his explorations in the Antarctic. And so we had a number with the girls flopping around the stage with a live penguin. Well, we took Pete the Personality Penguin on tour and he rode in the bus with the chorus girls, who fed him not herring, but salami and Polish sausage and crackers and lipstick and anything that came to hand.

Penguins are nonversatile performers, but with some ingenuity and a lot of herring, Todd and Goldberg made good use of Pete. Hidden behind a flat depicting an iceberg, he made his grand entrance in a miniature tuxedo, pushed from offstage down a shallow ramp—wearing roller skates. The featured comedian in the troop, Harry Savoy, was able to employ Pete, in one of the skits, as a most effective straight man. A herring in his back pocket guaranteed that wherever Savoy walked, Pete obediently waddled behind.

Todd accepted a substantial offer from the biggest New York night club, the Casino de Paris, for use of the Flame Dance as a featured act. This, and successfully touring *Bring on the Dames* around the country for a few seasons, meant that Todd, after only a couple of years, had developed show business contacts in every major city in the country.

My father was on the road during most of my early childhood, but we shared one memorable, if not historic, adventure when I was six or seven.

Danny Goldberg's older half-brother, who was totally dissimilar from him in character, personality and build, had been a championship boxer. His direct style gave him the unwieldy nickname of "Stick and Slug." Joe Sherman, the name he fought under, once battled Philadelphia Jack O'Brien in Denver for the light heavyweight crown. Sherman arrived two days before the fight. Joe explained away his defeat, saying, "He hardly laid a glove on me. It was the altitude that beat me."

From the early thirties through the mid-sixties, Sherman successfully operated a series of bars and nightclubs. He maintained an active interest in all sports and always had good seats for every major sporting event in Chicago. He was a Cubs fan and a season-ticket holder and had box seats in the first row beside the visitors' dugout, which, in Wrigley Field, is on the first-base side of the diamond.

The Cubs and the White Sox used to play three games a year called the City Series for sandlot charities, for the nominal championship of the city. Joe invited my father and me to be his guests for the deciding game of the year. Late in the contest the Cubs were behind a run and had men on first and second, with no one out. The Cubs' batter laid a bunt down the first-base line, and on a crazy impulse Joe picked me up, threw me over the low wall separating us from the playing field and told me to get the ball. With the impetus of his shove, I accomplished the outstanding athletic feat of my lifetime and beat the converging catcher, pitcher and first baseman to the ball, which was trickling down the line, still in fair territory. The batter easily got to first, while the astonished Sox players and the umpires stood in statuelike amazement as, following Joe's shouted instructions, I returned to the wall with the stolen baseball. He quickly plunked me back in my seat. Bob Elson, the Chicago White Sox sportscaster, was hysterical with excitement. The plate and first-base umpires chased after me and were shouting all kinds of threats as I sat holding the ball. Sherman stood up, imposing figure that he was, and made it clear that they were going to have to deal with him first if they contemplated laying a hand on me.

After walking quietly away, they were now confronted with the even weightier problem of making a ruling on the play. Both managers and most of the players joined the confused and noisy conference, giving their ideas as to what the only fair decision could be. The near-capacity crowd and the broadcasters were in a similar uproar. After about five minutes the umpires reached the not illogical conclusion that if a tiny kid could beat all three fielders to the bunt still in play, the hitter was deserving of a base hit and the runners could advance. Later in the inning a single drove in two runs, and with the score staying the same, it turned out that I had made the key play in the game.

Arriving home late that afternoon, my father and I were greeted by my mother at our apartment door. She had listened to the broadcast of the game and now excitedly asked if we had seen the little boy run out on the field and steal the bunted ball. Wordless for once, my father grabbed my right hand, which was holding the ball, and held it triumphantly in the air.

Joe Sherman was the source of even greater excitement in our household. One Christmas he gave me a windup train. During the holidays my father brought him home one evening for supper. I was playing with Joe's gift in the living room when they walked into the apartment. My mother was in the kitchen preparing the meal. My father went into the bedroom. Joe was pleased that I was having such fun with his windup train. "Hey, Mike," he said, grabbing me with one hand by the back of my shirt, "we can have even more fun playing airplane." He propelled me with my arms outstretched around the room. He suddenly decided to make the game even more thrilling and opened the window. We lived on the seventh floor. Still holding me with just one of his massive hands, and making a zooming sound, he swooped me once more around the room and then out the open window. My mother chose that moment to walk in the room, and before Joe had the chance to pull me back inside she fainted.

As a child in Minneapolis, one of the first live shows that Todd treated himself to was *The Mikado*. The Gilbert and Sullivan operetta was a worldwide favorite, especially in the United States, where it was in the public domain. With his profits from *Bring on the Dames,* Todd put together a legit production of *The Mikado* and signed for his star one of the popular opera names of the day, Mary McCormic. This evergreen faded in the subzero temperatures of a Midwest winter.

Todd's first brush with serious theater left him with nothing but a tired collection of costumes and sets. He used them for a condensed version of the show entitled *The Hot Mikado*. With an attractive line of girls and jazzed-up set of orchestrations, he made a modestly successful abbreviated tour of those presentation houses that needed a fill-in attraction.

Indirectly I provided him with an idea for his next road-show venture. Like millions of kids around the country, I ran to the radio every weekday afternoon to listen to the adventures of the Lone Ranger. Todd decided that for a weekend and holiday matinee attraction he'd put together a few simple inexpensive acts to surround "THE FIRST LIVE APPEARANCE OF THE LONE RANGER"—and make a fortune. The idea was a natural, and the bookings poured in.

A near riot broke out at the first performance in Peoria, Illinois, when parents of hundreds of disappointed children were unable to get tickets.

When the show started, the children were mildly appreciative of the acts that preceded the Lone Ranger's grand entrance, but their sense of anticipation was so great that they became restless and noisy until the theater was darkened and the announcement was made:

"For the first time live on any stage anywhere (to the swelling chords of the *William Tell Overture*) THE . . . LONE . . . RANGER!" The curtains parted, revealing a beautiful white stallion and the Masked Stranger. Total silence, followed by a growing crescendo of moans. The youngest kids were literally crying with disappointment. Nothing on any stage anywhere could reproduce the Lone Ranger that each child had conjured up in his own imagination.

Whatever his experience with the Lone Ranger cost Todd, he was repaid many times over eight years later. During the height of his Broadway success, he owned a few legitimate theaters. One, the 48th Street Theatre, he had bought at a bargain price. It had gone years without a single hit and was considered jinxed. His first booking was a play he produced entitled *Pick-up Girl*, which had a mildly successful run. However, he made a fortune with the next attraction, the Pulitzer Prize–winning play *Harvey*. Todd went up to Boston to see the opening. It was a marginal success but lacked both the critical and audience reaction required for a smash hit. The producer of *Harvey* was Brock Pemberton and the star Frank Fay. There was a big, beautiful six-and-a-half-foot pink rabbit at Fay's elbow during most of the play. After a series of conferences on how to strengthen the show, Todd got Pemberton aside and told him that not a line needed to be changed.

"All you have to do, Brock, is get rid of the goddamn rabbit and substitute a pin spot on the vacant stage wherever the rabbit is scripted to appear." Pemberton protested, saying, among other things, that the rabbit costume had cost him $300. Todd reached into his pocket. "No problem, Brock—I'll buy the costume from you," and peeled off three $100 bills and gave them to Pemberton.

Pemberton wound up keeping both the $300 and the rabbit costume. It was used most effectively without damaging the fragile whimsy of the play. The rabbit appeared only when Frank Fay took his last curtain call, and provided a gigantic, warm laugh to ring down the final curtain.

The week after the show opened to rave notices, Pemberton went up to Todd's office to thank him for his idea: ". . . and I'm especially delighted to be doing business with Mike Todd and for once not to be dealing with those kike Shuberts." Todd replied, "Thank you very much, Brock, but you must be the only schmuck in New York that doesn't know I'm Jewish."

When *Harvey* closed after 1,175 performances, it was the fifth longest running show in the history of Broadway. Todd sold the theater during its run at a substantial profit.

On one rare occasion Todd became wholeheartedly involved in a normal sort of father-son activity. While purchasing some army surplus lenses for a business project, a six-foot airplanelike kite caught his eye, and he bought it as a surprise for me. It had been used for aircraft gunnery practice during World War I. His eagerness to try it out was almost as great as mine.

The following Sunday he had an early brunch at eleven o'clock, and we went out to the vacant lot around the corner to try our luck. The kite wasn't easy to manage, but its size and the impressive three-foot drum of cord that came with it immediately attracted helpers. I was reduced to being a spectator almost from the start of this spectacular. I helped to set things up, but the launching of the massive kite became cumbersome and my father took command.

A fleet-footed teenager and the always cooperative strong wind coming from the lake, the other side of the South Shore Country Club, quickly got the kite airborne. For the first 150 feet or so it was still my kite. But as it gained altitude, the kite became a neighborhood spectacle, attracting almost everyone in a several-block radius. On the strong wind it went up and up, to the delight and admiration of the couple of hundred spectators now gathered around us. Even with several strong teenagers anchoring the stand, the cord was reeling out so fast that no one made an attempt to hold on to the winch. No one's disappointment was greater than mine when the last of the 2,000 feet of cord ripped off from the reel and the kite disappeared in the general direction of Whiting, Indiana. For me, it was a fabulous toy gone forever. For Todd, it was a thoroughly delightful experience. He had amazed and entertained hundreds with the most grandiose kite flying anyone on the South Side of Chicago was ever likely to witness. There was no reason to keep the empty reel, so we abandoned it. Walking back to our apartment, my father was in great spirits, but gradually he began to appreciate my mixed feelings about the whole episode.

From the start of his show business career, it was Todd's ambition to make a name for himself with a hit on Broadway. Danny Goldberg said:

> Todd kept badgering me. He said, "We have to go to New York and do a show." I told him I was quite contented here in Chicago, but he kept insisting, "Let's do a show, let's do a show in New York." I said, "We don't have a property." He said, "We'll write one . . . we'll write a play someday and we'll do it in New York." So about five o'clock that Friday, he came into the office and said, "We're going to write the play." I said, "How are we going to write a play? I've got to be back in the office on Monday." He said, "We'll go away for the weekend and we'll come back with the play."

To save time and, even more important, money, they took a train over the border to Wisconsin and locked themselves in a hotel room and came back with a play . . . of sorts. As Danny Goldberg explained:

> *Call Me Ziggy* was a play to do inexpensively—a play about a struggling impresario producing a play. The action took place during a rehearsal on a bare stage, with just a couple of odd flats leaning against the back wall of the theater. It ran for three nights, which is one day longer than it took to write it.

Todd later claimed: "*Call Me Ziggy* was the only show in history to close after the first-act curtain—no one came back from the intermission."

Call Me Ziggy opened February 12, 1937, at the Longacre Theatre and closed February 13. Its star was Joseph Buloff, a talented actor from the Yiddish theater, who was to win praise and long-term employment as the peddler in *Oklahoma!* His performance in *Call Me Ziggy* was the only element of the show to get favorable review mention.

Burns Mantle of the New York *Daily News* originated the star system of rating shows, four stars being the top rating. Mantle gave *Call Me Ziggy* one star and later said that this was only because the curtain managed to go up on the show. The unanimous verdict was concisely expressed by Richard Lockridge of the *Sun:* "*Call Me Ziggy* is a bad play within a bad play." Robert Coleman in the *Daily Mirror* was not so gentle, calling the play ". . . an amateurish and preposterous charade." John Anderson in the *Evening Journal* pulled out all the stops. "I think the actors will carry the scars to their graves, their memories seared by the lines they had to memorize and their souls upbraided by this harsh experience."

Todd pulled the Flame Dance out of mothballs, rented a few sets of old costumes for a new line of chorus and show girls and hired a few acts. He put together another road show, called *At Home A Broad,* having appropriated the title of a successful Broadway revue, *At Home Abroad,* which had recently completed its run. *At Home A Broad* made some money for Todd, but he made more while preparing this show to go on the road.

Rehearsals for such a show were minimal, but putting the whole thing together with the production numbers required the use of a stage. He had made friends with Harold Costello, who controlled the operation of the Oriental Theatre and who had put some money into *Call Me Ziggy.* The final rehearsals were to be held on the stage of the Oriental after the feature had played its last show. From the Loop to where we lived, the Illinois Central had slow, intermittent train service in the small hours, and so Todd spent the last two nights of rehearsal at a hotel a few blocks from the theater.

As a weekend treat that Saturday, my mother took me and her teenage sister Ethel to the Loop. Ethel and I were going to catch the first show at the State-Lake Theatre. Mother was going to visit with Dad, and then we would all have dinner at Henrici's.

After the show Ethel and I walked the few blocks to the hotel where my father was staying. As we came into the lobby, we heard my mother screaming and ran to where we heard her voice. She was being held by a man at the door of the manager's office. Inside, I could see my father lying at the foot of the desk; he was being held by one man and kicked by another. My father looked up and saw me and then shouted to my mother, "Bertha, take him away! Don't let him see me like this!" I ran into the office and gave a kick in the shins to the man who had been kicking my father. My father smiled momentarily and then started to cry and again tearfully asked my mother to take me away. The man restraining her let her go, and she took me out to the lobby. She explained to Ethel and me that the whole thing had been a dreadful mistake, and it would soon be straightened out.

Years later I found out that two house detectives had followed my mother up to my father's room. As he was registered as a single, they assumed that she was a prostitute and subsequently burst into the room. Bertha and Todd were outraged, but were forcibly taken downstairs to the manager's office, where the scene developed that Ethel and I walked in on. The house detectives' mistake cost the hotel a settlement of several thousand dollars.

At Home A Broad, the hotel settlement and another investment by Harold Costello, as well as investments from a few other Chicago friends, provided the bankroll for Todd's next attempt on Broadway. He bought the American rights to a French comedy set in Budapest that he thought would showcase the versatile talents of Joseph Buloff, the star of *Call Me Ziggy.*

Buloff played a Walter Mitty-type clerk who leads a double life by economizing all month for a one-night splurge on the town. Todd prevailed upon Danny Goldberg to do the adaptation with him and secured the services of one of the leading directors of the period, Harry Wagstaff Gribble.

The Man from Cairo opened in Boston in April 1938 to excellent notices and did very good business. The notices, the business and Gribble's reputation defeated Todd and ultimately the play itself. Todd was dissatisfied and wanted to make changes in the play while in Boston, but Gribble prevailed and told Todd not to tamper with success.

The play opened in May in New York. Buloff got unanimously good reviews, but the play received poor to mixed notices. Both Atkinson of the *Times* and Coleman of the *Mirror* acknowledged that the audience thoroughly enjoyed the play, but Coleman summed up the critical consensus when he wrote, "We regret that we failed to share the audience's enthusiasm."

The negative comments pointed to the very weaknesses Todd had wanted to try to correct in Boston. The play ran for two and a half weeks and only reinforced my father's determination to have a hit on Broadway, and soon. He later said that *The Man from Cairo* taught him two lessons—to act on his own judgment, and never to trust anyone with three names.

In less than a year Todd had a hit on Broadway that remained, of all his shows, his personal favorite. It was a lavishly produced and freshly orchestrated all-black version of *The Hot Mikado*, which starred Bill (Bojangles) Robinson. Having made a big score with a clever gimmick, he was able to perfect his idea of jazzing up the Gilbert and Sullivan operetta.

Bill Doll, the press agent Todd hired for the show (beginning a lifetime association) got an enormous amount of publicity for *The Hot Mikado*. Doll called it the musical financed by Santa Claus.

For years Joe Sherman had a novelty item in his bar called the Girl in the Goldfish Bowl. On a shelf above the bottles there was a wide goldfish bowl with fish swimming in it. Lying in the bowl was a naked girl, less than six inches long, who moved and was clearly alive. A four-inch-square submerged section at the back of the bowl was replaced by a reducing lens, behind which a naked girl reclined on a bench in a cubicle in back of the bar wall. For years my father had been frustrated because he knew that I, like any child, would be captivated by seeing a living human figure that was only inches tall. Soon after the closing of *The Man from Cairo,* he got the idea of how to convert the Girl in the Goldfish Bowl into a children's attraction.

The lenses needed for the illusion had been designed during World War I for use in photo reconnaissance. He tracked down several dozen sets of these army surplus lenses. With Yermi Stern, an acquaintance who provided the necessary financing, he put together a demonstration unit. A snow-covered dollhouse, two and a half feet high, was set up on a small platform against the wall of a room. The toy-department buyers were invited to see "Kute Kris Kringle, only three inches tall. . . . He lives, he breathes, he talks." The dollhouse had a picture window through which the buyers could see the miniature Santa Claus in a room full of toys. Instead of the awkward and time-consuming tradition of sitting on Santa's knee, the child had the novel opportunity of speaking to the miniature Santa on a telephone placed next to the picture window of the dollhouse.

Kute Kris Kringle was leased to department stores all over the Midwest. Marshall Field's had the exclusive in Chicago. During Christmas of 1938 Kute Kris Kringle netted Todd and Yermi Stern a small fortune.

It was a spectacular Christmas for me as well. The avalanche of gifts didn't arrive until several days after Christmas—when the Kute Kris Kringle displays had been dismantled—but when it did, I was the envy of every kid in the neighborhood.

With a decent bankroll Todd went first class with the production of *The Hot Mikado*. Bill Robinson, one of the most popular black stars of the era, was appearing at the Cotton Club in New York, which was run for the mob by Jack Dietz. Todd convinced Dietz to release Robinson to play in the show and did such a sales job that Dietz became an investor as well. This was the beginning of a lifelong friendship and association.

Todd sold Robinson on appearing in the show by saying that he could have the deciding voice in the selection of the sixteen dancing girls and a say in the selection of the show girls. Robinson's agent, Marty Forkins, was sold simply by the magical phrase "two Gs a week."

Todd hired Nat Karson, the costume and set designer for the Radio City Music Hall, known for its lavish and spectacular stage shows. Todd had a spectacular notion of his own for a set late in the second act—a gargantuan soapsuds waterfall. Every musical production Todd was to create for the rest of his life had one standout set or effect in it. *The Hot Mikado* waterfall not only produced a fascinating cascade of soapsuds but also a lot of free publicity.

Todd and Bill Doll issued press releases covering every aspect of the operation of the waterfall, real and imaginary—that the Procter and Gamble laboratories had created a special formula, that so many hundreds of pounds of powder were used in a week, and so on. It was perfect Sunday-supplement material.

Todd was sensitive to the fact that the sophisticated critics in New York might be touchy about a practically unknown producer from Chicago tampering with a Gilbert and Sullivan classic. He hired the services of one of the most prestigious directors of musical shows, this time a man with only two names—Hassard Short. Short had staged the first three Music Box revues,

Jubilee, The Band Wagon, As Thousands Cheer, Roberta and other hits of the era. Among his later successes were *Lady in the Dark* and Todd's two Cole Porter musicals.

Todd and Doll created an original stunt to herald the opening of *The Hot Mikado.* On his sixty-first birthday a city permit enabled Bill Robinson to lead his own celebration by tap-dancing from Sixty-first Street down Broadway to Times Square. Newsreels and photo coverage of the event were seen nationwide.

Todd and Doll pulled another stunt that got almost as much publicity. The first animated sign had just been unveiled in Times Square. Several thousand light bulbs were timed in a sequence to produce a short bit of action. Todd had Douglas Leigh, the man who owned the sign, create a thirty-second repeating display depicting Bill Robinson doing his famous staircase tap dance. The evening it first appeared Doll squired Bojangles, attired in his customary derby, spats and flashy three-piece suit, to the corner of Broadway opposite the sign. Robinson, in feigned or actual delight in seeing himself and his famous routine immortalized in lights, began a high-spirited version of his dance on the curb, attracting a crowd of spectators that eventually stopped traffic. Robinson was arrested for creating a public nuisance. Doll made sure that the proceedings, both that night and in court the next day, were well covered by the papers. Robinson told the judge he was so happy to see himself in lights that he broke spontaneously into dance. He was acquitted.

There was, however, a cloud over the seemingly rosy prospects of the show, and indirectly Todd had been the source of it. His condensed touring road-show version of *The Hot Mikado* had preceded and most likely prompted a government-funded W.P.A. production called *The Swing Mikado.* The W.P.A. show had originated in Chicago, had a black cast and was touring the country without plans to play on Broadway. Nevertheless, fearing possible competition, Todd offered to buy the show. Government bureaucracy couldn't cope with this novel offer and rejected it. With the publicity Todd and Doll were generating for the Bill Robinson version of *The Hot Mikado,* Todd's worst fears were realized when *The Swing Mikado* suddenly booked a theater and opened in New York while he was still in rehearsal. It got respectfully good notices and, even worse for Todd, the house was scaled so that a ticket cost a third as much as for *The Hot Mikado*. Another galling aspect of this situation was that *The Swing Mikado* moved from a location on the edge of the theater district to the 44th Street Theatre, on the same street where *The Hot Mikado* was housed in the Broadhurst Theatre. Compounding the problem, the 44th Street Theatre was east of the Broadhurst and closer to Broadway, so that *The Swing Mikado*'s marquee would be the first seen and more conspicuous to the passing crowds on Broadway. To remedy this, Todd made arrangements with the man who occupied an office a floor above and on the Broadway side of the 44th Street Theatre to hang a flagpole out his window. On the flagpole was a huge, brightly colored banner with an arrow indicating that *The Hot Mikado* was playing down the street at the Broadhurst. The banner completely hid the Broadway side of the 44th Street Theatre's marquee.

Rehearsals were not going well. As there was to be no out-of-town tryout, Todd had no alternative but to push back the opening. With this postponement Todd needed more money. The competition from the successful *Swing Mikado* dimmed the prospects of Todd's *Mikado*. Todd's first two shows on Broadway had been in Shubert theaters, and he had become friendly with the younger of the Shubert brothers, "Mr. Lee." Shubert was amused and charmed by Todd's audacity and developed an almost paternal relationship with him. At the time—totally out of character and contrary to his legendary tight-fisted, calculating approach to business—Mr. Lee offered Todd the money he needed to get open—of course for a generously proportioned piece of the show. Todd politely rejected the offer, and Dietz came through with the extra money.

The Hot Mikado opened on March 23, 1939, to rave notices. Burns Mantle in the New York *Daily News* wrote: "Michael Todd, a producer of somewhat obscure professional record, offered a version of the familiar classic under the descriptive title of *The Hot Mikado*. Something of moment has happened in the theatre. . . . They have dressed it beautifully, cast it expertly and staged it with such perfect timing and in such excellent taste that it stands absolutely unrivalled so far as my playgoing experience is concerned." The *World-Telegram*'s critic called the show "magnificent, the loudest, craziest, hottest and most brilliantly organized jam session of this cockeyed jazz age." Atkinson in the *Times* and Watts in the *Herald Tribune* gave the show great notices and pulled out all the stops in their praise of Robinson's performance. John Mason Brown in the *Post* wrote, "This *Hot Mikado* turns out to be an infinitely more professional show than its Federal Theatre rival. . . ." The other critics, with one exception, agreed that it was a much better show than the *Swing Mikado*. The *Daily Worker*'s critic preferred the W.P.A. version.

In the review and stories that followed the opening, Todd's name was prominently mentioned and he was given the lion's share of the credit for the success of the show. His ambition to make it big on Broadway had been fulfilled. However, fighting the lower-priced *Swing Mikado* and generally slack theater business, the gross in the first several weeks was only good, and then began to tail off rapidly to below a break-even figure. Unless a miracle came along, the show would not earn back a fraction of its cost. Todd could not meet the weekly overhead. On the Saturday the show was scheduled to fold, Todd paid a visit to Grover Whalen, the president of the New York World's Fair.

Grover Whalen had for a number of years held high positions in New York City government, including that of police commissioner, and was the dignitary who greeted all V.I.P. visitors. Virtually all pictures of him in the press showed him in a morning coat. He was reserved and aristocratic to the point of being pompous, and the image of Todd—who in those days often dressed in loud checked suits—propositioning him is almost ludicrous.

The fair had made a huge investment in a 4,000-seat auditorium called the Hall of Music, in which ballets, symphonies and classical concerts were the attractions. Most performances had more artists on the stage than customers in the audience. The idea of this expensive cultural showplace was primarily Grover Whalen's, and huge operating losses had forced him to shut it down. Whalen was in trouble, but Todd was really "calling from the police station."

Bill Doll picks up the story:

> Mike had reached the end of the line. He didn't even have enough for the final week's payroll. I remember that Saturday night the rest of the staff and myself—who hadn't been paid in weeks—were sitting in Mike's office, and it was a borrowed one at that. We were all depressed and no one wanted to leave. It was pouring outside. We heard someone

get off the elevator and come sloshing down the hall. It was Mike—he was drenched. He was carrying a wet brown paper bag. He had been to the fair and Whalen had given him ten thousand dollars to move the show. It was an utterly unbelievable thing for a show to get a reprieve—when they close, they stay closed. He came in and took this soggy bag and flipped it up in the air and it was full of money. Ten-dollar bills, five-dollar bills, and the money came raining down. It was a very beautiful sight. And Mike said, "Go ahead, fellows. Help yourself." So we were all snatching money out of the air.

CHAPTER 3

TODD BELIEVED THAT timing was everything, and the opening of *The Hot Mikado* at the fair on June 20, 1939, was a case of perfect timing. The show had opened on Broadway in late March and at the fair in mid-April. Until the beginning of June, *The Hot Mikado* was making money on Broadway, although not much. With the chilly and rainy weather of early spring and vacation time two months away, attendance at the fair remained so low that there was a distinct possibility that not only the Hall of Music but the fair itself was going to be a big flop. *The Hot Mikado*'s run on Broadway had gotten it past the uncertain early spring weather, and by the time Todd had contrived the move to the fair, the good weather had arrived and with it the first influx of large crowds.

The two-hour-and-twenty-minute Broadway version of the show was condensed to a "tab" version that ran an hour and a half, so that three shows could be done weekdays and four on weekends. With a ninety-nine-cent top scaled down to forty cents, *The Hot Mikado* packed them in and many weeks came close to grossing $75,000, a figure double the biggest-grossing hits in the history of the American theater to date.

Immediately a serious problem cropped up. The actors' union, Equity, provides that its members do eight performances a week, with additional performances paid for pro rata. On the new schedule at the fair *The Hot Mikado* cast under Equity rules was entitled to almost three times its original scale. Practically none of the cast of *The Hot Mikado* had been in a Broadway show before and were not particularly agitated about the

Equity demands on its behalf. Nevertheless, an adjustment was clearly called for.

Bill Doll was ecstatic about the big business the show was doing and hardly had to inflate the figures when he put out his first press releases claiming a gigantic success. The company manager, Joe Glick, was appearing before the Equity board, trying to work out the best deal possible for the increased schedule of performances.

One day, on the theatrical page of the *Daily News,* a story appeared in column one quoting a Doll press release saying that *The Hot Mikado* at the fair was chalking up the largest grosses in the history of the legitimate theater. A little lower on the same page, in column three, was a story reporting statements by Joe Glick at Equity that *The Hot Mikado* was struggling and that if the Equity demands were met the show would have to fold immediately. Early the next morning Sam Zolotow, the theatrical editor for the New York *Times,* got Todd on the phone and asked him if he had seen the *Daily News.* Todd said he had. "Well, how do you explain the contradiction of your press agent saying your show is doing record-breaking business and your company manager saying that the show is going to have to fold, both quoted on the same page of the same paper?" "Where's the contradiction?" Mike replied. "Each department is functioning perfectly."

Late one afternoon, shortly after the show moved to the fair, there was a rehearsal to smooth out a few of the rough spots remaining in the abbreviated version of the show. Only a piano had been used for the run-through, and the full orchestra was only now assembling for the second show, which was to go on shortly. Todd walked out to the box office to see how the ticket sale was going. A few minutes later Sammy Lambert, the stage manager, rushed to the ticket window and told Todd there was big trouble in the auditorium. Coming into the theater, Todd saw Bill Robinson standing on the apron of the stage, waving a .45 at one of the musicians in the pit. From the back of the auditorium, Mike called out in a steady voice, "Bill, I've got to talk to you for a minute," and calmly walked down the aisle as if nothing untoward was happening. Robinson said, "Mr. Todd, this ain't none of your business." "Bill, it's very important I speak to you," Todd answered. When he got to the stage Todd walked across to Robinson and took the gun out of his hand. He put his arm around Robinson and led him to his dressing room.

Once inside, Robinson turned to him: "Mr. Todd, you just saved us both a lot of trouble, 'cause I was going to have to shoot that man."

Robinson had heard that a trumpet player was chasing one of the girls in Robinson's chorus line. Robinson considered all the girls in the show, but particularly those in the chorus line, his exclusive domain. There is little doubt that Robinson would have pulled the trigger, since he had been involved in several shootings in similar circumstances.

The union problems were resolved and with the attendance at the fair now averaging a half a million upwards a day, *The Hot Mikado* was packing them into the Hall of Music, and in a few weeks the show had paid off its production costs.

Todd was receiving a lot of publicity, and a personality conflict developed between himself and the fair's most famous impresario, Billy Rose, which caught the fancy of the newspapers and was dubbed the "Battle of the Midway."

The two smash hits at the opening of the fair had been the General Motors exhibit, the World of Tomorrow and Billy Rose's Aquacade. Rose had made a big investment and staged a lavish spectacle in the outdoor auditorium built by the fair on the edge of an artificial lagoon. The show had a huge cast and starred Johnny Weissmuller, Morton Downey, Gertrude Ederle and Rose's wife, ex–Olympic swimming champion Eleanor Holm. Rose demanded and got special treatment from the fair management, who were only too willing to cater to the producer of the biggest crowd getter on the midway. Rose was undoubtedly a bit miffed when Todd rescued the Hall of Music and stole some of his limelight.

The back of the Hall of Music faced the Aquacade entrance, and while Rose couldn't object to Todd's billboarding his show on the back of the theater, he did object to Todd's plastering every other available space and lighting pole in front of the Aquacade with *Hot Mikado* posters. The fair management told Mike he would have to remove all these additional postings, at which point Todd installed a pair of powerful loudspeakers on the roof of the Hall of Music. Hard-sell messages for the show were interspersed with music from the *Hot Mikado* score. Todd had a box office built at the rear of the Hall of Music, where it would catch the overflow and exiting patrons from the Aquacade. Rose put up his own speakers to combat the Todd barrage, but Todd had the advantage of fifty feet of elevation over Rose's speakers. Todd then escalated the loudspeaker war by continuing to keep them in use during the performances of the Aquacade, which of course interfered with Rose's show, since it was in an open air auditorium. Rose vehemently complained to the fair management. Grover Whalen told Todd that he would have to desist and suggested that he and Rose get together to see if they could settle their differences amicably. Todd suggested to Rose that they have lunch at Lindy's. Bill Doll had been getting big coverage, publicizing each new development of the Battle of the Midway, and now let slip to several newspapermen the time and place of the peace conference.

In return for Todd's diminishing the volume and duration of his amplified pitches and restricting his billboarding, Rose agreed to do a series of "cross plugs." Each would do promotional announcements for the other's show and prominently display each other's posters. The "Treaty of Lindy's" was concluded, and the awaiting world was duly notified by the press that there would be peace on the midway.

The Todd-Rose feud became a legend on Broadway in the forties and fifties. Everyone considered it to be the real thing. But as far as Todd was concerned, a feud with Rose, the most prominent and publicized showman of the time, was just a means to elevate his own status and provide a lot of free publicity. Todd kept goading Rose in order to keep the feud going during the second year of the fair, but once he had made his name on Broadway he ignored the whole business.

Bill Doll, convinced by his own early flow of propaganda, always considered the feud to be genuine. Rose carried a grudge against Todd for years, and made the occasional snide remark to columnists and newspapermen that kept the alleged feud alive. Todd was amused that Rose, and particularly Bill Doll, who had contributed so heavily to its fabrication, believed it to be the real thing.

He would have been even more amused had he known that Rose felt he was getting revenge on Todd by secretly hiring Doll to do occasional jobs for him. Rose gave Doll lavish fees and paid in crisp $1,000 bills taken from a wall safe in his home.

When my father brought my mother and me to New York a few months before the opening of *The Hot Mikado*, we lived in a rather seedy furnished apartment on the Upper West Side.

After the opening, we moved to a small suite in the St. Moritz Hotel, where the show's company manager, Joe Glick, had lived for years. From that time on, whether my father was flush or deep in debt, we always lived well. After the success of *The Hot Mikado* at the fair, we subleased the furnished apartment of the Yiddish musical star Belle Baker in a modish twin-tower building called the Century Apartments, which occupies the block between Sixty-second and Sixty-third streets, facing Central Park West.

Our apartment had a terrace facing the YMCA on Sixty-third Street housing the McBurney School, which I went to a year later. My mother became friendly with a girl from a well-to-do family, Sylvia Sirota, who was several years younger than mother, and had had a bit part in *The Man from Cairo.* She had recently married a theatrical producer, David Wolper, who was about the same age as my parents. A few years later Wolper produced a very successful musical, *Follow the Girls,* which gave Jackie Gleason his first starring role on Broadway and enabled Gleason to put burlesque and vaudeville behind him. David Wolper's nephew, David L. Wolper, is the well-known television and film producer. In addition to finding Sylvia Wolper an amusing companion, Bertha felt that the Wolpers would make a wonderful couple to join herself and Mike in building a new and extended social life in New York. Todd found them pleasant enough, but he was unwilling to play any part in Bertha's social plans.

Once settled in the new apartment, and with plenty of money to spend for the first time in over ten years, mother rented a house in Bermuda for the summer of 1939, which we shared with Sylvia Wolper. The idea was that my father and Wolper might join us for a week or so during the summer, but neither put in an appearance.

With the exception of the Aquacade and *The Hot Mikado* and a new thrill ride called the Parachute Jump, almost everything in the amusement area was struggling. Todd felt sure he could convert some of these losers into winners and, as always, was bristling with ideas. He had no reluctance sharing them with Grover Whalen and Harvey Gibson, a well-known New York banker of the era and a former ambassador and cabinet member, who supervised the financial side of the fair. Whalen and Gibson listened to the man who had saved them a great deal of embarrassment with the Hall of Music and began discussions with him about the lame ducks Todd wanted to take over the next season.

Gibson felt that since Todd would be playing an expanded role in the amusement area the following summer, he should be invited to the full-dress banquet he was throwing for the principal financial backers of the fair at the restaurant in the French Pavilion. A renowned French chef, Henri Soulé, had been brought from France to run the establishment. The food was justifiably acclaimed to be the best in America, and the restaurant at the French Pavilion became the most chic spot at the fair. Todd and Doll regularly entertained the most important visiting journalists there. Based on the reputation made at the fair, Soulé opened and operated for a number of years one of the most highly acclaimed restaurants in the country, Le Pavillon, on East Fifty-seventh Street.

Dick Williams, a close associate of Bill Doll's who was originally, but not exclusively, a photographer, worked for Bill and Todd from the inception of *The Hot Mikado*. He remembers that Todd was so pleased and flattered that he had been invited to Gibson's banquet that he went out and bought himself tails, top hat and a full set of formal gear.

At the end of the function, a little worse for wear, Todd went back to the Hall of Music to check on the evening's take. Bill Doll spotted him in the box office in his top hat and tails and told Dick Williams to grab his camera. Dick Williams remembers:

Mike was a bit tipsy. As a matter of fact, he was just plain drunk. He never really drank in those days. By the time I got back with my camera, Mike was in the lobby, just before the break. In addition to a souvenir program, we had a thing called the Bojangles Dancing Doll, all decked out in a gold suit. We sold a ton of them. Bill had talked Mike into getting up on the edge of a table to demonstrate the doll and do the pitch during the intermission. Then he whispered to me, "Grab a couple of shots of this." Well, Mike's top hat was at an angle and he had a cigar butt clenched in his teeth and altogether, with the dancing doll, he looked a little silly. Afterwards, we had him pose for a couple of other shots without the cigar butt and with his top hat straightened out.

A few days later Mike recalled my taking the pictures and asked to see the proofs. He liked one of them, with the top hat and all, a very stiff, posed shot. Then I said, "Hey, how about this one?" He looked at it and said, "My God, I look a little drunk there. Besides that, it's a *stupid* picture. And, in addition, if it's printed anywhere, you and Bill Doll are both fired!"

I asked Bill, "What should I do with the picture?" Bill said, "Put it in the file, maybe we'll use it someday. Mike will forget about it."

Near the end of the fair, Lew Funke of the *Times* called and said Grover Whalen has been raving about this man and the *Times* was going to do a big Sunday piece about Mike and what he's going to do next year at the fair. Funke asked for all the photos we had of Mike. Now understand, Bill and I didn't have any responsibility for this. . . . We were in the city, and we called out to the fair and told them to send in all the photos of Mike to the *Times*. And with a couple of hundred pictures to choose from, what picture do you think the New York *Times* selected? There it is on the front page of the drama section. Early Sunday morning, Mike calls up Bill and says, "Get a hold of Dick and listen to me carefully— when you get him, tell him *you're both fired!*"

That was the first of a couple of dozen times that Todd fired Bill Doll. Everyone Bill ever worked for fired him several times. Drink was Bill's problem. He became very nasty and critical when in his cups. With Bill, "in his cups" was not just a figure of speech, because his staff knew he had fallen off the wagon whenever they caught a glimpse of him sidling up to the water cooler to remove a handful of paper cups. He would take these back to his office and pour himself a snort from a bottle stowed in his desk, crumple up the cup and gracefully throw it in the general direction of a wastepaper basket. The cups were a sure sign that everyone was in for a siege—if Bill hadn't already shown it by turning surly. At the surly stage, which came more quickly in later years, he would begin making long-distance telephone calls to newspaper pals. Once he asked a secretary to get "Lolly" on the phone for him. When he was told Louella Parsons was waiting on the phone, he slowly enunciated into the receiver: "Hello . . . Lolly. This . . . is . . . Bill . . . Doll. You are some son of a bitch," and then hung up, ending his conversation with America's most important movie columnist.

Bill worked for some of the top film and stage producers in

New York—in later years most notably for Joe Levine and Alex Cohen. He was occasionally fired because of his drinking, but always rehired for his outstanding ability and flair for publicity.

Bill handled a good many of Joe Levine's films, from the earliest Steve Reeves exploitation pictures through some of the Fellini masterpieces. At various times Bill represented the Steel Pier, the Moscow Circus, the Lippenzanner horses, Holiday on Ice, Ringling Brothers, the New Jersey State Fair and many lesser traveling shows and carnivals. Fellini, who was fascinated with circuses, had a real affinity for Bill and his approach to publicity and they became friends.

With one of the Fellini pictures, Bill had safely gotten through all the preopening interviews and screenings without a drink. Feeling the account was safely tucked away for the run of the picture, he allowed himself a couple of quick ones during the final preopening screening. There had been scores of good pieces about Fellini, who had come over for the opening, and good feature articles heralding the new masterpiece. At the end of the screening, the audience gave the film a gigantic round of applause. Levine came out into the vestibule all smiles, and went over to congratulate Bill on the fine job he had done. Bill was hovering next to the water cooler when Levine, a short, rotund man, threw his arms around Bill's waist in an appreciative gesture. Bill, wobbly at this point, reached for the cooler to steady himself, knocked it over and fell to the floor, pulling Levine down with him, dousing themselves and others around them. Exit Bill Doll from Joe Levine's payroll for six months.

Fellini got Bill the job of handling the premiere of his film *Juliet of the Spirits*. On the phone, Bill was asked by critic Judith Crist to briefly describe the picture. It was Fellini's first film in color, with many lyrical shots of art nouveau interiors. "Well, Judy . . ." Bill briefly groped for a handle, never easy for a Fellini film, "it's all about . . . Tiffany lamps."

Bill, over a period of years, became close friends with almost every newspaper critic and columnist in the country. When they visited New York, he would get them tickets for any show in town and buy them drinks and a meal. More important, if they had lost their jobs, he would hire them for a short stretch while trying to get them more permanent work. No one had more or better contacts with journalists throughout the country.

When Todd first hired Bill Doll for *The Hot Mikado*, he insisted that Bill work for him exclusively. Bill had a few other accounts at the time and, knowing the hazards of show business, was not about to give them up for the uncertain future of *The Hot Mikado*. One day, when Bill was busy with the producer of another show, he returned to his office to find Dick Williams in a nervous state. "Mike Todd's called four times asking for you. What the hell am I supposed to tell him when you're not around?" "It's simple," Bill replied. "Just tell him I'm out at the papers." For the next ten years this excuse was used to cover any unexplained absence of Bill's when Todd was trying to get in touch with him.

In 1956, several months before the opening of *Around the World in 80 Days,* when the photography had been completed and he was in the midst of the postproduction work, Todd took a trip to New York, primarily to engage Bill to do the publicity and to tell him how he wanted it handled. He took Bill to lunch at Dinty Moore's. Todd planned to road-show *80 Days* and give it the full treatment of a legitimate show. This was going to require Bill's full attention, and they would have to take on a large staff. It was going to be a big smash and Todd said he could not only afford but insisted upon having Bill's services exclusively. He asked Doll to drop his other accounts and said he'd make up the difference. Todd asked Bill to list them and then say how much they were netting him. Bill had three legitimate shows, a circus, a state fair, the Steel Pier, two summer theaters, three restaurants, many toy accounts (including the Little Drinking Duck, Silly Putty and big manufacturers such as John Tigret and Louis Marx), the sports and fine arts divisions of Sears Roebuck, personal publicity for several singers, a hypnotist, a lyricist, and on and on. Todd kept interrupting the litany of accounts, asking for the "bottom line." Bill did a little quick figuring and told him what he needed to work exclusively on *80 Days.* Mike got up from the table and said as he walked away, "Forget it, Bill. Just don't spend too much time at the papers."

No promotional stunt or publicity scheme was too bold for either Todd or Doll to attempt. Their association, although intermittent and sometimes stormy, was close and tremendously successful. Todd always said, "I am a product of paper and ink." He gave Bill a picture of himself, inscribed, "You made me what I am today, but I still love you." They had great confidence in each other's ability. Despite their frequent association with others, their names were indelibly linked during the forties and fifties as the best producer–press agent team in the business. As

Dick Williams said, "They were two guys going up the same street."

Todd had the Hall of Music for the second year of the fair and took over the leases of several of the first season's costly failures. He had elaborate plans for turning these losers into big winners. He bought the title and rights to *Streets of Paris,* a successful Broadway revue, intending to put his own revamped version into the Hall of Music during the second year of the fair. The star of the show on Broadway had been Carmen Miranda, "the Latin American bombshell." Todd was not taken with her fruit-laden turbans and Miranda, who had gone from Broadway to big money in the movies, would cost a lot more than Todd wanted to pay. He wanted the biggest name French variety artist he could get to headline the show. He cabled Maurice Chevalier an offer of the then lordly sum of $2,500 a week. Chevalier turned it down. Todd was delighted. Now he had an excuse to go to Europe. He would charm Chevalier into signing a contract and scout out a variety of European acts to feature in the other areas of the amusement section he had inherited. Todd obtained from Whalen and Gibson letters of introduction that gave him a quasi-ambassadorial status as a representative of the fair.

Soon after my mother and I returned from Bermuda, my father was off to Europe on a Pan Am Flying Clipper. In those days of the so-called false war—before Dunkirk—life was continuing almost normally. Todd had a wonderful time making himself known to the leading impresarios in London and Paris, but when he got down to business, Chevalier insisted on seeing an advance and a contract greatly in excess of what Todd was prepared to offer.

Before leaving France to catch his return Clipper from Lisbon, he made a stopover at Biarritz and had his first crack at casino gambling in Europe. As a child he had heard endless tales of his maternal uncle, the first of the Hellermans to go to Minneapolis, who had lost his share of the family estate at the roulette tables in Monte Carlo. He considered it a slow and finicky game, suitable only for old ladies. In Biarritz it was chemin de fer that immediately caught his fancy. Huge sums could be won at the turn of a card and a single player could take on all comers. First-time lucky, he won enough francs to pay for his entire trip.

As Todd left the casino, he was stopped by a Frenchman who said he had seen him at the tables and admired his style and luck. He asked where Todd was going next on his travels. When Todd said Lisbon, the Frenchman was delighted. He said he thought the false war would soon become a very real one, and he had a great deal of money in cash that he could not legally take out of France himself. Would Todd be so kind as to carry it across the Spanish and Portuguese borders and return the money to him in Lisbon—for a reasonable consideration? Todd was extremely wary, figuring this was just some kind of elaborate con to detach him from his fresh winnings. However, the Frenchman pulled out a huge roll of bank notes and handed them to Todd, who was intrigued enough to take a chance.

Crossing the French border, he was required to make a customs declaration, stating how much cash he was carrying. Mike made his declaration, but he was detained by the police. Confused, angry and alarmed, Todd was handed over to an English-speaking customs officer who told Todd that he had seventy-five francs more than he had declared. Todd, who was carrying about $35,000 worth of francs, breezily told the officer in charge, "Keep the change." This was interpreted by the French official as an attempt at bribery, and he was thrown in jail. Fortunately, his letters from Gibson and Whalen stood him in good stead and he was released the next day.

On his delayed arrival in Lisbon, he was warmly greeted by his now nervous French acquaintance. Much to the Frenchman's delight, Todd returned his bankroll intact and waved away the honorarium the Frenchman offered.

In Lisbon, Todd found that he was at the end of a long line of people clamoring to get aboard unavailable seats on Flying Clippers to the States.

He discovered that the Italian liner *The Rex* was in the Mediterranean, heading for New York with a lot of unfilled space. He bribed a reluctant Italian Line representative to cable the captain of *The Rex* to tell him to stop in Lisbon to pick up Todd. The reply came back that under no circumstances was *The Rex* going to detour to Lisbon; it could stop briefly in Gibraltar, but of course not for only one passenger.

Todd scurried around Lisbon and contacted the long list of Americans and Europeans trying desperately to get to the United States—among them, the Hungarian playwright Ferenc Molnar, Chaim Weizmann and Todd's cash-laden acquaintance from Biarritz. Within a few hours, Todd had a list of sixty-three people ready to join him on *The Rex*.

Todd told the Italian Line representative to cable the captain that there were now sixty-four paying passengers ready to book passage for the trip to New York. The wary representative said he would do this only if Todd put down a deposit representing 50 percent of the total passage money. Todd said he would be back in half an hour.

He found his French friend and said that he had trusted him once with his whole bankroll, would he now lend him half of it for a couple of days? Todd went back to the Italian Line representative and said, "Here's the deposit. Tell the captain to put some champagne on ice—I'm throwing a party after we board in Gibraltar."

Molnar said that he wouldn't be able to board; he had no funds to pay for the trip. Todd treated.

When the ship stopped, the captain was so pleased to pick up this unexpected crowd of passengers that he gave Todd the royal suite. On the voyage to the States a grateful Molnar offered Todd a free option to the American rights to any of his plays. Todd said he was flattered by the kind offer, but would of course pay the going rate and would contact him after Molnar had settled in New York. Todd made a note to himself to read a translation of Molnar's collected works at his earliest opportunity.

Dick Williams described Todd's return from Europe:

When he got back to New York after chartering *The Rex*, he created quite a stir and was feeling pretty cocky. He'd met a lot of important people, but had booked only a few acts in Europe. He had tons more space at the fair, and he started hiring people. We were in the RKO Building, but of course we had to have much bigger offices now. He wanted to let everyone on Broadway know he had been to France. He came back with this huge box of Charvet ties—there must have been a couple of hundred—and he tells us that some people like patterns, some people like stripes, but he's going to do it right and let everyone select a few that suited their own taste. So he calls in his secretary, Lillian Leff, and he says, "Lillian, call the messenger service. I'm gonna send all my friends a couple of Charvet ties." The first name on the list was Colonel Eagan, who ran Madison Square Garden. "Okay, Lillian," he said, "have the messenger take the box over to Colonel Eagan and tell him to take what he likes—compliments of Mike Todd." Well, the boy came and took the box and after lunch Mike yells to Lillian, "Has that messenger come back with the box of ties?" She tells him no, and he says, "Call up and see what the hell happened to him, for chrissakes. Madison Square Garden's only a couple of blocks away." They called the messenger service and the boy says Eagan kept the box. Mike's a little put out, but he figures Eagan's busy and wants to take his time to make his selection. But the next day a note comes over from the Garden and it says: "Thanks, Mike. The ties are great. Colonel Eagan."

The second year of the fair he had *Streets of Paris* lined up for the Hall of Music, only he got Gypsy Rose Lee to be the star of the show instead of Carmen Miranda or Chevalier. And he signed up a practically unheard-of comedy team called Abbott and Costello to back her up. But now he had literally acres of new area to fill with attractions. And these were huge places—almost like half of Disneyland today. So he started devising things. Of course, what he was talking about in October '39 was a lot different from what came to pass in the spring of '40.

Bill Doll and Gypsy Rose Lee describe the broad narrative of events during the second year of the fair, with some help from Dick Williams.

Bill Doll:

One of the places Mike took over was a thing that had been floundering around the first year called Merrie England, with tabloid Shakespearean plays and the changing of the guard, pubs and so on. Mike took it over and called it the Dancing Campus, and we filled the place nightly with thousands of jitterbugs. He had all the big bands—fellows like Harry James, Charlie Spivack and Les Brown, who had a kid vocalist named Doris Day. And then there was a bouncy little singer named Betty Hutton, who we all thought had a great future.

Dick Williams:

Mike told Bill and me he wanted some stories about the Dancing Campus having the biggest dance floor in the world. Bill added that we'd found an inventor who was putting springs under the entire dance floor. A guy from *Popular Mechanics* calls right away and says, "Hey, I wanna do a story about the springs." We tell him, "Oh no. It's a great big secret. Maybe when the season's over we'll show it to you." And you know, at the end of the summer, he remembered and wanted to come out and do the story. We had to tell him the inventor had pulled out all the springs and gone home.

Bill Doll:

Mike hung up some old Spanish moss and a little scrimshaw and changed George Jessel's Little Old New York into Mike Todd's *Gay New Orleans*, with marvelous restaurants, saloons, the Sazarac Bar and the Absinthe House. [Bill loved the word *scrimshaw*, and the fact that it is jewelry made from whale ivory did not prevent him from using the word to describe the iron filigree that adorns New Orleans balconies. Or, on another occasion, to say that Gene Fowler's prose was loaded with scrimshaw.] In Gay New Orleans they had shows that went right around the clock, winding up with a Mardi Gras show at midnight. They had Carrie Finnell, the lady credited with inventing the striptease.

Ms. Finnell, well into her fifties and very matronly, had retired to her husband's pig farm in Indiana at the time of the fair and was definitely the acknowledged master, if not the innovator, of the lost and forgotten art of tassel twirling. As she advanced in age she developed her art, but wore more clothing, substituting for displays of the flesh an unbelievable muscular manipulation of her covered but unharnessed breasts. She could bounce them in tandem, clockwise, counterclockwise, but, most incredibly, alternately in rhythm.

The second season of the fair only the French Pavilion had better food than the Original Absinthe House in *Gay New Orleans*. Todd had brought in the head chef from the Hotel Roosevelt, and the menu featured pompano *en papillote*, Gulf shrimp and oysters, which were flown in daily, souffléd potatoes and a whole range of other New Orleans gourmet specialties, all at very reasonable prices. Putney Dandridge, a famous jazz pianist of the era, was brought up from the Vieux Carré, and three singing waiters from the Sazarac Bar. Absinthe was still legal and adventurous souls could drink all they dared, poured by Lucian Casbonne, the head bartender, borrowed for the summer from the original establishment in New Orleans.

With such food, drink and ambiance, Todd had little difficulty persuading Harvey Gibson to hold his bankers' banquet the second year of the fair at the Original Absinthe House. As dessert was being served, Todd stood up in his tuxedo—tails were not required for the less austere surroundings of Gay New Orleans—and introduced Mrs. Henrietta Longstreet, a member of the National Executive Board of the D.A.R., who was going to give the assembled gentlemen a woman's reaction to the various exhibits at the fair. This unscheduled speaker was an unpleasant surprise for everyone, but especially for Harvey Gibson, who gave Todd a severe and questioning look during the introduction.

Starting with a dull and ponderous commentary on some of the more educational exhibits, Mrs. Longstreet suddenly gave a massive flip to her left breast. The few financiers and bankers, who at this point were paying attention, couldn't believe what they had seen, and nudged their dozing and inattentive neighbors. A sentence or two later, Mrs. Longstreet's right breast virtually jumped across the room, to the stunned silence of all assembled. As she gained the attention of the entire room and continued her dry appraisal of the fair's attractions, her bosom began an incredible gymnastic display. When it became clear, which it did in a matter of seconds, that this was no accident or nervous mannerism, the dignitaries collapsed in hysterical laughter, and at the completion of her little talk Mrs. Henrietta Longstreet, née Carrie Finnell, was given a standing ovation.

There was only a twenty-five-cent flat admission charge for *Gay New Orleans*, which was spread out over several acres and boasted a variety of small attractions and inexpensive food stands. The big show, a fifty-minute spectacle staged by Hassard Short, included original musical numbers, a chariot race and variety acts. "To dramatize the fact that all this stuff was available for twenty-five cents," Bill Doll said, "we made a Michael Todd quarter, which we gave to the press and other guests. It was made of wood, and instead of George Washington we had a caricature of Mike wearing a wig with a cigar in his kisser on one side, and the legend 'In Todd We Trust' on the back. It was the biggest entertainment value ever, and we packed them in." The midnight performance included the Flame Dance. This was the end of Mike's professional and romantic association with Muriel Page.

While there was scant business during the day, the Dancing

Campus was booming at night. At the Hall of Music, *Streets of Paris,* starring Gypsy Rose Lee, proved to be as big an attraction as *The Hot Mikado* of the previous year.

Gypsy, describing her summer at the fair:

> The fair was everything Mike told me it was going to be. My picture was even bigger than Stalin's—forty feet tall. It towered above everything else—that is, until the night of the big storm. The picture was done in sections, four sections, and I buckled in the middle. Oh God, I remember when we opened—it rained for sixteen days in a row. Everybody at the fair was crying. Everybody but Mike. He stayed cheerful through the whole thing. The cane, the noise, the loudspeakers going. "Here it is folks! Step right up! The only dry show on the midway! The only show indoors!" And, of course, we were. But right across the street from us was Billy Rose's Aquacade. And Billy would be standing there in the rain, livid. So he finally went to the head of the fair and said, "You've got to make Mike Todd stop ballyhooing his own show!"

In the summer of 1940, with the acquisition of the Dancing Campus and Gay New Orleans, which covered the flanks of the Aquacade and the Hall of Music directly facing it, Todd had Rose completely surrounded. Todd directed his loudspeakers toward the entrance of the Aquacade and, while fulfilling the Treaty of Lindy's by not blasting his pitches during the performances of the Aquacade, he kept them loud and continuous at all other times and made Rose feel that he was under siege. This produced the expected result of protests and countermeasures from Rose and kept the so-called Battle of the Midway alive in the press for the second season of the fair, providing Todd with an extra measure of publicity, aside from what was generated by the success of his attractions.

As Bill Doll summed it up, "If Mike had been around on Broadway and producing shows, it would have taken him twenty years to get to the point where he was when the New York Fair of 1939–40 closed. Everybody in America had heard about Mike."

Todd made a lot of money that summer and settled into a way of living and spending that he continued throughout the rest of his life. His partner on *The Hot Mikado,* Jack Dietz, did almost as well, but took his profits from this, the Cotton Club and other ventures and went west and started producing a series of successful "B" movies. Todd started playing high-stake gin at the Friars and thought nothing of gambling a thousand dollars or more on a single race at the track. He acquired a vast wardrobe and began storing cigars at Dunhill's. Mike started palling around with Walter Winchell at the Stork Club, joining him on his early-morning rounds, chasing after exciting and dangerous police calls. He became Damon Runyon's frequent companion at the track and at Dinty Moore's. He had arrived.

As always, he had a variety of plans, but the enjoyment of his success kept him from getting any of them going. Dick Williams tells a story about this interim period:

> After the fair, to pick up some quick money, he made a booking for *Streets of Paris* with the state fair up in Syracuse. What he was really doing was just booking Gypsy, throwing in a few acts to showcase her. I was sent up to do the publicity. Mike told me to be sure to keep his name out of it. He didn't want to be known as just Gypsy's producer or booker. He came up at the end of the date to collect the money, and he said, "I'm going to drive back to New York tonight. You come along with me." This was just when gas rationing had started, and I said, "Jesus, it's pretty late. You better watch your step. There's not gonna be many gas stations open, and you know you can only get two gallons." He had this big Cadillac. "Don't worry about it," he says. We start off from Syracuse and it's real late and I don't know how the hell we're going to get to New York. On the way, we stop off at Grossinger's—he loved Grossinger's. Anyway, we eat and he sees people there and then on we go. I looked to see how much gas we had, and I said, "You're hitting empty. We're not going to make it." "Okay," Mike says. "We'll stop and get gas." "Yeah, but where?" It was really late. "Oh, we'll work it out. Will you *stop worrying*." We're on Route Seventeen, and we come over this hill, and way down the line we see this general store that's open that has a gasoline pump in front of it. Well, Mike puts his foot down, and we start going like a bat out of hell, and he roars in with the brakes screeching and slides right up to the pump and jumps out of the car. A kid runs out of the store to see what's happening, and Mike screams at him, "Quick, fill her up! The cops are after us!" The kid looks at him, fills it up, Mike throws him a fin, and off we went.

CHAPTER 4

TODD HAD ARRIVED but found himself with no place to go at the close of the second year of the fair. That summer he had put aside any plans for future productions in order to enjoy his hard-won and spectacular rise to fame. As he put it, he was just "spreading a little sunshine," which meant he was spending money as fast or faster than he was making it.

While he was now acquainted, if not pals, with most of the leading journalists in New York, and his name was constantly in print, he was still not well acquainted with the major creative talents of the legitimate theater. By the close of the fair in the fall of 1940, only a few manuscripts and projects had been offered to him, none of which he was enthusiastic about.

He had probably made as much or more money than Billy Rose at the fair, but came away with just a small fraction of his profits. Rose saved and invested his Aquacade earnings and years later was reported to be the largest private individual owner of A. T. & T. stock. Todd never bought a share of stock in his life and never had a savings account. Any investments he made were in his own projects.

With a greatly diminished bankroll and no show to produce in New York, Todd went back to Chicago. His old friend and backer Harold Costello had offered him the chance to pick up some quick bucks with a minimum of effort. Mother and I remained in New York. He was going to be gone just a short while. He'd be back producing shows on Broadway in no time.

Just a few years before he had shared a bare office in the Oriental Theatre Building with Jule Styne, but now Costello was pleased to give him the lofty-sounding position of general manager of the Oriental Theatre. Todd was to get a modest salary and a generous piece of the profits his bookings produced. He had free rein to book any kind of attractions and movies that would bring in customers.

Even Todd's imagination could not overcome the monopoly on the pick of Hollywood products that the Balaban and Katz chain of theaters had in Chicago. B. and K. controlled most of the major first-run showcase theaters in the Loop and the majority of the key neighborhood sub-run theaters in the city and suburbs. This was years before independent theater owners, by government decree, could risk their necks bidding for individual films.

Todd could book only the B. and K. leftovers. B. and K. could afford to buy the best stage shows as well. Totally frustrated, Todd announced, after the screening of *Gaucho Serenade,* a forthcoming attraction at the Oriental Theatre, that the critics had just witnessed motion picture history. They had kindly and patiently sat through the worst movie ever made. Some of the critics sympathetically mentioned Todd's opinion, and business was a bit better that week, as a few film buffs didn't want to miss *Gaucho Serenade.*

Todd traveled extensively, assessing the road units in the Midwest, to see if he could find novelty attractions to boost the take at the Oriental. On a trip to Detroit he ran into an organizer for Gerald L. K. Smith. Smith, a former lieutenant of Huey Long's, was making a tidy personal fortune as the leader of a neo-Nazi, anti-Semitic group.

Smith's organizer was complaining to Todd about the increasing opposition and difficulties he was encountering. Todd lent a sympathetic ear—he was curious and wished to explore the peculiar workings of such a mentality. He attended a meeting, was introduced to Smith and allowed himself to be recruited into the organization.

Several weeks later the organizer called Todd and bemoaned the fact that pressure from some "goddamned kikes" had forced the cancellation of a booking they had for an auditorium in Chicago. Could Todd possibly find another location? Todd went to Costello and secured the use of the Masonic Hall in the Oriental Theatre Building for the Gerald L. K. Smith meeting.

The same Jewish activists who had forced the previous cancellation learned that Todd had made the substitute Masonic Hall booking. A few days before the Smith appearance several tough

Jews lying in wait cornered Todd on Randolph Street at night, pulled him into an alley and gave him a severe beating. Todd gave them no explanation and silently took his lumps.

The meeting was held with the battered Todd in attendance. As Smith left the platform that evening to the frenzied cheers of his supporters, he was detained as a dangerous subversive by FBI agents. Through his brother Frank, who was friendly with senior agents in the Chicago FBI office, Todd had arranged to have the FBI at the meeting. Smith was sufficiently intimidated by his Chicago experience to substantially tone down his blatant support of fascists. During the few months Todd was in the organization, he fed inside information to Walter Winchell, the most famous news columnist of the era, who publicized detailed exposés of Smith and his organization on his radio program and in his column. To take the heat off and steer clear of the FBI, Smith now turned his attention to the menace of communism.

Todd was getting nowhere booking the Oriental Theatre, and his tab unit of *Streets of Paris*, starring Gypsy Rose Lee, was touring and barely breaking even.

Todd heard about a huge barn of a place, miles north of the Loop in Chicago, that was once a jai alai fronton and had been vacant for years. Todd had the inspiration of turning it into the world's largest nightclub. Joe Sherman, a longtime successful operator of nightclubs, told Mike he was insane—it was miles off the beaten track and no nightclub patron would go there, even if they could find it. "That's the whole idea," Todd explained. "I'm not after the Chez Paree crowd—I'll get them later, out of curiosity. But this'll be the world's first nightclub for families." Sherman was convinced that lack of activity and his recent beating had scrambled Mike's brains.

Todd signed a lease and went ahead with his plans for Michael Todd's Theatre Café. He would lavishly redecorate and redesign the fronton, installing a gigantic stage and dance floor. He built up his tab version of *Streets of Paris* with specialty acts and a large chorus line, and he signed Hassard Short to direct and present the biggest show ever performed in a nightclub—a family Folies Bergère. There were millions of people in the Chicago area who would be curious about and interested in going to a nightclub if it was made appealing and inexpensive. Todd had no interest in running the food and liquor end, beyond dictating the policy of the operation—they must be ultra-scrupulous about not serving drinks to minors. Todd wanted to concentrate his attention on producing the show and handling the promotion. His own bankroll was short, and to get the place opened he farmed out the catering end to Joe Miller, a successful Chicago nightclub operator who was willing to gamble a sizable sum that Todd's crazy idea would work. Todd insisted, contrary to custom, that waitresses be used, as his kind of customer would be intimidated by a waiter. Todd was aware that Miller had "connections" and probably had little doubt as to where Miller's hefty capital contribution was coming from. Todd was to control the entire policy of the operation, produce the shows and in return get a sizable salary and a large chunk of the profits.

Gypsy Rose Lee concisely related the history of Michael Todd's Theatre Café:

> When the fair closed, instead of disposing of the scenery and costumes as most producers do, Mike saved every scrap, and he opened the biggest nightclub in the world in Chicago. It used to be called the Rainbow Gardens—it was a huge arena. Our customers used to arrive in the streetcar. The whole family—a man, his wife, the kids, everybody. I'd be out there doing the number and the kids were swinging back and forth on the railing. . . . Champagne cocktails for twenty-five cents. Mike wrote all the ads himself. A full-course dinner for seventy-five cents and champagne cocktails for a quarter. "All of this and Gypsy Rose Lee too." We ran for about, oh, twenty weeks. Smash business. Fifty-five thousand dollars a week. Unheard of in those days. And then, all of a sudden—I don't know what exactly happened. Mike tried to do it his way and it just evidently wouldn't work. Gangsters or somebody came in. Whatever it was, we closed.

He used other parts of the Gay New Orleans show, and from the Dancing Campus he took the Les Brown Band. Not only did he steal from his own shows, but he took the hit comedy routine from Billy Rose's Aquacade. This was a hilarious slapstick act that had survived vaudeville, Willie, West and McGinty, which, in Keystone Comedy fashion, mimed a hazard-prone construction crew.

Remembering the success of Pete the Personality Penguin, Todd inserted a novelty gimmick into the show that was a great delight for kids. When the curtains opened, two penguin statuettes were seen at either side of the proscenium arch. At the conclusion of the finale they came to life and waddled offstage. Of course, midgets were inside the statuettes and shortly before the Theatre Café opened for the holiday season at the end of 1940, Sammy Lambert, the stage manager, asked Todd to fire them. Lambert reported that they were fascist bastards who kept making anti-Semitic remarks. Mike told Sammy to keep them on: "They're such tiny Nazis. How much trouble can they make?"

As was often the case with any Todd venture, money became extremely short prior to the opening. While Mike had a Chicago press agent to handle the Theatre Café, his association with Bill Doll had proved so successful that he wanted Doll to come out from New York to handle the opening.

He wired Lillian Leff in New York: "WANT DOLL HERE. HAVE HIM TAKE TWENTIETH CENTURY TONIGHT."

Lillian phoned Bill and read him Todd's wire. Bill said he would come to the office and pick up the money for the trip. Lillian said, "Mr. Todd didn't say anything about money, and I don't have enough in petty cash to buy the ticket."

Bill sent Mike the following wire: "ANTICIPATE ARRIVING CHICAGO AS SOON AS I RECEIVE RAILROAD FARE."

Todd's return wire read: "BILL, PLEASE, YOU'RE MAKING ME LOSE CONFIDENCE IN MYSELF."

Bill arrived in Chicago the next day.

Todd's lunatic long shot came home a big winner. He invited the mayor and the police commissioner to the opening. The police commissioner was quoted the following day in the newspapers: "It's the only nightclub in the world I would take my children to." The Theatre Café opened at 5:00 P.M., and the dinner show began at 6:15, giving parents the chance to get their kids to bed at a reasonable hour. As much as anything else, the idea of a champagne cocktail for a quarter dramatized the concept of lavish nightclub entertainment being made accessible to all. Gypsy's routine, along with the rest of the show, was suitably tailored for the younger clientele at the first show and was risqué for the late show.

Both the Chicago papers and the national press pulled out all the stops, lavishing praise on the show; they emphasized the unique bargain price and family-oriented policy. Overnight Michael Todd's Theatre Café became a Midwest tourist attraction.

Seating almost five thousand and doing near-capacity business, Todd's offbeat nightclub rolled up gigantic grosses.

Shortly after the opening a bizarre incident occurred when Grandmother Goldbogen came to see the show. She was then in her seventies (she lived to be ninety-six) and while extremely lively and talkative, she seldom left her home at 2034 West LeMoyne. As much as she lived in the past, dwelling on her father's wealth and vast holdings in Poland in the previous century, she was aware of her sons' successes and was particularly pleased by "Avrumele's" fame—her neighbors were continually bringing her newspaper clippings about Todd. Her own reading was confined to the Hebrew-language paper. She was a bit vague about what exactly Todd did, never having seen anything he produced. After the tumult of the holidays had died down, Todd was able to coax his mother and his simpleminded sister Edith to get dressed in their finest and spend an evening at the Theatre Café.

Mike had leased a limousine to take Gypsy to and from her hotel. On the evening of my grandmother's excursion, he sent the limo to pick up her and Edith. As it was a week night, with no third show, they were ready to go home at about half-past twelve. Todd put them into the limousine, which was parked, as usual, in an alley by the stage door. Coming out of the alley, the car was stopped by three hoods. The chauffeur was dragged from behind the wheel and knocked unconscious. This was the first time my grandmother and aunt had been in a limousine, and they assumed that the flurry of activity that followed their departure was a routine part of the service. The thugs made a fast getaway and it was a few blocks before they took a close look at their passengers. They were severely disappointed. They thought they had kidnapped Gypsy Rose Lee. Instead, they had my grandmother and simpleminded aunt. The surprised kidnappers started to ask questions. My grandmother understood English but habitually conversed in Yiddish, and my Aunt Edith took little or no interest in most conversations, so they could shed no light on the situation. The thugs gave the whole thing up as a bad job and abandoned the limousine. After waiting fifteen minutes for a driver to reappear, my grandmother and aunt became impatient and completed the trip home by trolley.

After the chauffeur regained consciousness, the police were notified and they began searching for the limousine all over the city. Todd spent several nerve-shattering hours before the police found the empty limousine, and a phone call home cleared away the mysterious conclusion of his mother's night out.

With the operation of the Theatre Café running smoothly and the money pouring in, Todd returned to New York to find a show to produce on Broadway. He flirted with the notion of making a musical of Ferenc Molnar's play *Liliom*, but decided there was no way to make the protagonist sympathetic enough to keep an audience interested in his story and rooting for him. Five years later, Rodgers and Hammerstein made *Liliom* into the hugely successful *Carousel*.

Before Todd could find a project, he got word that Joe Miller, who was left in charge of the operation of the Theatre Café, had instituted policy changes; and with the weekly gross beginning to slip, Mike went back to Chicago to check things out.

The first thing he saw when he walked into the club floored him—a "26" game had been installed. All Chicago nightclubs had an attractive girl stationed in back of a green felt box near the entrance, usually adjacent to the hat check counter, where a seemingly innocent little game of chance involving a handful of dice could be played. The odds in this game are much worse for the player than in craps—a sure sign that the joint is out to clip the customer. Nothing could more clearly contradict the policy Todd had carefully established and successfully sold to the public. Drink prices had been raised, a minimum imposed, and several false economies—such as cutting the number of waitresses—had been instituted. Todd was furious and told Miller the "26" game had to go that minute, and everything else had to revert to the way it was when Todd left Chicago.

Miller took Todd aside and explained that Todd's contract gave him control of the show and the right to set the overall policy, but that Miller's "connections," who had put up almost all the money to open the place, exercised control of the "catering" and the front of the house. These "connections" wanted to get their money back quickly and see that everybody involved made more money—and this of course included Todd, with the sizable chunk of the profits he was getting in addition to his salary. Todd insisted that everything go back to the way it was or his name would come off. Miller said his backers were hard men to reason with, but he would try.

The next day Todd was visited by Joe Fusco and Frank Nitti, Al Capone's successors and the heads of the Chicago mob. They said it was their money in the club and everyone was doing well, so what was his complaint? Todd politely explained his position. When it became clear that Fusco and Nitti were not about to change their position, and that Todd, although frightened, was not about to change his, a settlement was agreed upon. Todd would get a small—but, under the circumstances, generous—lump-sum payment—and his salary and percentage of the profits would cease with the withdrawal of his name from the club.

Todd's name was dropped from the ads, signs, programs and menus, and while there was no publicity about the fact, it was circumspectly alluded to in the columns. Within a few weeks the first fines were imposed for serving liquor to minors, and within another month the place was closed down.

When Todd returned to New York from Chicago in the spring of 1941 he had little cash but great determination to find a show to produce on Broadway. He put Gypsy back on the road with some of the elements of the Theatre Café show. One Sunday night Bill Doll phoned Todd from Buffalo and said that he, Gypsy and the unit had arrived after a long, tiring bus trip, but the manager of the theater had booked another unit. What had happened? Todd sheepishly admitted he had never confirmed the verbal booking for the Buffalo theater with a written contract and that they would have to lay off for a week before the next engagement. During the enforced vacation Doll sent Todd a scenic postcard with the message: "Having a wonderful time. Wish you were Sam Harris."

Todd spent several months trying to put together a revue entitled *And So to Bedlam*, but it never came to life and expired without a Pepys. A show he worked on for months did get to Broadway, but not under his aegis. It was entitled *Beat the Band* and was written by George Marion, Jr., with a score by Johnny Green, and was eventually produced by George Abbott. The show had a catchy jump tune called "The Steam Is on the Beam," which was a hit, but the show was a failure.

Todd's involvement with *Beat the Band*, however, proved to have a significant effect on our lives. Dick Powell was perfect for the lead and would be a big draw on Broadway. Todd paid Powell's expenses to come to New York so that they could audition the show for him. Powell brought along his wife, Joan Blondell. Todd was unable to sell Powell on doing *Beat the Band* and shortly afterwards gave up on it himself. During the couple of days that Powell and Blondell were in New York, Mike took a fancy for Joan.

At about this time, Joan's already tenuous marriage to Powell was beginning to disintegrate. Joan didn't spend extravagant sums on herself, but was a free spender fixing up a house and catering to everyone else's comforts. Few women ever had a stronger nesting instinct. She made no use of decorators or pretentious furnishings, but whatever she purchased was of the finest quality. Any room she decorated looked lived in. There were no fragile antiques, but large comfortable sofas and armchairs—books, flowers and chintz, lots of sturdy polished wood and the smell of furniture wax.

Powell was a nice man—unpretentious and very likable, but extremely tight with a buck. He was insecure and reserved. To him a home was an investment. He devastated Joan by selling several houses out from under her after she had put her heart into turning them into homes. If Powell could see a substantial profit on a house they owned he sold it—furnished. Their problems and Powell's insecurity were heightened at this time because he was making the difficult and uncertain transition from a musical comedy star to a straight dramatic actor, while Joan's career was thriving. Another consideration was that June Allyson was beginning her campaign to win Powell's affections. To top things off, Joan indicates in her thinly disguised autobiographical novel, *Center Door Fancy*, that Powell was an infrequent and lackluster lover.

During the winter of 1942–43, when Mike made some business trips to the coast, he and Joan saw each other and there were blind items in the gossip columns linking them.

In the summer of 1943 Todd produced a play entitled *The Naked Genius*, written by Gypsy Rose Lee, which starred Joan Blondell. Early in September Joan brought her children, Norman and Ellen, to Boston for the premiere of the play. My father brought me up from New York. It was a bit of a tryout of another kind—to see how we all got on together.

On the evening of the dress rehearsal, Dick Powell and I took a taxi together from the Ritz, where we were staying, to the Wilbur Theatre. We sat together during the torturously long dress rehearsal. The show had a lot of trick effects, which Todd and George Kaufman, the director, were using in an attempt to paper over the defects of the play. In the hallowed tradition of the theater, everything went wrong.

Powell made a few attempts at lighthearted conversation during the ride, but he was clearly preoccupied. As we sat watching the dire proceedings on stage, Powell tried to make a few encouraging remarks, but these soon gave way to an occasional sympathetic glance in my direction. I had the vague impression that we were sharing more than a depressing evening in the theater.

Although I failed to make the connection then, my father had told me just days earlier that he would like to get a divorce. I was devastated by this announcement, although I knew my parents' relationship had been chilly for years. I wanted my parents together, not divorced. He immediately saw the futility of trying to reason with me and said he would try to work things out with mother. I knew his heart wasn't in it, but for two and a half years there was no further mention of a divorce. My mother was delighted. She loved being Mrs. Michael Todd and, even more to the point, she loved my father. Her principal dissatisfaction with him was that he wanted out.

From the early spring of 1941 until the early spring of 1942, all of Todd's efforts to get a show going on Broadway were unproductive. After he closed the touring tab version of *Gay New Orleans,* he had no income from any source.

Fiorello La Guardia, the mayor of New York from 1934–45, was a reform candidate who strenuously and successfully waged a battle against both political and moral corruption in the city. Open prostitution and avenues lined with smut shops would have been unthinkable during his administration. His cleanup of New York and Broadway went so far that by 1942 Minsky's and other burlesque shows in town, which today would probably get a PG rating, were completely shut down.

Todd, who had been profitably associated with Gypsy Rose Lee for two years, got the idea of doing a burlesque show on Broadway designed for the carriage trade. At this point in her career, Gypsy's act was a classy and nostalgic distillation of burlesque. She still did a strip, but her accompanying monologue was wry and sophisticated—the essence of the kind of high-class burlesque show Todd wanted to present. The title he picked, *Star and Garter,* clearly indicated the kind of show he was going to produce—"tall dames and low comedy."

Todd hired Bobby Clark as the comedy star of the show. Bobby, originally of the famous vaudeville act Clark and McCullough, always appeared with eyeglasses painted on in black grease pencil, a trademark as famous on stage as Groucho Marx's grease-penciled moustache was on film. Clark often walked in the same low crouch as Groucho, but with the added flourish, when successfully propositioning a comely lass, of growling and shuffling his feet like a purposeful dog. He often portrayed a comic lecher, but one who was even more harmless than Groucho. He was as good a juggler as W. C. Fields and a much better acrobat. In addition, he could misplay almost every musical instrument to great comic effect. It was twenty years since Clark had last appeared in burlesque, but he proved able, in *Star and Garter,* to get more laughs out of hackneyed burlesque sketches than anyone dreamed of. By this time, having appeared in a dozen Broadway productions, his name and presence in the show—like Gypsy's—took it out of the realm of ordinary burlesque. Todd still ran the risk that La Guardia's watchdogs would not share this view and close the show. His added insurance against this possibility was using Hassard Short again to direct. Short's classy musical comedy reputation was another step in elevating Todd's show above regular bump-and-grind burlesque. Lavish costumes and sets, as well as booking the show into the prestigious Music Box Theatre, would further justify charging Broadway prices.

Mike built a big production number around the Johnny Mercer and Harold Arlen hit "Blues in the Night." His big stage effect involved a huge papier-mâché crescent moon that was hung above the stage by wires. At the end of the production number, the eye of the man in the moon winked at the audience as the last nearly nude, statuesque show girl exited the stage. For comic insurance Todd hired Professor Lamberti, one of the classic acts of vaudeville. Lamberti, in shabby and mismatched formal attire, with a wild fringe of hair about his bald pate, is revealed as the show curtain opens, standing behind a xylophone. With false confidence and a few asides, he announces his program for the evening. As he ineptly plays his first selection, a gorgeous girl silently begins a striptease behind him, out of his sight. As his first number is completed, she disappears behind a curtain, having just begun to disrobe. Lamberti is surprised and pleased by the warm response of the audience (prompted by a claque of ushers in the rear of the house). Each short number he plays, accompanied by some whimsical self-deprecating remarks, gets an increasing amount of applause as the girl behind him gets closer to the bare essentials. Carrie Finnell was in the show, to give it some extra bounce.

Star and Garter also contains the most suggestive musical number ever presented on a Broadway stage, entitled "The Bunny." On one hand the chorus girls wore small, furry objects like muffs, which they stroked gently with the other hand, while the singers began to softly intone the lyrics:

> *Bunny, bunny, bunny*
> *Pretty little bunny.*
> *Who'll buy my bunny,*
> *So soft and warm.*

And this was only the beginning. Mike referred to *Star and Garter* as one of his great cultural achievements.

As Todd said, he was "down to his Abes" (only pennies in his pocket), but on the strength of his World's Fair reputation he was able to find enough investors to capitalize the production. (The ten shows Todd produced in the following five years were done principally with his own money.)

Substituting previews in New York for out-of-town tryouts is now a fairly common practice, but it was something of an innovation when Todd, who was short of money, scheduled one week of previews in New York. The dress rehearsal and first preview were disastrous, and the backers were extremely nervous. One of the backers demanded the return of his investment. Todd postponed the previews and the opening of *Star and Garter* in order to get the show into some semblance of shape. The show was in danger of folding before it ever opened. Gypsy described the situation this way:

> During the time that Mike was doing *Star and Garter,* he had a backer—I don't remember his name—who couldn't understand why his friends couldn't watch all the rehearsals—just sitting there talking, giggling and serving martinis to one another, so we had to get rid of him. And after all that excitement, I learned that the man had a miserable five thousand dollars in the show. So I said, "Well, that's nothing, Mike. I'll put up the five thousand dollars." So . . . suddenly there was a different look in Mike's eye. He said, "You mean to tell me you've got five thousand dollars?" I said, "Of course, I've got five thousand dollars. You think you're playing with kids?"

Actually, things cost a lot more than that, because we had to put up the equity bond. So I had to hock one of my annuities. And this of course involved lawyers now. [Gypsy's lawyer was Bill Fitelson, the leading theatrical attorney of the era. After the initial $5,000 buy-out, Gypsy came up with another $25,000 to get the show open.] I said, "I don't know anything about percentages. What I'd like you to do is make me a pie. Yes, just make a big round circle like this and put a mark like that and say, 'That belongs to Mike Todd.' Put another mark over there. Then that belongs to the other backers. And whatever is left is mine. Is that all right?" So, of course, all these great big expensive lawyers look at each other, and Mike said, "Will somebody please make the dame a pie? *Make the dame a pie!* She doesn't know from arithmetic." So they made the pie, and I looked at it, and it looked like I had a pretty good share of the show, and I said, "Now shade me, so I know that's mine." And they shaded mine darker, and I said, "Now Mike, you put your initials on my side, and I'll put my initials on my side." And we both initialed it, and that was my contract.

It was a very beautiful show and the time was ripe. It was wartime, and it was the first girlie show that had been done on Broadway in a long time—beautiful girls, scanty costumes, low comics. Low comics . . . it was Bobby Clark, the greatest comic in the world. And it was a wonderful show. It was beautiful, lush, extravagant and wonderful. I remember one matinee, one of the ladies was leaving—my dressing room faced the street—and there were some friends waiting for her when she came out. She said, "Mabel, I have just seen without a doubt the dirtiest, filthiest show I've ever seen in all my life. Don't miss it."

Star and Garter, which became Todd's longest-running Broadway show, opened at the Music Box Theatre on June 24, 1942. It ran until 1944 and was his second biggest moneymaker. The show received very good notices, although not raves. However, of greater importance, they were "money reviews." Louis Kronenberger in *PM* called it "a leg and laugh show with plenty of good filthy fun." The New York *Sun*'s critic wrote: "Mr. Todd's production proves a fast moving, sumptuous, dazzling and lusty show."

All the critics prominently featured Todd in their reviews. Lewis Nichols in the *Times* and Richard Watts in the *Herald Tribune* both commented at length on how Mike Todd had figured out ingenious ways to get around La Guardia's ban on burlesque.

From this point on in his theatrical career, everything he produced was dominated by his personality. No matter who wrote, directed or appeared in one of his productions, it was treated—critically and publicly—as the "new Mike Todd show."

Everyone in the business who knew about Gypsy's investment in *Star and Garter*—and it was fairly common knowledge—assumed, because of her extreme tightfistedness, that she and Todd must be having an affair. Over the years, whenever talk got around to *Star and Garter* or Gypsy, it was clear to me that most of Todd's employees had little doubt that Mike and Gypsy had slept together. I'm almost certain they weren't lovers, and even if they were, the earth never shook. Gypsy's son, Eric Preminger, is almost certain they had an affair. Sammy Lambert, who was the stage manager for *Streets of Paris* at the fair and in Chicago, and for *Star and Garter,* and who saw Mike and Gypsy together more than any other individual, was certain they never went to bed together. Jule Styne, who knew both very well, is unequivocal in his view that their relationship was primarily a business one and that they did not have an affair. David Lawlor, who worked for Todd in various capacities from the early forties through 1950, said, "I don't think they spent all that time just talking business." My mother was extremely jealous of Gypsy and very suspicious of my father's relationship with her.

Once, while we were discussing the women in his life, Elizabeth Taylor told me that my father had listed for her all the women he had ever slept with, and Gypsy was singled out and specified as not being on that list. Joan Blondell in her book indicated the same. From my observation, Mike and Gypsy admired and respected one another and got a kick out of each other's company, but that was as far as things went. I'm sure Mike considered Gypsy to be one of his closest friends. She may well have had even stronger feelings for him. There were probably times when their friendship might have developed into a romance, but various restraints on both sides kept this relationship from ever heating up. Although Gypsy was seven years younger than Mike, she seemed to him like an older sister who had a savvy understanding of the theatrical world, accumulated during her lifetime in show business. He appreciated her breezy style and wit. They had a well-developed knack for creating a colorful image and making good copy. Getting publicity was second nature to both of them.

Today Todd would be considered a male chauvinist because he needed and expected deference and dependency from a woman. Gypsy was much too cool, clever and independent ever to provide this. Mike talked and dealt with her as if she were a man. And although she was a sex symbol of sorts, she always struck me as someone who had a minimal interest in sex. It certainly was a secondary consideration to making money. There was a vast difference in their ideas of what to do with money, and in the last analysis, this difference between them— if nothing else—was irreconcilable. It was axiomatic for Gypsy that money was to be saved; Todd's only use for money was to spend it.

One Sunday, during the run of *Star and Garter,* I went with my father to visit Gypsy at her home in Westchester. Shortly before we arrived at Gypsy's I spotted a popcorn vendor. I was still eating the popcorn when we reached her house. Gypsy always had a collection of disagreeable little pets—a small monkey that used to bite visitors in her dressing room and, at this time, a group of ill-tempered Chihuahuas. She and my father were talking, and I carelessly dropped several kernels of popcorn on the floor. The next day we found out that one of her dogs had choked to death on the popcorn kernels. Gypsy was as nice as could be about the matter and told my father he should keep the news from me. It was my mother who told me about Gypsy's dog.

Star and Garter did smash business for almost two years on Broadway. Other than expensive costumes it was not a costly production, and it paid its way in a couple of months. Todd had made a big success with *The Hot Mikado* at the New York World's Fair and capitalized fully on this success with a variety of attractions the second year of the fair. The money made was quickly spent, and in the next two years he was on the verge of slipping back into the obscure shadows of show business. Gypsy's last-minute salvation of *Star and Garter* fully revived his fortunes.

CHAPTER 5

TODD'S SUCCESSFUL COLLABORATION with Hassard Short, who had directed *The Hot Mikado, Gay New Orleans* and *Star and Garter,* now opened the door for an association with some of the most highly regarded names in the American musical theater—Cole Porter, Ethel Merman and Herbert and Dorothy Fields. Herbert Fields had been associated successfully from early days with Rogers and Hart as their librettist and recently in 1941 had teamed up with his sister Dorothy, a successful lyricist, to write the book for the Cole Porter musical *Let's Face It.*

Porter and Short had done shows together and were friends who saw each other socially. This was at a time when homosexuals had not come out of the closet and to the outside world maintained the facade that, in fact, there were no closets. During this period, when I occasionally saw Porter and Short together, they were chummy but each had his own young friend, always introduced to me as a nephew.

Porter was preparing a show with Herbert and Dorothy Fields entitled *Jenny Get Your Gun,* and together they had won the interest of Ethel Merman in playing the lead, with Vinton Freedley to produce. As work progressed, Freedley became increasingly disenchanted with the book of the show and bowed out.

Todd's success and publicity prompted Porter to ask his friend Hassard Short what this new wunderkind was like. Short spoke well of Todd, and Porter and the Fields offered him their new show, which was retitled *Something for the Boys.* Todd recognized an opportunity when he saw one and was ready to sign without reading the book or hearing a song. Hassard Short was signed to direct.

The story involved a trio of cousins who inherit a ranch in Texas. One cousin, a sidewalk pitchman, was played by Allen Jenkins, a popular movie comedian. Another cousin is a night-club performer, played by a comparatively unknown deadpan comedienne, Paula Laurence. The remaining cousin is a Rosie the Riveter defense worker, played by Ethel Merman. When the cousins meet, they discover that their ranch adjoins an air base, Kelly Field, outside of San Antonio. They decide to convert their new home into a boarding house for officers' wives. The Ethel Merman character, Blossom Hart, makes use of her mechanical know-how and also sets up a small factory on the ranch, to manufacture "joining links" for the war effort. Naturally there is a romance, and one of several story convolutions involves the boarding house being mistaken for a bordello by the military authorities. All the plot complications are resolved when it is discovered that the Carborundum that had become lodged in one of Blossom's fillings when she was doing defense work has enabled her to receive radio messages through her teeth. At the end of the show Blossom gets her man, and the cousins are going to manufacture radio-receiving Carborundum caps for the armed forces. As Merman proudly announces in the show's last line of dialogue, "We're gonna put a cap in every yap!" For the finale she leads the entire ensemble in a reprise of the title song:

> We're always doing something,
> Something for the boys.

With *Lady in the Dark* recently setting a new musical comedy standard on Broadway for sophistication, and *Oklahoma!* for substantive librettos, Vinton Freedley might well have wondered what fate awaited a show with such a book. But the dialogue was sharp and funny. The story line was silly, but it was well constructed, and beautifully integrated with the musical numbers. Like *A Funny Thing Happened on the Way to the Forum*, there was an almost magical prologue that perfectly set the tone and pace of the show and got it off to a rollicking start. *Something for the Boys* had a very melodic and enjoyable—

though not memorable—Cole Porter score, a talented cast, good dancing and Ethel Merman. What more could a diversion-seeking wartime audience desire?

Howard Bay, the set designer of *Something for the Boys*, recalls:

> It was one of those greatest of all theatrical rarities—a trouble-free production. Cole Porter brought a group of his friends to see the final run-through before we moved to Boston. Porter had been around only for the music rehearsals. He and his friends came in late, sat in one of the boxes and his man served champagne. They sat there and laughed and applauded. They chatted amongst themselves. They had a marvelous time and greatly enjoyed the show.

Only the most minor adjustments had to be made during the Boston tryout. During the first performance before an audience, a benefit preview, Howard Bay went backstage during the intermission:

> When the curtain went up on the second act, Merman was standing in the wings on the other side of the stage from me, arms crossed. Betty Garrett, a little girl they had picked out of the chorus, was singing a soft solo opening number. Any coughing from the audience stopped—you couldn't hear a sound. I saw Merman watching, and listening, and listening. . . . The number was changed the next day.

Todd's major contributions to the show were one deletion and one addition. "At the heavy expense of the management," Todd demonstrated to the Fields, Short, Merman and Porter that a scene and number they liked just didn't work. He maintained before rehearsals started that the number should be cut, but to satisfy his collaborators, he had the necessary set and costumes made, and in Boston Todd won his point. This experience stood him in good stead when the next show he did with Porter and the Fields came a cropper in Boston, and changes he requested were made with the minimum of discussion.

His addition to the show was a spectacular scenic effect that he was now in the habit of putting deep in the second act of any Todd musical. The starring act of a vaudeville bill was always placed "next to closing." Todd's scenic effect in *Something for the Boys* was the penultimate scene. It was the interior of a bomber that was seen bouncing about in a thunderstorm. Fittingly, the *deus ex machina* makes its appearance in this scene. When the bomber's radio conks out, Blossom Hart receives emergency landing instructions through the Carborundum-laden filling in her tooth.

On the opening night in New York, Todd committed an unprecedented act of theatrical *gaucherie.* Hassard Short and Herbert and Dorothy Fields, who were watching the performance from the back of the standee rail, thought Todd had gone berserk when they saw him go down the aisle and grab the arms of two critics who were leaving the theater. Todd wanted to make sure all the critics saw his bomber. It was a practice of some critics on the morning papers to leave before the final curtain to ensure getting their reviews in the earliest editions of their papers. The two who had tried to leave so liked the show that Todd's youthful exuberance scarcely affected their excellent notices.

Something for the Boys opened in New York at the Alvin Theatre on January 7, 1943. It got the best set of notices of any show Todd had ever produced. There was not a single poor or even mild review. A couple were excellent, but the rest were all-out hats-in-the-air raves:

> All season long, the world has yearned hopefully for a big, fast, glittering musical comedy. It has it now, for last evening the fabulous Mike Todd brought in *Something for the Boys*.
> —LEWIS NICHOLS, New York *Times*

> Michael Todd went to town with *Something for the Boys* at the Alvin last night. Men growing old ungracefully wept to see what they never hoped to see again—the staging of a musical show as glamorous, kinetic, balanced and seductive as the still lamented Ziegfeld in his heyday used to stage them.
>
> —BURTON RASCOE, New York *World-Telegram*

> A big brash musical show has arrived at the Alvin . . . this Michael Todd production should be the answer to playgoers' prayers for a long time to come.
> —HOWARD BARNES, New York *Herald Tribune*

All the critics lavished praise on all aspects of the production, especially Merman's performance, but no one mentioned Todd's bomber.

Partially from patriotism and also to settle an audience before a performance, it was Todd's custom to have the orchestra play the "Star Spangled Banner" immediately before launching into the show's overture. *Something for the Boys* was a very entertaining show, but Ethel Merman was unquestionably its biggest attraction. On the few occasions that she was ill, a notice in the *Playbill*—or worse, a card in the theater lobby—announcing her absence from the performance would have caused a wholesale demand for refunds or exchanges. Todd sneaked Merman's absence by an audience and almost made them feel fortunate to have missed her. The leading man in the show, Bill Johnson, played the role of a staff sergeant.

Immediately before the playing of the "Star Spangled Banner," Bill would come out in uniform and announce, "An unfortunate illness will prevent Miss Merman from appearing this evening." Bill dramatically read the speech Mike had written, and none of his lines gave him as much stage opportunity as the illness announcement. As soon as the groans from the audience died down, Bill would say: "There's a little girl who has been waiting in the wings since the show first opened who will appear this evening in the leading role. Tonight that little girl, Betty Garrett, will have her chance. Perhaps you'll see a new star find her place in the Broadway galaxy." The orchestra immediately started the national anthem and, of course, the audience stood at attention. The combination of the star-being-born speech made by a handsome young man in military uniform and the playing of the "Star Spangled Banner" made anyone thinking of a refund feel stonehearted and unpatriotic. During the run of the play, with Merman missing a handful of performances, there were less than a couple of dozen requests for refunds.

As it happened, Betty Garrett did go on to have a successful career on Broadway and in the movies.

Something for the Boys had a show-stopping comedy number entitled "By the Mississinewa," a duet featuring Ethel Merman and Paula Laurence, who were fitted out in Indian maiden costumes. With a good reception and encores anticipated, it opened in Boston with four choruses. By the time the show closed Porter had to provide a dozen, and audiences still wanted more.

Ethel Merman played even the most tender love duet looking straight out at the audience, leaving her leading man rhapsodizing into the back of her neck. It was a physical impossibility for any performer to try to top Merman. Paula Laurence tried. Every bit of comic business that Merman was provided with, or that she improvised in this number, Laurence tried to match. This only spurred on Merman to a peak of comic invention. While supposedly a number done by friendly cousins, it became a deadly but hysterically funny duel. Merman ignored Laurence onstage and off until the night before Laurence left the show; at the end of the Mississinewa number, Merman bopped Laurence on the top of her head with a prop rubber hatchet.

Paula Laurence was replaced by a wonderfully personable dancer and comedienne, Betty Bruce, who became a close friend of Merman's, and then of Joan Blondell's, when they toured together in the road company of the show.

When *Something for the Boys* opened, Bill Callahan, the lead dancer, was barely sixteen, although he looked much older. He was tall and quite handsome. In almost a competition, he was taken on by practically all the chorus girls in *Something for the Boys* and *Mexican Hayride,* which opened in 1944, when Bill was still underage for the draft.

With the success of *Something for the Boys,* Todd was now the fully accredited boy wonder of Broadway. A few weeks after the opening of the show Runyon devoted a full column to him:

> Mike Todd is the greatest natural gambler I've ever known and the most spectacular of all the many colorful figures that have passed through the Broadway producing scene in the past thirty years or more. . . . Mike is strictly a Broadway fellow. . . . He hates to go to bed and will stay up as long as he can find anyone to stay up with him. He is a gin rummy fiend and will play until the cows come home. . . . Todd is a bundle of energy and craves action. . . . He is enormously good-natured, worldly-wise in every way and one of the mob, as the saying goes.

Runyon at the time was carrying the torch for his second wife, from whom he was separated, and was living alone in a hotel. He stayed up most of the night every night, and for years, when he had nothing better to do, would accompany Walter Winchell on his early-morning round of chasing police and fire calls. Runyon was devoted to any and all forms of gambling. Winchell had no interest in gambling. Todd's amusing line of chatter, combined with his knowledge and almost full-time dedication to gambling, his free hand with a buck and his theatrical prominence made him an ideal companion for Runyon. He would go to the track with Todd in the afternoon and join him at gin rummy all night. They were good knife-and-fork men as well. Runyon had found himself a perfect playmate.

Bertha had gone through twenty years of marriage, making do with little money most of the time, and had lived through Todd's long affair with Muriel Page. Todd had finally arrived, and Bertha was now totally satisfied with his success. But with the time and money he spent gambling and his developing affection for Blondell, he was now slipping away from her.

During this period my father was home for dinner at most once or twice a week. As mother made nothing of this, I accepted it as the norm. Mother was efficient in the kitchen and produced good plain food. She was an excellent housekeeper, and without a fuss our apartment was kept neat and functioning smoothly. My father slept late, and on most weekdays the only time I saw him awake was when I came home at noon for lunch, when he would be having his breakfast and getting ready to go to the office. We occasionally ate out together as a family, but always alone, and most often at Peter Luger's, Lindy's, Lüchow's, Ruby Foo's or the Stork Club. The Thanksgiving after he spoke to me about a divorce my father took us to Toots Shor's. As a family we were never big on holidays, but I suppose he was making a special effort to make this Thanksgiving a family affair. I remember mother seemed happy enough; she was flattered by the special attention we were getting from Shor. The occasion, however, was somehow offkey and depressing for both my father and me. Toots Shor's insults to all the patrons as they entered somehow didn't capture the Thanksgiving spirit.

While I rarely ate out with both my parents, I often dined with them individually. Mother and I almost always ate together at a ladies' restaurant, Jane Davies, which I loved because they served popovers throughout the dinner. My meals with my father were noisy and frequently interrupted affairs. As a prodigious tipper and a famous Broadway personality, he always got the best table and fantastic service. But at Lindy's, where the waiters were renowned for their casual attitude, the service was unbelievable. Todd's favorite kind of pickles and selection of bread and rolls were on the table before we were even seated, and at least one or two waiters were trying to anticipate the order, making likely selections before Todd had a chance to order. Table-hopping was common at the Stork Club, but there friends would merely exchange greetings as they passed by. At Lindy's we barely had time to put the napkins on our laps before acquaintances would be sliding into our large booth, and quite often they were comedians who sprinkled their conversations with their newest one-liners.

I was somewhat of a celebrity at Lindy's myself. Soon after we moved into our apartment at 25 Central Park West, I met an elderly gentleman in the park walking his dog. He would stop and throw a ball for the dog to retrieve. The dog was not a great retriever, and when the ball went under a bush, the dog sat and stared at it; and so I retrieved the ball and gave it back to the gentleman. This happened on several occasions, and each time the man offered me a dime for my help. I always declined the tip. When my father first took me into Lindy's, "the elderly gentleman" and I recognized each other—he was Leo Lindy. He made quite a fuss for such a quiet and shy man, telling my father about our encounters in the park—"What a nice little gentleman your son is." Lindy insisted then, and whenever I went into the restaurant, on giving me one of the gigantic red apples that were always part of his window display.

During this period Todd never went to the movies. He saw films on his increasingly frequent trips to the coast, in private screening rooms, or at the studios, but movies were definitely not his idea of an evening's entertainment. He and mother dressed formally and went to opening nights of the important Broadway shows, but otherwise he never saw an entire performance. He did, however, drop in to catch a few minutes of any show he had not seen on opening night that had a run. If the show or a performer caught his fancy, he would drop in at the theater again and over the course of a few weeks see most of the show and his favorite bits several times. He was continually dropping in on his own shows to make sure that the changes the stars were making worked.

Todd often made minor changes himself after visits to his shows, but primarily he was making sure that performances didn't slip. His principal stage manager, Sammy Lambert, was extremely tough and observant, so that Todd didn't often find things to carp about.

My father had no real interest in spectator sports but he liked boxing. He went to every championship fight and had the best seats in the house because he was friendly with the top people at the Garden and with Mike Jacobs, the top promoter of the day. There were at least a couple of good fights, with top contenders, held in New York every month, and Todd attended all of these, usually sitting with Damon Runyon in the press section. He would bet anything from a few hundred dollars on a dull Friday-night card to a couple of thousand on a championship bout; but measured against the scale of the rest of his gambling, these bets were child's play, and he made them only to have a rooting interest. A night at the fights was a social event more than anything else. He and Runyon would have a leisurely dinner at Lindy's or at one of the many steak houses in the area of the Garden. Ostensibly to skip the preliminaries, but mostly as a mark of snobbish prestige, they would arrive only a minute or so before the main event. The fact that I insisted on seeing some of the preliminaries made my presence a nuisance. Even so, I was brought along four or five times a year.

Two or three times a year my father took me to a baseball game during the forties, but by that time baseball was nothing to him but a tediously slow bet. He was itching to leave by the sixth or seventh inning, having arrived in the second or third. He was one of those pariahs baseball aficionados scorn, who go to the World Series, are disinterested in the game and, most irritatingly, occupy the best seats.

In 1943, with two sellout shows, money was rolling in even faster than Todd could draw it out. He had I.O.U. pads printed and would pick up a few thousand for "walk-around money" from either of the box offices almost daily. On one occasion he had drawn more than the production's share of the weekly receipts from both shows and gone off to the coast, without telling anyone where he was going or staying. In the midst of capacity runs, Equity threatened the closure of both shows when the payrolls, which had to be in cash, could not be met. The managers scrounged around town borrowing money, and were finally able to pay off the casts almost twenty-four hours late. When he returned the following week, Todd was astounded by the fuss; he had forgotten to tell anyone he had left $35,000 in cash in the office safe to meet the payrolls.

My Aunt Ethel remembers a trip she made to New York in the early forties. Bertha wanted to give her young sister a special treat. Tony Martin was the big heartthrob singer of the period. He was appearing at Ben Marden's Riviera, a huge nightclub perched on the Palisades, just north of the George Washington Bridge. Todd had arranged for Tony Martin to come over to the table after his performance, and Ethel was almost delirious with delight when Martin gave her a peck on the cheek. Not so delightful, but even more memorable, was Todd's taking her in to see Marden's gambling casino. While Ethel and Bertha were looking around, Todd excused himself, but without his knowing they followed a discreet distance behind. He walked over to the baccarat table and without even sitting down made a $25,000 bet on the next hand. He lost and walked away without a change of expression. It took less than five seconds to lose the $25,000. Ethel says she was in a state of total shock as they walked back to their table for a nightcap but Todd, who was unaware that they had observed him, was as jaunty as ever. Ethel couldn't help thinking that $25,000 would have comfortably supported the entire Freshman family through the Great Depression.

One day Todd had a pretty good afternoon at Belmont and came back into town with a tidy profit of $17,000. He and Runyon had dinner at Dinty Moore's, and then he went around the corner to check on business at the Music Box Theatre, where *Star and Garter* was playing. Todd knew that his general manager, Joe Glick, kept a safe deposit box at his hotel. He gave Glick the $17,000, telling him to put it in his hotel box until he asked for it. Three days later Joe Glick died.

At the funeral Todd was terribly embarrassed when the stage-struck rabbi, after a few perfunctory words about Glick, moved on to Glick's employer and launched into a twenty-minute tribute to Todd. A former employer of Glick's, the thorny Broadway producer Jed Harris, who was becoming irritated and bored by the rabbi's long eulogy of Todd, turned to his companion and in a stage whisper asked, "Say, whose funeral is this?"

When Todd had hired Glick to be the general manager of *The Hot Mikado,* Glick circulated cards reading: "I take great pleasure in announcing to my friends that I am no longer associated with Jed Harris."

The day after the funeral Todd went around to the St. Moritz to retrieve his $17,000 from Glick's safe deposit box. The box was sealed, and he was informed that the surrogate court would take custody of the contents. Finding out that Joe's estranged wife was his sole heir, Todd made what he knew would be a futile attempt to recover his money. Of course, he got nowhere.

When Todd was in New York, he ended up most nights at the Friars Club playing gin rummy. The highest-stake players during the early and mid-forties were Todd, Lou Walters, the owner of the Latin Quarter (Barbara Walters's father) and Benny Davis, a songwriter. Davis really didn't belong in the high-stake category of Todd and Walters. However, as Davis was commonly acknowledged to be the best player in the club—if not on the eastern seaboard—he would give parts of his action to other members, who were all too glad to take it.

Damon Runyon wrote a column about one Davis-Todd confrontation:

> The syndicate's gin rummy champion [Benny Davis], a sharp-looking fellow, plucked a card from the deck. This was the setting: A long table in the center of a brightly lighted room.
>
> Seated on one side of the table, a dark-browed chap [Todd]. To his left a cadaverous fellow with a gin rummy score sheet in front of him.
>
> But where the dark-browed chap had just his personal scorer and one other guy, a friend [Runyon] on his side of the table, behind the sharp-looking gent the kibitzers stood ten deep.
>
> They were his backers, each with an interest in his game ranging from a penny a point to ten cents a point. They were the syndicate against the dark-browed chap, whose total play was for seventy cents a point. [The stakes were surely at least two or three times this amount.]
>
> As I say, the syndicate champion plucked a card from the deck. He studied his hand briefly, shifted a card here and there and discarded. The syndicate members swayed slightly as one man.
>
> The dark-browed chap drew a card, then rather unexpectedly laid his hand down, the cards spread in sequences, asking:
>
> "Is four good?"
>
> The syndicate chief did not answer at once. He accor-

dioned his cards in his duke so no one could see them and gazed up at the white faces around him and said, without heat:

"I don't like it. That is all there is to it."

The syndicate members remained silent.

"What happened?" asked the dark-browed chap.

"Somebody grunted," said the syndicate representative. "I don't like it."

One of the syndicate members turned to the man next to him half accusingly and demanded:

"Did you grunt?"

"Me? No," said the man.

"Who grunted?" asked the member, addressing all his associates collectively.

There was a general shaking of heads and a murmur of disclaimer.

"Somebody grunted," insisted the syndicate player firmly. "I don't like it. I don't want no grunting around me."

"I didn't hear nothin'," said the dark-browed chap. "How about giving me a count?"

"Mr. Runyon," said the syndicate player addressing me, "did you hear somebody grunt?"

"Who, me?" I asked. "Why, no."

"It was true. I did not hear a grunt, though of course I would not have admitted it if I had. One of the first things a kibitzer must learn if he wishes to enjoy life is to profess ignorance about any and all arguments that may develop in a card game.

"What if somebody did grunt?" I whispered to a fellow kibitzer. "Why is he making a big *tsimmis* out of a grunt?"

"Why," said the man, "maybe he drew such an important card that it brought out the grunt or maybe it was such an unimportant one that it had the same effect, and in either event the grunt tipped his opponent off that it was a good time to knock."

"Did you hear a grunt?" I asked.

"No," he said, "but a gin player's ears are keener for grunts or any other noises around him than anyone else's. Sometimes a player can hear what the kibitzers are thinking."

"Look," said the dark-browed chap. "Do you mind giving me a count. I mean, after all, I am entitled to know what I caught you with."

"I do not like grunts," said the syndicate man. "I am playing here for important money and I do not want any grunting around me. If anybody feels like grunting again let them go somewhere else."

"You hear what he said," the dark-browed chap said to the syndicate members. "Grunts are out. Now, please, do you mind letting me know how many you've got in your hand so we can get on with the game?"

The syndicate man unfolded his cards and spread them on the table.

"Forty-eight," he said.

It was a two-game blitz.

I had a small piece of the dark-browed chap's play, and to save my neck I couldn't help grunting.

One morning after waking up and getting ready to go off to school, I discovered my father playing gin rummy with the comedian Lou Holtz at our dining room table. They gave a brief nod in my direction. Todd was somber with fatigue, and Holtz was not in the greatest humor either. I was surprised, as Todd never played cards at home. My mother pulled me into the kitchen and explained that Holtz was down a fortune when they had closed the Friars Club early in the morning, and to give him a sporting chance to get some of his money back, my father had brought Holtz home to continue the game.

They were still playing when I came home for lunch. It seemed that my arrival was a previously agreed upon stopping point. My father got up from the table.

Holtz said, "Mike, you can't do this to me."

Todd stretched and rubbed his five o'clock shadow. "Lou, we agreed. All right, I won't get any sleep, but I've gotta shave and pack. The plane leaves at three."

Suddenly inspired, Holtz stood up. "Mike, is there any law that says I can't go to California with you? What are you going to do for twelve hours on the plane?"

"Sleep."

Holtz protested further, and Todd offered to cut his loss in half and call it quits. After lunch, I went into my parents' bedroom to kiss my father good-bye before his trip. He was showered and shaved by now and was packing things in an open suitcase that was on the bed. Holtz was standing on the other side of the bed, still pleading his case.

When I got home from school that day, I asked my mother what had happened with Holtz. She said he had rushed out to his apartment to throw a couple of things in a bag and was flying to California with my father.

When Holtz left our apartment, he was $40,000 down. They played on the trip out. Holtz stayed with Todd at the home of movie mogul Joe Schenck, where Mike was allowed unannounced-visitor privileges. Todd's business took three days to complete, and Holtz had him playing every waking moment that he wasn't working. They played on the return flight until the cabin door was opened in New York—the agreed-upon *final, absolute* end of the game. Holtz had cut his losses to $10,000 and told Todd, "Another trip to the coast and I'm ahead."

One night, coming into the Friars Club, Todd was approached by Al Lackey, Sophie Tucker's ex-husband. Lackey had been having a rough time and told Todd that he was going to be locked out of his room if he didn't square his hotel bill immediately. Todd gave him $200, and Lackey headed straight for the door, presumably to go around the corner to the Hotel Edison to settle his bill. After a few hellos, Todd went to the card room, where Benny Davis and a large group of his supporters were impatiently waiting for him. Todd was about to cut the pack for the first deal when he noticed Lackey at the rear of the large group standing behind Davis. Todd stood up and asked, "Al, what are you doing here?"

"Nothing," Lackey mumbled. "Play."

Todd turned to Davis and asked, "Benny, does Al have a piece of your action?"

"Yeah, he's got a couple of cents—cut, Mike."

Todd stared at Lackey. "Al? . . ."

Lackey grumbled, "Mike, don't tell me how to spend my money!"

In a few years Todd found himself on the Lackey side of the story, but scaled upwards to Todd-like proportions. He was in the midst of bankruptcy proceedings to the tune of a million dollars and was short of walk-around money, or for that matter any kind of money.

Todd got along very well with both J. J. and Lee Shubert, a rare accomplishment, as they went years without speaking to each other. Both Shubert brothers had a well-deserved Scrooge-like reputation.

One day Todd was walking east on Forty-fourth Street with his press agent and companion of the time, Max Gendel. While excitedly describing the plans for his current project, he grabbed Max's arm and pulled him into the Sardi Building, saying, "I've gotta see Mr. Lee for a minute." In the elevator and while waiting in the outer office, Todd carried on his rapid-fire dissertation and continued talking as they were shown into Shubert's office. Max was trying to piece together the gist of Mike's monologue, when Todd briefly turned to Mr. Lee and addressed a few remarks to him. The next thing Max knew Mr. Lee was pushing a small pile of $100 bills across the desk to Todd—the cash had been taken out of the office safe at Shubert's instructions. (Both Shuberts had office safes containing lots of currency.) Max failed to catch what Todd had said to Mr. Lee. Going down in the elevator, Todd resumed his spiel. To this day, Max regrets his lack of attention in Shubert's office. "I saw theatrical history being made and I have no idea what Todd said to pry two thousand dollars out of Mr. Lee's grasp."

That evening, Todd was dining in Le Pavillon, probably the most expensive restaurant in New York, and saw Mr. Lee at a corner table with Gloria Swanson. Todd sent over a bottle of champagne to Mr. Lee, with his compliments. With his mahogany complexion and hatchet nose, Mr. Lee bore a striking resemblance to a cigar store Indian, but his facial expression was less animated. With the tiniest nod, Mr. Lee indicated his acknowledgment of Todd's bottle of champagne.

The next morning Max was sitting at Todd's desk when a call came in from an irate Mr. Lee. Normally he spoke in an almost inaudible voice, but Max could hear Mr. Lee on the phone from six feet away: "It's bad enough to see you walking into Pavillon! But then, to buy me champagne with *my* money . . ."

Gerry Schoenfeld and his partner, Bernie Jacobs, now run the Shubert Organization, but were formerly J. J. Shubert's attorneys. Gerry states that Mike was the only person he ever knew who addressed his former employer simply as J. J. Gerry says there were several occasions when each of the brothers did extraordinary favors for Todd that would never have been extended to anyone else:

Mr. Lee defied a court order in 1950 and had to face contempt proceedings when he released box office receipts to Mike during the run of his revue *Peep Show*, after they had been attached by Hassard Short for royalties due him. In 1956, J. J., holding the mortgage on the Harris and Selwyn theatres, permitted Todd to demolish the proscenium arch in the Selwyn for the installation of Todd-AO. It was an unthinkable thing to ask of J. J.—he wouldn't have allowed anyone else to touch the bulb in an aisle light. . . . Mike would come bouncing into the office, when everybody else would stand on the threshold fearful of their lives. Just one look from J. J. would put anyone else on the defensive. But Mike wasn't intimidated at all. After Mike had left, J. J. would make some remark like, "That fresh son of a bitch—he used to sell me blotters in Chicago when he was a kid." Mr. Shubert always used to smile when he spoke about Mike. And J. J. was not a man for smiling.

However, Todd was closer to Mr. Lee. Although Mr. Lee kept track of his empire down to the last penny and was ruthless in all his business dealings, he admired Todd's boldness and had a special fondness for him. On several occasions Mr. Lee maneuvered the bookings of hit shows to give Todd his choice of Shubert theaters.

In the late fall of 1943 Todd asked Mr. Lee to make the Winter Garden available at the end of January for his new musical, *Mexican Hayride. The Ziegfeld Follies,* produced by the Shuberts, starring Milton Berle, was doing standing room only in the Winter Garden, and for once Mr. Lee wouldn't accommodate Todd. In mid-December Todd bought the much less desirable Broadway Theatre from Mr. Lee for $400,000 to house *Mexican Hayride.* After a lot of doctoring in Boston, when it was clear that *Mexican Hayride* was going to be a hit, Todd went to New York to plead his case for the Winter Garden with Mr. Lee. Mr. Lee said his hands were tied, as Milton Berle would never agree to a move. Todd gave Berle two vicuña coats and Berle's wife, Joyce Matthews, a sable. Berle no longer had a strong objection to moving *The Ziegfeld Follies.* Mr. Lee grudgingly gave Todd a contract for the Winter Garden, and the *Follies* moved over to the Imperial. With his musical houses all booked and several shows heading for New York, Mr. Lee now needed the Broadway Theatre. After owning it just over a month, Todd sold it back to Mr. Lee for a $30,000 profit. Mr. Lee was outraged—but amused.

During the height of his Broadway success, Todd's most constant companion was Runyon, but he spent long evenings with Winchell at the Stork Club with a crowd of hangers-on they always attracted. But because of their mutual interest in gambling and Runyon's sense of humor—Winchell was humorless—Mike preferred Runyon's company to Winchell's. Also, Todd and Winchell were two of the most gigantic egos of the era, and as Olympic nonstop talkers, they were always competing to be the center of attention.

All during the forties the world stopped for fifteen minutes at seven o'clock on Sunday to hear Winchell's radio program, which ranged from the leading international news story of the moment to New York and Hollywood gossip.

One Sunday night in 1948, when Mike's last Bobby Clark show, *As the Girls Go,* was trying out in New Haven, Todd and Howard Bay, who designed and directed the show, drove to New York. Bay said:

> We had many serious problems with *As the Girls Go,* and we were discussing them on the trip down. I was exhausted. We had a lot to do in the morning, but Mike insisted on our stopping in at the Stork Club. As we passed Winchell's table, he grabbed Mike and said, "What did you think about that story I had about Dewey tonight?" Mike said, "I'm sorry, Walter, but we were driving down from New Haven and didn't hear the broadcast." Winchell shouted, "Well, you've got a radio in your car, don't you!" Winchell was furious. . . . That kind of ego is not to be found today. Once I was sitting in Mike's offices, waiting to see him, and that chunky assistant Winchell had come in and started flashing a gold ring he was wearing. "Today's my birthday," he said. "Look at this ring Walter gave me." I looked at the ring and said, "Gee, that's handsome." It had W.W. engraved on it!

My father and I ran into Winchell one spring Sunday evening as we were returning home after enjoying ice cream sodas at Rumpelmayer's. It was shortly before eight, and we were passing the Plaza when Winchell came around the corner. He grabbed Mike and asked him what he thought of his broadcast that evening. Not wanting to admit that his craving for ice cream had taken priority over listening to Winchell, my father said we had been visiting friends and had been unable to listen in. Winchell grabbed Todd's arm and said, "Tonight I led off . . ." and then proceeded to do almost his entire program—never loosening his grip on my father's arm. Todd managed to look suitably absorbed for the whole ten minutes and profusely thanked Winchell for the rebroadcast. As soon as Winchell had turned his back and started to walk away, my father shook his head in disbelief. "I think we owe ourselves a treat. Let's go back to Rumpelmayer's and have a sundae for dessert."

Damon Runyon was a good listener and a great counterpunch conversationalist. And, of course, after his throat cancer operation, when he was at first barely able and then totally unable to speak, he made an even more ideal companion for Todd. I once asked my father the reason for Runyon's occasional moodiness with him, and he said that aside from Runyon being miffed when he spent some evenings without Runyon, "He doesn't seem to understand that sometimes I've got to do things to put some bread on the table."

With a string of moneymaking hits behind him, Todd bought an elegant town house to use for offices. He was impressed with himself at the time and delighted in showing off his new acquisition. Runyon's column on the subject was entitled "Titantic Todd":

> I spent a week one evening recently with Mike Todd, the theatrical producer, a rags-to-riches fellow, and I want to tell you the experience left me quite unnerved. It was really most terrifying.
>
> He has rented a haunted house in West Fifty-sixth Street not far off Fifth Avenue for an office and he insisted on taking me there to show me my own photo in what he called a wall montage, only it was not there.
>
> "I guess they haven't got around to it," was his explanation of the blank. Then he added:
>
> "Stanford White designed this house."
>
> "Todd," I said, "never stay in this joint alone as they may find you some morning like they did Joe Elwell, as dead as a mackerel. It was in a house just like this."
>
> "Who would shoot me?" asked Todd.
>
> "Well," I said, "it might be someone who has seen one of your shows."
>
> Todd had found me in my cloister in the kitchen of Moore's restaurant entertaining a party of friends. There were seven of us huddled closely about one small table when he barged in uninvited, a short, chunky, dark dynamic fellow with a big cigar in his mouth.
>
> "Are you going to sit here, too?" demanded Eddie Walker,

the fight manager, rather subtly, I thought, as Todd wedged himself in between Bill Corum and Colonel Sammy Becker.

"I'll take the grunt," said Todd.

But of course I was too smart to let him bribe his way into my company by lifting a mere dinner tab. I am saving him for a lulu.

However, I made it clear to Todd that he is no longer in my good books since I discovered that he is at heart a snob. When I was in Hollywood he used to come out and be glad of a welcome in my set. [Runyon went to Hollywood as a writer-producer a year before Todd became a regular visitor there.]

Then he somehow wedged his way into the Beverly Hills upper crust and got to playing gin rummy with swells like Charley Feldman and D.O.S. [David O. Selznick], as we reverently refer to him out there, and from that time on all I got was the back of the Todd thick neck.

In New York, where he is a social outcast, he is always eager to be seen with me, as you will observe from the way he foisted himself on me in Moore's, but I have his number and why I fell for his suggestion that I spend the rest of the evening with him I will never know.

"First we will go around and look in a moment on the Mae West show," Todd said. "She is giving her hundredth performance tonight."

"I heard you weren't speaking to Mae West," I said.

"Well, I wasn't for a while," admitted Todd, "but we exchange hellos now. Small ones. You've got to say hello to anybody that runs a hundred nights, don't you?"

So we looked in on the Mae West thing [but] . . . I refused to pause at *Mexican Hayride* so Todd took me to the haunted house, and what is more conned me into climbing stairs up and down through seven floors chatting continuously all the while of his plans and himself taking a mean advantage, I thought, by first walking me out of breath so I could not reply.

I think it was midnight when I got in a word.

"Todd," I said, "you are a great man."

"Why, my goodness," he replied, "what do you think I have been telling you all evening?"

Todd had no interest in his home life during this period of the early forties, when he was one of the most famous and fastest-moving men about town. The comedian Joe E. Lewis said at the time, "Mike Todd definitely belongs on a runaway horse." He gambled and lost vast sums at the track and playing gin. His two smash musicals—*Star and Garter* and *Something for the Boys*—provided him with a bankroll bigger than even his high-stake gambling could dispose of. But his greatest pleasure and favorite form of gambling was on himself and his abilities as a producer and showman. From mid-1943 until early 1946, with six months off in Europe, he produced eight shows. He was happiest at work and—unlike most producers today—he controlled every aspect of his productions. He was at his best when the odds were against him and a show was in trouble and he needed to utilize all of his energy and ingenuity. During Todd's lifetime as a gambler, his best bet was always on himself.

CHAPTER 6

THE NAKED GENIUS was a perfect title for a stage comedy written by Gypsy Rose Lee. In 1940 Gypsy's intellectual and literary interests were immortalized by the showstopping number "Zip" in *Pal Joey*. Earlier that year Gypsy had taken up residence at a rooming house in the shadow of the Brooklyn Bridge, which was managed by W. H. Auden, who lived there himself, along with Carson McCullers and Benjamin Britten and his friend, operatic tenor Peter Pears. Residents and habitués of this mixed cultural ménage included at various times Salvador Dali, Christopher Isherwood, Thomas Mann's youngest son, Golo, Louis Untermeyer, Louis MacNeice, Oliver Smith, Marc Blitzstein and Richard Wright. When Gypsy went on the road with the tab unit of *Streets of Paris* and then to Chicago to star in the Theatre Café, she temporarily abandoned her typewriter and gave up her rooms in the Brooklyn Heights boarding house to Jane and Paul Bowles.

After the success of her mystery novel, *The G-String Murders*, published in 1941, and the appearance of some autobiographical stories in the *New Yorker*, Gypsy's writing abilities began to be taken seriously. The announcement of her first play was widely covered by the press.

George Kaufman, America's leading stage comedy writer and director, who was also known as the greatest play doctor of the time, was the ideal choice to direct *The Naked Genius*.

Joan Blondell, the saucy heart-of-gold girl from the Warner movie musicals, who was one of America's leading box office attractions and who had not appeared on Broadway for over a decade, was chosen to play the lead.

Mike Todd, who had two smash hits on Broadway and was being heralded as the new Ziegfeld, was further insurance that *The Naked Genius* would be a hot property.

Or so the thinking went in Hollywood. The studios were all bidding like mad for the film rights weeks before rehearsals were scheduled to begin. Todd spent a couple of weeks on the coast being romanced by studio executives for the film rights to his next hit. Although he had better offers elsewhere, he was reluctantly obliged to sell the movie rights for *The Naked Genius* to 20th Century-Fox because of a special relationship he had with Joe Schenck.

Todd had a free run of Schenck's home in Beverly Hills and almost always stayed with him when he was on the coast. The summer of 1946 I spent a month in Schenck's house with my father. Schenck was one of the pioneers of the motion picture industry. A few years after United Artists had been founded by Mary Pickford, Charlie Chaplin, Douglas Fairbanks and D. W. Griffith, Schenck was brought in to run the company. While he was the head of United Artists, he founded the theater chain of the same name, which was one of the largest in the country. In 1933 he founded Twentieth Century Productions, which he later merged with Fox to form the existing company. His brother Nick was the president of Loew's, Inc., the then parent corporation of M.G.M. Joe Schenck was a childless bachelor who had been married to one of the queens of silent movies, Norma Talmadge. Her full-length portrait, as she must have appeared in the early twenties, hung over the mantelpiece and dominated his imperial-sized living room. The house was a gigantic Spanish stucco mansion that sprawled over a triple-sized lot in the heart of Beverly Hills. The darling of the household was the butler's young daughter whom Schenck treated as if she were his own child. He was a quiet and gentle man and the only person I ever saw my father treat with great deference. Todd was a complete take-charge guy everywhere, but he was comparatively subdued in Schenck's presence.

There was an almost constant flow of top Hollywood executives to Schenck's home—most often to play in the high-stake poker and gin games that were the principal social activity of the household. Over $100,000 could change hands in a night and, for that matter, $100,000 or more could be in the pot for a single hand in the poker games.

Schenck received the admiration and respect of everyone he

dealt with, but particularly women, as he was very attentive to anything they had to say. He had a dignified but unpretentious manner and a gentle sense of humor. He was a homely man but because of his charm and personality, he was considered attractive. Schenck was seeing a number of comely young women who showed up at the house at all times of the day and night. During my visit there was a gorgeous girl who gave him Spanish lessons at breakfast three times a week.

Todd tried to talk Schenck out of *The Naked Genius* film rights purchase, but Schenck and 20th Century-Fox would rather run the risk of having their "bargain buy" turn out worthless at a later date, when it would escape Hollywood's attention, than to suffer the embarrassment of losing a current hot property. Todd's share of the film sale—subject only to the play's running four weeks in New York—was enough to guarantee him a profit on the venture.

It seemed only natural to the Broadway crowd that Todd would continue his profitable association with Gypsy. She had come to his rescue and was his partner on *Star and Garter*. It was generally assumed that he and Gypsy were lovers. Todd produced *The Naked Genius*, however, to have the chance to be with Joan. He could display his theatrical know-how to her, provide her with a triumphant return to Broadway and bring her to the city where he was king. She was obviously more than just interested in him, as doing the play would take her away from her two children, to whom she was truly devoted, and force her to turn down film offers that would earn her substantially more money than she could earn in the play. Dick Powell was not displeased to have Joan out of town, as his career was in transition and his ego bruised by Joan's being more in demand, and his romance with June Allyson was heating up. Mother was busy and pleased with her new life as the wife of Broadway's leading producer. Any lingering suspicions or jealousies she was harboring about other women in Mike's life were still directed at Gypsy—in spite of Gypsy's recent marriage to the actor Alexander Kirkland.

The Naked Genius defied the theatrical tradition of a disastrous dress rehearsal producing a brilliant first night. The Boston critics were accustomed to rough edges on a show and made allowances, but the hodgepodge with which they were presented left them no alternative but to pan it.

The story was about a famous stripteaser, Honey Bee Carroll, who wishes to enhance her intellectual image by writing a book. Her publisher's son falls in love with her and proposes marriage, and she accepts. At the end of the play, just before the wedding, Honey Bee decides her happiness and her heart belong to show business and her manager. Many incidents in the play were drawn from Gypsy's actual experience, but the story holding the material together was fictional and farfetched. Years later, when Gypsy stuck more closely to the facts of her early life, the book she wrote was a best-seller. *Gypsy,* the musical based on this book, was a smash hit on the stage and a successful film.

Todd sent handsome gifts to each of the Boston critics, which he would not have dared to do if any of their reviews had been even modestly kind. He enclosed notes thanking them for their constructive criticism and said that he, Kaufman and Gypsy would be working hard along the lines they suggested to fix the show. Critics normally expect, at the very least, hostility from producers of shows they have panned, and they wrote kindly follow-up pieces about Todd's unusual attitude. This favorable publicity, together with Gypsy's and Kaufman's names and Joan's strong box office appeal and the ticket-selling title of the play, resulted in excellent business, despite the bad reviews.

Under Kaufman's and Todd's direction Gypsy worked furiously, rewriting scenes and whole sections of the play. Todd, a great believer in stage effects, spent a lot of money on gimmicky props, such as a mantelpiece clock that went crazy for over a minute when it struck the hour. The clock in *The Naked Genius* rivaled the pinball machine in *The Time of Your Life.* The only difference between Todd's clock and Saroyan's pinball machine was that the latter had a well-constructed, absorbing play behind it.

There were daily dialogue changes and complicated revisions of Joan's stage business, which added no motivation or logic to her role. She could barely get through a performance. There was no improvement in the play, but business continued to be good throughout the Boston run.

Todd postponed the Broadway opening, and Kaufman and Gypsy made wholesale alterations to the script. Todd lined up theaters in Baltimore and Pittsburgh, cities in which burlesque still thrived, where he correctly anticipated *The Naked Genius* would find receptive audiences. The notices there were only slightly better, but the play continued to do good business.

The art for the billboards, window cards and display ads contained a line drawing of a scantily attired Gypsy-like figure sitting at a typewriter. For the additional tryout engagements he added the following message in large block letters across the ad:

GUARANTEED NOT TO WIN THE PULITZER PRIZE
IT AIN'T SHAKESPEARE BUT IT'S LAFFS

The show did have a fair number of laughs, but the plot was so contrived and the action and business so senselessly furious that the intervals between the laughs were not only boring but irritating. At the end of the Baltimore run, Kaufman felt that all further attempts to breathe life into the show would be futile.

Mike strived to the last. Gypsy always had a variety of pets around her, and Todd liked animal acts, so he added a small menagerie for the Pittsburgh engagement. It didn't help, but Joan forgot about trying to make any sense out of what she was doing onstage and let her warmth and personality come through, which did help—somewhat. At least Joan had regained her stage presence and would not be to blame.

Kaufman was inactive during the Pittsburgh run, feeling there was nothing more that could be done with the show. Gypsy had relied on Kaufman and all his know-how to turn the show around. When Kaufman gave up, she got together with him to beg Mike not to bring the show in. Todd said the show was opening in New York and that was that. Gypsy asked that her credit be changed to read, "Written by Louise Hovick" (her real name). "And Mr. Todd," Kaufman added, "change my credit to: 'Directed by Jed Harris.' "

The Naked Genius opened in New York at the Plymouth Theatre on October 21, 1943. This was the first time in his twenty-five years on Broadway that Kaufman skipped an opening night of one of his shows.

I was awakened in the middle of that night by voices in the hall outside my door. I went out to investigate and saw a couple of my father's assistants standing outside my bathroom. As I looked past them, I saw my father sitting in the tub. I saw him an instant before he noticed me. His head was nodding dejectedly on his chest. When he saw me he tried to slide down into the tub out of my sight. In a state of near panic, he cried out, "Please don't let Michael see me like this." The door slammed shut and I could hear my mother and another person speaking inside. I was petrified and couldn't imagine what was happening. After a few moments my mother came out and took me into my room, closing the door behind us. I was immediately reassured by her smile. She said the reviews in the morning papers had all been bad and that the advance word on the afternoon papers was no better. She told me that my father had gotten drunk for the first time in his life. She had needed help getting him home, and they'd put him in a cold tub in my bathroom, nearest the front door, to try to sober him up.

Max Gendel, one of his press agents, said, "Any show Mike produced was either a Mike Todd hit or a Mike Todd failure." *The Naked Genius* was a Mike Todd failure, his first in over five years. "In show business you invite criticism," Todd said. "If you can't accept it, you should find another line of work." He could handle failure, but he had let Joan down.

The next morning Todd was the only one in the office bustling around with a smile on his face. He put together a quarter-page quote ad for the show. In front of the Gypsy-like figure in this ad there were sheets of paper coming out of the typewriter, and those at the top of the ad contained the four usable quotes he could dig out of the dozen-plus reviews. The sheets closest to the typewriter diminished in perspective. You could read the names of some of the critics not quoted on the top, but their quotes were a mass of illegible small print. There was an asterisk beside the name of each critic. The asterisks were explained at the bottom of the page by the legend:

*DON'T STRAIN YOUR EYES—THEY DIDN'T LIKE IT ANYHOW.

Here are some of the quotes that Mike felt the readers should not strain their eyes to read: Burton Rascoe in the *World-Telegram* called it a "dreary witless mess." Howard Barnes in the *Herald Tribune* said it was "vulgar and boring." Nichols in the *Times* simply advised, "Mr. Todd: Take it off." John Chapman of the *News* noted: "Last week Mr. Todd advised the press that he was bringing his play into New York, despite the fact that the author, Gypsy R. Lee and the director, George S. Kaufman, had begged him not to. I figured it was another of Michael's smart gags. Now I report same out of fairness to the director and author."

Joan got decent to good notices, and again the show did surprisingly good business.

Cole Porter, Herbert and Dorothy Fields and Hassard Short were preparing Todd's next production, *Mexican Hayride.* He took them and mother on a junket to Mexico, ostensibly for background and inspiration, but really for rest and relaxation.

Several weeks after Mike's return from Mexico, *The Naked Genius,* on the fifth Saturday of its run, was still showing an operating profit. Todd closed the show. He again took quarter-page ads, this time in the form of a personal letter to the public, on his letterhead and with no artwork. It indicated that he had polled two full houses—an exaggerated account of the show's attendance—and found that only a little more than half the audience fully enjoyed the show, a substantial exaggeration of the show's popularity. The ad went on to say that since he planned to be around on Broadway a lot longer, he would rather close the show than have almost half his customers go away dissatisfied. The ad attracted a lot of favorable attention. The terms of the movie sale contract were met at the end of the fourth week, and with the show in the black during its run on the road and in New York, Todd was money ahead on the venture. Gypsy came away from *The Naked Genius* with over a hundred thousand dollars to ease her literary disappointment.

Playing the lead to half a house in a frenetically paced comedy that went nowhere was not doing Joan's disposition or career any good. By closing the show while it was still making money, Mike could build character with Joan, releasing her to go back to the coast to her children.

Todd often said that there are no rules in show business, and he believed it. Anything done really well had a chance of succeeding. His own view of entertainment, however, was that you had to have somebody to root for. This idea made him feel uncertain about a William Saroyan play he had optioned entitled *Get Away, Old Man,* which humorously mirrored some of Todd's own Hollywood experiences.

He visited Saroyan several times in Ohio at the army camp where he was stationed, ostensibly to discuss rewrites. Todd wanted to believe that Saroyan could overcome the basic fault in the play and he so enjoyed Saroyan's company that he continued to visit him, with the vain hope that some of Saroyan's exuberant charm would be transferred to the script.

Get Away, Old Man was a caustic play about Hollywood. Todd's encounters with the industry, from his construction days in the twenties to his recent dealings, gave him a contemptuous view of the industry and most of the people in it. Saroyan's play effectively embodied Todd's viewpoint but left him with no one to root for. Todd let his option expire. It was produced on Broadway at the end of 1943 and was a failure.

I went up to Boston during my Christmas vacation in 1943 a few days before the premiere of *Mexican Hayride*. Everyone anticipated a pleasant repetition of the previous year's experience with *Something for the Boys:* same collaborators—Porter, Short and the Fieldses—same time of year, and Todd had the same elegant suite in the Ritz, overlooking the Common. The cast as well had a close relationship with Todd's past successes. The star, Bobby Clark, had been taken out of *Star and Garter,* which was still running. The female lead was June Havoc, Gypsy's younger sister. And Bill Callahan, the precocious hoofer, was taken out of *Something for the Boys,* which was also still running.

At a time when even the most opulent musical productions cost $200,000, the *Mexican Hayride* budget was $300,000—all Todd's own money. There were large and complicated multilevel sets, notably a section of a bullfight arena; and for his big second-act production splash the central square in Taxco, with overhanging balconies able to hold the weight of props and actors. Todd was even more lavish with the girls' costumes, which cost a fortune.

The story was an effective vehicle for Bobby Clark's comedy and for the colorful production numbers. Clark played the part of a con man who is hiding out in Mexico after narrowly escaping arrest for running a numbers racket in the States. He attends a bullfight and is by chance made a representative of Roosevelt's Good Neighbor policy when he catches a bull's ear, which had been cut and thrown at him by June Havoc, who plays a lady toreador, and he becomes the "Amigo Americano." Havoc also happens to be the sister of Clark's deserted wife, with whom she did a rodeo act in the States, which had been mismanaged by Clark. Now Clark teams up with Havoc's Mexican manager to run an illegal lottery, and a State Department representative— who provides the love interest for Havoc—discovers the real identity of the "Amigo Americano" at the end of the first act. (Three years later, when he was starring in a revival of *Sweethearts*, Bobby Clark stepped over the footlights to confide to the audience: "Never has a thin plot been so complicated.") Clark and his Mexican accomplice spend the entire second act in various disguises, hiding out from the Mexican and American authorities.

During the rehearsals in New York, the individual elements of *Mexican Hayride* seemed wonderful. When the show was put together in Boston for its opening, nothing meshed. In several numbers the chorus girls wore huge Mexican hoopskirts, which were difficult to maneuver smoothly around the cumbersome scenery. Bobby Clark, who had not done a book musical for many years, seemed inhibited and overcome by the large and complicated production. The songs worked, but the score seemed to lack punch. The dancing, now confined by the big sets and a large cast, lost the verve it had had in the bare New York rehearsal halls. It was soon apparent that *Mexican Hayride* was not going to duplicate the smooth success of *Something for the Boys*.

The point was sadly and emphatically made when the trouble-ridden first rehearsal in Boston was suspended to give the cast a breather. Todd called for the first complete run-through of the music by the entire orchestra assembled on the stage. This run-through allows the composer, arranger, director and producer to hear the score played by the full orchestra for the first time. It was such a large orchestra that some of the string section spilled over into the adjacent box at the right of the stage. Before the overture was completed, a cello player seated in the stage-side box fell over backwards. I was sitting in the middle of the house, near Cole Porter's and Hassard Short's "nephews." As the problems connected with the staging of the show became apparent, the nephews had begun to snicker at the proceedings. When the cellist keeled over they started to giggle, and in a stage whisper one of them said, "What next?" Todd, who was sitting in the third row, next to Porter and Short, immediately jumped up and ran to the box. It was soon obvious that the cellist had suffered a stroke. Sammy Lambert, the stage manager, phoned for an ambulance. That evening we heard that the man had died on the way to the hospital.

At the end of the musical run-through, when the technical

points had been cleared away and the theater largely emptied, Todd had an impromptu conference with Porter and Short in the front of the darkened house. Mike was grim.

"Cole, we need a simple, straightforward ballad."

Porter was a bit offended. The nephews stopped whispering and sat up and paid close attention.

"What do you have in mind, Mike?" Porter asked in a slightly challenging tone.

"I would like you to write a song called 'I Love You.'"

Porter smiled with disbelief. "But Mike, there's already seventeen 'I Love You's.'"

"That's all right. We'll call this 'Cole Porter's I Love You.'"

Todd walked away, and that was the end of the conference. Early the next day Porter pulled Todd aside. "I've written that song you wanted. I'll play it for you now."

They went down to the lounge, where a rehearsal piano was available. Hassard Short, the nephews and I followed. Mike stood with one hand resting on the top of the piano as Porter began to play. Short stood to one side with an impassive expression. But Porter could barely keep from smiling.

"'I love you'
Hums the April breeze."

(Muffled snickers from the nephews seated on a banquette against the lounge wall.)

"'I love you'
Echo the hills,"

(More snickers.)

"'I love you'
The golden dawn agrees."

(Porter is now smiling broadly, and the nephews begin to giggle.)

"*As once more she sees . . .*"

(Porter suppresses laughter. Nephews laugh.)

"*Daffodils.*"

To the accompaniment of soft but unrestrained laughter of the nephews:

"*It's spring again
And birds, on the wing again,
Start to sing again
The old melodie.*" (Porter embellishing) "dee, dee, dee, dee, dee, dee, dee." (Now unrestrained laughter from the nephews as Porter finishes.)

112

> " '*I love you*'
> *That's the song of songs*
> *And it all belongs*
> *To you and me.*"

(Final appreciative burst of laughter from the nephews as Porter takes his hands off the keyboard and puts them in his lap.) "That's it, Mike."

"Absolutely perfect. We put it in the show immediately." And Todd briskly headed for the stairs.

So that his friends and admirers would know he was only kidding, Porter later wrote the following verse:

> *If a love song I could only write,*
> *A song with words and music divine,*
> *I would serenade you ev'ry night,*
> *Till you'd relent and consent to be mine,*
> *But alas, just an amateur am I*
> *And so I'll not be surprised, my dear,*
> *If you smile and politely pass it by*
> *When this, my first love song you hear.*

"I Love You" was the only breakaway hit Porter wrote for a Todd show.

Mexican Hayride opened in Boston on December 28, 1943, at the Shubert Theatre to poor reviews but pretty good business on the strength of the names involved—Cole Porter, Bobby Clark and Todd.

Three straight lines and two circles drawn on a man's face with a black grease pencil was the major factor in turning *Mexican Hayride* into a smash hit. Bobby Clark had always worked with a pair of spectacles painted on his face. But everyone had considered it inappropriate for him to appear in this contemporary book musical with his painted-on glasses. He felt naked without them; like Groucho Marx's grease-penciled moustache, they were not only his trademark, but his whole stage character seemed focused and dependent on them. *Mexican Hayride*'s gigantic staging problems were soon smoothed out, but the driving force that got the show moving and made it fun throughout was a rejuvenated Bobby Clark. Porter had written a delightful song with a rousing melody for Bobby to do with all the girls in the company, appropriately titled "Girls." A sample of the lyrics:

Girls to the right of me,
Girls to the left of me,
Girls in front of me,
Girls behind,
Girls all over me,
I don't mind!
Oh, what a rogue am I,
So much in vogue am I,
Simply smothered in kisses and curls,
By the girls, girls, girls, girls, girls!

This number was now a showstopper. Without his painted-on spectacles, Bobby was any middle-aged man awkwardly playing the fool. With his glasses and restored sense of identity, he was the lovable and harmless roué.

As he did in all his shows, Bobby would patiently apply his acrobatic and musical talents to his role and greatly multiply the laughs. In *Mexican Hayride* Herbert and Dorothy Fields provided Bobby with a plot that vastly accelerated the process, since he spent most of the second act in various disguises. He was seen as a flute player in a mariachi band and later as the bucktoothed wife of his Mexican cohort when they are masquerading as an Indian couple selling tortillas. In no time Bobby was doing assorted musical and acrobatic tricks with the flute. As the tortilla vendor he worked with a big glob of dough that he twirled and spun about like a master pizza chef. When approached by some tourists, he flings the dough onto a hook attached to the tortilla wagon. Facing the audience, he played the business and dialogue of the scene, turning around each time just at the second the blob was about to fall off the hook onto the stage. It took him three weeks during rehearsals in New York to get the tortilla dough to exactly the right consistency. In Boston Bobby tried out several different sets of novelty-store false teeth, but he was unhappy with them and wound up spending a considerable sum out of his own pocket getting exactly what he had in mind from a dentist. He also had himself fitted out with a papoose who was his spitting image, down to the painted-on spectacles and the cigar clenched in his teeth.

During the run of *Mexican Hayride* Bobby worked up dozens of additional bits of business and jokes, and its closing performance was the funniest show I have ever seen. Bobby won the

New York Drama Critics' Circle Award for the best performance by an actor in the 1943–44 season. A pretty high achieve-
ment for a low comic.

Mexican Hayride opened in New York January 28, 1944, at
the Winter Garden to great notices: Howard Barnes in the *Herald Tribune* wrote: "Bobby Clark has a comic field day." Robert
Coleman in the *Mirror* called the show "another Michael Todd
hit. A smash hit. Beautiful, bountiful, tuneful and amusing."
"Bobby Clark and June Havoc make a joyride of *Mexican Hayride*," said John Chapman in the *News*. Burton Rascoe in the
World-Telegram wrote: "Aladdin Todd rubbed his wonderful
lamp last night and lifted us into a dream world of splendor,
mirth, melody and enchantment." Robert Garland in the *Journal-American*: "Broadway in general, and the drama critics in
particular, can continue their custom of writing the word 'Fabulous' in front of the name of Michael Todd . . . the fabulous Todd
produced a musical comedy so funny, so tuneful, so beautiful,
that you could hardly believe your ears and eyes." In the *Times*,
Lewis Nichols's lead was: "Let this morning's news from Broadway be all to the good for a change. Bobby Clark is back."
Nichols went on to say, "Of Mr. Porter's score, the best number
bears the title almost startling in its forthrightness, 'I Love You.'
. . . With the arrival of *Mexican Hayride*, everything is in order
at the Winter Garden. Bobby can begin laying in a large supply
of cigars now."

Bobby smoked twenty-cent cigars. Mike smoked dollar cigars.
One day during the Christmas holidays of 1944 my father had
me come down to the Winter Garden. A photographer posed
us next to each other in the middle of the empty auditorium.
With tremendous disdain Todd took the cellophane wrapper off
a twenty-five-cent cigar and with great repugnance lit it. He
handed me one with the wrapper still on, and told me to hold
it near my chin as if I had been smoking it. We were having our
pictures taken for a father-son cigar ad campaign. Bobby either
heard about the picture-taking session or saw the first appearance of the ad, which came out a few weeks later. He asked
Mike if he was receiving any cigars for the endorsement and
Mike told him, yes, they were going to send him a couple of
boxes each week for a year. Bobby nodded and said, "That's
nice." Two weeks later he appeared at the office, saying that if
Mike didn't mind he intended to use the office as a mailing
address for certain business he was conducting. It was well

known that Bobby spent most of his leisure time at the Lambs Club and used it for his mailing address.

Bobby returned to the Todd office a week later and asked if he had received any letters. After being told he hadn't, he said, "I'd like to say hello to Mike if he isn't busy." Todd had anticipated the visit and had four boxes of cigars on his desk. After exchanging greetings, Mike saved Bobby the embarrassment of asking. "Bobby, I'll never smoke these cigars—why don't you take them?" After mildly protesting, Bobby accepted, saying there was no sense letting them lie around. Bobby came up every Thursday afternoon to ask if he had received any mail. After a brief exchange of pleasantries with Mike, Bobby would hesitantly accept the two boxes of twenty-five-cent cigars Todd forced on him. This ritual was repeated without variation for a year.

Todd always said that he smoked the occasional dime cigar to remind himself that if he flopped he would be forced to smoke them the rest of his life. Bobby took the opposite view of life and never accepted one of Mike's expensive cigars, saying that he was fearful he would get used to them and be stuck if he ever hit hard times again.

Bobby lived in an inexpensive rent-controlled apartment on West Fifty-fifth Street until his death in 1960. He had no children and left his wife Lucette an estate in excess of two million dollars—much of it cash—and considerable real estate on Coney Island.

Todd now had three hugely profitable hits running on Broadway simultaneously. A year and a half later the Gallup organization took a nationwide poll asking people to name as many motion picture producers as they could. Todd's was the third-most-mentioned name, after Samuel Goldwyn and Cecil B. De-Mille. The poll was taken at a time when he had never produced a motion picture. Little wonder he was offered generous contracts at several of the major studios.

For the fun of being romanced by the studios and to see Joan he was going to the coast more often. There were mentions in the press and on radio that Joan's marriage to Powell was breaking up and that she would next marry Todd. I neither saw nor heard whatever mother's reaction was to these reports. I was only aware that my father was away a lot and that mother's brittle disposition was not mellowing.

Todd knew he could produce successful motion pictures, but he wanted a degree of autonomy that none of the studios would offer a novice movie producer. They kept trying to tempt him with increasingly extravagant salary offers, but he was making much more money on Broadway and was deeply involved in plans for a number of new productions. He didn't need or want to get involved in moviemaking at this time, although he was listening to the escalating offers. He was sure he had more ability and theatrical sense than most of the producers and studio executives he was playing cards with at Joe Schenck's.

At a studio screening of a Columbia film, Todd was astounded at the end of the picture when everybody went up to the producer and Harry Cohn, the boss of Columbia, and congratulated them on the sensational picture they had made. Todd had found it boring, a horrible mishmash that had required all his patience to sit through. At the end of several minutes of adulation from others, Todd had the temerity to ask a few questions about the elements of the picture that had confused him. The film producer started to answer when Cohn interrupted. With heavy sarcasm, Cohn told Todd to sit down—he would explain it all to him. A small and appreciative group of Columbia executives quietly gathered around, ready to see Cohn put this big-headed Broadway producer in his place. As if talking to a child, Cohn spent ten minutes explaining the story to a respectfully silent Todd. At the end of his dissertation, Cohn asked with exaggerated patience, "Now do you understand, Mike?"

"Yes, perfectly. Now, all you have to do is go around the country to every theater the picture plays, grab anyone who sees the movie and give them the same explanation."

While none of the salary offers at the majors tempted him, an unusual deal being discussed at Universal did. The studio had been struggling for years, and in an indirect way Todd had played a minor role in keeping it alive. In the spring of 1940, shortly after *Streets of Paris* had opened at the World's Fair, Abbott and Costello had been offered a movie contract and Todd had released them to Universal after only a couple of weeks of the run, even though he had a contract with them for the entire summer engagement. The string of Abbott and Costello comedies in the early forties and the Deanna Durbin pictures were all that kept Universal from going under. The new heads of the studio, Leo Spitz and William Goetz, were trying to pull Universal up into the ranks of the majors. In the process of wooing Todd, they not only offered him a top salary and the independence to produce what he liked, but money to invest in any Broadway shows he was planning. Todd took them up on the last part of their offer.

June Allyson's romance with Dick Powell was common Hollywood gossip late in 1943. Joan and Powell continued to live in the same house although their marriage was falling apart. To have more time with Joan and to get her away from the mess at home, Mike put her in the Merman role in the road company of *Something for the Boys* early in 1944. That July Joan filed for divorce.

In 1944 Todd had a large staff. Aside from press agents, company and general managers for the shows and an accountant and several secretaries, he had a general business manager, James Colligan, who tried as best he could to maintain some semblance of order with Todd's various Broadway enterprises. There were the finances of shows that were running, as well as for the shows that were being optioned and produced. The leasing, buying and selling of theaters. The maintenance and supervision of an office staff, with large payrolls to be met. And then there were Todd's personal finances to keep track of, an immeasurably complicated job, as he was always making irregular draws of cash from the box offices, most often to pay off gambling losses. Todd was traveling to and from the coast and Chicago and usually neglected to tell Colligan what money he was taking, spending or committing—or, for that matter, his whereabouts.

On the New York staff Todd had a full-time assistant and part-time companion named Harry Bloomfield, who handled all dealings with theater brokers and concessionaires. But more important, Harry was the sounding board for most of Todd's New York financial dealings and was privy to a lot of Todd's gambling adventures, as he often had to scramble around the following day to cover a previous evening's losses. Colligan relied on Bloomfield to keep track of financial dealings Todd neglected to inform him about.

An assistant of Todd's, Harriet Kaplan, who had the title of talent scout and story editor, read and liked a script entitled *Elizabeth Versus You and I.* This was a courtroom drama about a teenage runaway girl who, after various misadventures in New York City, is arrested as a prostitute—not exactly Todd's idea of entertainment. However, the script was well written, and, more to the point, he had recently acquired the 48th Street Theatre and had no play to put in it. Partially to disassociate himself from a message melodrama and partially because he now felt it befit his stature in the theater, the production credit for this show read: "Michael Todd's Staff: Harry Bloomfield, James Colligan and Harriet Kaplan present." Todd made a sizable contribution to the venture, aside from the money and the theater: he changed the title to *Pick-Up Girl*. The play opened on May 3, 1944, and the majority of critics gave it excellent notices. The minority that didn't like it couldn't rap it very hard, as it had such praiseworthy intentions. The heading to Robert Coleman's review in the *Daily Mirror* got it right: "PICK-UP GIRL GOOD BUT DEPRESSING."

Todd often said, "There are no geniuses in show business, except the unconscious genius, the public." The "unconscious genius" saw through the play's title and were scared away by the threat of the moralistic message that the good reviews and quotes implied. The play closed after a six-week run, but because it was inexpensive to produce—it was a one-set courtroom drama—and had no stars, and it would have been costly for Todd to keep his theater dark, he actually came out a few dollars ahead on the project.

On one of his trips to the coast, Mike heard that Mae West had been working on a play about Catherine the Great as a starring vehicle for herself. He contacted her and read the play. It didn't read all that well, but the subject matter and situations gave ample scope for Mae West to have a royal romp. The dialogue and gags could be sharpened, and Mae West need only be herself to bring in one of the best farces Broadway had ever seen. He provided the show with a lavish production and a bevy of big good-looking men that Miss West could disport herself with onstage and off. There was, however, a gigantic misunderstanding that became apparent only after rehearsals began.

Howard Bay, the scenic designer, describes how work on the show started in New York:

> We had this delicate little fellow as director. His job was
> to show the one other woman in the play how to move—and
> that's all he was allowed to do. Miss West took total charge
> of the thirty or so men. One day Miss West was giving the

director, in no uncertain terms, her interpretation of a scene. He kept backing away from her and fell into the orchestra pit. He went off to the hospital, and that was the end of his directorial duties.

It turned out that Miss West wrote and performed as if the play were a serious dramatic work. Todd always maintained that comedy, satire and even farce had to be seriously acted to be most effective. Although there was a great deal of unconscious humor in Mae West's portrayal of Catherine the Great, Todd felt that her pretension of presenting a serious dramatic work made him the victim of a perverse practical joke. All attempts Todd made during rehearsals to get Miss West not to treat her portrayal of the empress as drama were to no avail. Flattery, bombast, humor and cajolery were all deflected by Miss West's ironclad bodice and will. She told Todd that the smoke from his cigars made her ill and that he would have to do without them in her presence. He was smoking fifteen to twenty cigars a day and was not about to give them up for the doubtful pleasure of having futile conferences with Mae West, the author. After the first few days of rehearsals, Todd temporarily abandoned his attempt to convince Miss West that her play would succeed only as a farce.

When the show opened in Philadelphia, it received the bad notices Todd had anticipated. He felt this would convince Miss West that he should be given a free hand to change the tone of the play and have the dialogue reworked. He was amazed and disheartened to discover Miss West felt that the solution was to make the play even more serious and dramatic. Todd was soon made aware that even threats of closing out of town would not get Miss West to change her views.

Howard Bay recalls:

Mike was very frustrated in Philadelphia. West wouldn't rewrite. She spoke of herself in the third person as the Empress. When Mike suggested something, she'd say to him "The Empress would never do that." Mike got desperate. He was still negotiating a deal with Universal, and he had a lot of money in the show from Spitz and Goetz. He owed it to them to get the show to New York in the best possible shape—otherwise, I feel he surely would have closed it in Philadelphia. Mike would come out of her dressing room exhausted. One night he said, "Do you know what she just told me?—'I'm afraid, Mr. Todd, that what you want is to take all the spiritual qualities in this production and flush them down the toilet.' " We'd go to Bradford's and have a drink together, and Mike wasn't a drinker.

Todd pretended to play it her way. He conned West into making a series of minor changes on the basis that it would strengthen the drama and her serious portrayal, all the while accomplishing the opposite. Maintaining her imperial dignity, she went along with many of Todd's ideas. Both pretended they were trying to heighten the drama and serious nature of the work. A few more laughs were added, and despite her desire to showcase herself as a dramatic actress, Mae West couldn't help being anything but Mae West. It was just possible that no one would take Miss West or her play seriously.

Howard Bay was backstage before the final preview performance in New York. "Mike came out of West's dressing room, shaking his head, and said, 'You know, I wish she'd exile me to Siberia.' "

Although Todd was not terribly hopeful, he figured he could give the play a better chance if he staged a gala premiere. Perhaps Miss West and the play would be carried along by the gaiety and excitement of the evening. Opening-night tickets were allotted in accordance with the amount of War Bonds a premiere patron purchased. Several million dollars' worth were sold. *Catherine Was Great* opened in New York August 2, 1944, at the Shubert Theatre. The play and Miss West were roasted by the critics. Lewis Nichols in the New York *Times* wrote: "As the authoress, Miss West has tried to blend history with a leer . . . Broadway as of last night would have settled for more leer and less history. . . . When Mike Todd produces a show he gives it the works. In this case the trappings surround emptiness." Chapman in the *News* said: "I'm afraid *Catherine Was Great* will be a bust, which will give Miss West one more than she needs." Howard Barnes in the *Herald Tribune* called it "expensive and awful." Coleman in the *Mirror:* "Less Majesty and more West is what it needs." Louis Kronenberger of *PM* summed up the proceedings, saying, "Mae West slips on the steppes . . . the siren of sex lies self-slain by her pen."

Surprisingly, the show was a big hit at the box office. The fanfare and publicity overshadowed the reviews. Mae West as Catherine the Great in a lavish production was the theatergoing public's idea of a Mike Todd show, and there was the satisfaction in seeing Mae West in person, still successfully portraying her charade of a sex goddess at an age well past the half-century mark. There was enough humor, much of it provided by the imagination of the audiences, to keep the show running profitably. *Catherine Was Great* chalked up 191 performances on Broadway and had a successful road tour.

In less than ten months Todd had produced four shows on Broadway. Though in big trouble in Boston, *Mexican Hayride* was an unqualified success in New York. Despite good notices, *Pick-Up Girl* was not well received by the public. *The Naked Genius* and *Catherine Was Great* deserved and received devastating reviews. By most standards three of the four shows were failures. Yet through various circumstances Todd made money on all of them and they enhanced his reputation with the public as Broadway's most successful producer.

CHAPTER 7

THE MCBURNEY SCHOOL was very convenient when we lived across the street, on West Sixty-third Street, but when we moved to a more fashionable apartment my mother found on Park Avenue, McBurney seemed less desirable in many ways. Eyebrows were raised more than a little at home when I reported that the purchase of War Bonds was discouraged by two of the teachers as a poor investment. One of these teachers told us that Hitler was misunderstood and not really the villain portrayed in the American press. My parents decided that perhaps I should be going to school elsewhere.

Although my father took great pride in claiming that his last full year of schooling was in the fifth grade, he was intent on my getting a good education. A friend of his, Gradwell Sears, who was then the general sales manager of United Artists Pictures, had a son at Lawrenceville. Checking out its reputation, Todd found that it was considered one of the best prep schools in the country. Early in 1944 he "went to research" and sought out every graduate of the school and "heavyweight name" he could line up to recommend me. Some of the references on my application were Lloyd Lewis, a distinguished historian and an editor on the Chicago *Daily News;* Lewis's boss, the owner-publisher of the Chicago *Daily News,* Frank Knox, who at the time was Secretary of the Navy; and Lloyd Lewis's neighbor in Libertyville, Illinois, Adlai Stevenson, who was then special assistant to Frank Knox in the Navy Department.

My first year at Lawrenceville I played on an intramural football team, and the last game of the season preceded the fall prom weekend. The orchestra was budgeted at $750, and the

123

prom committee, with my father in mind, had asked if I could get any kind of name band at that price.

While mother and I maintained a regular correspondence, I was in closer touch with my father, who called me from his office several times a week. I passed on the prom committee's request to him, and he was delighted to have the chance to get involved and help improve my lowly new-boy status. He called me back within an hour to say that Les Brown would fill the date. When I asked him how he'd swung it, he told me that Brown owed him a favor and this would be it.

I later found out that in 1940, when Brown's band was on the verge of breaking up, my father had given him a long and profitable engagement at the Dancing Campus. Brown was pleased to play our prom for less than a third of his regular fee.

Late on the Friday afternoon before the prom, I was playing defensive end for my house football team. The single wing, Princeton's favorite, was the offensive formation being used by our opponent. On the last play of the year for me, they lined up strong on my side of the line and ran an end run around me or, to be more precise, over me. I met the three-man interference head-on. The last thing I recall was one of my teammates tackling the ball carrier directly over my head.

Twenty-two hours later I woke up in the Lawrenceville infirmary and saw Betty Sullivan, my date for the prom, sitting on a chair looking rather bored and confused. My father was sitting next to her, bedraggled and distraught. He had been notified of my injury and had not told my mother for fear of scaring her out of her wits. He had rushed to the school and had instructed a brain surgeon to see me if I didn't regain consciousness soon, as the school's doctor had assured him I would. Betty had arrived at noon, not knowing about my brush with the single wing. Hearing me talk and seeing that I had no physical complaints, my father began to take the incident more lightly.

He shaved and showered, having sat by my bedside all night, and then took Betty to dinner. He arranged for one of my dateless housemates to take Betty to the dance, and he went himself as my proxy and had a grand time. From that evening on Todd lost his reverential timidity about the school and felt as comfortable there as the most devoted and generous alumnus. In fact, he pledged $1,500 to the school's building fund that night—a pledge that he never got around to fulfilling before he went into bankruptcy for over a million dollars three years later.

The next morning my father visited me before and after breakfast, and then drove Betty back to New York. Betty, Ed Sullivan's daughter, lived two blocks south of us on Park Avenue.

Two years later, when I was trying out for the varsity football team, I was inexplicably cut after the second day's practice. It was not until graduation that my housemaster, who was also the school's football coach, explained that I had been cut at my father's request.

My father often came down on a weekend and took me and my roommates to Bookbinder's in Philadelphia or Hackney's in Atlantic City for lobster. We ate buckets of steamers, followed by the largest lobsters we could manage. I managed a seven-pounder one Sunday at Bookbinder's.

As one could leave the school only if accompanied by a parent and our favorite restaurant was in New York, my father would occasionally make a four-way trip on a Saturday so that we could eat at Peter Luger's steak house at the foot of the Williamsburg Bridge in Brooklyn. We and a lot of other people thought they served the best steak in the world. The restaurant was then run by Peter Luger's two aging and irritable bachelor sons, Carl and Peter junior. They slammed their doors shut at 6:00 P.M., and brooked no impertinence or familiarity from their customers.

On one occasion during the war, at about a quarter to six, Carl was called to the phone booth by one of the waiters. They didn't have a private phone. In his heavy German accent, he erupted with the following: "Tell your Colonel Darryl F. Zanuck we close at six sharp and we don't open the doors one minute after for General Dwight D. Eisenhower." He slammed down the receiver and was still growling when he unlocked the door to let us out of the restaurant half an hour later. Mike of course gave no sign that it was he who had introduced the audacious Colonel Zanuck to Peter Luger's.

One Saturday afternoon Mike got around both Carl's stern code of customer conduct and my timid, law-abiding nature. When we arrived at the restaurant, he asked Carl if the rest of our party had arrived. Carl said no and seated us at a table for six. Mike then ordered tomatoes and onions for six and three double steaks, two medium rare and one rare. Carl said he would hold the steaks until the rest of the party showed up so that they wouldn't get overdone. When I asked my father who was joining us, he told me no one else was coming—he just wanted to see how much steak I could eat. During the war restaurants could serve only single portions of meat. I almost lost my appetite for fear that Carl would bar us from the place for life. After we were halfway through our tomatoes and onions, Mike asked Carl to put the steaks on, saying that the rest of the party would arrive momentarily, but Carl was adamant about waiting until they were actually seated at the table. I nervously awaited the outcome of this stalemate. A few minutes later, with Carl watching, Mike went to the telephone booth. When he returned, he told Carl that his friends had left fifteen minutes ago. Carl reluctantly had the steaks put on the fire. When they were cooked, Carl stood by irritably while they were served. Carl said he wouldn't accept responsibility for the steaks being cold, and he wouldn't overcook these, or provide new ones. Indignantly he walked away. As we were about to finish the first steak, Carl came back to the table with a phone message that one of the waiters had received: Mr. Todd's friends had been in a minor auto accident and wouldn't be able to join us. Mike frowned and said it would be criminal to let these magnificent steaks go to waste—we'd just have to try to eat them ourselves. As we were eating away, I asked my father about the message Carl had delivered. He explained that when he left the table he had phoned his secretary, Belle Postal, and told her to call back in fifteen minutes with the bogus message. Every time he passed the table, Carl gave us a menacing glance, but was mollified when he saw we had polished off all the steaks.

My mother never joined us on any of the eating expeditions. She didn't enjoy long drives, and there grew to be a tacit understanding among us that I did certain things with my father and others with her. The three of us were seldom together. When I was home on weekends or vacations, I went to the theater with her when I didn't have a date. We most often ate alone, as Mike would be away or out for dinner. He lived at home, but was spending very little time there. In effect, they were in a state of semi-separation. No one ever suggested, least of all me, that there was anything wrong or unusual about this arrangement. We were all willing to leave well enough alone.

One of Mike's greatest triumphs was his visit to school on Father's Day my second year at Lawrenceville. Some fathers came Friday night to take part in our Saturday morning classes. In English we were discussing *Crime and Punishment*. Todd seemed to enjoy the discussion, but made no effort to be a part of it. I was relieved that he wasn't going to try to compete with my classmates' fathers, who were all college graduates.

When the instructor asked what event in Soviet history mirrored Dostoevski's life and the portion of the book we were discussing, everybody sat slightly stunned. No one had a clue. No one except my father, who leaned over and whispered his idea to me. I gave him a dirty look, as his idea was ridiculous. A few more moments went by, and the teacher plaintively said that the answer was quite obvious and someone should have thought of it by now. More embarrassed silence followed. Then the instructor, who had noticed my father whispering to me, said, "Perhaps Mr. Todd has an idea." Because of my visual rebuff Todd was apologetic when he said he thought the Moscow purge trials illustrated the points under discussion. "Of course!" cried the instructor, and he took the class to task for not immediately recognizing the parallels. He and my father spent the next ten minutes discussing the similarities between the Moscow trials and the about-face in Dostoevski's beliefs. At the end of the period the instructor thanked all the fathers for their attention and my father for his stimulating participation. I was pleased, but felt that Todd had pulled off an incredible long shot and told him he shouldn't try to press his luck in the next class.

This was a course in modern European history, taught by Mr. Shea, one of the most interesting and devoted masters in the school. He and his wife were from extremely wealthy Pittsburgh families, and he worked at Lawrenceville for a dollar a year. He had built a lovely house on the campus, which he was bequeathing to the school.

When the class began, Mr. Shea launched into a lecture about the reunification of Italy. Midway through the period, when no one had spoken except Mr. Shea, Todd suddenly bolted upright in his seat, raised his hand and started speaking: "You just said that Mazzini was one of the triumvirate who took over the Roman republic in 1848." I slumped down in my chair as he continued: "In 1848 Mazzini was involved in the liberation of Milan. He didn't take office in Rome until the following year, 1849."

Mr. Shea smiled politely and said that he had been teaching this course for twenty years and that he had always been under the strong impression that Mazzini went to Rome in 1848—but there was no need to speculate. Mr. Shea walked over to the bookcase to find the appropriate reference book. Todd grinned confidently as Mr. Shea thumbed through the book. Mr. Shea looked up from the book and stared at my father.

"My God!" he said. "You're right. It *was* 1849!"

Todd always had a fully conceived concept of any project he proposed. He would enthusiastically describe his ideas as if they were almost accomplished realities, but all the while he was testing the reactions of people whose opinions he valued. Sometimes he talked about projects for months and even years, gradually modifying his own concept. But each revised version was presented as better than the last. Finally, either he abandoned the project and it was never heard from again—or he did it. He was uncharacteristically diffident about an idea he had for his next musical.

During the period *Mexican Hayride* was in preparation, Todd read a book about Boss Tweed's incredible looting of the New York City treasury during his reign as Tammany Hall chief. Todd was particularly intrigued by the fact that Tweed and his cronies had pocketed millions during the construction of Central Park. Todd thought a good musical might be based on Tweed's shenanigans with Central Park and his subsequent downfall, brought about by a New York *Times* exposé. This was his first original idea for the plot of a show since his initial foray on Broadway with *Call Me Ziggy*. It was a period piece, far away from the meat-and-potatoes kind of musical with which his name was most closely associated, and he had no specific story ideas. He lightly threw the concept at Dorothy and Herbert Fields.

Once *Mexican Hayride* had settled in for its successful run, Dorothy Fields gave some thought to Todd's idea. It was particularly appealing to her as her reputation had been built as a lyricist, not as a collaborator on librettos. She had won the Academy Award with Jerome Kern for the song "The Way You Look Tonight" and had written the lyrics for such hits as "I Can't Give You Anything but Love," "A Fine Romance," "I Won't Dance," "On the Sunny Side of the Street," "Lovely to Look At" and many more. The kind of show Todd had in mind was really an American operetta, not a Cole Porter show, so she could write the lyrics as well as collaborate on the book.

Dorothy and her brother Herbert devised a Romeo and Juliet story—the girl, a daughter of a Boss Tweed underling, and her

128

lover, an investigative reporter trying to expose the Tweed gang. Todd liked their ideas, and in the summer of 1944 they decided to go ahead. Todd's conceptions were predominantly visual, not verbal or musical. *Up in Central Park* was to have a "Currier and Ives flavor." He had had a good working relationship with Howard Bay, who had done the sets for *Something for the Boys* and *Catherine Was Great.* Bay, an excellent artist, was knowledgeable, efficient and a good listener. He readily absorbed Todd's capsule descriptions of what he wanted and executed detailed sketches—without lengthy discussions.

The most logical choice for a composer—immediately agreed to by Todd and the Fieldses—was Sigmund Romberg, the acknowledged dean of American operetta. Romberg was born and raised in the Austro-Hungarian Empire prior to World War I. In thirty years, after immigrating to the United States, he wrote the music for over thirty American shows. Many of the most successful were presented by the Shuberts, had made them a fortune and were the keystone of the producing side of their empire. Most of Romberg's smash shows had been produced in the twenties: *Maytime, Blossom Time, The Student Prince, The Desert Song, Rosalie* and *The New Moon.* His last success, *May Wine,* was produced in 1935 and was nowhere near as well received as his big hits of the twenties. He was almost sixty when approached by Todd and Dorothy Fields to write the music for *Up in Central Park* and by this time had been labeled, if not stigmatized, as a composer of Strauss-like operettas. Romberg was delighted to have the opportunity to do a show with a book set in America and with a hot team of collaborators.

Todd thought the show would look best played against painted backdrops with a sprinkling of appropriate props and that the costumes needn't be elaborate, only colorful. The cost of producing this show would be a fraction of one with a heavy production. The story and structure of the show would be carried by the music, dancing, the setting and period flavor, and would not require high-salaried stars.

An even more enticing commercial consideration evolved in Todd's mind. For a number of years the Shuberts had a theater, the New Century, on the west side of Seventh Avenue, between Fifty-eighth and Fifty-ninth streets, that they found nearly impossible to book. It was five long blocks away from the outermost fringe of the theater district. Even at peak periods—and this was one—the Century lay idle and dark.

The Shuberts looked at everything but the dental records of the cast before accepting ironclad cash guarantees for the bookings of their theaters. Todd went to see Mr. Lee prior to announcing the production of *Up in Central Park*. Mr. Lee was totally taken aback when Todd talked to him about leasing the Century Theatre.

No matter what trick Todd had up his sleeve, Mr. Lee was more than ready to unload the Century on a "four wall" basis, as Todd proposed. This means that the renter (Todd) pays a fixed weekly sum for the rental of the theater—without staff, services or utilities included. The theater owner does not participate in any percentage of the gross of the attraction and in exchange is guaranteed a specified sum for an agreed-upon number of weeks. With the real squeeze on theater availability at the time, the total cost of booking one in the theater district would be about twice as much as the four-wall deal Todd made for the Century. Todd figured that the proximity of the Century to Central Park would actually *help* his show. There was, of course, one risk in personally guaranteeing Mr. Lee a number of fixed weeks' rental—the show had to be a hit.

In the late fall of 1944, when *Up in Central Park* was in rehearsal, *Mexican Hayride* was nearing the end of its run. Although it was still doing good business, it had a large and expensive cast, a huge crew of stagehands and a large orchestra. It had already paid back its heavy investment but now was netting Todd only a few thousand dollars a week. *Star and Garter* and *Something for the Boys* had been closed over half a year and had made huge profits. His three straight plays were not hits but had made him some money. Not counting the fortune made at the World's Fair, he had made almost two million dollars the previous three years on Broadway. Even after taxes, not all of which he paid at the time, Todd should have been in fabulous financial shape. He was, however, spreading a lot of sunshine and gambling heavily. By heavily I mean that almost every week during this period he had ten to twenty-five thousand dollars in action, or up to six-figure amounts in a single poker session at Joe Schenck's.

In the fall of 1944 Todd should have been able to finance the production of *Up in Central Park* out of his own pocket, especially since it had a comparatively inexpensive budget for a musical—$150,000. But he was short of cash, since on top of everything else he had bought the expensive town house at 10 West Fifty-sixth Street for his offices. It was elegant, but a grandiose gesture, as he had four times the amount of space he needed. Todd would have no difficulty securing investors for *Up in Central Park*, but he wanted total ownership and control. Having assets that greatly exceeded the size of the loan he needed, he had no compunction about borrowing the money from Joe Schenck, who wrote him a check without blinking. To maintain the posture that it was a business, not a personal, transaction, Todd insisted on paying a nominal rate of interest on Schenck's loan.

Todd's self-confidence was dented when *Up in Central Park* got mixed notices in Philadelphia, where it opened for the out-of-town tryout. Perhaps it was confusing to have Todd's name linked with Sigmund Romberg. Certainly the Philadelphia critics were not totally taken with the sentimental flavor of *Up in Central Park*. Two key production numbers—as might be expected at a show's out-of-town opening—had not gone smoothly. These were intricate dance routines that Todd hoped would keep the public's and critics' minds diverted from the show's skimpy physical production. One was a simulated ice skating ballet and the other a maypole dance, both done full stage in front of painted backdrops. These numbers required precise timing and execution to achieve the desired effect.

Howard Bay recalls:

> Mike was nervous about the cool reception we got in Philadelphia. The show was only a modest hit. After all, we had no stars. We had a big preopening benefit performance for some hospital. The tickets were fifty dollars apiece, which was a gigantic price then, and the wives had pulled their husbands there by the lapels of their dinner jackets. The audience sat there glum. It was solid glum, not a sound from them the whole night. I had brought a scenic artist and his crew down to work on one of the sets. After the show we were backstage touching it up. They were all painting away; nobody was saying anything. An old Italian fellow who had a wry sense of humor broke the silence. He looked up and asked, "That audience tonight—were they all one family?"

Todd was worried about the New York opening, so he scheduled it for a Saturday night (January 27, 1945) and invited the critics and the first-night audience to an all-night party at the Tavern-on-the-Green in Central Park. The critics would have all Sunday to write their reviews. A heavy blanket of snow enhanced the atmosphere of the evening. He hired almost every horse-drawn carriage in the city and had them lined up waiting to transport the entire audience to the party. Riding through the moonlit snowy park in a horse-drawn carriage seemed to be a continuation of the show. There was a lavish buffet supper. Two orchestras provided a continuous flow of music, much of it from the score. Todd invited all of the cast as well. The chorus appreciated this unusual invitation to an opening-night party and exuberantly filled the dance floor throughout the night. In addition to an endless supply of mixed drinks, 127 cases of champagne were consumed. The party was still going on at dawn. Sunday afternoon it was difficult to remember where the show stopped and the party began, but both the show and the party were widely acclaimed by the press.

Todd hired and had waiting enough taxis to pick up all the guests when they were ready to leave. Earl Wilson wrote: "I have attended Evalyn Walsh MacLean's lavish parties in Washington but even she never paid her guests' way home."

Todd's close but sometimes peevish friend George Jean Nathan, who was always an honest and impartial critic, wrote: "Just why Mr. Todd, whose show was a sufficiently good and surefire one, should have deemed it necessary to ingratiate himself with reviewers by wining and dining them I cannot understand."

Except for Louis Kronenberger's review in *PM*, all the notices were good to excellent, with a couple of raves thrown in. But raves weren't needed to make this show a gigantic financial success. The timing was perfect. The war was drawing to a close, and where earlier, bawdy entertainment had been a welcome diversion, the imminent return of the armed forces made sentiment and nostalgia the order of the day. John Chapman in the *News* said the show was "warm, gentle, and affectionate" and called the skating number "a complete delight" and the maypole dance "utterly charming." Otis Guernsey in the *Herald Tribune* wrote, "Todd has assembled a flawless production in his first try at operetta." Burton Rascoe in the *World-Telegram* called it "one of the most charming musicals ever staged." In the *Sun*, Ward Morehouse wrote, "It is Mr. Todd's most ambitious, and perhaps his most creditable contribution to the local stage." Robert Coleman of the *Mirror* said, "Michael Todd brought another musical hit to town last night. . . . Oh go ahead and supply your own favorite superlatives. . . . It's got everything, and Todd's got another gold mine."

After the nine weeks it took Todd to pay off the show and the party, he netted over twenty thousand dollars a week during the first year's capacity run of *Up in Central Park*. This money flowed out as fast as it came in.

David Lawlor worked for Todd during the height of his Broadway successes and was often the person carrying cash to him. He described Todd's free and easy manner with the receipts from his shows:

> The company manager would put an I.O.U. into the box office and sign Mr. Todd's name to it, and I would bring the money over to the office or to him at his apartment. In many cases, when a show was nearing the end of its run, the theater couldn't throw him out because he owed more money than was coming in. Mr. Lee would scream at the treasurers when Mr. Todd got too far ahead.
>
> There was no box office treasurer in this town who couldn't and didn't go by the Burberry Shop and pick out any coat he liked, sign for it and Mr. Todd would pay for it. He could get tickets for any show, any time he wanted them, without even going through the Shubert office. And Mr. Todd never had a problem getting a drawing room or a compartment on a train going anywhere in America, at a time when there were people standing in the aisles on every train that left New York. Any conductor could call Mr. Todd and get whatever he wanted—theater tickets, a coat, money, anything. His friends from the Midwest—the Florsheim brothers, Al Strelsin—when they couldn't get accommodations on a train, Mr. Todd could get them on a moment's notice.

The huge amount of money he made on *Up in Central Park* made it less painful for Todd to make a costly pullout on two shows he had in production.

Todd had enjoyed a series of short stories in the *New Yorker*, written by Arthur Kober, about a Jewish family that lived in the Bronx and the romantic ups and downs of their daughter. Kober did the script and Elmer Rice directed. The play, *Bella's Got a Fella*, was smoothly adapted by Kober from his stories, and all indications were that it would be filled with laughs. A theater was booked for the Boston tryout and for the opening in New York. The show seemed to be shaping up very well, but Mike was nagged by an uneasy feeling throughout rehearsals. Howard Bay tells what happened next:

> The day we finished the set and it came out of the studio, we did a run-through. We were seated together in the theater—Arthur Kober, Elmer Rice, Mike and myself. At the end of it, Elmer said, "What do you think of it, Mike?" Now, most people waltz around—they'll say, "Well, you do this. You fix that. You replace so and so," and they dodge the issue. All Mike said was, "I know you fellows put a lot of work into this, but it comes out anti-Semitic and it's cheap. I'll give you back the rights, the set and what I've invested in it for free." A very simple statement. He got up and walked out.

Bella's Got a Fella never opened, but there were many occasions, both before and after, when his interest in or option on a property was picked up after he had abandoned it. Molnar's *Liliom* was successfully produced by Rodgers and Hammerstein as *Carousel*. *Beat the Band* and *Get Away, Old Man* were both unsuccessfully produced by George Abbott. After Todd dropped his option on "Tevye's Daughters" and other Sholom Aleichem stories, Rodgers and Hammerstein tried unsuccessfully for five years to work them into a musical. Sixteen years later the material was transformed into *Fiddler on the Roof*. When presented to him by Herbert and Dorothy Fields, Todd was too busy in Hollywood to produce *Annie Get Your Gun*.

The other show Todd abandoned in this period was a musical comedy adaptation of Jules Verne's book *Around the World in 80 Days*. Orson Welles was to write, direct and star in it. Cole Porter wrote the score.

When Mike did the film a decade later his favorite description of the property was "It's a fairy tale for adults." This was the concept that he and Welles shared when they started to do the musical together.

The production of this show would be a vivid contrast to *Up in Central Park* with its light production. To create this fairy tale for adults, Todd and Welles agreed that Phileas Fogg's adventures must be made to seem real, with the most impressive stage effects they could devise. The enthusiasm

Todd and Welles shared for the project was a show of its own.

I was home on vacation when Mike and Welles were spending hours together every day, excitedly exchanging their thoughts on how to stage various episodes in the story. I walked into my father's huge office one day to pick up some shopping money. Welles was lying on the floor with his head resting on a wastepaper basket and Mike was pacing in wide circles around him. I stood there for a while, fascinated by their conversation—their excitement was like that of two boys contemplating the construction of the world's most elaborate model train setup.

Howard Bay tells about his brief involvement with the show:

> There were lots of conferences. Orson talked very well. But all he had was an outline with a description of the scenes. It was February of 1946, and I had just finished a show. It was the first chance I'd had for a vacation in years, and the day after my show opened I took my wife off to Cuba. Mike had given me Welles's outline and asked me to make a budget for the scenery and costumes. It wrecked my vacation. When I got back I called Mike. I told him that if Welles's outline was followed, the scenery and costumes alone would cost over four hundred thousand dollars. Well, that would be four million dollars today. That was the last conversation Mike and I ever had about the show.

Ten years later Todd explained his decision to give up on the *80 Days* musical:

> I have only one superstition about show business—you can't start rehearsals without a script. We were three weeks away from rehearsals and despite a long series of promises, Welles still did not have a single word written. When I kept pressing him, he said, "Don't worry, Mike. I've got it all up here," pointing to his head. "That's great," I said, "but I want it on paper." A week later when there was still no script, I told him I was abandoning the show. He said, "You can't, Mike. You've already got forty thousand sunk into it!" "Yes," I said, "but by next week it will be sixty thousand, and the week after eighty. I'm quitting now."

In exchange for the movie rights, Welles was able to get Alexander Korda, the boss of London Films, to provide financing. The show had a huge model train and collapsing bridge, a ship in a storm at sea, a circus with jugglers, acrobats, a tightrope walker, a magic act (a Welles specialty), an Indian attack that was broken up by a troop of soldiers who marched down the aisles of the theater to the rescue and a bigger-than-life-sized eagle suspended from a steel cable that carried an actor across the theater in its claws. There was so much scenery that some of it couldn't be squeezed into the Forrest Theatre in Philadelphia during the out-of-town tryout. The New York reviews were mixed, and one critic noted that Welles's show had everything in it but the kitchen sink. During its eight-week run, Welles remedied this complaint by taking his curtain call with a kitchen sink. The show was a financial disaster.

When the United States entered the war in 1941, Todd was thirty-four years old and had four financial dependents—mother, myself, his mother and his sister Edith. Except for a chronic case of colitis, Todd had no health problems. In September of 1944 I was told about the possibility of his enlisting in the navy, and he was scheduled to take a physical. I asked mother, when I next came home from Lawrenceville on a weekend, what my father's status was with the navy. She seemed embarrassed and brushed the question aside by saying he was deemed unfit for active service. From conversations I overheard, I had the impression that he could get a job in Special Services as a noncommissioned officer but that he wasn't going to enlist in the navy unless he had some gold to wear on his sleeve. Several months later, early in 1945, to be in on the action when the war ended, he secured a position as a consultant to the Special Services branch of the army.

At that point his involvement in the war had been limited to using his shows to sell War Bonds and putting together a few units to entertain soldiers in army camps.

In February 1945, Todd went to Europe in an army uniform made by his tailor, with one star on each shoulder. He held the assimilated rank of brigadier general. The fact that he was not really a general or a part of the regular army was apparent only to anyone who had occasion to look at his I.D. card or closely inspect his orders. So the star on his shoulder and the single star painted on the jeep assigned to him allowed him to freewheel around pretty much as he pleased. His assignment was a self-created one, which was to devise entertainment for the armed forces in the European theater. After spending a few days with friends in London and checking out what new plans were afoot for the entertainment of troops, he was dispatched to Paris to work under the command of the regular army general who headed Special Services in Europe.

The few things Todd did accomplish, and a few things he failed to, all came shortly after the war ended. His most dramatic idea was to hold the annual all-star baseball game in Nuremberg Stadium, the setting of Hitler's biggest rallies and most frenzied speeches. There was immediate acceptance by everyone involved, and arrangements had begun when a serious hitch developed. Despite Todd's protests, the senior medical authorities would not waive the requirement for immunization shots. Players who might develop a strong negative reaction to the shots would not only be incapacitated for the all-star game itself, but might be put out of regular season play. The immunization requirement killed off this beguiling way of exorcising the ghost of Hitler. Another piece of Americana that Todd wanted to transplant to Germany was the idea of having a showboat on the Rhine, but this proved impossible, as the river wasn't navigable because of fallen bridges and sunken craft.

Among his few accomplishments was the patching together of several variety bills, ranging from a circus to a selection of opera highlights.

His wanderlust and desire to get away from the confines of the Paris Special Services headquarters put him on the road, where he came up with a workable idea. A perfect bit of casting provided Todd with a driver, Sergeant Bosco from Bayonne, New Jersey, who could easily have served as the prototype for Sergeant Bilko. With nothing more in mind than seeing a bit of Europe, he and Todd took off in the jeep.

Todd's orders were broad enough to get him almost anywhere he wanted to go, but to ensure his freedom of movement he accumulated a sheaf of official-looking letters and documents, only some of which properly belonged to him, and smeared them with a variety of rubber stamps he found lying around at Paris headquarters. It would take hours, if not days, for any authority, military or civil, to sort out what Todd's position, mission and orders truly were.

During a quick tour of Switzerland a couple of weeks after the war ended, Todd noted that every resort in the country was deserted and desperate for business. He decided that linking up war-weary G.I.s with the empty resorts in Switzerland was a natural. Many thousands of soldiers spent their first post-war furloughs in the deluxe hotels of Switzerland at a fraction of the usual rates, and the Swiss government and hotels earned a lot of goodwill and got their moribund tourist industry moving.

When Patton's swoop through southern Germany accelerated to the point where no one knew quite how far he had penetrated each day, Todd and Bosco left Paris. The Allied troops linked up with the Russians at Torgau on the Elbe River, about sixty miles south of Berlin. Hitler committed suicide. When the Russians began to breach the last defenses of Berlin, Todd figured he and Bosco should go there to greet them. In the final days of the war, the American advance was so rapid that there was no orderly or contiguous front line. Todd's general's uniform and jeep and thick sheaf of ambiguous orders easily got him past the few sentries and military police he encountered on his dash to Berlin. The last two days of the war Todd and Bosco were behind the German lines, such as they were. The only resistance or hindrance they encountered was various splintered German units dashing west and south, away from the Russians. They all tried to surrender to this unauthorized mobile advance consultant unit of the U.S. Special Services. Todd found that his fairly fluent command of Yiddish was sufficient to explain to the Germans that he wasn't taking prisoners, and that they had to push on to surrender.

The day the war ended, Todd and Bosco were stopped ten miles outside of Berlin by Russian troops. The official American military party was arriving in Berlin by plane to join the Russians in ratifying the German unconditional surrender. At gunpoint Todd and Bosco were taken to an English-speaking Russian officer who wanted to know who they were and what they were doing in Berlin. Todd was telling the partial truth when he explained that his orders gave him free access to go anywhere to accomplish his mission. The Russians held him for three days but treated him with great hospitality. As the sole American comrade-in-arms available, he was invited to various vodka-drenched victory celebrations and was allowed under escort to sightsee in and around Berlin while the Russians were getting through to Paris to verify that he was who he claimed to be and was on official duty with the U.S. Special Services.

When asked to explain his unauthorized presence in Berlin, Todd told his commanding general that he had made a wrong turn at Aachen.

By midsummer 1945, Joan's divorce from Powell became final. When Todd returned from Europe, his objectives, personal and business, had shifted from New York to Los Angeles. He knew he would be successful in Hollywood, once he took the plunge, but first he had some unfinished business in New York.

While Todd was overseas, *Mexican Hayride* had ended its profitable fifteen-month run on Broadway. Among Bobby Clark's varied credits were his somewhat surprising successful appearances in two Broadway productions of classical comedies, Congreve's *Love for Love* and Sheridan's *The Rivals*. Not only did Bobby create almost all of his own stage business, but quite often revamped sections of his dialogue. For years he had considered doing his own adaptation of a classic. Soon after Todd's return to New York, Bobby indicated that he would like to star in his own adaptation of a Molière comedy. Todd said he'd be delighted to present it.

A best-selling book that year was a humorous novel entitled *January Thaw*. Todd's staff suggested that it could be successfully adapted for the stage and he told them to proceed.

When Bill Doll was released from the service—among other duties he was the press representative for *This Is the Army*—he suggested that a Maurice Evans version of *Hamlet* that had toured the South Pacific during the war might, if suitably produced, go on Broadway. Todd thought it was a good idea and got in touch with Evans.

Gossip columnists on both coasts were speculating as to how long Todd was going to keep Joan waiting. By this time, Bertha was beginning to realize that she wouldn't be able to hold on to Mike much longer. She and Todd began protracted discussions about a settlement and the arrangements for a divorce.

Up in Central Park was still playing to packed houses. Playing uptown out of the theater district had not hurt business a bit. Evans's *Hamlet* was a condensed version tailored for G.I.s and it was this aspect that appealed to Todd—Shakespeare for people who had never seen Shakespeare. The new audience Todd hoped to attract with a painless Shakespeare would not think twice about going to a theater comparatively far removed from

Shubert Alley, and the carriage trade would go anywhere to see a critically acclaimed *Hamlet*. He picked a theater in Columbus Circle that was as little used as the Century had been prior to leasing it for *Up in Central Park*. He secured a favorable lease, partially paid to refurbish it and called it the Columbus Circle Theatre (immediately overcoming any possible confusion as to its location).

Maurice Evans's G.I. *Hamlet* opened on December 13, 1945. Howard Barnes's headline in the *Herald Tribune* read: "TO BE . . . A HIT" and he went on to call the production, "an ingenious piece of showmanship." Louis Kronenberger's headline in *PM* read: "THE GIs KNEW A GOOD THING," and he continued: "It is a swift-moving, cleanly blocked-out version." Robert Garland in the *Journal-American* called it "the greatest show in town," and the *Post*'s critic, Wilella Waldorf, found it "stirring, moving and impressive." In the *World-Telegram* Burton Rascoe led off his review: "Michael Todd is an eclectic and impartial impresario, nothing concerning the theatre is alien to his generous purse. He has lavished just as much care and money upon his production of Maurice Evans' G.I. *Hamlet* as if it were a drama like *The Naked Genius* or a musical like *Something for the Boys*."

All the reviews were outstanding, and they played up the fact that this was a zingy, entertaining and nonpretentious Hamlet. But Todd took no chances about attracting the people who were scared of Shakespeare: he arranged for Toots Shor to provide a verbal critique for some of the leading New York columnists. Several of them used Shor's intermission comment: "I'll bet I'm the only bum in the joint who doesn't know how this comes out." And his final assessment: "This is real good cops and robbers stuff."

Maurice Evans's G.I. version ran longer (seventeen weeks) and grossed more money than any previous production of Hamlet in the history of the theater.

In three and a half years Todd had done eight shows on Broadway—four plays and four musicals. The plays made him some money (about a quarter of a million dollars), but the musicals made him a fortune. Incredibly, he was just barely in the black.

Through a friend in Chicago, Colonel John Gottlieb, Todd was introduced to Henry Crown, the owner of the Material Service

Corporation, the largest supplier of basic construction materials in the Midwest. Crown became one of the principal owners of the Rock Island Railroad and the largest private shareholder of General Dynamics. Among varied real estate dealings he became second only to Conrad Hilton in ownership of Hilton stock. He was involved with William Zeckendorf in the purchase and sale of the land on which the United Nations was built. Crown owned the Pierre Hotel and bought and sold the Empire State Building. He was one of America's wealthiest men.

Using real estate as security—his office building off Fifth Avenue, the theaters that passed through his hands and eventually the Del Mar Racetrack—Todd made a series of personal loans from Crown that finally amounted to over half a million dollars.

The Would-Be Gentleman opened in New York at the Booth Theatre on January 9, 1946. Todd put an insert into the *Playbill* that took the form of a letter of personal apology to Molière for taking certain liberties in the translation and adaptation of his comedy masterpiece, explaining that this was his season for presenting the classics for Toots Shor. The next day Shor's critical assessment of the play was quoted in one review and in several columns: *"The Would-Be Gentleman* is even funnier than Hamlet."

The reviews told two stories, as indicated by Lewis Nichols in the *Times* and Howard Barnes in the *Herald Tribune*. Nichols wrote: "Seventeenth-Century satire, even freely edited, is not the dish for Bobby Clark." Barnes said: "A great clown has been meddling with a classic and has come forth with a wonderfully funny show." Bobby received great notices for his performance and mild criticism from the dissenters as the play's adapter.

The hard-core Clark fans packed the house for the first seven weeks of the run. They loved Bobby and the play. But then the regular theatergoing public took the view of the dissenting critics, that it was "more horseplay than play" and that it "did not make for a full evening's happiness in the theatre." Attendance dropped off sharply and the show was soon in the red. Regretfully, because he hated to injure Bobby's pride, Mike closed *The Would-Be Gentleman* after a ten-week run.

Of the three shows Todd had decided to produce when he returned from overseas, *January Thaw* gave him the most concern. He wasn't sure that the material would appeal to New

Yorkers. It had a contrived plot and rustic humor. The props included oil lamps and chamber pots, and the cast included two piglets.

Todd deliberately picked a date for the opening of *January Thaw* to coincide with the premiere of what he anticipated would be one of the biggest shows of the season. He scheduled the out-of-town tryout for Newark, which despite its proximity to Manhattan would provide a less sophisticated audience. As a final twist he invited the critics to see the last performance of *January Thaw* in Newark on Saturday night, February 2, so that they would be free to attend the other show's opening two nights later.

Both as a matter of pride and custom, critics at that time based their reviews on the opening-night performance and would not go near a show during an out-of-town tryout, or at a New York preview performance. Todd was well aware that the first-line critics would not write a review based on what they saw in Newark and would pass up his play to go to the other opening on Monday, February 4. Second-line critics would be reviewing *January Thaw* and they, given the chance to see his play in Newark (with Todd supplying a limousine to and from the theater as well as a meal and drinks), would take it, whether or not they also went to see the show Monday night in New York, since they would have all of Sunday and Monday to polish their reviews. And, of course, as was also the case, *January Thaw* would play better on a Saturday night (always the easiest audience, with no concern about going to work the next day) in Newark than it would on a Monday night in New York.

The second-line critics saw through Todd's ploy but nevertheless availed themselves of the opportunity to see the play in Newark and were influenced to some degree by how well the audience received it there. Of the nine major New York dailies (nine!) and five lesser ones, six papers gave it good notices, four their qualified approval, and four were outright pans—but these latter included the *Times,* the *Herald Tribune* and the *Journal-American.* The good and qualified reviews all noted, however, that the humor was unsophisticated and sometimes unadulterated corn. The dissenting critics felt they had been exposed to a bucolic plague.

In the *Morning Telegraph* review there was a quote that was typical of the favorable notices: "The woman behind me said, 'It's as good as a movie, there isn't a dull moment.' Personally,

I think she was stretching the truth, but certainly the audience never stopped laughing, and this critic laughed right along with them—most of the time."

Much of the humor in the play came from lines delivered by a crusty, self-reliant farmer and his old-fashioned wife, at the expense of a family from the city. Within the year the Hollywood studio with which Todd was associated, Universal, produced the movie version of the best-selling book, *The Egg and I*. Two of the supporting characters in the film, Ma and Pa Kettle, got most of the laughs. At a studio screening of the movie, Todd, mindful of his experience with *January Thaw*, told the studio bosses they had a gold mine with the Ma and Pa Kettle characters and should be thinking of building a series of films around them. This offhand comment turned out to be the only positive contribution Todd made to the studio's fortunes during his stint at Universal.

January Thaw did moderate business the first few weeks and limped along for a run of forty-eight performances. It was a one-scene, low-budget production and so amounted to no more than a bad day at the track for Todd.

If nothing else, Todd's judgment about the play opening opposite *January Thaw* was indeed accurate. Garson Kanin's *Born Yesterday* was one of the biggest hits of the decade.

Todd reached an agreement with Bertha about the terms for a divorce. After the opening of *January Thaw,* he wound up his personal and business affairs in New York and headed for the coast.

CHAPTER 8

THE TYPICAL SCENARIO is that a creative Broadway talent goes to Hollywood and for enormous wages sacrifices his integrity and artistic standards. Todd abandoned his career as Broadway's most prolific and successful producer and went to Hollywood for a contract that offered him independence but greatly reduced his income. He never budged an inch on his concepts, and his self-assurance grew even greater. He came back to New York from the coast after a year and a half, a total failure, without ever having made a movie, and was soon in bankruptcy proceedings. But he was convinced that he could be a gigantic success in the film industry, and though it took him the rest of his life, he did just that.

In February 1946 Todd took up residence at Joe Schenck's. Todd's high-stakes gambling, his familiarity with the most powerful studio executives and his Broadway reputation enabled him to start his movie career just short of the Hollywood pinnacle.

Louis B. Mayer, Jack Warner, Harry Cohn, the Schencks—the pioneers and "moguls" who still owned and controlled the major studios—were at the top of the heap. At the next level were the production bosses of the major studios and the owners and heads of the lesser studios—David O. Selznick, Darryl Zanuck, Howard Hughes.

Todd created for himself a rather new position at the next level—an independent producer who ostensibly has complete financial backing to make whatever pictures he pleases, in whatever manner he cares to. As the movie business has evolved, the independent has become increasingly important and autonomous. But for the early independents, as Todd was soon to find out, the promise of autonomy and backing was always subject to a few "minor" qualifications. Basically this boiled down to convincing a studio that one's movie concepts were sound—and would ultimately, as films, make money.

Todd's friendship with Joe Schenck and the fact that 20th Century-Fox had bought the film rights to *Something for the Boys* and *The Naked Genius* made it seem logical that Todd would become a producer at Fox. However, Darryl Zanuck's strong personality and his control of all production decisions at 20th gave insufficient room for Todd's ego and his desire to be his own boss. Similar considerations, despite lucrative offers, kept him away from some of the other majors.

Universal, now one of the giants, was then in a narrow middle ground, along with RKO, between the majors and the "B" studios—Republic and Monogram. Here he would be a big fish in a middle-sized pond.

Universal-International was run by Leo Spitz and Billy Goetz. Spitz made all the business decisions, while Goetz was in charge of production. Goetz had been a successful producer for a number of years and was a son-in-law of Louis B. Mayer. (David O. Selznick was married to Mayer's other daughter.) Spitz and Goetz were endeavoring to elevate Universal to the status of a major, and bringing Todd into the studio was part of the buildup.

He was given a large bungalow containing several offices and what he thought was *carte blanche* to develop and produce what he wanted. He started with three properties in hand: his musical *Up in Central Park;* his play *Pick-Up Girl;* and Edna Ferber's most recent novel, *Great Son,* published a year earlier —a family saga set in Seattle. Anticipating his move to Hollywood, he had acquired the film rights to *Great Son* at the time of publication. His option on the Ferber book was assurance to Spitz and Goetz that Todd's head was in the right place.

Edna Ferber's novel *So Big* had won the Pulitzer Prize in 1924. Her novel *Show Boat* had been adapted into one of the great musical stage successes and then into a film in 1936 (there was a remake in 1951). She had written over half a dozen plays (mostly in collaboration with George S. Kaufman), notably *Dinner at Eight, The Royal Family* and *Stage Door.* Her novels were great critical and popular successes. Many of her works were made into successful movies.

While *Great Son* was a short novel, the story spanned four generations and would be difficult to adapt for the screen. It required a large cast and a diversity of sets, costumes and locales. Major work was needed to prepare it for production.

Up in Central Park was just finishing its Broadway run, and a national road tour was in the works. Todd was in no hurry to get this property on the screen when it might compete with or kill off his profitable road company.

Universal was not particularly thrilled with his idea of making a movie of *Pick-Up Girl*. They agreed, however, that it was a commercial title and that with the obvious ways of opening it up for the screen—all the play's action took place in one courtroom set—the moralistic and preachy character of the story could be minimized.

Todd's major contribution to any show he produced usually began at the start of rehearsals; he didn't get into top gear until a show began its tryout performances. He thought best on his feet, under pressure. As Dorothy Fields said, "Give Mike Todd bad notices in Boston and you're really in business." Sitting around a bungalow holding long story conferences was not his style. His ideas about a property were always handled in a few succinct phrases. Many years later, when he finally did get around to making motion pictures—half of *This Is Cinerama*, and *Around the World in 80 Days*—he produced them as though they were legitimate stage shows: *Cinerama* as a revue, and *80 Days* as if it were a stage musical with a thin book, freely manipulating the material to produce the most effective running order. While his screenwriters were struggling with *Great Son* and *Pick-Up Girl* and he was stalling the production of *Up in Central Park*, he was looking around for other properties.

Soon after settling in on the coast, Todd hired an associate, Jack Moss, an actor, writer and producer, who became a friend and sounding board for his production plans. Moss had been the production manager for *Citizen Kane* and a majordomo for Orson Welles. He was an avid reader and always carried a book around with him. One day Todd dramatically held up his hand to Jack and mysteriously announced, "That's it."

"What's what, Mike?"

"*Under Cover*, the book you're reading. That's going to be the first movie I make."

"But Mike, it has no story."

"It's a great title. We'll create a story. We'll use a 'March of Time' technique and make it almost like it was a newsreel."

Under Cover, a best-seller of 1943, was about Nazi subversive activities in the United States. Mike's idea of how to film *Under Cover* gave him a handle for another property that interested him, *The Brick Foxhole*, a fictional work dealing with anti-Semitism. It also could best be produced as a movie in the "March of Time" documentary style.

Todd informed Spitz and Goetz that he was going to launch his production career with three low budget, black-and-white, documentary-style movies—*Under Cover*, *Pick-Up Girl* and *The Brick Foxhole*.

The first big box office success set in this documentary style of filmmaking was *The House on 92nd Street*—released in 1945—which depicted the capture of a German spy network in New York City. Todd told Spitz and Goetz that its success proved that the public was ready for the kind of films he wanted to make first. Spitz and Goetz argued that the critically acclaimed Robert Flaherty documentaries *Man of Aran* and *Nanook of the North* had never made a nickel and that *The House on 92nd Street* was not a success because of its documentary style but because it was a spy story—which was always box office.

Todd persisted and said he was going to go ahead and make the three low-budget films, without big-name stars or directors, while *Great Son* and *Up in Central Park* were in preparation. Some of the Hollywood names Todd was bandying about to assist him were politically far to the left: Jack Moss and a young director-writer, Jules Dassin. Although Todd was clearly a free-wheeling capitalist, his proposal to make "message" pictures—dealing with anti-Semitism, juvenile delinquency and fascist conspiracy—in a style commonly associated with Russian propaganda films made Spitz and Goetz nervous.

So the man known on Broadway for his lavish productions of light entertainment went ahead with his plans for three weighty pictures. He would launch his Hollywood career by starting a new trend in moviemaking. And because his contract gave him a generous share of the profits of his movies, the success of his low-budget program would make him a fortune. Spitz and Goetz believed Todd was perversely setting out to make controversial "B" pictures instead of the big, splashy movies they had brought him to Universal to produce.

As work progressed on the films, preliminary budgets were prepared. One day Todd noticed an item for $10,000 labeled "Want-to-See Survey." "What the hell is this?" he asked. He was informed that the titles of all pictures being produced at the studio were tested by the Gallup organization in Princeton. He stormed into Spitz's office and demanded that his pictures be excluded from "Want-to-See" testing. Spitz explained that the manufacturers of consumer products and their advertising agencies had proven the value of test marketing. Todd stated that the task of determining what the public wanted to see was his exclusive responsibility as the producer of the film and that testing a title on the public was nonsense. As a case in point, Todd said, RKO's big picture of the year, *Sister Kenny,* would undoubtedly get a huge "Want-to-See" rating. Spitz indicated that as a matter of fact RKO had tested the title and that it had an extremely high rating. Todd bet Spitz two vicuña coats that no matter how many people said they were dying to see a picture about Sister Kenny, they would stay away from the box office in droves. (*Sister Kenny* got good reviews and lost money.) Todd demanded that the charge and survey be omitted on his pictures. Spitz tried to make a conciliatory gesture and told Todd that even though the testing would be done and the item would remain on the budget, Universal would privately pick up the cost and not charge it against his productions. Todd said this was not a satisfactory arrangement and that his reputation as a showman was besmirched by title testing. He wanted no part of the whole business. Spitz said the testing was now studio policy and they couldn't make Todd an exception.

After a moment's reflection Todd said he wanted to make a picture called *The American Flag.*

Spitz asked what the story was about and who was going to star and direct. Todd said that his contract gave him the freedom to produce any film he liked. He would package the property after the Gallup people had tested the title.

He was positive that no one would deny wanting to see a picture entitled *The American Flag*—no one would have the balls to say no.

Universal tested the "Want-to-See" on Todd's pictures without the item appearing on the budgets.

When the first-draft screenplay and preliminary shooting budget of *Pick-Up Girl* were completed, Todd was not thrilled with the script; neither was the studio. They were also not pleased by the fact that Todd planned to shoot his first picture for $350,000. Trying to coax him into their way of thinking, they told him that while the script was being reworked, he should open it up more and make it a bigger production. At a million-plus it could be an important picture.

Two days later, Todd sent through studio channels a new budget for *Pick-Up Girl* at $1,350,000. This was the original budget, plus a cash item for $1 million under the category "Exploitation and Promotion." This item immediately caught Spitz's eye. Wary of the answer, but still in a conciliatory mood, Spitz asked Todd what his intentions were with regard to the extra million.

Todd told Spitz that since Universal was determined that *Pick-Up Girl* be made for over a million dollars, they should get full value for the money. If the extra money was spent on production, it would ruin the picture. *Pick-Up Girl* made for $350,-000 would look grimly real, but at over a million it would become a Hollywood confection. Todd said that to get full value for the additional money he would throw a huge press party. He would have the million dollars, all in singles, piled in a huge stack in the back lot. While the press was enjoying drinks and a buffet, he was going to put a match to the pile of dollar bills and there would be a wonderful bonfire. "That way, we'd at least get a million dollars' worth of publicity out of the extra money. The picture of the bonfire would be on the front page of every paper in the country."

To show that he had a sense of humor and was not easily provoked, Spitz replied that it was a federal offense to destroy U.S. currency: "We don't want your career beginning with a long stretch in Leavenworth."

"Then I'll tell you what we do, Leo. We'll add the ten Gs you were gonna spend on the 'Want-to-See' test and give it to some fall guy to light the fire."

Todd's Hollywood career was not getting off to an auspicious start. None of the scripts in preparation looked very promising.

For fear of compromising Joan Blondell and himself, he was able to see her only on the sly. In those days a movie star just didn't go around publicly with a married man. Now that his wife had finally agreed to a divorce, Todd had no wish to antagonize her by flaunting his relationship with Joan. He had yet to tell me about his intention to marry her. Joan had been divorced from

Dick Powell for almost a year, and although she was good-natured and easygoing, she was understandably desirous for Todd to get moving and set the date.

The first week of June 1946, when I came home from Lawrenceville for the start of my summer vacation, my father told me that mother had agreed to give him a divorce. Approaching the age of seventeen, I was now prepared to accept this decision and could appreciate that it was senseless for him to continue his unhappy marriage. I was surprised that my mother was reconciled to giving him up. They had agreed on a settlement, and mother was to go on a long South American cruise while I spent the summer vacation with my father in California. As the time drew near for my father and me to go to the coast, my mother began to vacillate, first saying that she would not give him a divorce, and then that she would, but only on vastly improved terms. Finally, they reached a revised agreement. He and I got out of town before she could have another change of mind. My father made no mention to me of Joan or of his intention to marry her. Being naive and reading nothing but the sports pages of the newspapers, I was unaware that Todd and Blondell were an item. When my father and I went to California together I moved in with him at Joe Schenck's house. Now Joan could not even see him there.

While in New York Todd optioned H. Allen Smith's *Rhubarb*, a best-seller about a cat who inherits the Brooklyn Dodgers. When script troubles delayed his other projects, Todd conjured up a few more. Al Jolson to star in the life of Stephen Foster. Charles Laughton to star in a film adaptation of Brecht's *Galileo*. A movie based on the life of Tchaikovsky—Toscanini had agreed to conduct. Discussions with actors, agents and writers began on these and other projects. Universal, not unreasonably, asked that before Todd had everyone in Hollywood on the payroll, he first get satisfactory scripts on *Pick-Up Girl* and *Great Son* completed and into production.

Howard Bay, who had signed a contract with Universal as an art director and had arrived in Hollywood shortly before Todd started his stint there, recalls:

> It was coincidental that Mike and I were both at the same studio at the same time. Instead of going for a cocktail at the end of the day, I'd go over to his bungalow to find out what today's project was. It was fun, and he was exhilarating, but

151

of course nothing ever got much beyond the talking stage. The one he really should have done was *Great Son*. I'm a Seattle fellow, so I'm prejudiced, but it was a fine story. Of course, I didn't see all that much of Mike at the studio because I was actually making pictures. In fact, the most memorable thing Mike did while he was at Universal was the party he threw at Joe Schenck's when he first came out. I forget the occasion, but Mike didn't need an occasion. It was a lovely party out on the lawn—he had Don the Beachcomber cater it. [Mike was so in love with the Beachcomber food that he took an option to lease a building in New York to open a second Beachcomber restaurant. Money trouble later forced him to abandon these plans.] Bill Doll and I were the only stags at the party, and there were lot of starlets and those great rum drinks.

At Universal, despite everything, Mike got on very well with both Spitz and Goetz. But he had much too ambitious a program. Spitz was the businessman; he was an ex-lawyer. Goetz was very intellectual and quite social—I think he was more pleased that he had stolen Zanuck's cook from Fox than of anything else he did at the studio.

While waiting to get going at Universal, Todd came across a story in the Hollywood trade papers that Arnold Grant, the attorney who had represented him in his dealings with Henry Crown, was taking over the Del Mar Racetrack. Bing Crosby, who held the controlling interest of the track, wanted to buy a piece of the Pittsburgh Pirates. The bylaws of baseball prohibited anyone connected with the game from having any involvement with professional gambling. Pat O'Brien, who had bought into the track with Crosby, and several other minority stockholders, joined Crosby in selling their share to give Arnold Grant control.

Todd called Grant and asked if he could buy into his deal. Todd certainly knew his way around racetracks and had lots of ideas about promoting and managing one. Grant said he was not interested. Todd called his friend in Chicago, Colonel Gottlieb, who had been his original contact with Henry Crown. They worked out a complicated deal whereby Crown loaned Todd the money to buy into Del Mar, with Crown holding an option to buy a third of the shares at the end of the first track season. In his earlier dealings with Crown, when Arnold Grant had represented him, Todd had detected a keen interest on Grant's part in Crown—in his prestige, money and power. When Todd told Grant that Crown would be involved in Todd's end of the deal, Grant said Todd could come in as a partner, as long as he promised not to do any gambling at Del Mar. The operation of the track should prove to be great fun for Mike, a source of prestige in Hollywood and keep his name in print until his movies were completed. Also, he could park me in a place where I would be happy and busy, so that he could see a lot more of Joan.

Del Mar was to Los Angeles what Saratoga was to New York—in terms of proximity, its summer holiday racing season and resort facilities—with one notable exception: Saratoga attracted top-quality horses, and despite the wide-open illegal casino gambling at the spa, the track itself had a deserved reputation of integrity and honesty. Del Mar's program for the most part had been made up of cheap claiming races, and with sore-footed platers contesting most races there was the reasonable suspicion that the races were occasionally fixed. During the war the physical plant had been neglected and was in ragged condition.

Charles Carr, a former U.S. attorney with a Dewey-like reputation for crime busting, was installed as the president of the track. The most famous trial attorney on the West Coast, Jerry Giesler, was a former chairman of the California Racing Commission and was prominently publicized as a director of the newly named board. The facilities were completely refurbished, and cameras and other security devices were installed to discourage dishonesty. Purses were increased to attract better horses and races were named after movie stars, to attract their attendance and generate publicity.

The opening-day press party was lavish, and Todd's gimmick of giving away a leather-bound collection of Damon Runyon's racing pieces, *All Horse Players Die Broke*, to all opening-day patrons produced national press coverage. With lots of wartime money still in circulation and consumer products still in short supply, the freshly painted and promoted Del Mar Racetrack, "Where the Surf Meets the Turf," did record-breaking business.

Todd was only a partner in the operation of the track, albeit a prominent one. The irony was not lost on him that his successful promotion of Del Mar made it all the more likely that he would lose most of his piece of it—Crown would exercise his option. It was not one of Todd's shrewdest deals, but he craved action.

153

Shortly after the opening of the track, when I was settled into a house my father had rented for the season nearby, my mother showed up in Los Angeles—she had never gone on the South American cruise. She said she was not going to give my father a divorce unless he escalated his settlement offer. My father told me he would be willing to meet her new demands, although they were now becoming unreasonable, but he was convinced she would never give him a divorce on any terms, and he felt he had no option but to file for a divorce, even though he knew it would be bitterly contested by mother. He had Jerry Giesler start proceedings. To avoid a threatened scene with my mother and to duck inquisitive reporters, he joined me in Del Mar for an extended weekend. My mother came down the next day and took a room in the Del Mar Hotel. My father had Jack Dietz, who had always got on well with Bertha, call her at the hotel to see if an amicable settlement was still possible. Dietz reported back that she was relatively calm with him on the phone, but that it was very clear that there was no chance of an amicable settlement. The next day we found out that my mother was belligerently patrolling the track in search of my father. That night a taxi rolled up to our rented house. Mother got out and when she came through the door, we could see she was drunk —she was not a drinker. She let fly a rather incoherent torrent of abuse. My father kept his distance, and when he had the chance he tried to talk her into returning to the hotel. He promised to meet her in the morning to see if they could quietly discuss their situation. Exhausted by her outburst, mother sat in a chair, but even then my father stayed a safe distance away. Mother ignored what he was saying and was alternately amused and angered by his physical fear of her. She asked me to get her a drink. I tried to talk her out of having one, but this only made her angry again. She stormed into the kitchen and began slamming cabinet doors, trying to find the liquor. Suddenly her eye was caught by a rack of kitchen knives. She pulled out the largest one and headed back into the living room. I grabbed her by the arms and held her. She shouted at me to let her go; hearing the commotion, my father peered into the kitchen. Mother pulled away from me and went after dad, who ran for the front door. She was a few steps behind, and as he was getting out she made a frightening but ineffective lunge for him with the knife. It stuck in the door molding, and her hand slipped off the handle and caught the blade, cutting the palm of her hand by the two little fingers. She screamed, and I saw that her hand was bleeding. She stopped and looked at it. My father was standing outside on the driveway. I put my arm around mother's shoulder and guided her to a chair. I wrapped my handkerchief around her hand and shouted to my father to call a doctor. The handkerchief wasn't stopping the flow of blood, so I asked him to bring a towel from the kitchen. When he brought it over, mother tried to hit him with her left hand. He retreated to the driveway. When the doctor arrived he stitched and bandaged mother's hand and gave her a mild sedative. While he was treating her I went back out to the driveway. My father and I decided that she would stay with me; he would check into the hotel for the night and we would talk in the morning.

When mother woke up she indicated that she was going to fight for her rights and that I should not interfere. After having juice and a cup of coffee she left to go back to Los Angeles. Newspapers reported that there had been a domestic battle between the Michael Todds involving a knife. The phone rang repeatedly. My father said mother had cut her hand while slicing an orange and refused to make any further comments. We stayed in the house until he returned to Los Angeles on Sunday.

On Monday Bill Doll phoned and said that my father wanted me to come up and meet him in Los Angeles on an important matter. I asked if anything was wrong; Bill assured me everything was fine but that my father was tied up and unable to come to the phone.

When I arrived I was taken in a limousine to a hospital in Santa Monica, where I saw my father standing on the front steps with a few members of his staff. His face was ashen. I jumped out of the car, and as he raced down the steps he began to cry. He put his arms around me and told me my mother was dead.

She had gone into the hospital that morning for minor surgery to repair the tendon of her little finger that had been severed by the knife, but before the operation began she had had a fatal reaction to the anesthetic.

We left the hospital and went to a nearby hotel, where we were able to let ourselves go. We tried to comfort each other as best we could. I had little to say. I was totally bereft. He said she had been a fine woman and a marvelous mother and he was stunned that their marriage had ended this way.

The Santa Monica coroner conducted an immediate autopsy, and when he felt that its findings were inconclusive he ordered an inquest. My father and the doctor in Del Mar had reported that she had injured her hand "while slicing an orange," which was also the story mother had used when explaining the accident to the doctors in Santa Monica. The coroner was reported to have stated that if Mrs. Todd were left-handed the story would appear reasonable, but as she was right-handed further investigation was required. Headline stories across the country implied that my father was somehow implicated in mother's death. I was never questioned and the investigation simply verified that she had had a fatal reaction to the anesthetic. Her death was ruled as accidental, and no guilt was attributed to anyone. But this official verdict was not published until ten days after her death, and the few newspapers that bothered to report it buried it in their back pages. Meanwhile, a story came out that mother's furs and jewelry, valued at $80,000, were missing. They had, in fact, disappeared. The grisly publicity continued, with lurid headlines in the nation's tabloids. Even to this day, whenever a biography or article about Elizabeth Taylor refers to the death of Michael Todd's first wife, there is a shadow of guilt cast on him. Mother's chance-in-a-million fatal reaction to the anesthetic would not by itself have implicated him in her death, but the phony story he used to explain her knife injury did. He could have immediately ended the mystery and innuendo by revealing what really happened. But to save me the nightmare of having to testify at an inquest, and to bury his wife without revealing the cause of her injury, he stuck to the story he had told the doctor in Del Mar—that she had cut herself while slicing an orange.

When it came time for me to return to Lawrenceville in late August 1946, my father accompanied me. Instead of flying, we took the train; he wanted the leisure of the long trip so that we could talk and make plans for the future. He told me that he thought mother had been an excellent parent and had done a wonderful job raising me. He was proud of me but felt he had been negligent in the amount of time and attention he had given me. Without referring to his unhappy life with mother, or his coming new life with Joan, he indicated that we would now be closer and he would try to build a family life. Given his nature and interests, I felt he had been a great father, and I had no complaints. I told him so. Since we were being so honest, I told him he spent too much time and money gambling. He promised that part of his shift in interest to family life would include his giving up heavy gambling.

Back in the New York apartment we keenly felt mother's presence. It seemed much more her home than ours. I had lived there only a year before going away to school, and my father hadn't spent much time there either. It had represented her dream of material and social success, and now it seemed that years had passed since June, when mother had finally agreed to a settlement. It struck me that mother had not even attained her modest ambition of having an established home; most of the furniture was rented from the previous tenant. I asked my father if we could keep the apartment as it was. Selfishly I wanted a place to go to in New York. And, to fulfill one of mother's wishes, I asked him to buy the furniture. This was an expensive whim on my part, but my father acceded to it without comment. Ironically, in a few years my request to purchase the furniture would become an adverse turning point in his contested bankruptcy proceedings.

Todd's impatience with getting his moviemaking career going not only got him involved in the Del Mar venture but caused him to disrupt the only smooth-running area of his business operations. In April 1946, *Up in Central Park* had finished its hugely profitable fifteen-month run on Broadway and its national road tour was successfully launched in Chicago. It could surely play over a year on the road and make him a lot of money. But he decided to postpone, or at worst partially sacrifice, this almost certain income for a unique theatrical engagement.

The Hollywood Bowl, an amphitheater seating 16,000, played only a limited number of concert attractions, which were very warmly supported by the public. In the balmy California climate an evening of entertainment under the stars was a popular diversion. No one had ever attempted to stage a musical comedy in the Bowl.

Up in Central Park was one of the biggest hits of the decade. In mid-July Todd secured a booking for the Bowl for over a month at the beginning of September. Scaling upwards from a dollar a head, it would be possible to almost triple the largest gross of any previous stage attraction anywhere. The idea of building gargantuan sets and restaging the show for the vast expanses of the Hollywood Bowl appealed to his sense of the spectacular. He wouldn't have the time to put together and rehearse a new company, which meant that he would have to break off the successful Chicago engagement and piece together a subsequent road tour in place of the one that had already been penciled in with the Shuberts. But the profits and prestige of the Bowl engagement would more than make up the profits of the originally planned road tour.

Todd and Bill Doll made the opening of *Up in Central Park* a civic event. They were able to assemble practically every major marching band in the state, who viewed the parade as a warm-up exercise for the forthcoming football season. Floats were eagerly contributed by companies and charities to promote themselves. It nearly rivaled the Rose Bowl parade and got full police and civic cooperation. There was tremendous newspaper coverage—all to celebrate the arrival and opening of a road company.

Although from the rear of the Bowl the cast looked like insects crawling around the huge sets, the sound system and acoustics carried the music and dialogue to the outer reaches of the audience. The reviews were marvelous and business was outstanding. The first week's gross was close to the $150,000 Todd had hoped for. He began formulating plans to perpetuate what promised to be a highly successful annual event.

But the weather turned cold and rainy, and the balance of the engagement turned into a washout after the record-shattering first week. Todd lost a couple of hundred thousand dollars; in addition, the Shuberts, who at the time controlled most of the musical houses throughout the country, had been furious when they were forced to find substitute attractions, where they could, for *Up in Central Park*'s canceled tour. When Todd put his show back on the road, the Shuberts made no effort to arrange suitable bookings. The show now faced huge jumps and split weeks and had to play in many secondary theaters. The road company tour of *Up in Central Park*, which surely would have earned over a quarter of a million dollars' profit, was now a dead loss. Trying to make a splash in Hollywood with his latest Broadway hit cost Todd half a million dollars.

A few months later Todd lost almost as much betting on the horses at one race meeting. He did keep his promise to Grant and had not made a single bet at Del Mar, but Bertha's death, the Hollywood Bowl fiasco and the frustration of getting nothing accomplished at Universal pushed him into a betting binge

158

of epic proportions. At Hollywood Park during a forty-day period he bet a couple of thousand dollars on also-rans in almost every race. An uncharacteristic quirk impelled him to save all his losing pari-mutuel tickets from this episode. Years later, in the midst of contested bankruptcy proceedings, he naively produced a suitcaseful of pristine fifty-dollar pari-mutuel tickets to show the I.R.S. and his creditors where the money had gone. I knew that while he would bend down to pick up a penny (to emphasize the principle that no one should be disrespectful of money—an extravagant case of penny wise, pound foolish) he would never stoop to pick up a discarded pari-mutuel ticket. There was no doubt in my mind that he had lost all this money, and the tickets were proof. But legally, of course, they had less significance than tissue paper.

While I never saw my father gambling during this time, I imagine he was in a trancelike state similar to the one I saw Eddie Fisher fall into when he was losing several hundred thousand dollars in long sessions at the crap tables in Las Vegas, shortly after Richard Burton had taken Elizabeth Taylor away from him. But I would prefer to think that Todd maintained some animation and didn't totally lose his sense of humor while he was gambling the money away. In later years Todd could joke about his gigantic losses at this time: "A lot of guys have dropped a bundle on the horses, but I'm the only guy I know to blow a racetrack. I lost Del Mar at one meeting of Hollywood Park."

Joe Schenck, who was aware of Todd's heavy gambling, bet him $50,000 that he couldn't give it up for a whole year. The offer went further: Schenck said he would give Todd $50,000 for every year after the first that he continued not to gamble. It wasn't really a bet, but a bribe on Schenck's part, since Todd had no obligation to pay $50,000 to Schenck if he did gamble. By the end of 1946, Todd had run through all the cash he could put his hands on and the loans from Crown had come to an end. He was tapped out and was down to the $5,000 a week he was drawing from Universal. He finally took up Schenck's offer. However, they agreed to exclude playing gin for less than a nickel a point from their understanding; this was not gambling but child's play. At these stakes, the most Todd could win or lose was $500.

At Thanksgiving my father flew in from the coast to spend the holiday with me in New York. He thought that staying at our apartment would make a gloomy family holiday, so he arranged for us to stay with Damon Runyon, who had a two-bedroom suite at the Hotel Buckingham on West Fifty-seventh Street. He felt that keeping Runyon company was doing him a favor as well as ourselves, as Runyon had recently been divorced and was carrying a torch for his former wife. I knew Runyon fairly well and enjoyed his company. My father and I dined with him often and the three of us had gone to a lot of prizefights together. I liked his manner and enjoyed his sense of humor. Either Runyon's personality, or his reputation for being a collector of colorful characters, or both, encouraged Todd in Runyon's presence to be extravagantly flamboyant. Runyon and I loved working together as a team, needling Mike. The previous spring Runyon had written a column about a lunch he had with Todd at the Colony restaurant on an unseasonably hot day. He wrote that Todd had picked on him endlessly for being so gauche as to appear at a classy restaurant in a seersucker jacket. Runyon tried to defend himself on the basis that his coat was neat in appearance and sensibly cool. Todd persisted that seersucker was inappropriate in the Colony, no matter how hot the weather. Todd continued by saying that Runyon might not consider his opinion an informed one, but that Runyon should be willing to accept the judgment of Todd junior on the subject, as he was attending an extremely fashionable eastern prep school and should be knowledgeable about such matters. In the article it was agreed that I should resolve the question when I came to join them for lunch. The piece ended as I walked in seconds later wearing a jacket made of the identical blue and white striped seersucker.

When we arrived at Runyon's suite, we were both shocked to find him haggard looking and in bed, attended by both a nurse and a doctor. He was heavily sedated and clearly in a very bad way. He made a real effort to greet us and to play the host, scribbling out a few lighthearted messages to us on the small pad he used to communicate. While he apologized for and made light of his current indisposition, it was clear we had no business being there. To make other arrangements now would only acknowledge his grave illness, which he obviously wanted to ignore. Even getting out of bed to eat would have been too much of an effort, so aside from keeping him company for brunch, we had our evening meals, including Thanksgiving, at restaurants. We saw a few shows and tried to keep ourselves busy, but the specter of Runyon's fatal illness completely overshadowed the long weekend. I went back to school and my father returned to the coast. Two weeks later Runyon died.

My father and I spent a weekend in December "auditioning colleges." He was in extremely high spirits. Always ready to forget the past without a backward glance, he was looking forward to my going to college and was making great plans for our future. The deans of admissions we saw barely had the chance to ask me a question, as Mike interrupted his ebullient monologues just long enough to throw them a few quick questions. We liked Dean Wilson at Amherst best—he was easygoing and personable. The campus and atmosphere also impressed us, and I was particularly intrigued by its location—seven miles from two large women's colleges. As Mike later said, "My son went to Amherst and majored in Smith and Holyoke."

I spent my Christmas holidays with my father on the coast at Joe Schenck's house. Things were very quiet in Mike's bungalow at the studio; most of his projects were at a standstill. Jack Moss was there in attendance, but the bustle and traffic I had seen the previous summer had disappeared. Mike's enthusiasm for his film career had drained away; he was unable to sustain even the briefest spiel about his movie-making plans. His lethargic silence now was a sure sign that the death watch had begun.

The final break with Universal came a few months later. Richard Brooks's *The Brick Foxhole* was made in 1947 by RKO with the title *Crossfire* and was very successful. Brooks wrote a screenplay entitled *Brute Force*, which was directed by Jules Dassin and released by Universal in 1947. In 1948 Universal released a film directed by Dassin entitled *The Naked City*. These films were in the genre proposed by Todd and were quite successful. Brooks and Dassin went on to very distinguished film careers, both as writers and directors. Mike was a bit early with his idea and took the wrong approach with the studio to see it through. The scripts on *Great Son, Pick-Up Girl* and *Rhubarb* never came right. With none of his primary projects getting before the camera, work on his multitude of follow-up projects never got beyond the talking stage. Finally, to get something going, they started preproduction work on *Up in Central Park*.

This became the breaking point for both the studio and Todd. According to Mike, Leo Spitz had a special fondness for a young actress, Yvonne DeCarlo, whom the studio was trying to build up into a major box office attraction. They requested—more like gently insisted—that she be tested for the role of the pert inge-nue lead. The character, Rosie Moore, is the daughter of an Irish Tammany Hall politician, and sings and dances and has a major speaking role. With her dark, sultry looks Miss DeCarlo seemed singularly unsuitable for the role; but the test was made. After looking at it, Todd contended that not only was she unable to satisfactorily sing, dance or act, but she could not even walk naturally. For Todd, this was the last straw, demonstrating the studio's inability or unwillingness to understand and support his ideas. For Universal Todd was a costly nonstarter. Attempting to salvage something from its expensive interlude with him, Universal eventually and unsuccessfully produced *Up in Central Park* with Deanna Durbin and Dick Haymes.

At the time the biggest and most lavish New Year's Eve party for the Hollywood elite was thrown by Sam Spiegel, who then called himself S. P. Eagle. My father took me to this gala, and it was the highlight of my Christmas vacation of 1946. At seven-teen, it was difficult to be blasé about rubbing elbows with most of the major motion picture stars. I spent the first part of the evening talking with Jimmy Stewart, who, with the exception of my father and me, was the only bachelor at the party without a date. When I told him I went to Lawrenceville and had consid-ered applying to Princeton, Stewart told me stories of his under-graduate days. We then drifted into a conversation about the partygoers, which soon evolved into an appraisal of the individ-ual merits of the large collection of starlets in attendance. How-ard Hughes, who arrived solo in a tuxedo and white sneakers, stood for fifteen minutes with Stewart and me, listening to our conversation. Hughes began to seriously survey the field, add-ing a few brief comments of his own, and then took off in pur-suit.

From the glimpses I caught of my father, I could see he was glum and distracted. He had no interest in the proceedings. Here your social standing was directly proportionate to the success of your last picture. Todd had established himself only as a big gambler and a good-natured loser. Losing was not highly regarded in Hollywood.

Shortly after midnight I started dancing with one of the star-lets. After a few minutes my father saw me, took me aside and said, "I think you've seen enough Hollywood high life. It's time to go home." As we were waiting for the car to be brought around, John Garfield drove up in a Cadillac convertible with four girls. Their fearful attention was focused on Garfield, who was blankly looking around at them, without even a glance at where he was driving. The car seemed to drift to the curb, as if it were on casters and driven by the wind. When they all got out of the car, Garfield was unable to stand by himself and was carried into the party supported on the arms and shoulders by two girls on each side.

I drove myself back to Schenck's. My father stayed at the party, saying he would have someone give him a lift home. Undoubtedly he had a delayed New Year's Eve celebration with Joan; he certainly wasn't enjoying the party.

Late in the winter Todd came east. He phoned from New York and said that he would pick me up at school early Sunday and we would drive somewhere for a meal. He said he would prefer if I didn't invite any friends to join us; he wanted to spend the day alone with me. He was in a very subdued mood when he arrived.

We took off for Atlantic City—he loved strolling on the deserted boardwalk in the winter. I loved the steamers and lobster at Hackney's.

On the drive down, after I had talked myself out, he began a long and hesitant reprise of the conversation we had had in August on the train trip to New York, about the new life we were going to build together. This went on a while, and then he arrived at what sounded like a concluding statement: "I'd like to spend more time at home and for us to have a warm family life." He looked at me, then asked the question: "Do you mind if I get married?" I had some idea who he had in mind, but I had not seen Joan since *The Naked Genius* in 1943, three and a half years earlier, and he had never so much as mentioned her name to me since. Who, I asked him. "Joan Blondell," he answered. And before I could comment, he went into a long description of her many wonderful qualities: her warmth, her sense of humor, her abilities as a homemaker, her "juiciness," her human understanding, her zest for life, how wonderful she was with her two children and her great sense of fun. As his description of Joan progressed, he gathered enthusiasm and continued nonstop, with little illustrative stories, and by the time he paused for breath, his mood had turned around 180 degrees. I was all for it. He was delighted.

A few months later, in the spring, my father appeared without warning at my room in Lawrenceville and announced that he had a surprise for me. Outside, when I opened the car door, I saw a figure crouched in the back. Half-amused and half-concerned, Mike asked Joan if she had been scrunched up on the floor for the half hour it had taken him to sign me out. She popped up and with a nervous grin said she had—a lot of boys had passed by and she didn't want her presence to embarrass me. Joan joined us in the front seat and we went off to Hackney's.

During the drive we made plans for the summer. My father would come east for my graduation, we would then fly back to the coast, and a few days later they would get married. I planned to take a cross-country auto trip with a roommate from school that summer. My father was not sure where our new family would settle, but he thought it would be in the East. In any event the decision would be clear by the end of the summer, when I had finished the trip and arrived in New York.

We had a marvelous time at Hackney's. As we were leaving the restaurant, my father noticed a series of bathing suit pictures of every year's Miss America contestants. Reading his mind, Joan tried to pull him away. "No, Joan, let's find you." My father was looking at the group photographs from the late twenties, and Joan hesitantly pointed to an earlier year, explaining that she had lied about her age and was only fifteen, not eighteen, when she was stranded in Texas with her family's vaudeville act and a girl friend had talked her into entering the contest. Joan, shyly staring at the photograph, was well over twice the age of the chubby bathing beauty in the picture, but was now far more attractive.

My father and I were both in high spirits at my graduation. I was looking forward to the summer, the auto trip and college, and we were both anticipating life with Joan and her kids. Mike was clearly moving from one phase of his career and personal life to another. It seemed as much his graduation as mine.

As we were about to leave New York, my father had some last-minute business to attend to that forced us to miss our flight. We took the next plane, which left an hour later. When we arrived in Los Angeles, we were shocked to hear that the first plane had crashed, killing the crew and all but a few of the passengers.

One of the few survivors, a dancer whose career was ended

by severe injuries to a leg and foot, later became Bill Doll's second wife. As a consequence, Bill would travel by plane only when circumstances absolutely required it. And when my father acquired a private plane, Bill was always able to find an excuse for not setting foot in it.

We lived at Joan's house in Hollywood, where I had my first opportunity to get to know her and the children. Norman was thirteen and Ellen was eight. They were attractive, intelligent and friendly. Despite our age differences, we got on well together. Joan was everything I had been led to anticipate. Her home was lovely, but I was pleased that plans were pretty well settled to move east. Joan seemed not to care about actively pursuing her movie career and, while it was not discussed, Todd's failure in Hollywood made it likely that he would need to reestablish himself on Broadway.

To avoid a lot of fuss and publicity, he and Joan decided to get married in Las Vegas. With a few overnight bags the five of us set off in my father's convertible the afternoon of July 4. When we stopped for something to eat, we spotted a double rainbow off on the horizon. None of us had ever seen one before, and we took it to be an extraordinary good luck omen. At nightfall we were still in the desert, a good distance from Las Vegas. It was one of those clear moonless nights and, driving with the top down, we could see every star in the sky. I pointed out to Ellen the few stars and constellations that I could identify. Occasionally we saw a meteor flash across the sky. I told her that once in a very great while a huge meteor called a fireball would enter the earth's atmosphere and spectacularly light up the whole countryside, almost as if it were daylight. There was a second's pause, and then in her innocent little girl's voice she said, pointing towards the sky, "Is that one?" Suddenly the whole desert was lit up. It was a fireball; a million-to-one shot if ever there was one. Mike stopped the car and we marveled at the glorious display. We were convinced that here was another spectacular good omen about our great future together.

The wedding took place later that evening, shortly after we arrived at the El Rancho Vegas, which was the oldest hotel on the Strip and less garish than the newer hotels. Since our arrival on the coast, everyone, especially Mike, had been full of high spirits and enthusiasm, but we were all on edge when we assembled in the huge banquet room of the hotel, where the ceremony was to take place. Joan whispered to me that Ellen, who had been exhausted by the long trip and all the fresh air, had fallen asleep in the bath. Ellen looked uncomfortable in a new dress and was barely able to keep her eyes open. Joan was jittery and anxious to get Ellen to bed. On an enormous table the wedding cake and buffet supper looked lost—which is how we felt in that oversized room. Mike was upset about the arrangements and the way things were going. He seemed confused and was unable to exert his usual confident control over events. We were joined by the hotel owner and manager, who were the legal witnesses for the ceremony—which was short and simple. Ellen had a taste of the wedding cake and then Joan put her to bed.

The car trip to Vegas had seemed jolly and most auspicious, but between the time we had arrived, bathed and dressed and assembled for the ceremony, the magic had dissipated.

CHAPTER 9

THE MORNING AFTER the wedding, to amuse Norman and Ellen, we all spent a half hour looking around a small ghost town that was an adjunct of the El Rancho Vegas. The concessions were closed and there was no staff to be seen. With the July midmorning temperature well over one hundred degrees, we were the only people drifting around the deserted structures. The exhibit was a ghost town in fact.

The trip back to Los Angeles was a painfully long and dull drive. The next day my Lawrenceville roommate arrived, and two days later we started our cross-country tour in the convertible. We had a marvelous time, but my finances got stretched thin at the end of the seven-week trip by a series of tire troubles. I dropped my friend at his home in Wilmington, Delaware, and drove to New York, where I caught up with Mike and Joan. My father had kept the apartment on Park Avenue, but they were in the process of closing it out so that we could move to a wonderful house in Westchester they had bought.

I had arrived in New York with a quarter of a tank of gas and a dollar and twenty cents left from the generous sum my father had given me to cover the trip's expenses. He was incredulous and couldn't restrain his laughter about how close I had cut it. I explained that I had had to buy three new tires, but he persisted in wanting to know how I could go the last few weeks with so little reserve. I had started off proud of making ends meet, but became embarrassed when he kept making fun of me in front of Joan. He asked what I would have done if I'd had to take the slightest detour, been delayed anywhere, wanted to eat an extra meal, had to make a long-distance call for help or if the car had required an extra quart of oil or half a tank of gas. He kept laughing as he enumerated all the possibilities that would have left me broke short of New York. Three weeks later he went into bankruptcy for over a million dollars.

His bankruptcy proceedings began in September 1947, and it was five years before he had the major effects of it behind him and had either paid off or settled with his creditors. He never reached a final agreement with the government during his lifetime for the federal taxes he owed from the 1940s. It wasn't until several years after his death that this tax bill was settled, and it was many years later before it was paid.

During the period of the bankruptcy proceedings, judges and attorneys for some creditors—particularly Arnold Grant, who now represented Henry Crown—accused him of perjury, fraud and felonious concealment of property, but no criminal charges or proceedings were ever made or initiated against him. He was reckless and careless with the money that passed through his hands, but not criminally or morally culpable. There are only three areas in his bankruptcy where he could be considered morally negligent, and of these only one that most people, myself included, would seriously fault him for—that is, gambling with borrowed money.

It was the understanding among the people he played cards with that losses were paid off in cash. To do this, Todd would write himself a check to cover the amount owed and often some extra for walk-around money. When his bankruptcy was contested, he was questioned about all the checks he had written and cashed himself. He explained that practically all of it was used to pay off card debts, but then had a convenient loss of memory when asked what he had paid to whom. If he had studied the checks, which totaled about two hundred thousand dollars, he could have told the court, within a couple of hundred dollars, how much he had paid and to whom. But the point of paying off card losses in cash was to avoid having to report winnings to the I.R.S. The court and some of the creditors' attorneys took the position that Todd was lying and had hidden away the money from these checks against the day he went into bankruptcy.

After moving back to New York in August 1947, Todd contemplated going into voluntary bankruptcy so that he could wipe the slate clean for his new marriage and career. His debt to Henry Crown constituted over half of the almost one million dollars he owed in excess of his assets. When Todd's friend, Colonel John Gottlieb, who had first made the introduction to Crown, became aware of Todd's intentions, he told Todd that to preserve his name he should square his debts as best he could, but not go into bankruptcy. Todd promised Gottlieb that he wouldn't.

Todd had made a hasty promise to Gottlieb, and, after reflecting on his situation he ducked behind a device to renege. It was Todd's desire and intent to pay off all his smaller creditors; but apart from his relationship with Gottlieb, he did not feel a strong obligation to pay Crown. Most of the money he had borrowed from Crown went into the Del Mar Racetrack purchase, and Crown had come out ahead on this deal. And Crown could use Todd's bad debt as a tax write-off. So, after giving his situation serious second thoughts, Todd went around the corner on his promise to Gottlieb and had some friendly creditors put him into involuntary bankruptcy. This appeared to be what it was—a devious way out. Arnold Grant, who had been involved with all of Mike's dealings with Crown, soon took action, on Crown's behalf, to contest the bankruptcy.

The crux of the legal proceedings in the next few years was: what happened to all the money that had passed through Todd's hands? Had he hidden any of it to withhold from his creditors? The fishy smell of the involuntary bankruptcy, the sloppy or nonexistent accounting for the money that went personally through his hands, Todd's unwillingness and stated inability to name the people to whom he had lost money at cards and his incredible naiveté in trying to account for his losses on the horses with his collection of pari-mutuel tickets created a picture in the court's mind of a man fraudulently trying to hide funds from his creditors. I played a role in completing this portrait.

Apart from coming down hard on his gambling losses, the court and attorneys for the creditors attacked his purchase and sale on my behalf of the furniture in our Park Avenue apartment. My father had asked me at the end of summer 1947—although the question was rhetorical at that point—if I had any objection to his selling the furniture in the apartment to the new tenant. The apartment, its furnishings and its memories were a closed chapter. We were all to begin a new life in Westchester, and of course I had no objection to the furniture being sold. The transaction on Mike's books indicated that he had laid out the money for the purchase of the furniture against the insurance money on mother's jewelry, which was lost at the time of her death and which my father regarded as my part of mother's estate. To the court and the creditors' attorneys it looked as if he had created a fiction about my wanting to own the furniture and then my agreeing to sell it, so that he was, in effect, siphoning off money that passed through his hands and keeping it from his creditors by putting it in trust for me.

My father called me at Amherst one Friday in the spring of 1949 and told me I would have to come down to New York the following week to testify in his bankruptcy proceedings. On the way to court my father and his attorney, Samuel Becker, refused to give me any background information or suggestions and instructions about the testimony I was about to give. They said that all I had to do was tell the truth about the purchase of the furniture. I was a terrible witness and gave long, disjointed answers to the questions, trying to remember the exact events. At one point I used the unfortunate figure of speech "To tell the truth—" The attorney for the creditors cut me off, saying that it was obvious the rest of my testimony was pure fabrication— concocted and rehearsed. I must have contradicted some of my father's testimony concerning minor details of the furniture purchase and sale. To the judge and opposing attorney it seemed to be highly unlikely that I had asked my father to purchase the furniture and a strong indication that Todd was siphoning off funds from his creditors.

In his declaration of bankruptcy Todd had liabilities of slightly over $1,100,000 and assets of a bit more than $250,000. Approximately $750,000 in cash had passed through his hands in a two-and-a-half-year period, over half a million of which he lost gambling. Between his assets and his liabilities Todd was short something in excess of $800,000; the court and attorneys for some of his creditors alleged that somewhere Todd had hidden most of this money. The $6,500 from the sale of the furniture, which was being held in trust for me, was the only amount they could come up with of the fortune Todd had allegedly stashed away.

It was a bum rap all the way. Todd should have been able to wipe the slate clean. While trying to get a fresh start he had to carry the burden of these debts. It took a number of years, but eventually Todd paid off all the small creditors in full and settled with Crown for slightly more than 25 percent of the $640,000 he owed him.

It was Joan's money that paid for the dream house that we moved into in August 1947. It was a magnificent red brick English manor house with marvelous grounds and views, located in Irvington, twenty-two miles north of New York on the Hudson River. The rooms were large and graceful and there were so many that Mike thought we should affect a kind of pretension and never stoop to count them. The living, dining and sun rooms all had French doors opening onto a terrace atop a gently sloping meadow that led to the river two hundred yards away. Each bedroom had a commanding view of the river, which swept around the slight promontory on which the house sat. We had an unimpeded view of Nyack and High Tor on the west bank of the river, and of the entire Tappan Zee, the baylike widest section of the Hudson. To the south we could see the Palisades on the far side of the river, and on clear days and nights we could see the George Washington Bridge.

There was a five-room guest cottage at the bottom of the meadow. My father and I were surprised to discover that on one side of the guest cottage was a pair of apple trees, which produced the mammoth red Delicious apples that Leo Lindy used for decorating the front window of his restaurant. We looked at each other in amazement. We never expected to see this bigger-than-life fruit actually growing on a tree. To own two of these trees was the ultimate proof we had settled in Eden.

A hundred yards from the house was a courtyard with a six-car garage and a tool and tractor shed. There were two sizable apartments above the garage and sheds. Midway between the garage and the house was a brick kennel and fenced-in run, which could comfortably accommodate a dozen large dogs. All of this was set on twenty-seven beautifully landscaped acres. Todd had an aerial photograph taken of the estate for a Christmas card, which bore the legend: "Seasons Greetings from *Jemmen-on-the-Nut.*" *Jemmen* was *J* for Joan, *E* for Ellen, double *M* for the two Michaels, *E* for "an added starter" and *N* for Norman. "On the nut" is a theatrical term referring to unrecouped production costs. While Mike could make light of his financial straits, it nevertheless must have upset him deeply that Joan was bankrolling Jemmen and would continue to do so for more than a year.

Neither Mike nor Joan ever made reference to the fact that money was tight. I had been unaware of my father's initial bankruptcy proceedings and was surprised to discover, when we traded in the old Cadillac convertible for the new fishtail model, that it was being purchased on time—the only credit purchase I ever knew my father to make. He blithely tried to pass this off as the American way of buying.

The entire estate was purchased for the now unbelievable sum of $27,500 from an insurance company that had contemplated, twenty years ahead of its time, moving their headquarters to the suburbs. When they decided to stay in the city, they unloaded their white elephant for the best offer they could get.

The outward sign that we were over our heads was that no attempt was made to completely furnish and decorate the house. The kitchen was fixed up and modernized. A sizable breakfast room was cozily decorated, and we had practically all our meals there. Only a token attempt was made to decorate the large dining room, which was used on just a handful of occasions during our three years in the house.

The library adjacent to the front hall was the only one of the main rooms that was ever completely furnished and Joan did a marvelous job with it. The room was a preview of what the entire house would look like when Todd was back on top, but in the meanwhile, as he said, "we're not exactly camping out."

Joan did not go in for gourmet cooking, but there was always a plentiful supply of top-quality groceries. In June of 1948 I came home from college weighing one-hundred-sixty-five pounds and left in September, thirty pounds heavier. If one of us had the flu, Joan would boil down twenty pounds of prime beef to make one cup of health-restoring broth.

The bedrooms for Norman, Ellen and me were comfortably furnished. My father and Joan's bedroom was never completely done. An unused bedroom adjacent to Ellen's room on the second floor was fitted out as a sewing room and upstairs parlor. A large open hallway on the third floor, outside Norman's and my bedrooms, was furnished as a comfortable sitting room for us. The attic was made into a recreation room, and as a surprise Joan had a number of her Hollywood chums autograph pinup photos for Norman and me. When the pictures were hung Joan asked if there were any other stars that we would like signed photos from. She gave me a strange look when I asked for one of Myrna Loy, but it soon arrived in the mail.

Many years later I was visiting Joan on the coast and we got to talking over drinks about the house in Irvington. She started

172

laughing about the Myrna Loy photo and told me that my request had put her off telling me then about an experience of hers:

I was doing a USO tour during the war, and they flew us into some godforsaken place up in Canada—Gander, I think it was. Snow and ice up to your derriere. After the show we were all huddled around a stove in a Quonset hut, and I noticed a tall, thin boy staring at me, and I could tell he was just too shy and nervous to approach me. He was standing by the door, shivering. So before he froze to death, I went over to him and said hello. He was from the South, and he said he had a terrible problem and could I help him. He was engaged to this marvelous girl, but all the guys in his platoon were saying that with him being away and her being in show business, she was probably seeing other fellas. "Now, Miss Blondell," he said, "you're in show business. Just 'cause I'm away doesn't mean she isn't gonna wait for me, does it?" I told him to pay no attention to his friends and said that it was just an old-fashioned notion that people in show business were fast. He was terribly relieved and practically in tears thanking me. When we were ready to go and I was walking out to the plane, he ran up and said, "Miss Blondell, you've made me so happy. I just want you to see a picture of my girl." He handed me an eight-by-ten glossy. There she was in black lace underwear with her things bursting out of her brassiere, and she had a black boa that she was holding between her legs, trailing behind her. Her name, Trixie Dixon, was etched in white in the corner, and her manager's name and phone number was printed at the bottom. At the other corner, in ink, was the inscription:
Honey—I really love you No Shit
Trixie

Joan generated tremendous enthusiasm for our new home and tried to instill this feeling into Norman and Ellen. They had been shunted about from one luxurious house in Los Angeles to another, and now they had to get used to living in the East. Soon, however, they adjusted happily to their new life. Joan worked tirelessly at getting us settled. I was crazy about her. My father was tremendously pleased with this ambitious new start in our life. I went off to college equally pleased.

That first autumn I couldn't wait to bring home someone so that I could show off our magnificent new home. My first opportunity was Thanksgiving. I invited a date to spend the long weekend with us in Irvington. When I told my father, he reminded me that the spare bedrooms and the guest cottage had not been furnished yet, so there was no place for her to stay.

Joan's mother had come east and was living in one of the apartments over the garage. She had joined a bridge group, and made other social contacts and arranged for my date to stay with the family next door.

When we arrived in Irvington late Wednesday night, I discovered Joan, the rest of the household and even my father in a flurry of excitement at the prospect of entertaining our first guest. There was only a quick hello that evening, and then I deposited my date at the neighbors' house.

The next day I took her on an appetite-building walk around the estate. She was suitably impressed, but when we did the tour of the house, she didn't know how to react when she saw that half of it was barren. The dining room was bare except for the table and chairs and a few impromptu autumnal decorations Joan had strung up on the walls. Joan was effusive and amusing while supervising the final preparation and serving of the meal. It was a perfect Thanksgiving dinner, and the spectacular views of the river overshadowed the lack of furniture in the room. My father joked about the state of the house and about his first attempt at carving a turkey. Brushing aside suggestions from Joan, he did a unique job of carving up the bird.

At Christmas, with everyone decorating, roaring fires and marvelous food, we were brought together as a family for the first time. The day after Christmas it began to snow. My father and I rushed to the tool shed, where his greatest prize was stored—a Ford-Ferguson tractor, which had come with the estate. We had used the sickle bar attachment during the fall to mow the twelve-acre meadow in front of the house and had fought to take turns at the wheel. The grass was mowed so often it barely had a chance to grow. The tractor had a snow plow attachment, and we started to clear the mile of road we had on the property. Although we plowed the entire afternoon, we couldn't keep ahead of the snow. This was the start of the big blizzard of 1947.

By next morning, over two feet of fresh snow had fallen. We had enough supplies in the house to last the crew of an aircraft carrier a month, but my father and I tramped half a mile through the snow, pulling behind us a large toboggan, which had been one of the Christmas gifts, to stock up on such essentials as black olives, wild rice and clam juice (which Mike regularly drank for breakfast). We worked until suppertime the next four days, pitting the tractor against the drifts of snow on our roads. Then we plowed out a few of our neighbors. When the roads were cleared, Mike used the tractor to haul us up the hill during long tobogganing sessions. He spent almost the whole vacation happily shifting gears. Later in the spring he had two blue denim tractor suits tailor-made to his own design. The jackets were patterned after the type General Eisenhower had worn. Like the Soviet hero laborers of the period, Todd had fallen in love with his tractor.

As far as he was concerned, Broadway was a step backwards, but his inability to make a name for himself in Hollywood left him no option now but to produce another show. He was reluctant to approach Herbert and Dorothy Fields; he had turned down their offer to produce *Annie Get Your Gun* and, more to the point, he still owed them royalties from the debacle at the Hollywood Bowl and the disastrous tour of *Up in Central Park* that followed. He had to reestablish himself on Broadway, starting practically from scratch, and come up with his own idea for a show. Nobody was coming to him with properties. There was real doubt that he could raise the money to produce a show. The word was out that he was broke.

He had a great relationship with Bobby Clark, who was not temperamental and worked like a Trojan on "business" and dialogue to build laughs. There had been no shows for the tired businessman since early 1944, when Mike had done *Mexican Hayride* and David Wolper had produced *Follow the Girls*. Broadway was ready for tall girls and low comedy.

In the spring of 1948 Todd was struggling for an idea for a show to build around Bobby. One night, to amuse Mike, Joan read aloud a newspaper anecdote about Bess Truman. It referred to her not as the First Lady but as the "First Gentlewoman of the Land." Joan slipped and said, "Bess Truman, the First Gentleman of the Land—" Mike let her go no further. "That's it—Bobby's married to the first woman President, and he's the first, First Gentleman of the Land." All kinds of situations for Bobby in this role immediately came to mind. And the idea was timely—it was a presidential election year.

That night Mike phoned Bobby, who was on tour in a revival

of *Sweethearts*. Bobby loved the premise and immediately ad-libbed several situations he could see himself in, playing the role. They agreed that Bill Roos, who had helped Bobby with the script of *The Would-Be Gentleman* and was flexible and fast, would be ideal to write the book. The next day Todd called Roos, and they met later in the week and started to talk out the situations and plot. It was full speed ahead.

The biggest song in the country at that moment was "It's a Most Unusual Day," written by Harold Adamson and Jimmy McHugh, both of whom lived and worked on the coast. After sketching out the bare bones of the plot with Roos and coming up with the title *As the Girls Go*, Mike flew to California and summoned Adamson and McHugh to his suite in the Beverly Wilshire Hotel. With no introduction or warm-up, he told them he was going to do a show and he wanted them to write the score. He explained the idea and told them to get to work. They would consult by phone, and they should plan to be in New York by August 1 with the songs.

Then Mike called Fred Astaire and asked him who he thought was the best choreographer around. Astaire recommended Hermes Pan. Todd contacted Pan and signed him for the show that same day.

As work progressed on the book, Mike signed Howard Bay to be the director as well as scenic designer.

Igor Cassini, who wrote a nationally syndicated newspaper column under the pseudonym of Cholly Knickerbocker, had a brother Oleg, a fashion designer who was making a big splash on Seventh Avenue and was prominently in the news, having recently married Gene Tierney. Mike signed Oleg Cassini to do the costumes.

Years later, Bill Roos pointed out that Todd had hired a book writer who had never done a musical, a musical team and choreographer who had worked almost exclusively in pictures, a scenic designer to direct and a costume designer who had never before done a show. They were all as anxious as Todd to prove themselves, and not likely to be aggressive about money.

When Harold Adamson and Jimmy McHugh came east, they stayed with us in Irvington at the guest cottage, which had a piano in the living room. Not only was this convenient, it cut down on expenses. They came with the title song and the ballads, which excited everyone, and went to work on the specialty numbers.

176

A good part of the work was done at the guest cottage. The isolation and comfort, the pleasant surroundings and Joan's lavish catering and general helpfulness more than made up for the inconvenience of being forty-five minutes from New York. Joan's other contribution was putting up the front money for the show.

He invited all the production team and their wives and Lucette and Bobby Clark to spend the Fourth of July with us. He chartered two forty-foot cabin cruisers for an excursion up the river. As the outing began, everyone settled down with a drink on the cabin decks. I noticed that Bobby was standing alone on the rear roof deck of the other boat. He seemed lost in his own thoughts, content merely to gaze at the passing scenery. I paid no further attention to him and got involved in a conversation.

A short while later, Bill Roos took me by the arm and said, "Look at Bobby." From atop his perch on the roof deck, he was gracefully directing the flight of the sea gulls that were following his boat. It was as though the birds were watching him and carefully obeying his commands. Bobby would slowly and majestically swing his arms back and forth as the gulls caught the current and eddies of the winds. Then, abruptly, he'd use an intensive flurry of motion to underscore and highlight an occasional landing or the sudden veering off of one of the gulls. The hustle and movement of the rest of the party continued beneath the roof deck on Bobby's boat; they were oblivious to the unusual performance going on over their heads. Bobby went on with his virtuoso display for several more minutes, unaware that Roos and I were watching. When one group of birds seemed out of tune with his conducting and when he started to direct more of his attention to them, he caught us watching him. Without a break in rhythm Bobby continued, but manifested increasing concern over the discordant flock of gulls between our boats. He created the effect that he was patiently trying to coax his dissonant section into harmony with the rest of his ensemble. When repeated efforts failed, he threw up his hands and turned his back on his unruly disciples. As he was wheeling about, he hunched his shoulders, turned his palms up and grimaced to us, indicating the futility of trying to work with a bunch of amateurs. He marched over to the ladder in disgust and joined the party below.

Thirty miles upriver we anchored out of the main stream. Some of us went for a swim while the buffet luncheon was being

laid out. Todd acted as cruise director and supervised the proceedings, busily swimming between the two boats—mostly on
his back, to keep his cigar lit. He made sure that everyone
sampled Joan's potato salad and that they had some of the lox,
sturgeon and Nova Scotia salmon that had been driven up by
limousine early that morning from Barney Greengrass's delicatessen. Todd was in action. It was the first time since he and Joan
were married that he seemed to have completely regained his
high spirits and cocky ways.

Harold Adamson told about an evening when we were standing around on the terrace, watching the sun set across the Hudson:

> Joan, Michael junior, Hermes Pan, Jimmy and I were hav-
> ing a drink and enjoying the view when we heard Mike roll
> up. He came running around the corner of the house and
> said, "Get that whiskey off the table and get out the vodka.
> I've got Madame Karinska with me." [Madame Karinska,
> who had worldwide experience with stage and film produc-
> tions, executed Oleg Cassini's designs for the show.] Mike
> had a fifty-dollar tin of caviar with him, and he started
> spreading it out bountifully to all of us. Suddenly he turned
> to Michael junior and said, "Do you want to try a little caviar,
> Michael?" Junior replied, "Gee, Dad. I don't know whether
> I like caviar or not." So Mike put a speck on a cracker and
> said, "Here, try a half a buck's worth."

Irene Rich, a movie actress and a big radio star, was cast in
the role of Madame President. Bill Callahan, the lead male
dancer of *Something for the Boys* and *Mexican Hayride,* who
was just twenty-one, was cast as the male romantic lead—the
eldest child of Madame President and Bobby Clark.

Todd had great difficulty raising money for the show. His only
source thus far was a conservative investment counselor, Bill
Richardson, who had discretionary powers over a large capital
sum that came from several clients, all of whom were expecting
the most cautious management of their money. Initially this
investment was to be little more than a "rooting interest."
When Todd was unable to get money elsewhere, this rooting
interest grew to become the principal backing for the show.
Richardson was the kind of man Mike described as a guy who
had white piping on his vests. Todd was working on him all
during the preproduction period and rehearsals, raising the

ante bit by bit. Both Richardson and Todd were feeling guilty about the now heavy investment in the show, but they were both locked in. David Lawlor, the assistant company manager, said that Al Strelsin and the principal heiress of the Johns-Manville fortune, Lorraine Manville, were also backers of the production.

As the elements of the show were falling into place, Joan, my father and I had dinner one Sunday with Bill and Audrey Roos, Harold Adamson and Jimmy McHugh. We had a large table in the back garden of Bertolotti's restaurant in the Village. Halfway through the antipasto, Todd glanced at his watch, held up his hand and said, "Wait a minute, we've got to listen to Winchell." The headwaiter brought a radio to the patio entrance, where there was a wall socket, and we gathered around to listen. After the major world issues were disposed of, Winchell got to his gossip items, and in his distinctive shouting way he announced: "Tunesmith Jimmy McHugh in New York preparing Mike Todd's new show has been seen squiring champion aqua beauty Anita Lohest around town." Jimmy's tan turned ashen. He reached out and turned off the radio. For years he had been the steady escort of Louella Parsons. In a husky voice and with a cautionary finger in the air, he said, "For God's sake, don't any of you whisper a word of this to Lolly."

Just before rehearsals were to begin, Todd had the uneasy feeling that not enough use was being made of the girls in the show. Someone suggested there ought to be a beach number to get the girls into bathing suits; Adamson came up with a song title that he said he could get a lot of play out of—"American Cannes." McHugh's eyes lit up immediately. "I can almost hear the tune now."

Early the next day McHugh gathered everyone to hear the melody for "American Cannes." We stood in pleasant anticipation around the piano and Jimmy enthusiastically launched into the number. But as Jimmy, totally absorbed, pounded the keyboard with great exuberance, we began to exchange worried glances. At the finish of the number Jimmy looked up expectantly; we tried to hide our thoughts behind blank expressions. The pause became painfully long, but no one wanted to say what we were all thinking. Jimmy began to look worried.

Finally, Harold came out with it. "But Jimmy, that's 'Valencia.'"

Jimmy smiled radiantly again. "No, no, no. *This* is 'Valencia.' " And he began to demonstrate the difference in the two tunes. The tempo and melody were identical except for one note at the end of a phrase, which in Jimmy's "American Cannes" melody went up, where in "Valencia" the note went down. The number stayed in the show, but Harold—under the pretext of requiring an accommodation for his lyrics—had Jimmy alter the melody.

During the rehearsal period in New York, Howard Bay came up with the idea for the first-act finale:

> Bobby was to receive an honorary degree from a college. We used his old judge's bit, where he's doing the double-talk and falls off the platform, and then he starts a conga line with the chorus girls. Of course, none of it made any sense, but it did make a busy, cheerful first-act curtain. Now Bobby was the most unusual combination—a literal-minded pixie. He went up to Brooks' for a costume fitting one morning, and he came back looking very worried. "Howard, I *have* to talk to you." He got me off in a corner and said, "You know, I've just been up to Brooks' for the fitting of my gown and mortarboard." I said, "Yes, Bobby, I know." He said, "Do you realize the gown they made is the wrong color for the degree I'm getting?"

When Bobby was first presented with the script, he placed it in his right hand and bounced it up and down, getting the heft of it, as if it were a package of cold cuts. His immediate judgment was, "There's too much book here."

That was just one of the major problems when the show opened its out-of-town tryout in Boston on October 13. It ran forty minutes too long. All the Boston critics blasted the show. The out-of-town notices in *Variety* started with a succinct statement, which represented the conclusion of some New York ticket brokers and other knowledgeable show business types who had come to view Todd's comeback effort—"Dear Mike, close it and forget it."

Todd had to salvage *As the Girls Go,* or it would be back to selling shoes. He was personally in debt for over three-quarters of a million dollars. He still owed money on the sets and costumes and had no contingency funds for losing weeks in Boston.

When the show opened, there were several elderly male character actors portraying hack politicians. Todd said, "There's too many men walking around on the stage," and they were immediately dropped. Bobby had done a number with them entitled "I've Got the President's Ear," which was changed so that he now did it with the show girls. A big comedy scene was put in the second act, where some attractive girls try to get Bobby in a compromising situation in order to embarrass the President. A lot of the plot exposition, which took place in a barber shop, was leavened by having Bobby do variations of the material W. C. Fields used in his classic two-reeler of the same setting. Big hunks of the book were cut away.

Dick Williams describes the photo call in Boston the night after the opening.

There was the beach number, "American Cannes." All the girls were gorgeous. Cassini had them in the briefest blue bathing suits. They were like the first bikinis. But over these bikinis he had them all wearing beach robes. They were made of the flimsiest material, so you could see through them—but only some of the time. The girls hated the robes because they were floor length and they tripped on them. During the dress rehearsal they kept getting stuck in the scenery and were ripping and everybody said, "Damn these things." But Cassini said, "Leave them on."

So we were taking pictures, and it's getting down to about two o'clock—when you get into overtime. Johnny Bennewitz was shooting it, and he turns to me and says, "Hey, Dick, these girls are beautiful." We had Gregg Sherwood, who later married the heir to the Dodge fortune, Mildred Hughes and Abbe Marshall—she later changed her name to Abbe Lane and married Cugat. And a singer, Jo Sullivan—she married Frank Loesser. It was some line of girls. Bennewitz says, "Dick, with the shadows it looks like they're wearing overcoats." I looked around. The theater's dark. I asked, "Is Cassini still here?" It seemed everyone was gone. So I yell to Sammy Lambert, our stage manager, "Hey, Sammy, how about the girls taking those robes off?" Sammy says, "Cassini wants them on." So I said, "We can't see the girls' bodies. It's getting late. We gotta get a shot." Sammy finally says, "All right, girls. Take the robes off." And from out of the dark, a voice shouts from the back row, "AND KEEP THEM OFF." It was Mike.

Howard Bay recalls:

Of course, everybody on the production side, except Mike, had little or no experience with stage musicals. For instance, Hermes Pan, a very nice and talented guy, had never choreographed a number for more than two dancers . . . and one of those two was always Fred Astaire. At the beginning he was lost, trying to move around a stageful of people. . . . And so it went.

Bill Roos describes the tryout in Boston:

> The situation was frightening—we were doing absolutely no business and Mike needed money to make the changes. While he was reconstructing the show, he would take off to New York in the middle of the night or early in the morning. He'd come back in time for the conferences and the rehearsals. He'd be there when we tried out the new material and then go right out looking for more money. It got very mysterious. His beard kept getting longer and he kept getting more and more haggard. He looked worse, but the show started looking a little better. We tried everything. Somebody thought up a joke and Mike wanted to try it, but it involved hiring a dog act. I don't know where he found an act with twelve dogs overnight, but he brought it in, and we had one rehearsal, and it went into the show that night. It turned out not to be a very good joke, and the dogs were out after their first performance. The show seemed better, but we couldn't really tell, playing to so many empty seats.

After Richardson, the Boston investment counselor, realized he had made a mistake—he was not going to throw away any more of his clients' good money. Todd had to scratch around everywhere to come up with fresh cash. He had almost tapped out Joan during the past year, and he could not and would not go to her for more. He went to old friends, like Jack Dietz and Izzy Rappaport, a theater owner in Baltimore he had known since the *Bring on the Dames* days. David Lawlor reports that Todd sent him to New York to see Johnny (Blue Eyes) Aiello, a leading Mafia figure, who gave him an envelope containing $15,000 in cash.

Howard Bay says that Todd got Mr. Lee to come up and look at the show in Boston once it began to get into shape. Although it was still very rough and was playing to an almost empty house,

Mr. Lee—more out of compassion (a word seldom linked with the Shubert name) than for any good reason—made the Shubert Theatre in New Haven available for a further break-in period, on a promise and a personal guarantee from Mike, which at the time was totally worthless, as Mr. Lee fully realized.

My father called me at Amherst and told me he thought they had the show straightened out and that he had a booking in New Haven to break in the revamped version. The New Haven opening was on election night. He had a suite at the Taft with an extra bedroom for me and told me to cut classes and come down to the opening for luck.

Todd was skating on such thin ice that he wasn't able to make more than a token payment for the new sets and costumes and the move to New Haven had been made on his promises. Six hours before the curtain was ready to go up in New Haven, the sheriff was literally at the back door of the Shubert, having impounded the scenery and costumes. They would be released only when and if Todd had paid the bills the sheriff was holding. Mike was in a state of mental and physical exhaustion. He had been awake and in action almost continuously since the premiere in Boston three weeks before.

Mike was at the point of tears. He was convinced they had licked the problems and that he now had a winner. But the curtain was not going to go up. He went back to the hotel and made a desperate appeal on the phone to Bill Richardson to bring up enough cash to satisfy the claims. A check would not do, not even a certified one.

It was a freakishly warm day for the beginning of November. An hour and forty minutes before curtain time, Richardson arrived, agitated and breathless, sweat pouring off him, but with an attaché case full of cash. We met him under the marquee in front of the Shubert Theatre. Joan's eyes filled with tears when she saw him. When he said he had the money, she threw her arms around him and gave him a huge kiss. Todd almost fainted with relief. He turned over the cash to a very surprised sheriff. With only an hour before curtain time, we went next door to our suite in the Taft Hotel to dress and grab a bite to eat.

Todd had finished his shower and was in his shorts when our order from room service arrived. As I was signing the tab, he walked into the sitting room and, managing a tired smile, delivered his standard line, "Tip lavishly." He was still dressing when

Joan and I sat down to eat. We shouted at him to hurry up before his food got cold, but the next thing we knew he had the phone tucked under his chin while he was putting the cuff links in his shirt. I went into the bedroom to try to get him to cut short his call. He waved me off, and I overheard his end of the conversation.

"It's going to be a big hit."

(Long pause, during which I made another attempt to get him off the phone and in return got an angry nod.)

"That was Boston. It's a whole new show now . . . Look, have I ever stiffed you before? . . . It's my money—what'll you give me? . . . For chrissake, the papers are quoting fifty to a hundred to one . . . Okay. I'll be down to collect in a couple of days."

He had taken twenty-five to one and bet a thousand dollars that Truman would win the election.

The show seemed a bit ragged and disjointed, but Bobby was his old confident self and had a field day with his new material.

After eavesdropping on the departing audience's favorable comments, we gathered with the authors, Howard Bay, Hermes Pan, Oleg Cassini and Sammy Lambert at the back of the auditorium for an after-the-show conference. Barely able to keep his eyes open, Todd said, "We've got a hit. Take the rest of the afternoon off."

That evening there was a small but enthusiastic party in the hotel that went on into the early hours and became boisterous when it was obvious that those late returns that were supposed to turn the election around in Dewey's favor were never going to put in an appearance. Todd, like Truman, had gone to bed early.

The next day, the New Haven reviews were even better than we had anticipated:

> As the Girls Go is loaded with laughs and boasts a fabulous collection of beautiful show girls. . . . Clark is a one-man show in himself. . . . On Broadway it will undoubtedly go—in a big way!
>
> —New Haven *Evening Register*

Bobby Clark, with all his sprightliness, his painted eye glasses and his famous Clark leer, stars in a lavish musical which has the White House for its background. Last night the little comedian was in top form, romping through the

acts in his own inimitable fashion, pursued by or pursuing beautiful girls. . . . It's a typical Mike Todd production, big and expensive and a full evening's entertainment.
—*Journal Courier*

At a noon conference, Adamson and Roos told Todd, with mock concern, that they had a major problem. There was a sight gag in the finale with a Dewey look-alike returning to the White House for his homburg. Adamson and Roos asked what Todd was going to do, now that the show was a hit and Truman was elected. He said, "What do you think, you're playing with kids?" He explained that he had been so confident of Truman's winning the election that he found a Truman look-alike the last week in Boston and had him standing by in New Haven to go on in the matinee performance. The man did look like Truman and stayed in the show throughout its run, but his one line was dropped after the matinee, when it turned out he had a pronounced Boston accent.

Todd had his first good night's sleep in a month. He was too exhausted to really enjoy the twin triumphs. He told us that he had always known he was at his best when conditions were at their worst, but he had surprised himself by the incredible amount of energy he was able to sustain during the Boston crisis. Joan smiled. She told us later that she had been slipping pep pills into his coffee the whole time. Mike was outraged and refused to acknowledge that any pills had kept him going. Joan knew better.

Only minor changes were made in New Haven, and the performers had a chance to get comfortable with the revised show. It was doing great business in New Haven, but the heavy operating losses in Boston could not be recouped. The sheriff had held only a portion of the outstanding bills. Todd brought as many brokers as he could up to New Haven to counteract the bad word that had spread from Boston. The show would never open on Broadway if he didn't come up with a substantial amount of cash to pay off the existing debts and all the New York preopening expenses. *As the Girls Go* was playing very well and had received great notices in New Haven, but that didn't guarantee that the more sophisticated New York critics and audiences would similarly accept it. The stigma of the Boston disaster had not been totally erased. His winning bet on Truman gave him less than a third of the money he needed to bring the show in.

At the end of the week he convened a meeting in New York of all the ticket brokers. He wanted them to buy half of the orchestra and some of the mezzanine seats for the first four weeks of the run—in cash. A "broker's buy" is a huge gamble and ticket brokers, like bankers, are not in the business of taking big risks. They would be gambling that the show would be a hit. If it was, they would get the tickets without "ice," the illegal but normal premium brokers pay to get choice tickets to a hit show. Anything charged above the box office price would go into their pockets. If the show was a flop they had a four-week supply of tickets they couldn't give away. Todd never took a penny of ice during his glory days on Broadway—now he wanted a favor in return. Brokers are generally regarded as cutthroat operators who illicitly make big money from the theater without contributing to its health. Todd insisted they made a big contribution to the theater—they could make a lukewarm ticket hot and lengthen the run of a successful show. He appreciated their past efforts and the use of their talents on behalf of his shows, and now needed their help to bring in what he knew would be a big winner for them and himself. He made the sale.

The show opened at the Winter Garden on Saturday night, November 13. Brooks Atkinson began his review in the *Times*: "Eschewing art for the moment, the headmen of *As the Girls Go* have come up with a bountiful and uproarious musical show. . . . *As the Girls Go* is the peace offering of Mike Todd, the free-wheeling showman who, as an adjoining column once remarked, has recently been recuperating from prosperity. Interested in making a fortune, Mr. Todd has promised his clientele an old-fashioned fandango. . . . It is a gay and rowdy Broadway entertainment."

In the second most important review, John Chapman of the *Daily News* gave the show only a mildly favorable notice. In the other morning papers, Robert Coleman in the *Mirror* gave Bobby and the show a rave notice, and even though Howard Barnes's review in the *Herald Tribune* was a mild pan, good quotes could be extracted from it.

All the notices in the afternoon papers were good except for the review in the faltering successor to *PM,* the New York *Star.* However, its critic, John Lardner, praised Bobby Clark and liked the score and the "dozen or so tall, gorgeous tomatoes of early Gothic design."

Mike Todd, at age seven, posing with his brother Frank, sister Edith and their mother on the steps of the house in Bloomington, Illinois.

Her Imperial Highness, Mae West, as she appeared in Mike Todd's production of *Catherine Was Great.* The actress played it straight – and the show fizzled.

Gypsy Rose Lee, Todd and George S. Kaufman at a rehearsal break of *The Naked Genius*. Gossip had Todd and Gypsy romantically linked, but his secret love was Joan Blondell, the star of the show. – *Photo by Richard Tucker*

Mike Todd, with ever-present cigar, at the height of his Broadway success in 1944. As a property owner, he made a fortune when *Harvey* played at his 48th Street Theater.

The impresario's favorite photo of himself, when he was switching between cigar and pipe.

Father and son at Jones Beach, 1952, where Todd produced the outdoor spectacle, *A Night in Venice.*

Checking out a fine point with his ace cameraman, Lionel ''Curly'' Lindon, in London during the filming of *Around the World in 80 Days*.

On location in Arizona with director Fred Zinneman and Oscar Hammerstein II during the production of *Oklahoma!*, the first Todd-AO success.

Joan Blondell with her two children, Ellen and Norman, and Mike Todd, Jr., during an idyllic moment at ''Jemmen-on-the-Nut,'' Irvington, New York. Joan's money paid for the ''dream house.''

Movie mogul Joseph Schenck, co-founder of Twentieth Century-Fox, Todd's closest friend and father
figure.

The Stork Club was a favorite watering hole for Mike
Todd and his cronies, Walter Winchell, Damon Runyon
(with Dorothy Strelsin), Mike Todd, Jr. and his roommates from Lawrenceville.

The Todds enact an Eskimo number in the Place de la Concorde, Paris.

At 715 Park Avenue, Todd and Elizabeth Taylor just prior to doing Ed Murrow's ''Person to Person'' television show.

Family Christmas portrait, Palm Springs, 1957. Front row: Christopher and Michael Wilding. Middle row: Liza Todd, Elizabeth Taylor Todd, Michael Todd, Sr. Back row: Susan Todd, Sarah Todd, Cyrus Todd, Mike Todd, Jr.

The critics expressed hats-in-the-air enthusiasm for Bobby—"the funniest man in the world": "I'd rather be Bobby Clark than President," "comedy genius, irrepressible," "top of his form," "ideal vehicle for Clark's wonders," "rough, ready and uproarious," "nothing can top him," "incomparable, extraordinary clown," "inexhaustible fount of low and gaudy humor"—and much more.

There was a line at the box office on Monday morning. The brokers' gamble on Todd paid off handsomely. Todd was back in business at the old stand and things were definitely looking up. At home Joan partially furnished the dining room, put some finishing touches on the downstairs library and started to decorate the master bedroom. Mike and Joan were in especially high spirits and shortly before Christmas—out of the blue—they received a personal invitation from President Truman to his inaugural ball. Joan bought a lovely taffeta evening gown; this was the first money she had spent on herself in over a year.

Joan and Mike were big hits at the ball and enjoyed themselves tremendously. Although they had met before, Mike avoided greeting the President; he didn't want to embarrass Truman in case he couldn't remember the name of Joan Blondell's new husband. While Mike and Joan were dancing Mike felt a tap on his shoulder; he turned around to discover that he was facing the President. Todd was at a loss for words and was fumbling around for something to say when Truman said: "What's the matter, Mike? Why don't you say hello? Are you stuck up, now that you have another hit on Broadway?"

CHAPTER 10

AS THE GIRLS GO did smash business the first five months of its run, but as the warm weather approached, the box office receipts began to drop. By the middle of June it was barely making its large operating nut. The show had nearly recouped its production costs and the $75,000 it had lost during the Boston tryout. As usual, Todd had been tapping the box office, but he had yet to see big money from *As the Girls Go*. There was a good chance that the show could run profitably after Labor Day, when the theater came alive again, but it surely would lose money during July and August, the off season.

To acknowledge that the show was closing down for the summer would be the kiss of death. Always cooperative, Bobby Clark was willing to let Mike put out a cover story attributing a temporary shutdown to Bobby's poor health. With the connivance of a friendly doctor it was announced that the show was forced to suspend operations—in spite of excellent business—starting July 10, because Bobby was suffering from "faulty vision caused by a spasm in the main artery of his left eye."

Back in the good graces of Mr. Lee, he was allowed to store the production without charge, but since the Shuberts had another booking for the Winter Garden, *As the Girls Go* had to reopen in a less desirable theater, the Broadway.

In the five months following the arrival of *As the Girls Go*, two of the greatest musicals in the history of the American theater opened, *South Pacific* and *Kiss Me Kate*, and understandably relegated Todd's show, when it reopened in mid-September 1949, to being an also-ran. David Lawlor says, "By the late fall it was a continual struggle to meet the payroll—

Friday was a day given over entirely to seeing who could get paid what. I know there were times—which, of course, Lucette never knew about—when Bobby turned around and gave his salary back to Mr. Todd."

The initial critical and financial success of *As the Girls Go* went a long way to restoring Todd's Broadway reputation, but provided only the briefest respite from his gigantic financial problems.

When *As the Girls Go* temporarily shut down in early July, Todd had two other projects in the works. After the success of his own *Hot Mikado* and Billy Rose's *Carmen Jones,* he was preparing an all-black version of a Verdi opera, reset in the Civil War period, entitled *My Darlin' Aïda.* The score understandably was no problem, but the book never came right and Mike had neither the money nor the patience to see it through.

His other project was to present a "two-a-day" series at the Palace, the top showcase for talent during the heyday of vaudeville. Jack Benny was set for a four-week engagement to launch the policy. But the Palace was making money playing motion pictures, the rental was high and Todd couldn't come up with a sufficient guarantee for a lease. Todd felt that the Palace was the only theater that he could successfully use to get this concept across. Eight years later Judy Garland played the Palace, revitalized her career and launched an era of big stars in concert performances.

When we moved to Irvington, Todd and Joan politely turned down all local party invitations. They did not want to get involved in the Westchester social scene. Joan had only two close friends in New York. She had frequent phone conversations and an occasional lunch with Betty Bruce, who had been on the road with her in *Something for the Boys.* Her other friend was Glenda Farrell, a movie star of the thirties and early forties, who had married a doctor and settled in New York City.

Joan was close to her only sister, Gloria, a successful actress in California, and greatly enjoyed their weekly phone conversations and the few brief visits Gloria made to New York.

Joan's mother, Catherine, called Nana by the family, had the smaller of the two apartments over the garages. The larger apartment was occupied by the previous superintendent of the estate, who had become terminally ill with cancer and died a few weeks before *As the Girls Go* opened in New York. Joan's brother Ed and his family came from California and moved into the vacant apartment. Ed became a stage manager for the show.

Joan's mother was very unobtrusive; when Mike was around she never came up to the house unless she was invited. Nana was a wonderful grandmother to Norman and Ellen and arranged a date for me with the youngest daughter of the Weaver family, our nearest neighbors. I married Sarah Weaver five and a half years later.

Ed Blondell was a good-hearted extrovert who liked to have a few drinks at neighborhood taverns. On a couple of occasions when my father was busy in the city, Joan and I joined Ed and his wife, Gretchen, at one of his favorite haunts. Once, when my father was in particularly low spirits, we dragged him along, thinking we might jolly him up, although to avoid local attention we drove to a bar six miles away in Hartsdale. Our idea was a dismal failure—it was a mistake for Joan and me to think he could enjoy "having a couple" in a neighborhood bar.

Joan never neglected Mike, and certainly the limited time she spent with her family and friends was not at his expense. Nevertheless, he became increasingly and insanely jealous of any attention she paid to others. He would hear Joan laughing on the telephone with her family or friends, or she would casually refer to one of them in conversation, trying to cheer him up with an amusing incident, and this would only irritate him. Joan was scrupulously careful never to force their company on him, and later, catering to his paranoid jealousy, she kept her contacts with them out of his sight and hearing. Her sensitivity to his feelings was wasted. At first he made little jokes. These soon degenerated into snide remarks, until finally he was provoking vitriolic arguments about the attention she paid to them.

He began to launch long verbal assaults at Joan on some minor or invented pretext. The first year of the marriage I witnessed a few of these outbursts. The second year they became an occasional but nevertheless regular occurrence. At the start of the third year, we could count on his breaking out in a crazy rage at least once a week. I am sure he never struck her, but his verbal abuse was so loud and profane that it seemed more vicious and intimidating than a physical assault. Joan put up a minimum of defense and quietly tried to reason with him. When it became apparent that there was no deflecting his anger, she simply endured his abuse as long as she could. When she was no longer able to hold back her tears, she would lock herself into the sewing-sitting room next to Ellen's bedroom.

Todd was sensible enough to contain his rages until he was able to get Joan out of range of Norman and Ellen. But as large as the house was, they could still hear something of his tireless shouting. Ellen, of course, became very protective of Joan and wary of my father. He adored Ellen and was very disappointed to see his warm relationship with her dissolve, but he seemingly accepted this as part of the price he had to pay for working out his inner anxieties on Joan.

Norman, possibly as a psychological self-defense against getting involved in Joan's problems with Todd, but also due to a full schedule of school activities, became something of a stranger to the entire household. During his first semester in school he became friendly with a girl in his class, Ann McDowell, and soon was dating her steadily. Norman and Ann were married several years later, when Norman was a Cornell undergraduate.

Mike created issues with which to harangue Joan. He accused her of extravagances in shopping for food and other purchases. This from a man who tipped maître d's twenty dollars as he was greeted at the door. He hardly needed provocation to pick a fight.

Irrationally, Joan seemed to feel a sense of guilt about Mike's constant rages. She never understood them. During conversations I had with her over a period of years, she indicated that there may have been a flaw in her nature, even though she could not put her finger on it, that caused her three marriages to fail. Overoptimism obscuring a realistic approach to problems is the only flaw I can attribute to her after all this time, and I am still inclined to consider this more of an asset in someone's character.

David Lawlor, who was the company manager for a road tour of *Bye Bye Birdie* in which Joan starred and who knew her for twenty years, claims that she didn't always keep her temper under control:

> I was the one who picked up Joan from the Broadway Limited in 1943, when she came to New York to do *The Naked Genius*. I saw her and Mr. Todd together during the entire period of their relationship. In my book each gave the other the devil's due. On one occasion when they were living in Irvington, I came up in a limousine on an errand for Mr. Todd—to bring him some cash he had me draw out of

the box office. He and Joan were getting ready to go to an opening that night. Joan prided herself on the cheesecake she made, and in fairness it was very good. We were in the kitchen—they were having a drink before leaving—and an argument started. Joan picked up her homemade cheesecake and pushed it right in Mr. Todd's face and was not content just at that, but slid it down his dress shirt and tuxedo and walked out of the room. Mr. Todd said nothing, changed into fresh clothes and we went back to town in the limousine without Joan. I don't know if he went back to Irvington that night, but the next day was one of the few occasions I ever saw him in the office early.

To the very end he avoided creating scenes in front of Joan's children or an outsider, but he never hesitated to give her hell in front of me. From what Joan told me, my being a witness to these exhibitions only slightly moderated the ferocity of his attacks. Without exception I took Joan's part in these arguments, but to no effect. If he ever paid me any attention, which he seldom did, it was only to tell me to "mix out." In the last year of the marriage, he did admit that he was being unfair to Joan but that he was unable to control himself. Once he told me that he loved her more than ever but couldn't control his temper and that any minor irritations with her somehow threw him into a tantrum.

Apologies to Joan seemed halfhearted, as if he were holding a well-founded grudge against her. He couldn't acknowledge that his rages were unjustified. I think that his financial and career problems were a tremendous blow to his self-esteem, and since he was constitutionally unable to blame or analyze himself, he worked off his anxiety and frustrations by finding imaginary faults with Joan.

Joan appreciated my sympathy and ineffective attempts to help her, but scrupulously never tried to make me an ally. On a few occasions, she tried to work out her confusion and distress by talking to me; she was too embarrassed to discuss my father's irrational behavior with anyone else.

Mike never felt guilty about making Joan a hausfrau, and Joan didn't care about her movie career, but its abandoned potential highlighted his money troubles. On her own she could have been earning enough money to furnish and maintain several places as big as ours.

Starting with my sophomore year in college, I always had a

new car. When my father asked what I thought was a comfortable monthly allowance, I told him a hundred dollars. He insisted it was too little and made it a hundred and twenty-five. Although my tuition was occasionally late in being paid, there was never any other indication that he was short.

If he had been realistic about his financial situation, it would have led to our living on a more modest scale and, consequently, to reducing the image he had of himself; but it wasn't in his nature to take the ordinary and "realistic" view of adverse circumstances. He knew that he might be temporarily—or, in his view, *momentarily*—down, but he would soon be back on top. Joan believed in him and readily accepted his view of things. But the price they paid for his inability to be "sensible" and "realistic" was the terrible strain he put on their marriage by working out his anxieties on her. However, he never would have accomplished so much in his career, against such heavy odds, if he had been a "realistic" person.

It was at this time, when confronted by columnists with his financial plight, that he made his oft-quoted statement: "I've been broke many times, but never poor. Poor is a state of mind." And when asked why he continued to smoke one-dollar Havanas, his reply was: "I'm in hock for over a million. What am I supposed to do, switch to stogies?"

The referee in the bankruptcy was tenacious and diligently pursued any assets of Todd's he could get his hands on. Mike told Herman Odell of the firm of Berman, Becker and Odell, which represented him in the bankruptcy proceedings, that he understood the referee's responsibilities but: "You know, that son of a bitch found out about all the cigars I had stored in the Dunhill humidor, and the bastard attached them . . . he didn't have to go that far."

Joan toured in summer stock in 1949, ostensibly to keep busy and professionally alive. She and Mike treated the tour as though it were nothing much more than a diversion for us kids, who were going to troupe along with her. But had we not needed the money, she would not have been lured away from Irvington and semi-retirement. I went along as a sort of general manager and majordomo.

Joan played the lead in a sentimental comedy by Anita Loos entitled *Happy Birthday*, in which Helen Hayes had starred on Broadway a few years before. It was a warmhearted piece, and Joan was marvelous in it. Business was excellent. We stayed at the most luxurious hotel nearest each of the theaters. Mike was working on his projects in New York but joined us on weekends.

During the final engagement, Joan got involved in a silly situation that became a national news story. In the middle of a dress rehearsal, the director obstinately tried to get Joan to perform some bit of stage business that Joan felt was bitchy and totally out of character. Joan firmly refused to change the way she had been successfully playing the scene all summer. The director made the contretemps into an issue of an actress questioning and contradicting the authority of the director or, as Todd would have said, into "a Dreyfus case." The director made some unflattering personal remarks in a stage whisper for the benefit of the assembled company. Joan was outraged. She searched around frantically for something to throw at the man, and as he turned tail and began to run up the aisle, Joan could find nothing at hand except some Kleenex. She wound up and threw it at his retreating back. The wad traveled about eight inches before it fluttered to the ground. The director locked himself in the office and phoned the state police, alleging that Joan had physically attacked him. Nothing could dissuade him from swearing out a warrant for assault. Mike came in from New York, and the incident became big news. The local district attorney laughed the matter off after investigating the charges. The show went on and the publicity was a marvelous stimulus for business. My father decided to stay on and take a holiday with us.

He and Joan threw a farewell supper party for the members of the touring company. The next day we packed and drove back to Irvington. As we were nearing the New Jersey side of the George Washington Bridge we heard a siren behind us. A motorcycle policeman waved us over to the side of the road. He pulled out his book and belligerently stated that we were exceeding the speed limit by twelve miles an hour. While Todd was politely explaining that he had been distracted by a discussion he was having with his little woman, the policeman recognized Joan Blondell. In a deferential tone the policeman asked my father for his license and registration. He took the auto registration, which was attached to the steering column, gave it to the policeman and asked Joan to get his license out of the glove compartment. He did not have a driver's license and had never had one. Joan frantically searched through the glove compartment for the nonexistent license. With increasing impatience he waited for Joan to find the license. With a caustic comment he pushed her hand aside and leaned over to look for himself. After a few beats, Joan, on the verge of tears, admitted she had forgotten to put it in the car. Todd started shouting at her, telling her that if he had told her once, he had told her a hundred times, "Don't forget to put my license in the glove compartment!" The policeman started to take Joan's part, but Mike brushed him aside and went on yelling at Joan. She began to cry. The policeman by now was defending Joan and told Todd to please take it easy on her. Finally he relented and the policeman was so pleased he had rescued Joan Blondell from the wrath of her husband that he let Todd go without producing his license and without a ticket. As we drove off Joan gave the policeman a friendly wink. Before I could ask a question, Mike commented, "It took this one a lot longer to take the bait." When I asked what was going on, he said this was a routine they had improvised on a similar occasion a year earlier. It was one of Joan's finest performances. He wasn't too bad either.

With all of us going first class the whole summer, the tour did not net a lot of money.

When I came home for Thanksgiving in 1949, things were on the upbeat. They were full of optimism about projects on the horizon. Earlier Todd had talked about doing a revival of Sean O'Casey's *Juno and the Paycock*, starring Joan, but they had come across a superb new drama for her, which Mike was anxious to produce. It was written by a newcomer, William Inge, and was entitled *Come Back, Little Sheba*. This was even more of an offbeat role for Joan than her Aunt Cissie part in the movie *A Tree Grows in Brooklyn*. Also, he had started conversations with Betty Smith, the author of *A Tree Grows in Brooklyn*, about adapting the book as a musical, to star Joan. This was in the talking stage, but the script for *Sheba* was in hand. It would give them the chance to work together, and it offered Joan the opportunity of forever leaving behind her tired Warner Brothers image as the carefree wisecracking girl friend of the heroine. Now she could establish herself as a dramatic actress, capable of playing any kind of character role.

Todd also wanted to get up another musical right away. With no book show ready to go, he was planning to present one of his "great cultural achievements" on the order of *Star and Garter*. He did not want to reuse that title—Gypsy owned over a third of the show and would expect up to $1,000 a week for the use of it. That Thanksgiving weekend we went through the collection of books around the house to see if one of them might trigger an idea. We came across one that gave Mike just what he was looking for—*A Penny to See the Peep Show*. By the time I returned home for Christmas vacation, he had started the preproduction work on *Michael Todd's Peep Show*.

None of his projects was far enough along to require his full attention, and he felt we could all use some sun. After Christmas at home we went to Golden Beach, Florida, where we rented two bungalows on the ocean. We dressed up and had a family New Year's Eve dinner and celebration at the Boca Raton Hotel. It was a marvelous holiday, but I sensed some tension between them. She seemed reserved, and he seemed tentative and apologetic. There were no fireworks, but I had the feeling that Mike had been recently raging at Joan and that the family vacation was an attempt at a reconciliation.

At the end of January 1950 I decided, with my father's reluctant concurrence, to take off the following semester from school and ship out on a tanker. A classmate had introduced me to the captain of the Standard Oil of New York tanker fleet, who said he would give me a job on one of their ships. It took a week to get my Coast Guard papers and then I had to spend a couple of weeks commuting daily to the Battery, where I sat around a hiring hall, literally waiting for my ship to come in.

Todd had no big flare-ups with Joan during this period, but he was more tense and irritable than he had been over Christmas. He was still far from out of the woods financially—*As the Girls Go* hadn't proved the bonanza everyone had anticipated. Added to this, he was attempting to put *Peep Show* together without stars and full-time collaborators. He was really doing this one the hard way, but if he pulled it off, the operating costs would be comparatively modest, and his end of the take could be huge. Todd and Joan were still planning to do *Come Back, Little Sheba*, but *Peep Show* was to get on its feet first. Joan seemed distracted, but I felt this was merely a reflection of my father's fidgety state.

Finally I signed on the S.S. *Stanvac Durban*. The ship was to sail around the world and would be away from the States for about a year. It was cleared with the company that I would sign off somewhere in the Pacific in late summer so that I could return to college in the fall. My father, Joan and the kids gave me a farewell banquet at Peter Luger's.

The next morning I reported to the ship, which was anchored off Staten Island. About noon we hoisted anchor and set sail for what I knew was going to be a great adventure. An hour later we tied up in Port Newark. I spent the rest of the day carrying cans of paint aboard the ship. That night I was given liberty, so I phoned my father, rode into town on the Hudson Tubes and had a second farewell banquet with him at Peter Luger's.

At every port of call, there was a two- or three-page handwritten letter from Joan, with a few scribbled words from Mike, relating the news from home as well as a brief statement about his business activities.

From Port Said I sent home a vivid but not exaggerated account of a shipboard fight that involved a fire axe and ended when the instigator of the melee was knocked unconscious with a Rose's Lime Juice bottle. David Lawlor says that the day this letter arrived, my father spent the better part of a morning on the phone with the captain of the Socony fleet, who had given me the job, trying to get me fired and flown back to New York, with Mike volunteering to pay all expenses. Joan's long, cheery letters and my father's brief notes appended to them gave no indication of his desire to abort my cruise. A letter I received in Hong Kong from Joan indicated that my father was making great progress with *Peep Show* and that everyone was well and happy.

Then, mysteriously, the letters from Joan ceased. At first I took the optimistic view that rehearsals had started on *Come Back, Little Sheba,* although she had not mentioned the play in her letters.

When there was no letter from Joan at the next two ports, I wrote, asking if anything was wrong. Three weeks and two more ports without a reply had me really concerned. I made up my mind that if there was no letter at the next port I would phone or send a cable.

Two days before we were next scheduled to dock, I was called amidships, where the first mate handed me a cable. It was from my father, stating that he and Joan had been divorced and that a letter would follow. I cabled Dad back: WE'LL BUILD A NEW SAN FRANCISCO. ALL MY LOVE, MICHAEL.

This reference was to a joke he and I shared with several million people. On the only occasion I had been to the movies with my father and Joan, we had gone to White Plains one rainy night to see a reissue of the 1936 Clark Gable epic *San Francisco.*

After half an hour of the most spectacular effects depicting the 1906 earthquake and the devastation that followed, Clark Gable climbs to the top of a hill overlooking the smoldering shambles of the city and rallies the courage and fortitude of the shaken survivors with the pronouncement "We'll build a new San Francisco." Even for Clark Gable in his prime, this was a heap of courage and fortitude. The audience broke up with laughter.

At the next port I received a letter from my father. He wrote that one day Joan packed up and flew out to Vegas for a divorce. He said that it was probably his fault—that he had finally exhausted Joan's patience. He was sorry to have ruined such a good thing, but there was nothing that could be done about it now. He was pleased and relieved that I was still with him, no questions asked, and there was no doubt about it—we would build a new San Francisco together. He went on to say that *Peep Show* had received great notices in Philadelphia and was selling out. It would open at the Winter Garden on June 28.

Three days before the scheduled opening in New York, the Korean War broke out and there were rumors that our ship, now in the Pacific, would be pressed into service, transporting fuel to Japan and Korea. The next few days were anxious ones as we awaited further developments. I was also anxiously awaiting word from my father about the opening in New York. A few days later it became clear that Truman's bold action in support of the South Koreans was not going to spark a world war. No news from my father about the show, however, was a bad sign, and I sent him a cable asking about the reviews. Three days later an evasive reply came back, reporting that the first week's business was capacity and that everything looked good; but conspicuously absent was any word about the notices.

I was anxious to see how my father was getting on, so I signed off the ship at Suva in the Fiji Islands and took a plane to Hawaii. When I arrived in Honolulu, I was delighted to see that the show had earned a *Life* magazine cover and a favorable story inside. The piece related that Todd had signed the King of Siam to write a few numbers for the show, but that it was the low comedy and tall girls that sustained the evening's entertainment. I was at ease for the first time in weeks, knowing that things couldn't be too bad with a big cover story in *Life*. We exchanged cables. He indicated that the show was continuing to do capacity business. With that news I decided to take a brief vacation.

When I got back to New York a week later, I found my father in good spirits. He was philosophical and apologetic about the divorce. He accepted full blame but seemed unburdened by guilt. He felt it was just some strange quirk of his personality, or his circumstances, that had caused him to give Joan such a rough time. He looked back on his behavior as something entirely beyond his control, and while it was regrettable, there was nothing he could do about it. He understood Joan's inability to absorb any more abuse. He did seem surprised, though, that her breaking point was so sudden and decisive. I was perplexed that having said all this and given an honest and accurate analysis of their breakup, he seemed so detached and showed no signs of real regret. But then he never looked back or dwelt on either his failures or successes.

Mike had taken a duplex penthouse apartment in a brand-new building on Park Avenue at Seventieth Street, which was even less furnished than Jemmen. There were a few pieces of outdoor furniture on the large terrace. There was some furniture in the master bedroom, and he had the closet in his room expanded and cedar-lined so that it became a walk-in affair, with a line of four racks that held his seventy-plus suits. I was installed in a huge room on the top floor adjoining a spacious terrace that fronted the east side of Park Avenue. My room contained nothing but a convertible sofa and a reading lamp on a table from one of the sets of *Up in Central Park*. Mike had had the gilt furniture from the big second-act ballroom scene taken out of storage and delivered to the apartment. I am sure that in his mind's eye he saw the furniture as quite elegant. But the eighteen or twenty ballroom chairs and the few occasional tables only emphasized the lack of real furniture in the apartment.

Peep Show had received mixed reviews but was doing capacity business, and inasmuch as it had no stars it was clearing a lot of money. The costumes and sets were lavish, so there was a sizable production nut to recoup. Still, Todd was in action. He no longer seemed sullen and appeared to have regained his boundless self-assurance, which had dimmed perceptibly the last few years. *Peep Show* struck me as lively and funny, and I was curious as to why the New York critics had not agreed with their brethren in Philadelphia, who had given it such great notices.

He said that the show had played marvelously in Philadelphia and that the first-night audience in New York had given it the only negative response it had received. He took full blame for the unprecedented letdown at this one crucial performance. The day of the opening he worked late and didn't get home to shower and change until after six o'clock. When he was walking out the front door, it suddenly occurred to him that his musical conductor knew that he liked to have the "Star Spangled Banner" played before the overture on the opening night of all his shows. Todd knew that the one sure way to silence a noisy opening-night audience was to play the national anthem; and this took everyone's attention away from arriving celebrities and directed it to the front of the theater, where it belonged. The Korean War had broken out only a few days before, and everyone was concerned about the international situation, even about the possibility of an atomic war. Todd realized that playing the national anthem this evening would bring all these fears and tensions to the fore and cast a pall over the frivolous entertainment of the show. He rushed back into the apartment and tried to reach the conductor by phone, but the theater's lines were busy. He had a limousine waiting for him downstairs but traffic delayed him and he ran the last couple of blocks to the theater. As he arrived, he heard the first strains of the anthem, and he knew that overlooking this seemingly trivial detail would seriously handicap the chances for the show's success. The second act, however, played almost as well as it had out of town.

Hobe Morrison in his *Variety* review noted:

> *Michael Todd's Peep Show* is appropriately titled, even to the inclusion of the producer's name. For *Peep Show* is just about that, and it has Todd's personality stamped all over it. Moreover, Todd is one of the few Broadway producers whose name has box office draw. . . . The fact that the King of Siam has provided one of the songs has already been profitable as publicity, and will continue to be. . . . The combination of beauty, nudity, risque comedy and the intangible come on power of Todd's name adds up to a promising commercial bet.

The notices in the New York dailies were mixed but had plenty of good quotes and could fairly be said to be "money reviews."

The sketches were directed by Bobby Clark and written—or, in the case of the old burlesque material—rewritten by Bobby, Mike and Bill Roos. Two of them—poles apart, one original and one ancient—the critics agreed were very funny: "Rowdy and boisterous in its hearty fun is a slapstick travesty of Thomas Stearns Eliot's *The Cocktail Party* [which had opened earlier in the season] in which a couple of painters and paperhangers perform mayhem while hoity-toity Britishers drink drinks and chatter." "The 'I Hate a Parade' number turns into a drum solo —no words—with Peanuts Mann pounding away for dear life, and it becomes something very special. A really hilarious turn."

There were four dozen scantily clad gorgeous girls. There was a finger-snapping Jule Styne-Bob Hilliard tune, "Stay with the Happy People," which was one of the modest hits of the year. There was also a winsome number, performed in Mexican costumes, entitled "You've Never Been Loved (if You've Never Been Loved below the Border)." While the show was undeniably a bit raw in places, it was definitely a good evening's entertainment.

Howard Bay recalls:

> In Philadelphia Mike felt that we needed some spectacular scenic effect, preferably involving the girls. Well, he dreamed up this giant keyhole bubble bath, and it sort of made sense—*Peep Show* and all that. Besides, we had no real first-act finale. So I drew it up real fast and took it to New York and got it built. Mike flew in this soap expert from Procter and Gamble in Cincinnati. The keyhole had a rhinestone border all around it, and there was an aquamarine blue tarp with forty-eight holes with elastic so the girls could push through, and the whole thing was raked with bleachers, so that they either sat, kneeled or stood. And it worked very well . . . until one Saturday matinee the soap mixture went awry, and we had forty-eight girls with blue pubic hair— brilliant blue. Prophetically, the King of Siam's big song in the show was "Blue Night."

Peep Show was doing near capacity business the first few months of its run, and Mike was back in full swing again. TV was in its infancy, and he was able to sell NBC a variety hour, starring Bobby Clark, that would appear on alternate weeks of a series called the "Colgate Comedy Hour." Mike was busy preparing for this show, which was scheduled for the fall, as well as nursing along a play in summer stock that he was going to produce on Broadway.

One night, shortly before I was to return to school, my father called and ordered me to meet him for supper at the Stork Club. Coyly, he said he had a special friend he wanted me to meet. When I arrived at the restaurant I was surprised, almost shocked, when I saw my father seated at one of the banquettes in cozy tête-à-tête with Joan.

In reaction to my coolness, they became self-conscious. There was no reference to the divorce. Their behavior was back to square one, when I had found Joan hiding in the back seat of the car at Lawrenceville three years earlier. I was too put off by their inconsistency to try to understand their present situation— whatever that was. After we had dropped Joan off at her hotel, my father looked at me questioningly and said, "What's new?" He then proceeded to tell me that he realized how unfair he had been to Joan and that she was beginning to feel she had been too hasty pulling out. I had no comment.

My father almost always had total confidence in his business decisions and seldom allowed them to be influenced by others. However, on one occasion I was able to sway his judgment about a production, and the result was a failure.

While I was waiting to ship out early in the year, I read through a pile of scripts he had brought home from the office. One was by Garson Kanin and I thought it was great. I enthusiastically recommended it to Mike. Joan mildly supported me. Todd was unimpressed because the protagonist was a heel, and because of his belief that for any play, novel or movie to be a big commercial success, you had to have "someone to root for." Nevertheless, with my pushing him on, he optioned the play with the halfhearted conviction that it could be reworked to minimize the flaws he saw in it.

When I returned to New York from the Pacific, I was pleased to discover that he was going to produce Kanin's play *The Live Wire*. It was trying out in summer stock with the cast that was going to be used in the Broadway production. The first I heard of it was several days after my return, when Todd casually said we were going to drive up to Fairhaven, Massachusetts, and have a look at it. I was amazed by his indifferent attitude. He explained that Kanin, who was also directing the play, was refusing to make any changes. After seeing a performance, I was even more amazed by his lack of enthusiasm, as there was a steady stream of laughs and the audience loved the play.

The Live Wire was about a group of struggling actors who rent a lot on the East Side in mid-Manhattan (there were still such vacant lots at the time) and erect a Quonset hut, which they share. In effect they set up a commune, pooling all their incomes. The central character is the last one to join the group and he immediately starts lying and playing devious games to advance his own career. *Life* magazine decides to do a story about the group, and the heel manipulates the situation so that he is prominently featured in the piece and winds up with his picture on the cover. The *Life* story gains him a movie contract. There are several subplots, including a romance, but the gist of the play is how the "live wire" steps on his compatriots' shoulders to get ahead.

I asked Mike what changes he wanted that Kanin was rejecting. First, he wanted to change the single set of the play from a Quonset hut to an industrial loft. The play had been written shortly after the end of World War II, and Todd thought that in 1950 the idea of a Quonset hut in midtown was stale and pointlessly eccentric. He wanted to play down the commune aspect of the group and the heel's successful conniving, and shift the emphasis to the likable characters in the play, leaving the audience with the feeling that the good guys would make their way without dirty tricks. Obviously, Todd hadn't changed his basic distrust of the play, despite the fact that it looked like a big hit. He was wary, but I was convinced that I had touted him onto a big winner.

The play opened in New York at the Playhouse Theatre on August 17 and received only two good notices—in the *News* and the *Mirror*. The rest were bad, although a couple of notices commercially damned the play with faint praise. It had a marvelous cast and there were good notices for Jack Guilford, Pat Harrington, Murvyn Vye, Heywood Hale Broun and Peggy Cass.

Todd seemed as uninterested in the failure of the play as he had been in its potential success. It was not costly to produce, and by trying it out in summer stock, where it made money, his losses were minimized. *The Live Wire,* from start to finish, was a big yawn for him. Although it might sound extravagant, I think his major motive for optioning the play was to demonstrate his interest in me at a time when we were being pulled apart by his harsh treatment of Joan.

The mainstay of Todd's "Colgate Comedy" show were Bobby Clark routines from the Broadway productions he and Mike had done together. The show was done live from a theater that had been extensively remodeled for television. The entire balcony was converted into a control booth. Intensive lighting was required in those early days, and making room for the then cumbersome television cameras and sound-boom dollies had reduced the seating on the main floor by more than half. After almost forty years on the stage, Bobby's freewheeling antics were confined by bulky equipment, and he was upset by the difficulty of trying to play to both the camera and the audience. He was nervous and unable to establish a rapport with either. Bobby, one of the greatest comics ever to appear on the stage, lost his self-assurance, and he and the show misfired. After two more shows it was canceled by mutual agreement between Todd, Bobby and the network. Joan made a guest star appearance on one of the shows, and Todd was able to get a settlement of $100,000.

Peep Show ran thirty-five weeks and just about broke even. Jule Styne and the other composers were never paid full royalties for the use of their songs, but this was forgiven and forgotten because they liked Todd and knew he was having a tough time. Todd also stiffed the King of Siam.

In addition to drawing box office money during the run of *Peep Show,* two bits of luck kept Todd in walk-around money for the better part of two years during this period.

A minor stroke of fortune came one day when he was selecting a suit from his huge cedar-lined closet. He noticed that a pair of pants from a hanger in the back had fallen to the floor. He picked them up and heard a crinkling sound coming from the beltline. Looking hopefully into the gambling pocket that had been sewn into the back of all his pants, he found three crisp $1,000 bills. They had been there at least six years.

A major stroke of luck came when a flush member of the Friars Club got tired of ducking Mike and his own conscience and paid off seventy cents on the dollar on an old gin debt, giving Todd $35,000 in cash. Mike had not been pressing him, but out of the blue the fellow Friar came across at a time when he knew things were very rough for Todd.

Todd took a quirky and inconvenient way of concealing these assets. On the shelves in the back of our front hall closet he had put several hatboxes. It only seemed fitting that he stash his money in the bottom of the box that contained his top hat. He had a heavy lock put on the closet door and kept the key at the bottom of a jewelry box in a bureau drawer in his bedroom. Anytime either of us brought home a guest, we had to keep the visitor waiting in the front hall while we retrieved the key to open the closet, so that we could put away our coats. This provoked a lot of quizzical looks, but I don't recall anyone ever asking for an explanation. The money was in thousand-dollar bills, and occasionally he would take a stepladder from the kitchen, unlock the front hall closet, climb up to the hatbox and make a withdrawal. He looked and felt silly doing this.

One huge gambling debt owed to Todd was never paid. The owner of a big hotel on the Strip in Las Vegas welshed on a $125,000 gin loss. In 1947 Jack Dietz laid out a plan for Todd for recovering this loss. Dietz's credit in Vegas was good for that and even larger amounts. He proposed a visit to the hotel, gradually drawing on credit approximately $125,000 in chips. He would put in time at the tables at this hotel, but keep accumulating most of the chips he was drawing on credit and change them when he gambled at other casinos. Casino chips at that time were as good as currency in Las Vegas and could be cashed anywhere in town. Dietz proposed that when the hotel owner went after Dietz to make good on his markers, he would square the debt with an I.O.U. from Todd that transferred the owner's gin loss. Todd thanked Dietz but shrugged the whole idea off, indicating that Dietz would be blackballed in Vegas, if not worse.

From 1940, when we moved into our first luxury apartment at 25 Central Park West, we had a maid who worked steadily for us named Kathryn Baltimore. She continued to work for us when we moved to 530 Park Avenue and maintained that apartment after my mother's death. By the time my father returned to New York with Joan in the summer of 1947, Kathryn was happily married. After he and Joan had bought the house in Irvington, they asked Kathryn if she and her husband would care to come and live with us. She politely declined. When I returned to my father's new apartment at 715 Park Avenue in the summer of 1950, Kathryn was back in our employ. One day when we were alone, I asked her why she hadn't come to work for us in Irvington. After much tactful evasion she said that soon after Joan and my father came back from California Joan told Kathryn that it was too expensive to order all our groceries by phone from Gristede's. Joan had brought one of her cars from California, and she asked Kathryn to use it to shop in a supermarket in a less expensive neighborhood. Kathryn said that she knew Mr. Todd liked his food from Gristede's, but that in any case she didn't have a driver's license. Joan did the shopping herself. Seeing the size of the laundry bill, Joan asked Kathryn if she would launder my father's shirts. Kathryn didn't mind doing the laundry, but she told Joan that she would never be able to do his shirts, most of which were silk, as nicely as the French laundry did. A couple of other household incidents convinced Kathryn that Joan was attentive to the housekeeping responsibilities and that she had fixed ideas on how her home should be run. Kathryn knew that my father had equally fixed ideas, at least insofar as the management of the household affected him, and she felt Joan's style was going to conflict badly with Mr. Todd's and that she would be caught in the middle. So when my father persisted in asking her to come with them to Irvington, she finally answered, "Mr. Todd, you are going to be moving back into the city in two or three years' time. It will be easy for you to get another apartment, but I've got a great rent-controlled place in Harlem, and I'll never be able to get another one as good. I'll be glad to work for you again when you come back to the city."

Kathryn worked weekdays. On weekends when I was away and Max Gendel was not around, and before Mike started living with Evelyn Keyes, he occasionally would ask Kathryn to come in on a weekend morning, saying that he needed help in preparing a brunch for guests. Kathryn would drop everything, arrive at the apartment, go into the kitchen and look in the refrigerator and not see any food for the guests. Todd would call her into the bedroom, and while he was dressing or shaving would start a conversation. Kathryn would sit on the bed and occasionally nod or make an appropriate comment. When there was a pause, she would ask when the guests were expected and if she should call the delicatessen to make sure the food was on the way. My father would reassure her there was plenty of time. After he was dressed they would go into the kitchen, have a cup of coffee and continue their conversation. When he was ready to go out, he would make some lame excuse to Kathryn about his guests probably forgetting about the brunch date. There was the occasional real brunch, but after a half-dozen or so phantom brunches, Kathryn said, "Mr. Todd, you just called me down here because you wanted someone to talk to." He vehemently protested that that was not the case, but the practice continued and Kathryn never made any further comment.

When I came home for the Christmas holidays in 1950, Joan and Todd were once again an "item." I remained aloof to the renewal of their romance. I felt I had gone all out on the first go-around, and would wait until things became a little more official before I got worked up about their possible remarriage.

At the end of my vacation, I came back to the apartment late one evening and found my father engaged in a serious conversation with Joan. We had a short chat about my doings, and then I went upstairs. From the few words I exchanged with my father and Joan, I had the feeling that their rapprochement was reaching a definitive stage. Joan seemed to have lost her air of uncertainty with me and had resumed her attitude of affectionate respect, which had developed during the marriage. My father was relaxed—no longer the self-conscious suitor, but more like the comfortably settled married man he had never completely become. The whole situation struck me as perverse. Why hadn't they achieved this kind of serenity and developed such confidence in each other during their marriage? Now, when all our lives had been disrupted and our marvelous home sold, it seemed a little late for a reconciliation.

As I started to get undressed, I worked myself into a rage about their behavior, which seemed maddeningly inconsistent and irresponsible. Ostentatiously I threw my shoes on the floor, one at a time, taking a good dramatic pause between. I got myself into high gear and slammed around the few pieces of furniture in my room and banged the closet door. Then, in a burst of self-induced emotion, I sat on my bed and began to cry. As I had anticipated, my father found me in this maudlin state when he came up to investigate the disturbance. Reaching for the strongest ammunition I could muster, I sobbed out, "My mother had to die . . . to make all this possible." The desired effect was achieved. After the momentary shock wore off, he put his arm around me and said, "I'm sorry, son. I never realized how all this would seem to you." He then went downstairs, and

I heard the murmur of a brief conversation. The front door quietly closed, and I never again saw my father and Joan together.

Although my behavior was totally illogical, I think it had a reasonable emotional basis. How dare they disrupt my life, and Ellen's and Norman's and then get back together as if nothing untoward had happened. I had taken the divorce as calmly as my father had, but their reconciliation built up and released all the frustration and anger I felt about it.

Mike and Joan were both self-confident people, and if they hadn't had some deep uncertainties about their reconciliation, my misbehavior alone would not have deterred them; and sooner, rather than later, they would have reenlisted me as their ally.

A few months later Joan began a romance with Jimmy Cannon, a syndicated columnist for the New York *Post*. It was to be the last serious affair of her life. A few years later she told me that she had given up any notions of men or another marriage. From that point on she focused all her attention and affection on Norman and Ellen and subsequently on their children. By the mid-fifties Joan and I began an affectionate although intermittent correspondence and occasionally spoke on the phone. Once, long after we were back on the friendliest of terms and Mike was back in the chips, she said, at the end of a phone call, in a voice that was barely audible, "You know, your father still owes me sixteen thousand dollars and I wouldn't mention it to you or get you involved, but I could really use it now. Would you please look into the matter?"

That night I told my father about Joan's claim. He coolly dismissed it, saying, "She's completely goofy—I paid her everything I owed her years ago." I persisted: "Are you sure?" He replied, "I'm positive." And that ended the conversation. I felt reasonably confident that his answer meant that Joan had gotten her figures wrong and was asking only out of necessity, but I was surprised by his indifference to Joan's distress.

Joan and I became closer than ever after my father's death. When she worked in New York, she came for visits to my home in Dobbs Ferry. She had a grandmotherly interest in my children and took them to shows and bought them gifts. On almost all my trips to Los Angeles I visited her.

We continued our correspondence and visits. She never talked about the marriage, except to say that she knew Mike had been a wonderful father. For years she consistently refused to comment about him in interviews. Then in a magazine article in the late sixties, she stated that her first husband was her father, her second husband was her accountant and her last husband, Mike Todd, was the love of her life.

CHAPTER *11*

TODD BEGAN NOW what he later in life called his "giant three-horse parlay"—Cinerama to Todd-AO to *Around the World in 80 Days*. In six years he went from a fading has-been on Broadway to the pinnacle of success in movies. His first full-length motion picture won the Academy Award and earned him millions.

In his personal life, after achieving the marriage and family life he had been looking forward to for years, he unconsciously destroyed it, and without remorse or regret moved on to a pleasant and comfortable three-year affair with the actress Evelyn Keyes, which almost ended in marriage. He married one of the most beautiful women in the world—Elizabeth Taylor matched his zest for creating and having fun. He was delighted with the birth of his daughter Liza. He was less delighted about being a grandfather, but nevertheless derived some satisfaction from the arrival of my first two children. Just before his life came to an untimely and dramatic close he said, "I'm so happy that there ought to be a law against it."

Late in 1950, the Chinese invaded Tibet. In the middle of the previous year, there had been the occasional news and feature story about an expedition that Lowell Thomas, senior and junior, had made to Lhasa, the remote capital of Tibet. The drama of their trip had been heightened when Thomas senior was thrown from a horse midway on the trek out of Tibet and fractured his right leg in eight places. It was a month before he was carried out to civilization.

Todd heard that the Thomases had shot extensive footage of

their expedition. Lowell junior was planning to make a lecture tour featuring this footage. Todd got the idea that he would promote the lecture tour and give it a spectacular send-off by presenting it in Madison Square Garden, to as many as fifteen thousand paying customers. He visualized its becoming the most publicized and financially successful lecture in history and sold the Thomases his idea. As the promoter of the Garden appearance and subsequent tour, he could net a quick and needed buck. Since his start as a show business entrepreneur, he had never become involved in such a modest and uncharacteristic project. This almost whimsical interest in presenting a Burton Holmes–like lecture tour led directly to his spectacular three-horse parlay.

Todd went to have a look at the film. As travelogue material goes it was superior and built to a dramatic finish: getting Thomas senior out through the Himalayan passes after he had broken his leg. The Thomases' trip might seem gratuitously hazardous now, but at the time there was no form of public transport to Lhasa, and it was an almost impossible task to obtain the visas necessary to enter the country.

He saw the Tibetan footage in a small screening room and immediately realized then even blowing up the 16mm film to 35mm and projecting it on a normal-sized movie screen would be totally unsuitable for the vast proportions of Madison Square Garden. He said that for the Garden premiere they would need a huge screen. The elder Thomas said that he was getting involved with a new film process that had the largest screen ever built and that a demonstration unit could be seen in an indoor tennis court on an estate in Oyster Bay, Long Island.

Todd and his press agent-companion at the time, Max Gendel, drove out to have a look.

The giant curved screen was an integral part of a new film process called Cinerama, which had evolved over a period of years through the efforts of a motion picture technician and engineer, Fred Waller. Waller believed that motion pictures should approximate the human field of vision and not be limited to the comparatively narrow scope of existing screens.

Prior to World War II, Waller had developed a crude working model of his invention and obtained some backing to develop it. The process had a successful application during the war as an air gunnery training device. With eleven cameras, films were made of "attacking" planes coming in at all angles and speeds.

212

Trainees were placed in simulated gun turrets in a globular room. Waller's films were projected on the walls, so that the entire field of a gunner's vision was employed as he tried to sharpen his reflexes and timing in aiming his gun at the quickly passing targets.

To commercially exploit his concept for movies, Waller approximated the range of human vision (165 degrees horizontally and 60 degrees vertically) and planned to put a deeply curved screen within existing proscenium arches to roughly triple the width and double the height of normal screens. He needed three cameras and three projectors to produce a picture to fill his new screen.

One of the original backers of Waller's process was Hazzard Reeves, the owner of Reeves Soundcraft, one of the companies that pioneered "audio-engineering." Understandably, his principal interest in Waller's process was to make use of stereo so that sounds would come from the area of the huge screen where their sources were seen. Walt Disney had already used stereo for his film *Fantasia;* and while it had been well received, it had made no lasting impression, because *Fantasia* was projected on ordinary-sized, or only slightly enlarged screens. The most dramatic use of stereophonic sound was in the sequence of Stokowski's Philadelphia Symphony assembling and the individual musicians, at various locations on the screen, tuning their instruments. This effect, however, was vitiated when the audience's attention was shifted to the animated figure of Mickey Mouse darting about in the orchestra.

After World War II Waller's invention attracted a list of prominent nontheatrical investors, but despite Reeves's continued support, the other investors had dropped out, and the Cinerama company, by 1950, was almost a bankrupt corporation, with a concept that had gone no further than the demonstration unit.

Waller's film was shot in sepia and opened on a normal-sized screen with Waller making a dull introduction of himself and his new process. Then the masking opened to show Waller on the gigantic full screen as he continued to explain how he had accomplished what the viewer was seeing—with the use of three cameras and three projectors. The sequence that followed was set in a Long Island church and showed the parishioners filing into the pews, cutting to a reverse angle shot of the choir singing a hymn. The first fifteen minutes of the demonstration film were a fast cure for insomnia. Waller on the screen provided unnecessary commentary between sequences—his delivery was leaden. The first excitement was generated after Waller said that the process would be great for action shots, and then the viewer actually began to experience the roller coaster ride at the Rockaway Playland Amusement Park. A large number of motion picture executives had been dragged out to Oyster Bay to see Waller's new process. The first part of the film was not only dull but vividly demonstrated all the shortcomings of Cinerama: angular distortions and fuzziness at the two "seams"—where the three pictures were joined; and different light intensities and hues of the three pictures. All these shortcomings were minimized in the roller coaster scene, which everyone found exciting and novel. But by the time it came on the screen, the movie executives thought it no more than an amusing gimmick, because by then the ship had already sailed and sunk.

Max Gendel said that when the screen first opened up to full size, Todd went crazy with excitement and kept grabbing his arm and whispering in his ear: "This is the greatest thing since talkies. We're going to revolutionize the industry. We're going to make millions with this!" And on, and on. After the roller coaster sequence he quieted down, realizing he had to hold back in front of Waller until he could figure out a way to get control of the process.

Max described the drive back into the city:

> We tore along at the speed of sound—the sound of Mike explaining how he was going to take over and promote the process. When we got into town Mike turned on the radio to listen to Lowell Thomas's newscast. I remember, at the end of the program Thomas was saying that some vegetarian or other had just walked up a mountain and there were no more mountains to climb and so long until tomorrow. Todd stopped the car at Broadway and Fifty-second Street, ran into the Western Union office and sent a telegram to Lowell Thomas care of CBS, saying: DEAR MR. THOMAS, I KNOW OF ONE MOUNTAIN THAT YOU HAVEN'T CLIMBED. MICHAEL TODD.

Although Todd was already in close contact with the Thomases, it was a Todd touch to send the wire. It gave dramatic emphasis to his intended sales pitch and gave him a night to think over the proposition he was going to make Thomas.

All his interest in presenting Lowell junior's lecture was put aside the second the masking opened up on the huge screen in Oyster Bay. Cinerama from that instant on became the most important thing in his life.

When I came down from college for the midyear break in January 1951, my father was bubbling over with enthusiasm. Before I could get my bags unpacked, he had me in his car, driving out to Oyster Bay to see "the greatest thing since penicillin."

His excitement was contagious, and I believed him when he said that he would present the process in a way that would make it the new sensation of the movie business. It was novel and impressive to be practically enveloped by the pictures on the huge screen, and at times you had the almost eerie feeling of being a participant in the action. Nevertheless, the flaws in the process were very distracting. And except for the roller coaster scene it took an act of faith to imagine the process succeeding or having any impact on the motion picture industry.

Hazzard Reeves controlled Cinerama, and he and Mike got along very well. Through the years that Reeves and Waller had struggled to get Cinerama to the state it was in by the end of 1950, no motion picture executive or theatrical personality had shown anything resembling Mike's all-out enthusiasm for furthering the development and presentation of the process. Although he was broke, Todd still had a name with the public. Reeves correctly figured that Todd's precarious finances would make him struggle all the harder. Todd's drive and showmanship were needed to get Cinerama off the ground.

Lowell Thomas was part of one of several groups that were halfheartedly bidding to license the process for its initial public exposure. Thomas's expedition to Tibet had taken him away from his nightly newscast, as well as from his other business interests. He did not have the time to create and supervise the feature-length film that would introduce the Cinerama process. He, like Reeves, was swept off his feet by Todd. Years later Lowell Thomas said, "Mike performed a number of miracles with Cinerama. There's no doubt he was a man of unusual talents. He was a super salesman, a brilliant promoter and a master charmer of men and women." Todd talked his way into partnership with Thomas. They made a deal with Reeves for their company, Thomas-Todd Productions, for the license to make the first Cinerama film and, if it succeeded, an exclusive to use the process for a number of years thereafter.

Lowell Thomas and Thomas Dewey had big estates in Pawling, New York, and were close friends as well as neighbors. Lowell Thomas was respected by Dewey's political and business associates and dealt with them as equals. Thomas was one of the founding partners of Capital Cities Broadcasting, which owned radio stations and was getting into television, both on an ownership and production basis. Lowell Thomas's fame and his business reputation and connections, plus Todd's theatrical prominence, were more than enough to make Mike's financial problems of little consequence to this project. There was no difficulty raising the money needed to launch Thomas-Todd Productions and to finance the first film to be made in the Cinerama process.

Todd was ready to roll and get the Cinerama process launched. But prior to making the deals with Todd and Reeves, Lowell Thomas had promised his friend, Robert Flaherty, a fellow explorer and documentary maker (*Nanook of the North, Moana of the South Seas, Man of Aran*), that he would be the producer-director of the first Cinerama presentation. There were no specific plans for the production except that it would be a documentary. While Flaherty was formulating a concept, Todd was desperately searching for things to shoot.

Truman had just dismissed MacArthur for wanting to chase the Chinese across the Yalu River after they had entered the war in support of the North Koreans. It seemed that a majority of the American public and politicians supported MacArthur, and he was given a tumultuous hero's welcome and ticker tape parade in New York on his return from Korea. Everyone loves a parade, and Todd responded enthusiastically when the Cinerama assistant cameraman, Jack Priestly, held up the *Daily News* centerfold picture of the parade and said, "We should have shot this, Mike." Priestly says:

> Mike shouted, "Goddamnit, you're right. We blew it. But we'll go to Chicago." We packed up and went to Chicago for MacArthur's welcome at Soldier Field. We had the old-timer Robert Flaherty directing. And it rained to beat the band. It was pouring the whole time—everybody got drenched. And old man Flaherty got pneumonia and died."

With Cinerama entering his life, Todd abandoned plans for other Broadway shows. He jumped into the vacuum created by

Flaherty's absence. (After the Soldier Field filming in late April, Flaherty was bedridden until his death in late July.) If only to put together a better demonstration film, Todd and a small crew went out to grab some color footage to replace Waller's sepia sequences. Still taken with Priestly's idea of filming a parade, and to make a one-day job of it, he decided to go to West Point, where there would be scenic views of the Hudson in the bargain. Todd decided the sequence would be more exciting from the air. Jack Priestly recalls:

> We went up in a helicopter to get the dress parade on a Saturday morning. We're shooting it, and Mike keeps shouting, "Get lower! Lower! Lower!" We got so goddamned low that the cadets couldn't hear the band, and for the first time ever they were all out of step. It was total confusion. The police were calling us: "Get down, you're all gonna be arrested." We shot what we could and flew away, but it was a mess. We didn't get a usable foot of film.

When the Shriners held a convention in New York he seized the opportunity to film them in their crazy cars and funny hats. While this footage was being processed and edited, he decided to film Niagara Falls from a helicopter. Priestly remembers:

> We also shot from the Maid of the Mist with Fred Waller along. Mike and Fred were arguing constantly. Mike always wanted to do a lot more than Fred thought could be done with the process. Waller was not a fan of Mike's, Fred was low-keyed and Mike was a showman and came in and took over the whole shebang.

By the time I came home for summer vacation, these last two sequences were edited and ready for viewing. Nobody loved the parade, not even Todd. But the footage of the falls was fabulous. The idea in the back of his mind—and there were no better ones being put forth—was that he could shoot a series of festivals, fairs and musical events, with a sprinkling of scenery thrown in, and do a documentary called *This Is Cinerama*. The core of his argument was that the roller coaster ride was so startling and exciting—it was literally a dizzying experience—that if you led off with that, practically nothing you could do from there on would be wrong.

Mike now told me to take the crew and go out to Far Rockaway and shoot the roller coaster sequence in color. Harry Squires, the cameraman, felt this was merely an exercise and was to be used only to replace the sepia footage in the demo film, so he brought out only a collection of "short ends" instead of full thousand-foot rolls of films. It took about two hours to securely bolt the bulky camera on the roller coaster. Using the short ends meant we had to take the ride three times, but that was no bother. I promised the proprietor program credit, so the use of the roller coaster cost us nothing. Not including salaries or lab expenses, the production cost of the sequence was thirty-two dollars. For the rest of his life Todd never tired of telling people that "Michael shot the most famous sequence in motion picture history for less than it costs me to get a haircut." (He went to a barber shop tucked away upstairs at 21, and even in those days a shoe shine, manicure and tips cost him over twenty-five dollars.)

The roller coaster ride in color and the Niagara Falls footage both looked terrific and convinced Todd that his plan to have the roller coaster as the first full-screen sequence, with good travelogue material behind it, would be enough to introduce the process to the public. Todd was in overdrive, but his partners and associates were undecided how to proceed, except for Hazzard Reeves, who shared Todd's enthusiasm and was anxious to introduce the process to the public. With no better ideas in the offing, Todd was hesitantly given approval to proceed, as long as production costs were minimal and sufficient funds were left to shoot a different film if his idea failed.

Max Gendel puts a different slant on this decision-making process:

> Todd was not what you call an organization man and he couldn't put up with a board of directors. He used to say, "I'm too old to put up with stupidity and politeness." He wanted results. I remember once that there was some argument with the board of Cinerama, and he said, "Listen, you guys are only putting up your money. I've got my life riding on this." He believed it, and he was right.

Under Todd's insistent demands that they get on with it, arrangements were made for us to shoot festivals and a variety of other events in Europe that summer.

We and a crew of five—Harry Squires, the cameraman; Jack

Priestly, his assistant; Dick Peachman and Fred Bosch, the sound men; and Marty Philbin, the grip—flew off with the equipment to Scotland to film the Edinburgh Festival and Highland Games.

A strange but symptomatic relegation of responsibilities occurred before we left for Scotland. The Cinerama board gave me control of the funds to cover the production costs. This was due partially to Todd's boasting about my grabbing the roller coaster sequence for next to nothing. But as later became self-evident, there was a total lack of confidence in his ability to handle money. Lowell Thomas, Thomas's business manager and the member of the Wall Street underwriting firm who sat on the board sensed an Ivy League kind of kinship with me that inspired their confidence. My father never made any comment, but seemed pleased that I could shoulder this responsibility. He later told me that he had been so irritated by the board's haranguing him about production costs and the limited funds they would advance that he told them, "Well, if you don't trust me with the dough, let Michael handle it."

Most of the footage we shot in Scotland was unusable, either because it was dull, or because we had not yet learned how to deal with the most glaring fault of the process—the horizontal lines that crossed the three picture panels had to be shot head-on and kept in the center of the frame or they would unnaturally flange up or down. This fault, and the ever-present although considerably reduced fuzzy two seams where the pictures met, caused Todd such dissatisfaction that he was thinking about developing a whole new process, if necessary, a full year before *This Is Cinerama* opened.

The principal accomplishment in Scotland was to establish a loose working pattern that served us well the rest of the trip. Mary Martin describes Todd at work in Edinburgh:

I had just finished two and a half years on Broadway in *South Pacific* and was on vacation in Scotland with Richard, Heller and Larry. [Her husband, Richard Halliday; their daughter, Heller; and her son, Larry Hagman.] On our first day in Edinburgh, we came out of the hotel, and there was a tremendous crowd and a lot of excitement, so we tried to cross the street to see what all the commotion was about. Thousands of people were moving towards us. Suddenly we were able to see a man hunched over a camera, walking backwards, shouting all kinds of instructions. Richard and I looked at each other and said, "Oh no, we came all the way to see the Old World, and some Americans are making a bloody movie." We were hemmed in on all sides by the crowd—and the shouting man who was hunched over the camera backed right into me. He swore like mad and turned, ready to say some more, when flash went the teeth, and the steel gray-blue eyes lit up like stars, and he said, "Mary! What the hell are you doing in Edinburgh?" I said, "Mike, I might ask the same of you." He started to tell me, then stopped and shouted, "Everybody break for lunch." The thousands of extras were just spectators like us who had been interested in seeing what was going on. Mike was ordering them around and when he yelled, "Break!" they all went off. Mike took us for lunch and explained that this was the beginning of a whole new world in the motion picture business, a new process called Cinerama. We had the most wonderful four days following him about, although most of the time he was on the phone—I think even to Moscow for some reason or another. He said, "Mary, I'm going to stage the Edinburgh Tattoo just for you and your kids." Well, we had to get up to the castle at four o'clock in the morning, and it was freezing, but thrilling. And, of course, there were a couple of thousand people up there as well that he had conned to provide a background crowd for the marching bagpipe bands and all.

He promised that we would be his guests to see the premiere of Cinerama in New York, and, bless his soul, he remembered and kept his promise.

Much of the rest of the summer's filming was ad-libbed. The pattern that evolved was that Todd would leave me and the crew and go ahead to make arrangements for the next sequence to be shot. If there were two or more sequences to shoot at one stopover, he would remain for the filming of the most important and then go on, leaving me behind to shoot the secondary events.

From Edinburgh we went to Salzburg, where we were to film some of the festival. As beautiful as it is around Salzburg, Todd was dead set against shooting scenery without some kind of interesting action to justify its inclusion, as he wanted to avoid making the film a straight travelogue.

The festival authorities in Salzburg were rather sticky about our filming, but I am sure that he could have worked things out if another event hadn't fired his imagination.

After Salzburg we were going to Vienna, where one of our biggest and most expensive sequences was to be shot. Elisabeth Schwarzkopf had been engaged to sing an aria, backed up by Wilhelm Furtwängler conducting the Vienna Philharmonic. A secondary event was to do a sequence with the Vienna Boys' Choir.

In 1951 the cold war was going strong, and Austria was still a divided country, with the Russians in control of the eastern half. Vienna, like Berlin, was an enclave in the Russian zone under the authority of the four powers—Russia, the United States, England and France. On a monthly rotation each of the four powers assumed supervisory control of the city. By the time the crew and I arrived in Salzburg, Todd had heard that in three days the Russians would be relinquishing their month's control to the United States and a ceremony would take place in which the Russian flag would be lowered and, with attendant guards of honor from both countries, the American flag raised. The chauvinistic appeal of this symbolic replacement of the Stars and Stripes for the hammer and sickle was an event that Todd rightly felt would pack a wallop with American audiences. The American military commander told him that the Russian general in charge was politically astute and would never allow us to film the ceremony. The challenge of getting the Russian commander's okay appealed to him a thousand times more than charming the Salzburg Festival authorities.

The loose rubble had been cleared away, but the postwar reconstruction of Vienna had hardly begun. The Vienna Opera House was still a shambles. There was no tourist travel to the city, as the Russians made it very difficult to get a visa, and as yet there were no facilities to cater to tourists. The few deluxe but now dilapidated hotels in operation were occupied by the military and civil authorities of the four powers.

Todd departed for Vienna with bravura assurances that he would readily have things in hand for us to film the flag-switching ceremony. To keep ourselves busy in Salzburg, we filmed some folk dancers on a terrace of a lakeside inn in the nearby mountains. The views, lunch and beer were marvelous, the dancers a bore. The footage wasn't used in the film.

The following day came and went without a word from Todd. The ceremony was to take place the next morning at nine o'clock; so by suppertime I naturally assumed—not having heard from him—that he had been unsuccessful with the Russian general, even if he had even gotten to see him, and that the crew and I would go on to Vienna, as previously scheduled, by train the following afternoon. Priestly and I went out on the town that evening. Having had a fair amount to drink, I fell immediately asleep when I returned to the hotel a little after midnight. Half an hour later I was awakened when Mike called from Vienna. The phone connection was poor, but I was sure from his slurred speech that he was completely sloshed. He said it had taken all night and several bottles of slivovitz (an extremely potent plum brandy), but he had finally gotten the consent from the Russian commander and I should show up with the crew and equipment at the Hotel Bristol by 7:30 in the morning—"Good night."

I phoned Priestly and asked him to wake up the rest of the crew and bring them to my room. The night porter said the concierge had long since retired. I told him that it was an emergency and to get the concierge up. The crew and the concierge arrived at my room in a few minutes. A fistful of schillings convinced the concierge that the logistical problem I was describing was going to be worth his while. I needed a truck for the equipment and a limousine to transport the crew to Vienna—in six and a half hours. Harry Squires, who had been the height of cooperation and geniality up to this point and who was the archetypal old-fashioned cameraman—with a pencil-line moustache, dapper outfits, glib dialogue and supreme self-confidence—was very ruffled by the proceedings. He stepped forward and asserted that this was the worst fly-by-night operation he had ever been associated with during a lifetime in the movie business. Union regulations required that they have first-class accommodations and regular rest and work periods, and everything else was "golden time" and so on. He was not going to be awakened in the middle of the night to be told that he had to be driven in an automobile through hostile territory and then be expected to put in a full day's work immediately following. He was as willing and cooperative as the next fellow, but either first-class sleeping accommodations were provided or he was not moving or working tomorrow.

With more schillings in sight, the concierge indicated there was an overnight sleeper to Vienna that most conveniently departed at 2:30 A.M. and arrived at 7:00 A.M. I told him to get on the phone and book sleeper accommodations for four. Marty Philbin, the grip, had indicated that he was willing to accompany me with the equipment on the truck. The concierge returned and told everyone to pack. He had been able to get one compartment and three bedrooms. Harry was appeased by having a compartment to himself. I settled up the hotel bill and gave a final installment of schillings to the resourceful concierge. On split-second notice we were all off to Vienna to grab the documentary sequence of the decade.

Marty and I were both able to fall asleep in the bouncy cab of the truck. We were awakened only at the Russian checkpoint and then again as dawn was breaking, when we pulled into the outskirts of Vienna. The truck driver knew his way and drove us straight to the Hotel Bristol, which was completely taken over by high-ranking U.S. military and diplomatic personnel. While I was still checking at the front desk on the whereabouts of my father, the rest of the crew arrived rumpled, groggy and extremely disgruntled.

They reported that although they had tickets that entitled them to bedrooms and a compartment, the train itself was more suitable for the transport of cattle, and every square foot of it was fully occupied by the time they boarded. There was not even room for them to stand up in the aisle of the car; they had to squeeze in and lie down in a freezing, sooty gangway corridor. They said they had not only been stepped over or on by most of the crowd on the train, but the Russian guards had viciously kicked them awake to inspect their passports and visas.

The porter at the reception desk, who was attired in striped pants and tails, haughtily announced, "Mr. Todd is in the Imperial Suite." Squires turned purple. Marty said he would wait in the lobby, but the rest of the crew, uninvited, angrily went up with me on the elevator.

We walked into the elegant sitting room of the suite, which could have held five single bedrooms of a modern luxury hotel. Exhausted, the crew sank into the silk brocade settees, but I could see Harry was getting ready to tell Mike off when he appeared. I looked into one of the bedrooms. It was empty. I crossed over to examine the suite's other bedroom. It was almost as large as the sitting room. Mike's clothes were strewn all over the floor and he was sleeping at an angle on the large double bed, with his head half hanging over the mattress. Glancing at my watch, I saw that, incredibly, it was exactly 7:30. Softly, but with tremendous pride, I announced, "It's seven-thirty." No reply. Louder, I said, *"Wake up! We're here!"* Nothing. Shaking him, I shouted, "FOR CHRISSAKES, WE SOMEHOW GOT HERE. WAKE UP!" One eye opened, but no sign of recognition. More shouting from me and a brief description of the hell we had all gone through to get there. Finally, he was barely awake, but when he started to speak, he was, if possible, even more drunk than when I had spoken to him six and a half hours earlier. He asked the time. "Seven thirty-three." He rolled over, saying, "We got nothing but time," and fell immediately back to sleep. I spent another few minutes trying to get him up. It was impossible.

I went into the sitting room where the crew was asleep. I woke up Jack and Dick, told Dick to order coffee and rolls for everyone and asked Jack to come into the bedroom with me. Jack and I dragged Mike out of bed—he protested every inch of the way. We got him into the bathroom, which miraculously had a shower. We sat him on the toilet, took off our coats, rolled up our sleeves, undressed him and held him under the shower. After five minutes, by which time Jack and I were drenched, he began to show the first signs of life. He explained that it had taken several dozen toasts, with full glasses of slivovitz, before the Russian general had even begun to come around, and finally, semiconscious, he had agreed to our filming the ceremony.

By the time Dad was dressed and we all had coffee, it was 8:15. He insisted there was still plenty of time to get there and set up and that even if we were late, he was such buddies with the Russian and American commanders by now that for him they would gladly delay the changing-over ceremonies, or even repeat the procedure. It was 8:30 by the time we were in the truck and cars ready to proceed to command headquarters.

We arrived and started unloading the equipment, picking our way through a crowd of spectators at 8:50. Mike was shouting at us to hurry and at the American and Russian soldiers to vamp until we were ready. Proceedings started promptly at nine. He was screaming at us, "Are you getting this? Are you getting this?" In the time we had you could hardly get set up with a modern hand-held battery-operated camera and sound equipment, let alone the Cinerama three-headed monster. The crew and I ignored Mike and tried to get the equipment ready to shoot. "ARE YOU GETTING THIS? ARE YOU GETTING THIS?" Mike shouted, as he jumped up and down. The Russian flag went down, the American flag went up, with bugles blasting and anthems playing, all barely drowning out his voice. Later his shouts could be heard clearly on the sound tape. We shot 141 feet of the tail of the Russian guard of honor disappearing into the crowd of spectators. Somewhat unsure, Mike turned to us and asked, "Did you get it all?" Almost in unison we nodded wearily. Harry was our spokesman: "Yeah, sure, Mike."

We went back to the Bristol and slept soundly for about six hours. The crew said not one word to either Mike or me for the rest of the day. I was furious—if he had gotten up only fifteen minutes earlier, we would have had the shot.

The next day Mike sat silently through the rehearsal and prerecording session with Schwarzkopf, Wilhelm Furtwängler and a slightly scaled-down Vienna Philharmonic.

He said he had to get to Venice to make the arrangements for our filming there, and without the usual fanfare and speeches, he quietly departed, leaving me to shoot the Schwarzkopf sequence and later the Vienna Choir boys.

With the dollar at its then almighty postwar level, the operatic sequence was going to cost the now laughable sum of $3,000, but thus far we had spent next to nothing. Logic would dictate that we film it in a theater. However, this meant we would need to produce a suitably dressed audience, build or rent an appropriate set and at great difficulty and expense we would have to import the necessary lighting equipment, which was not available in Vienna. So we were going to shoot the sequence outdoors on the steps of the Schonbrunn Monument.

With rainy weather and other complications, it took us two and a half days before we completed the Schwarzkopf sequence. It never appeared in the film. For the master shot, the camera was set about eight feet off the ground—approximately level with Schwarzkopf and the orchestra, who were positioned on the steps—but the long horizontal wings of the monument were about forty feet above us. When I saw the shot projected several weeks later, the wings of the monument in the side panels were distorted downwards at the seams. The Schonbrunn Monument in Cinerama resembled the TWA terminal at Kennedy Airport. Only one lab in New York was set up to do our work, and the demo unit in Oyster Bay was the only place where it could be projected. It took a week for anyone to see what we had shot in Europe and give us a report.

Our last day in Vienna was clear and lovely, as were the voices of the Vienna Boys' Choir, whom we filmed in less than an hour.

If you like that kind of thing, and several million Cinerama patrons did, you were almost totally immersed by the tow-headed congregation of lads with their angelic faces and voices.

The next stop was Venice, where we shot the annual regatta, a Rio Carnival–type parade, but set on water in the Grand Canal.

Dad had a suite at the Royal Danieli, where he introduced me to a fellow American guest at the hotel, Lorraine Manville. She and her brother Tommy were the principal heirs of the Johns Manville fortune. How and where he met her I have no idea, but at the time I assumed they had simply come across each other at the hotel.

David Lawlor says that Lorraine was an investor in both *As the Girls Go* and *Peep Show* and intimates that they had an affair. All my knowledge of their relationship indicates they never went to bed together, but that there was a romantic interest on Lorraine's part that she toyed with but never acted upon. Today Todd would certainly be considered a male chauvinist, insofar as he disdained the sexual attractiveness of older women. He found Lorraine lively and amusing and in the following five years she became a substantial backer of his.

Lorraine had been married and divorced three times and was using her maiden name. She was fiftyish and had a daughter—usually referred to as Lorraine junior—who was in her early twenties.

Lorraine senior was doing a continental tour and as a home base maintained a suite at the Hotel Meurice in Paris. She was traveling about in a black Chevrolet convertible with her chauffeur, Raymond, an ex-merchant marine sailor. Although she had thick ankles and shapeless legs she had a trim figure, a pleasant face that was often charmingly animated and the most beautiful skin I've ever seen on anyone over the age of three. A few years later, I found out that her annual disappearance for the month of February was to have the skin on her face peeled. I have heard that this was an extremely painful treatment, but it certainly produced the desired results.

The day before he was to leave for Milan, Mike, Lorraine and I were in the sitting room of our suite at the Danieli, and Mike was trying, with only partial success, to make a series of telephone calls. Lorraine was trying to converse with us, but I remained silent, well aware that Mike was becoming increasingly irritated with her idle chat while he was, with great difficulty, trying to conduct important business on the telephone. Before he could lose his temper, I took Lorraine by the hand and led her into our twin-bedded bedroom and started a conversation with her. There were no chairs in the bedroom, so we each sat on one of the beds. Relaxing, I propped up the pillows on top of the bolster on my bed and stretched out. Following my example, Lorraine kicked off her shoes and did the same on the adjacent twin bed. At a point in the conversation, undoubtedly because we were in Italy, we both were gesticulating with our arms when our hands touched. The twin beds were quite close to each other. For all of Lorraine's money, I cannot say what possessed me, but I kept hold of her hand. Although our discussion was about something innocuous, we held and caressed hands like twelve-year-olds. Absorbed with our hand holding and conversation, we were surprised when Dad suddenly entered the room.

He did a fast double take and asked, "What the hell is going on here?" In an innocent, sweetie-pie voice, Lorraine answered, "Just getting to know each other."

"Well, cut it out during office hours," he said. And while Lorraine was leaning over to put her shoes back on, he gave me a perplexed look.

Lorraine had no fixed schedule, so she volunteered to drive him to Milan. He loved convertibles and the weather was great, but he accepted the offer only on the condition that he could do the driving. Before they left for Milan, Mike told me that it could take a few days to set things up with the La Scala people. "But in the meantime," he said, "don't use up a lot of film shooting scenery. Do you hear me good? Don't shoot any film!"

The next morning I went sightseeing and discovered the beautiful little canals near the hotel. After lunch I found Harry Squires and asked him if he minded spending the afternoon with me. We rented a gondola and made a four-hour tour of all the canals close to the Piazza San Marco. Without my telling him, Harry knew what I had in mind and said, "Before he left, your father took me aside and told me not to let you shoot any scenery—but I think this is terrific stuff. Let's do it." Harry was still nursing a grudge over the train ride from Salzburg and the flag-changing fiasco in Vienna.

That night at dinner in the Royal Danieli I cornered an attractive American couple and asked them if they had a day to spare. We photographed them getting into the gondola and then did a full day's filming that edited down to a seven-minute sequence in *This Is Cinerama*. Aside from being beautifully scenic, it was a slow-motion roller coaster, as the canals were narrow and the buildings on either side hemmed you in; and, most fortuitously, they remained in the side panels, so did not bend unnaturally like the wings of the Schonbrunn Monument. Harry and I and the rest of the crew said nothing about the filming to Mike when we arrived in Milan a couple of days later.

As I had over a week left before the start of school, Lorraine volunteered to give me a jiffy holiday by driving me from Milan through Switzerland to Paris. I would have three days of a scenic drive and a day or two to sightsee in Paris for the first time. Before Lorraine, Raymond and I set off the morning after the crew and I had arrived in Milan, my father delivered a short farewell address. He told me how pleased and proud he was about the way I'd handled myself through the summer and that this was only the beginning of a long, successful and happy future we would have working together. Then, looking me in the eye, he said, "Now about this Manville dame. No funny business along the way. She's a grandmother. Pick on somebody your own age."

Shortly after we arrived in Paris a phone call came through from Mike in Milan. He said that he had made all the arrangements at La Scala and had lit both the stage and the house enough for some test shots. It would be a costly sequence to film, as he was using the full opera company and orchestra. He wasn't going to take any chances; he wanted to look at the test footage himself. He was flying to Paris the next day and that afternoon we would fly back to New York together.

When he arrived in Paris, he brought only a small overnight case that contained a change of underwear, his toilet kit and three cans of negative. Having shipped the Venice footage, I knew that it was a long and complicated process, getting the film out of Italy. I asked him how he had gotten through customs. He said he had timed his departure perfectly, arriving at the gate, case in hand, just as the ramp was being pulled from the cabin door. There was barely time to examine his ticket, let alone his bag.

On the plane to New York, the thought occurred to me—and I asked Mike—how he planned to get the negative into the United States, as I knew it was not a simple procedure. He said, "I'm just going to walk through." I said, "That's terrible. What if you get caught? It'll be a huge mess." He said, "Look, the film's not pornographic, it has no intrinsic value, it's just test footage and has no significance for customs. I'm just saving them and me all the trouble of going through the formalities."

In New York, as we were going through customs, he was practically waving his bag in front of the inspector's nose and said, "Boy, that dame had some nerve hanging that hunk of ice on her kid." Two days before a woman had been arrested trying to smuggle a big piece of jewelry into the country by putting it on her ten-year-old daughter as if it were a piece of junk kiddie jewelry. The inspector smiled and said, "You're traveling light," and waved him on. I was so nervous about the cans of film that I misplaced my yellow immunization card (at the time, a necessary document to enter the United States) and had to wait three hours for a health officer to come and give me a superfluous smallpox vaccination.

When I finally got home that evening, Mike said that the lab was rushing through the test footage and we would be able to look at it and everything else we had shot that summer the next day at Oyster Bay. He was going to return to Milan the day after, and I was to meet with the board to talk about the problems and practicalities of working with the equipment and to turn in my accounts.

Then, shaking his finger at me, he said, "You disobeyed your old man, didn't you? You shot a bunch of stuff in Venice as soon as my back was turned."

"We were just sitting around and didn't use that much film—"

He cut me off: "Well, they all seem crazy about it, but we'll wait and see for ourselves tomorrow."

The La Scala test footage was very murky, but there were no distortions. However, a huge amount of additional lighting would be required. (This was years before the development of high-speed color film.) Mike was thrilled about the prospect of shooting the highlights of *Aida* with the best opera company in the world—at a bargain-basement figure.

The sequence in the small canals had been nicely edited and looked great. In front of everyone at Oyster Bay, Mike gave me a tongue-lashing: "You've been totally disobedient and disrespectful," he said. "See that this never happens again . . ." And then, putting his arm around my shoulder, he said, ". . . or we will have to give you a raise."

After seeing the distortions in some of the footage we shot,

Todd took Waller aside and complained to him about not being forewarned that there were severe limitations to the camera angles that could be used. Waller told Mike that he *had* explained. However, Waller had always played down the various flaws in his process. Todd's enthusiasm had been so great that he had previously accepted Waller's vague explanations, but now he began to have questions about any broad use of Cinerama. His extreme displeasure, however, was only privately expressed to me at home that evening. He was still convinced, shortcomings and all, that *This Is Cinerama* would have a big impact and be a big success. But his growing awareness of the problems convinced him that something was going to have to be done to solve them. He told me not to discuss this with the board when I met with them, as he wanted to tackle this question in his own way when he finished the La Scala sequence and whatever else he might pick up in Europe. He also warned me that with the exception of Hazzard Reeves he was having his troubles with the board. I was to be very careful what I said to them.

While he had occasionally checked with me regarding the money being spent during the summer, he now asked me for "the bottom line"—through Venice. I told him it was $14,780. He couldn't believe it: "That's hardly even cigar money. Have you got all your own expenses in there?" I told him that there was just short of $500 from my out-of-pocket expenses in the figure—there was about $280 or $290 that I knew I had laid out, but I neither had vouchers for this money nor could I properly account for it otherwise. He said, "For Godsake, put it in, or I'm gonna disown you. Honesty is one thing, but you're overdriving the green."

He flew back to Milan with a few sample frames from the test footage, to show Harry Squires what they had. Jack Priestly tells about Mike's quick trip to New York from Milan:

> Mike said, "I ran out of cigars and I'm going home for the weekend. Here's a thousand dollars to cover the crew's expenses. Don't steal more than half." When Mike came back he asked me, "How much did you steal?" I told him, "Two hundred and fifty dollars." He said, "That's okay—take some and leave some."

Mrs. Manville's daughter showed up in Milan after Mrs. Manville drove off to Paris with Michael junior. The daughter was married to this Belgian nobleman, and I think she was divorced or in the process of getting a divorce from him. Anyway, she couldn't get her kid out of Belgium. Mike offered me ten grand to kidnap the kid. I was young and crazy, but not that crazy.

The day after he flew to Milan, I met with Lowell Thomas; Thomas's business manager, Frank Smith; Hazzard Reeves and the member of the Wall Street underwriting firm who sat on the board. They told me they were delighted with most of the sequences we had filmed. It was evident, although not specifically stated, that Todd's concept for the initial Cinerama presentation had been accepted and, barring unforeseen developments, would be carried through to completion. Despite Mike's instructions, I did not put in for my undocumented out-of-pocket expenses, as I wanted to keep the total under $15,000. Thomas and the other board members were amazed that so little money had been spent on the production. Then, to my shame, I was induced by the conspiratorial atmosphere of the meeting to acknowledge that, yes, Todd probably would be spending vastly greater sums completing the sequences he was going to shoot in Europe. They didn't actually say so, but I felt they were assuming that he would have to be closely watched.

Jack Priestly said that even though they had forced the exposure on the La Scala test footage and—as he and Harry Squires could see—the lab had souped up the processing, there was just barely enough light to see an image.

And, of course, we were in tight on the stage for the test shots, but when we pulled back we'd have to use every lamp they had in Italy and send over for a lot from England. While we were getting and setting up all the lights in the opera house, Mike couldn't sit still, so we went off to Barcelona to film a bullfight. He wanted to put the camera right in the center of the ring and let the bull charge straight at it. But it was the only Cinerama camera in the world then and Harry wouldn't let him. Even so, we grabbed enough to make a sequence that was in the film. To finally get the La Scala lit, we had three blocks of generators outside. Mike would do anything to get what he wanted.

Todd filled the opera house with a capacity audience in formal dress for only a thousand dollars. He hired the hottest concert pianist in Italy that season and advertised in the Milan newspapers that a piano recital and portions of *Aïda* by the La Scala company would be seen at the opera house free by anyone who arrived by one o'clock that afternoon in full formal attire. The opera house was quickly filled and thousands of angry Milanese in tuxes and ball gowns were turned away.

The La Scala sequence worked out beautifully. The quality and stereophonic effect of the sound system developed by Reeves was dramatically demonstrated. And Todd got two bites out of this cherry, as a ballet from the opera was used in the beginning of the film and the finale of act 2 of *Aïda* brought down the curtain on the first part of *This Is Cinerama*. (Todd's ideas of road-showing *Cinerama*, charging advanced prices, selling reserved seats and having an intermission were all used.)

When the filming was finished in Europe and Todd had returned to the States, a split between him and the board developed that was never healed. He was not used to working with boards of directors and he was in a hurry. His idea for the initial Cinerama presentation was working out, and he expected carte blanche to proceed as he planned. He was now also insisting that steps should be taken immediately to eliminate the seams and the problems that severely limited the angles from which any sequences could be shot. On Broadway, working with his own money or silent backers, his decisions were final. With Thomas-Todd Productions and Cinerama, Todd was providing his ideas and enthusiasm, but none of the money. What right did he have to yell and try to bully the rest of the board into doing everything his way and his way only? The board was now aware of the awkward filming problems and the imperfections of the seams, but with Waller's assurances that they would be minimized, they were in no rush to make extensive and expensive alterations to the process.

Aside from the irritation caused by Todd's domineering ways, there was an unfortunate personal twist that developed involving one of the key members of the board. This company director had a socialite wife who was bored and drank too much. One of the things that bored her most was her husband. Much to everyone's embarrassment—especially Todd's—she found Todd exciting and attractive. She made some very unsubtle public overtures to him. Although she and her husband were divorced a few years later, he was still trying at that time to maintain the facade of being happily married. Understandably, he resented his wife's play for Todd, even though Todd had not only done nothing to encourage her, but had ignored her to the point of being rude. Todd had neither the time nor the patience to respond to these overtures or to playfully dismiss them.

Of greater significance to his final position in Cinerama was the deterioration of his relationship with Lowell Thomas and his business manager, Frank Smith. Thomas was busy with his broadcasting and other business affairs and was willing to let Todd take an active role, but he wanted to be consulted and deferred to—he did not take kindly to being bullied and condescended to by Todd.

On a weekend visit to Thomas's home in Pawling, Todd told Governor Dewey that he lost the election to Truman because he never took his coat off and showed his suspenders during the hot summer's campaign. Dewey replied that if he had, the perspiration would have shown on his shirt. Todd said, "That's the trouble—you perspire, but the voters and Truman sweat. And your homburg was the final kiss of death. It was a guy wearing a homburg who foreclosed on mortgages during the Depression." Dewey and Thomas were not edified or amused.

On the day of reckoning Frank Smith was able to pay back Todd for his insolence.

The roller coaster, the Niagara Falls sequence and all the European shots Mike and I had filmed made up a satisfactory first act of a feature film. The board was convinced they could put together a good second act, without Todd and the aggravation of dealing with him.

Todd's financial situation was of great assistance in easing him out of Cinerama. It would be another year before his bankruptcy was settled; although there was a verbal understanding as to how much stock was his in Thomas-Todd Productions, none was actually issued, since it could be attached. For my work and contribution to the film, in addition to the $275 a week I received while I was working during the summer, I was given some stock. But this was only a fraction of what Mike was supposed to get.

Largely to get Todd out of the way and partially to reassure and compensate him while the production of *This Is Cinerama* was being put in other hands, Lowell Thomas and Dewey a match between Todd and Robert Moses. Moses, York City park commissioner, head of the Tribor Authority and the power behind the Long Islan

Commission, was the most influential nonelected official in the state of New York. For a full generation, Dewey and every other governor of New York—as well as the mayors of New York City—who had to fight for the funding for their projects had come to discover, to their irritation and chagrin, that Moses almost always got what he wanted; through the Triborough Bridge Authority and other bodies he had tremendous sources of revenue at his disposal. Dewey and Thomas felt they were throwing Todd into the lion's den. But, always unpredictable, Todd got along famously with Moses.

Robert Moses justifiably regarded the creation of Jones Beach as one of his greatest achievements. To further enhance this facility, Moses had an outdoor stadium of 8,200 seats built on the edge of a bay a few hundred yards from the east end of the beach. It was his intent to have musical spectacles presented here during the summer season to rival and surpass such similar facilities as the Kansas City Starlight Theater and the St. Louis Municipal Opera. Moses was delighted to have a showman of Todd's reputation as the impresario of his nearly completed theater, which would be inaugurated in the summer of 1952.

For Todd this was an enterprise he could carry out with his eyes half closed. And, with the necessary and heavy subsidization of the Long Island State Park Commission, principally in the form of a low rental, there was a chance to make a decent few bucks. While Todd was kept busy creating a show for the new stadium at Jones Beach, the board took over the production of the balance of *This Is Cinerama*.

The plan that evolved for the second act of the film was to retain General Merian Cooper to film the scenic wonders of America the Beautiful. Cooper, who was chief of staff during World War II for General Claire Chennault, creator of the Flying Tigers, was a distinguished longtime movie executive and producer of such films as *Fort Apache* and the originals of *King Kong* and *The Four Feathers*. With Todd still participating in the decision-making process, it was decided to open the second act with a tour of Dick Pope's Cypress Gardens, featuring its waterskiing show. An exciting and scenic variant of the roller coaster was put together with a camera in one of the motorboats whizzing through, around and over the little islands and peninsulas of the Gardens. Paul Mantz, the leading motion picture aerial-stunt photographer, was retained to take a series of daring low-altitude shots of America's various scenic wonders.

I won't get into the labyrinth of corporations and their interlocking relationships that were changed and manipulated from the beginning of 1951 until the end of 1952, but Thomas-Todd Productions, the licensee for the use of the process and the producer of *This Is Cinerama*, stood to take the lion's share of the profits to be derived from the film and the exploitation of the process. While nominally one of the major stockholders of Thomas-Todd Productions, Todd, by the end of 1951, was an outsider looking in.

Although he hadn't given up the struggle, Todd knew that the Cinerama board was going to call the shots and he wasn't. He was tired and largely resigned to his back-seat position, but not really dissatisfied, as they were following the course of action he had advocated. In this state of mind he proposed—when I returned from school for my Christmas vacation—that we go off to Golden Beach, Florida, again, to get away from it all.

Eddie Fisher was one of the most famous PFCs in the army during the Korean War. His recording career had just begun to boom. His single, "Anytime," had sold over a million records that year. Milton Blackstone, Jennie Grossinger's publicity genius, had become Eddie's mentor and manager. Blackstone asked Mike to look up Eddie and take him out to dinner while we were in Florida. Milton said that Eddie was a wonderful kid, but not ideally suited to military life, and he was undoubtedly missing New York and show business. A weekend visit would be a welcome break for Eddie from his army routine.

Blackstone said Eddie had unsuccessfully auditioned as a singer for *As the Girls Go* three years before. My father told Eddie that he remembered this audition, as well as his performances at the Copacabana, where he had been the club's production singer for over a year. Several years later Eddie told me that he had gone through the entire Copa chorus line at the age of seventeen. But while he had this and the first of his big recording successes behind him, he was still a shy and insecure young man when he joined us in Florida.

He appeared on the scene early one afternoon. Mike gave him a hearty welcome and told him to get into a bathing suit—we were not going to waste a minute of sunshine. He began to tell Eddie stories about Milton Blackstone and some of his promotional exploits and then segued into stories about Winchell and Runyon. Like a camp director, Mike insisted we go in for a long swim. He was crazy about the water and swimming was his favorite and almost only form of exercise.

After we had finished our swim, a couple of teenage girls recognized Eddie and ran off to tell their friends. We were in an area that even during the holidays was never crowded, but Mike sensed that the news of Eddie's presence was going to travel fast and that soon there would be a crowd of teenage girls hanging around. He told Eddie and me that we should get a move on—not to disappoint the expected gathering, we should build a little stage so that Eddie could do a medley of his hits. Eddie looked at Mike in total disbelief. Mike had already begun to gather up some driftwood and was using it to push sand in a mound, to form a stage in front of a dune at the back of the beach that would serve as a natural amphitheater. Mike told the girls, who had returned with some friends, that Eddie was going to give them an alfresco concert, but that they would have to help build the stage.

By the time Mike was satisfied with the arrangements, twenty to thirty girls and a few of their boyfriends had gathered. Mike made a grandiloquent introduction, and Eddie stepped forward and did half a dozen songs. He got a standing ovation. Eddie walked away, but Mike brought him back for an encore. Then we exited to tumultuous applause. Although nothing had been further from his mind, or more contrary to his natural instincts, Eddie had enjoyed giving this impromptu concert under Mike's spirited staging of the event.

Mike was occasionally playful but hardly ever mischievous, and he disliked practical jokes. On a weekend late in June 1952, however, he played a prank that backfired on a friend.

Sunday afternoon was sunny and warm and we had passed the time on our terrace, reading the newspapers. We had no specific plans for supper, and Mike called Max Gendel to ask him to spend the rest of the afternoon with us and then join us for a meal.

Max's plentiful supply of Broadway gossip always made him an amusing companion for Mike. At the end of the afternoon we went downstairs to have a cup of coffee before dressing to go out to dinner. Max and I were in the living room when Dad shouted from the kitchen.

"What time is it?"

"Six-forty," I replied.

He ran into the room smiling broadly and asked, "Who would you like to be the next President of the United States?"

I thought he was being silly and made no reply, but Max seriously pondered the question. After a few moments Max said, "Paul Douglas." [The junior senator from the state of Illinois.]

"That's an inspired choice," Mike said. "He'll fit perfectly. But listen, we've still got a few seconds. Why Douglas?"

Max replied, "I like his brand of politics, and I ran into him a few times while I was touring with *This Is the Army*, he seemed to be a nice guy."

Before Max had finished his explanation, Mike was dialing a number. "Hello, this is Mike Todd. I want to speak to Walter . . . I know he's on the air in a few minutes, but this is urgent. Tell him I'm calling . . .

"Walter, you've got to promise me that you'll never say who this came from, and even if you do, I'll deny it on a stack of Bibles, but the big boys are not going to let Truman call any of the shots, and they're going to dump both Kefauver and Stevenson. And now this is the real shocker. They're going to slide in Paul Douglas. Good-bye, Walter. I never spoke to you."

Max and I were both dumbfounded. Mike was smiling as if he could already visualize Douglas's inauguration. I was the first to say anything.

"Why is Winchell going to take your word on what the Democratic bosses are going to do at the convention?"

This was before primaries played an important role in the selection of nominees.

"Well, it just so happens, Mr. Wise Guy, that last night I'm at the Stork Club, and Jake Arvey is sitting at a table having a discussion with Jim Farley." [Jake Arvey was the Democratic party boss in Illinois at the time, and James Farley was an influential Democratic leader in New York.] "Arvey called me over to say hello and asked me what I was doing. I started telling him about Cinerama and in walks Winchell and sees the three of us sitting there, having what looks to be a serious discussion. We just cut up a few old touches, but Winchell is seated at his table and dying. I pretended like I didn't even see him come in the room. This goes on for about five minutes and when I leave Arvey and Farley, Winchell grabs me and says, 'What the hell were they saying?' I play innocent and actually tell him the truth, but Winchell felt sure that I knew something and wasn't talking. Now, wait and see what happens." And Mike turned on the radio.

Winchell's lead item was a self-proclaimed exclusive that was practically a verbatim repeat of Mike's phoned report to him. Max was worried about the possible repercussions, especially the alienation of Winchell. Half-seriously, I said, "This is a hell of a way to run a country."

"It's as good a way as any to choose a President, and it just so happens Douglas would make a hell of a good one."

The next day Truman was furious and took no pains to conceal his anger. He said that it was going to be an open convention and that neither he nor anybody else was going to select a candidate in a smoke-filled room. Douglas, of course, denied that he knew of any plans to make him a candidate and stated that he was not in the running for the nomination. The more denials Douglas made and the stronger he made them, the more publicity he got, which in turn produced more comments from Truman. For a ten-day period, a month before the Democratic National Convention, a segment of the press and public began seriously to consider Douglas as a possible candidate. At the convention it was a battle between Senator Estes Kefauver and Governor Adlai Stevenson, which the latter won on the third ballot.

About ten years later I was making frequent trips to Chicago; I was supervising the operation and booking of two theaters we had purchased there during the initial run of *Around the World in 80 Days*. I was in a restaurant with an associate, and a few tables away I saw "Honest Abe" Marovitz, an old friend of my father's whom I knew from my early childhood. Marovitz had been a prominent figure in Democratic circles and had been a Supreme Court justice in Illinois. My associate told me that Marovitz had recently been appointed to the federal bench. I went over and congratulated Judge Marovitz on his appointment. When I returned to my table, my associate told me that Marovitz's federal appointment had been a long time coming. Early in 1952 Senator Douglas had nominated him to the federal bench, and Truman had approved the appointment. Just before confirmation of the appointment had gone through, a rumor had come up out of nowhere that Douglas was being handpicked by the Democratic bosses as the presidential candidate to be sprung on the convention. Truman was furious because he thought that Douglas or his associates were behind the rumor, and he squelched Marovitz's appointment to the federal bench.

The more Todd was being eased out of the picture at Cinerama, the more vocal he became about the basic flaws in the process. He succinctly stated his position: "You can't spend your life on the roller coaster. Someday someone's going to want to say, 'I love you,' and the seams are going to get in the way." Of course, as a principal stockholder (by verbal understanding with all parties concerned) he confined his criticism to his fellow directors; he was not going to diminish his or their potential profits by publicly voicing his dissatisfaction. He was intent, however, on getting the process perfected to the point where after the initial success of Cinerama—of which he was supremely confident—they would be ready to shoot a spectacle with a story.

A Night in Venice, the show he was producing at Jones Beach, was based on a Johann Strauss operetta, which he freely adapted with a young couple, Ruth and Thomas Martin. It required a very free adaptation to fill out the vast expanses of the Marine Theatre stage and the ninety-foot lagoon that separated it from the 8,200-seat amphitheater. Todd filled the lagoon with gondolas, a water ballet and a submersible fountain and integrated a fireworks display into the show. The music, songs and dialogue were made audible by an adequate amplification system, but even with sets forty and fifty feet high, the action on the stage looked like a marionette show viewed from afar. An effect, in a ballroom sequence, of champagne bubbles floating into the sky was interpreted by John Chapman of the *News*, who was seated in one of the front rows, as an invasion of moths. Nevertheless, in deference to Moses and Todd and/or the refreshing breeze from the ocean, the show received good notices—with the words *spectacular, lavish* and *extravaganza* in liberal use to describe the evening's proceedings. Dewey made an opening-night dedication speech.

Except for Friday and Saturday nights, which were almost completely sold out in advance, the business directly corresponded to the daily temperature reading. Seventy-five degrees or below produced a quarter of a house. Anything over ninety-five degrees resulted in a turnaway crowd. Good reviews, word of mouth and extensive advertising and publicity produced all the business the thermometer reading allowed. At the start of the season Todd thought we were getting a short count and had me spend almost every night of that summer at Jones Beach, minding the store.

Lorraine bankrolled *A Night in Venice* to the tune of approximately $400,000. In the next five years her loans to Mike and "investments" in Todd's projects were to increase to over $2 million. She got it all back with interest; and although on the odd occasion—always when her accountant was in attendance—she made a cursory attempt at adopting a businesslike attitude about the money, she really suffered less anxiety about it than most people would have about the loan of a paperback book. She was not a pushover; she could be very tough when she wanted to be.

After her father's death in 1925, she fought her uncle for a much more substantial piece of the Manville fortune than he was willing to concede to her and her brother Tommy. Tommy had been ready to settle with their uncle early on for a fraction of what Lorraine finally, after a ten-year struggle, secured for both of them.

My father and I both had an easygoing relationship with Lorraine, but he was embarrassed by the fact that he was being bankrolled by a rich dame and quite successfully hid the fact from all but his closest associates. Midori Tsuji, who came to work for him during the spring of 1952, when he was preparing the production of *A Night in Venice*, and was to remain his secretary for the rest of his life, thought she was about to be fired just a few weeks after starting the job:

> We were at Jones Beach and Mr. Todd was in an office, having a production meeting. I knocked at the door, stuck my head in and announced, "Mrs. Manville is on the phone." He gave me an icy glare, came out and took the call, and then after he'd finished the meeting, he took me aside and chewed my head off. "Never announce her name," he said. "It's nothing to do with them." Well, I caught on, and I'd come in and whisper it in his ear, and then eventually we developed a code and I'd say, "It's thirty-one B calling." That was her penthouse suite at the Carlyle.

Lorraine never flaunted the fact that for five years she was Mike's big backer. She shunned publicity. As far as she was concerned, her playboy brother Tommy kept the family name too much in the news. Also, any publicity about her investment in Todd's projects would have produced a plague of promoters at her doorstep.

Mike was somewhat unfair with Lorraine; if she called him too often to find out what was going on, or just to have a chat, he would scold her—sometimes not too gently—for interfering with business. But when he ran out of other people to talk to and was keyed up, he would often call her at almost any time of the day or night and give her a report of what was happening.

Late in the autumn of 1952 I decided to become formally engaged to Sarah Weaver, the girl next door from Irvington. Dick Winston, a fraternity brother from Amherst, had gone to work at his uncle's famous jewelry establishment on Fifth Avenue. I went in and asked him to show me a selection of engagement rings. What I had in mind would have been appropriate as one of the side-setting stones for the smaller of the range of diamonds he brought out. I told him I'd look around before I decided. When I explained my predicament to my father, he said, "Call Lorraine. She knows more about rocks than Dick and Harry Winston combined."

Lorraine was delighted to take me to her jeweler, where she helped me select a flawless one-carat diamond that cost just what I intended to spend.

A Night in Venice ran as scheduled through Labor Day. It had made little more than its operating expenses, which was not too bad, considering that it had been a rather cold and wet summer. For an inaugural season, Moses and the Long Island State Park Commission were satisfied with the results. However, it was a profitless exercise for Todd. It was decided, and it became the policy of the theater, to play an attraction with any popularity for two consecutive summers. *A Night in Venice* did slightly better the second year, but paid back only a small portion of Lorraine's investment. As Todd vociferously pointed out, any semblance of intimacy, even for a huge outdoor theater, was destroyed by the ninety-foot lagoon separating the seats from the stage. No matter how much use was made of the lagoon itself, something had to be done to get the performers closer to the audience. A few years later a thirty-foot forestage was built, on which as many scenes as possible were played. This immeasurably aided the staging of shows at the theater. Moses and the commission realized after the second season that they needed to subsidize the shows to keep the theater going. This was of no assistance to Mike or Lorraine. But a dozen years later a two-summer run of a musical version of *Around the World in 80 Days* was put together by Harold Adamson; the composer Sammy Fain; a stage and screen writer, Sig Herzig; and me, and produced a healthy profit for all.

The whole summer of 1952 Todd was in a state of nervous agitation. *This Is Cinerama*, in the final editing stages, was turning out to be all that he had envisioned. But with his bankruptcy not yet settled, his participation in the anticipated bonanza was still not on paper. He could not take possession of his sizable share of Thomas-Todd stock until he squared away his debts. Equally frustrating was the cold shoulder he was getting from the board. By the middle of summer he gave up struggling with his fellow directors. He shut up, and kept his own counsel. Only to Max Gendel and me did he confide that if the Cinerama people were not going to try to perfect the process, he would get out and do it on his own. But first the picture had to open and the process be acclaimed before he could settle up and move on. After Cinerama was publicly unveiled, Todd borrowed some money from Joe Schenck and more from Lorraine and settled his bankruptcy. I got $127,500 for my chunk of stock, which I immediately turned over in the form of a loan to my father. His settlement was, in addition to the dubious pleasure of inaugurating the Jones Beach Marine Theatre, less than twice what I had received and was only a fraction of what his promised piece of Thomas-Todd Productions was then worth. Without a written contract he settled for what he could get.

This Is Cinerama had its world premiere in the Broadway Theatre on September 30, 1952. Mike got us two center-aisle seats in the last row of the orchestra. His settlement discussions had long since reached the insulting stage. He was not only going to be the first person connected with this motion picture milestone to get out of its corporate structure, but he saw to it that he and I were going to be the first people out of the theater, once he saw it was going to be a hit.

Lowell Thomas, pictured in the prologue on the small screen, projected the low-keyed authority and image of worldly wisdom that twenty-plus years of broadcasting had implanted in the American public's mind. When he told the opening-night audience that what they were about to witness heralded a new era in motion pictures, they believed him. When the screen opened up to its immense proportions, and they saw and felt they were on the Far Rockaway roller coaster, they knew that Lowell Thomas had calmly understated his prediction.

Not that there had ever been any doubt in Todd's mind, but he allowed himself a small smile of satisfaction as the audience gave a sustained and tumultuous reception to the opening scene. The process was a success, and motion pictures would never quite be the same again.

The first act was all the material that we had filmed. It was very well received. Mike did not want to see or talk to anyone, so we ducked out of the theater as soon as the first act was ending. We returned just in time to catch the beginning of the second act, which received as good if not even better audience response than the first act. Of course, nothing duplicated the initial surprise and excitement of the roller coaster. Thomas-Todd Productions received its appropriate film credit, as did my father and I for the first-act material. The opening-night audience was generous with its applause. Again, we ducked out of the theater without seeing or talking to anyone and went straight home.

A few hours later Max excitedly called to report that for the first time in history the New York *Times* was heralding a motion picture opening on its front page. Not even the introduction of sound or color had prompted America's most prestigious paper to run a front-page story. Bosley Crowther, the New York *Times* film critic, in his page-one piece wrote: ". . . it was evident that the distinguished gathering was as excited and thrilled by the spectacle presented as if it were seeing motion pictures for the first time."

Buried at the end of this story was Crowther's mention of the bug that was going to keep Todd busy for the next two years: "And the question arose as to what might, indeed, be done with this new panoramic system in the way of developing a dramatic story on the screen."

Practically all of the reviews were raves. The other critics, like Crowther, questioned whether the process could be used for a narrative film.

Mike had been grimly quiet from the time we had dressed for the opening until he had finished reading the last of the afternoon dailies eighteen hours later. His only indication of pride or pleasure was the thin smile he had allowed himself when the

243

audience started to roar with delight at the beginning of the roller coaster scene. The first horse of his parlay had come in a twenty lengths' winner.

Todd's simple concept of how to present Cinerama made it a gigantic success. *This Is Cinerama* played in only seventeen theaters throughout the world, and it was, when it completed its run, the third-largest-grossing motion picture in history.

Although Mike had told me about his plans on several occasions during the previous two months, I was confused by his reaction to the instantaneous success and impact of Cinerama—which certainly went beyond my expectations and, I think, even exceeded his. Aside from monosyllabic answers to my direct questions, he maintained a totally unnatural silence for almost a day.

By the middle of the afternoon following the opening, his silence was getting me down. I asked him what was on his mind. He looked at me, then smiled:

"We're going to build a new San Francisco."

CHAPTER 12

THE NIGHT AFTER *This Is Cinerama* opened, Mike asked me to phone Sarah whose family had contacts at Columbia University to find out who was the "Einstein of optics." The answer came back that it was Dr. Brian O'Brien, head of the Institute of Optics at the University of Rochester. He had developed the lenses and high-speed camera that had photographed the A-bomb test explosions. Within half an hour Todd had Dr. O'Brien on the phone.

Dr. O'Brien said he had never heard of Cinerama, but he had heard of Mike Todd. Mike explained the general nature of the Cinerama process, with its three cameras and three projectors, and told the scientist: "I want you to design me a Cinerama where everything comes out of one hole." Dr. O'Brien said he was flattered by the call, but he was very busy and didn't think he would be able to find the time to design a one-hole Cinerama, whatever that was.

Todd, of course, would not take this for an answer and insisted that Dr. O'Brien fly to New York, at Todd's expense, to see the process—they could sit down over some good groceries and discuss the matter further. Dr. O'Brien thanked him for his generous offer, but he had to decline, as his interests were already too diverse. Persisting, Todd finally got Dr. O'Brien to agree to send down an assistant to have a look at Cinerama, just to keep abreast of new optical techniques.

Two days later, Dr. O'Brien's assistant came down from Rochester. In his eyes, Cinerama was little more than a mechanical lash-ups of existing elements, although one that was clever and effective. The only original element was an oscillating saw-tooth border in the projectors that diffused the edges of the pictures at the two seams, and this innovation only partially succeeded. What did have a gigantic impact on Dr. O'Brien's assistant was the audience's tremendously excited reaction to the process. Although scientifically crude, Cinerama packed an emotional wallop, even for him.

Three more phone calls from Todd, following the enthusiastic report from his assistant, brought Dr. O'Brien down from Rochester to have a look at Cinerama. He was not the least bit impressed by the process, but he too was totally taken by the audience's response. He said that wide-angle pictures projected on a large screen made use of peripheral vision, and it was this that created the sensation of movement. By this time, he was aware of the avalanche of stories and articles that was heralding Cinerama as the advent of a new era in the history of motion pictures. Dr. O'Brien was now willing to talk to Todd about building a one-hole Cinerama.

"Everybody has two businesses," Todd said, "their own and show business."

At the time, Dr. O'Brien was finalizing a long-contemplated move, to become the head of research for the American Optical Company. Now that he was going to be involved with a commercial enterprise, Dr. O'Brien felt that if the motion picture industry was going to be transformed by a new process, he could provide one that had scientific innovations, rather than one that was just a mechanical potpourri. It would be a challenge to design new lenses, new camera equipment and new projectors—to perfect a Cinerama with no seams.

Now that Todd had sold him, Dr. O'Brien softened up the president and board of the American Optical Company. He arranged a meeting for Todd with Walter Stewart, the president of the company, and other senior executives at their headquarters in Southbridge, Massachusetts.

Mike took me along, and when we arrived in Southbridge, we were taken aback by the appearance of the American Optical headquarters and main factory, which were in the same building. It was a huge, square, late-nineteenth-century brick structure that looked like the many New England mills that were being closed and abandoned. On the way to Stewart's office I expected to pass Bob Cratchit perched on his stool, working away, quill in hand. Dr. O'Brien and the company's executives were in the president's office, awaiting our arrival.

During the introductions and social preliminaries I could see Mike sizing up Walter Stewart. I detected an impish expectation in Dr. O'Brien as he waited to see Stewart's reaction to Todd's flamboyant tide of Broadway rhetoric. He was obviously disappointed that there was no talk of creating a Cinerama that came out of one hole, or any of the other hyperbole Todd had used on him. Mike took the floor:

"The motion picture business is the only major industry in the country that's remained totally static for a quarter of a century. Not a cent is spent on research and development. Color and sound were developed over thirty years ago. The moguls—the geniuses—said the public wasn't interested in talkies or color. Public acceptance and demand forced their hands, or we still wouldn't have color or sound. Not to boast, but Cinerama was lying around for years before I saw it. I don't want to embarrass Michael, because he's a very conservative-type fellow, but for thirty-two dollars he shot the roller coaster, and it's going to start an avalanche of changes in the movie business."

He told them that he was not a scientist and did not have the benefit of an education, and that during the course of making *This Is Cinerama* he began to realize that it had serious shortcomings—it could never be used to tell a story. Even so, Cinerama was setting the public and the motion picture industry on its ear. With all of Cinerama's limitations—the heavy installation costs, with the three projection booths on the orchestra floor and the triple cost of projectionists—exhibitors were still fighting each other to get the process; and exhibitors were even more conservative and unimaginative than the film studios. His proposal was simple:

"You're bringing into your company a top man in his field. If you'll forgive my presumption, I'm told he is *the* top man in optics. You've got the technical know-how and resources and the oldest and best name in the business. Please forgive my lack of modesty, but I am a showman and I know how to sell something to the public. We should join forces and put together the first really new motion picture system in thirty years."

Stewart seemed favorably impressed by Todd and his proposal, but said that he wanted to consider the proposition with his executives and board of directors. He promised a speedy reply.

Horses for courses. Todd had correctly sized up Walter Stewart and the American Optical Company. Stewart, in his early fifties, was unpretentious, a no-nonsense businessman, but clearly had a sense of humor. He was confident of his own judgment and completely in charge of the company. Todd's concise and low-keyed pitch was in step with Stewart's style. However, there was a more subtle element to Todd's pitch that I'm sure he formulated only after he saw the American Optical headquarters. The company had been secure and profitable, but unadventurous. They had not diversified, like their biggest competitors, Bausch & Lomb and Polaroid. Everything Todd had to say about the motion picture industry was analogous to American Optical's position in its own industry.

Back in New York, he went right to work on something that had been in the back of his mind ever since he became involved with Cinerama. *Oklahoma!* he felt, had the greatest motion picture potential of any theatrical property around. He was not alone in this conviction. For the past nine years, since its opening in 1943, the major studios had been offering Rodgers and Hammerstein the top dollar and top stars, but none had been able to land the property.

Todd now approached Rodgers and Hammerstein and told them he was going to develop a new process that would have the impact of Cinerama, but none of its limitations. They had waited this long to make a deal for *Oklahoma!* and so were in no rush. However, they were not in the business of giving away free options. Todd said within six months he would give them a demonstration that would knock their eyes out. They indicated that they probably would not sell the film rights within that period and that Todd should keep them advised of his progress with the new process.

As promised, Walter Stewart came back quickly with a decision. If Todd could put together a group that had theatrical prominence and the necessary financing, the American Optical Company would embark with Todd's company on the development of a new film process. Mike had some news of his own. "Walter, the first film in the new process will be *Oklahoma!*"

Todd was on the phone continuously, when he wasn't commuting between New York and Los Angeles. He put together the required group and financing. No one had believed his boasts about the impact of Cinerama. Now everyone was listening to him. Joe Schenck was the first to come in with his money and name. Through Schenck's association with 20th Century-Fox, Todd had gotten to know Spyros Skouras, the president of

Fox. Skouras's brother, George, was the president of United Artists Theatres, which Joe Schenck had founded, although he was no longer associated with the company.

A process that had the impact of Cinerama without its gigantic installation and operating costs would be an exhibitor's dream. As Todd pointed out to George Skouras, part of the cost of acquiring the film rights to *Oklahoma!* would make Rodgers and Hammerstein partners in the venture—it would be in their interest to have *South Pacific* made in the process as well. Todd convinced Schenck and Skouras that the two properties in the process would be "a license to print money." United Artists Theatres put up the lion's share of the initial investment, and George Skouras became Todd's equal partner in the project.

The temporary name for the new company was the M.A.O.T. Corporation—Todd's initials with those of the American Optical Company's sandwiched in between.

In the midst of this frenzied activity, Todd squeezed in a weekend trip to Virginia to satisfy a whim. For years there had been the occasional newspaper feature story and even one *Life* article about a horse in Virginia named Lady Wonder, whose owner claimed it was psychic. Todd had spoken several times to the woman who owned the horse. At the time when he was planning to present Lowell Thomas Jr.'s lecture about Tibet in Madison Square Garden, Todd had entertained the idea of putting the horse on as a sort of curtain raiser, but the horse's owner had said that this would be impossible; the horse was sensitive and would answer only questions that were privately put to her, from individuals she liked. The owner also said she did not wish to commercialize her mare's rare and unusual gift.

By the fall of 1952 Lady Wonder was seventeen years old, and Todd figured that if he was ever going to meet her, he had better not delay.

Lady Wonder's modus operandi was that first her owner would lead a visitor to her stall. After a brief period the owner could usually detect if Lady was in tune with the visitor. If Lady was, the visitor would proceed and ask the mare any question about the future. Lady Wonder would then go to a gigantic "keyboard," which was mounted at her nose level at the edge of the stall. She would tap out an answer by hitting successive keys with her nose. The "keyboard" consisted of twenty-six planks of wood with a letter of the alphabet on each one-by-two-foot plank.

Todd was led to Lady Wonder's stall, and after he and Lady looked each other over, the owner said she thought Lady would respond if he asked a question. Todd asked, "Will my new project be a success?" Lady went to the keyboard and hit the following letters with her nose: M - O - A - T G - R - E - A - T S - U - C - C - E - S - S. Mike thought that Lady's transposition of the letters of his new company was the twist that gave the performance that extra touch of credibility.

One morning I was told to make up a list of names from which he would choose a final name for the M.A.O.T. Corporation. That evening, from about a dozen suggestions, he selected "Magna"—it sounded large and impressive.

The Magna board included Todd; Joe Schenck, chairman; George Skouras, president; Judge James Landis, who was Skouras's attorney, a former dean of the Harvard Law School and a former head of the Securities and Exchange Commission; Professor Charles Seligson, Todd's attorney, who had finally extricated him from bankruptcy; Lee Shubert; and Edward Small, an independent motion picture producer and friend of Todd's. When the process seemed promising, Rodgers and Hammerstein took seats on the board, as did the film producer, Arthur Hornblow, Jr., whom Rodgers and Hammerstein wanted as the producer of *Oklahoma!*

One of Dr. O'Brien's earliest technical decisions was that in order to preserve a high-quality picture on the giant screen, a larger picture negative would have to be used, now that Cinerama's three 35mm cameras were to be replaced by a single camera. By doubling the width of the film to 70mm and increasing the height from the four-sprocket hole height of a frame on 35mm to six sprocket holes, there would be more than four times the area of film negative, resulting in a picture even clearer and of higher resolution than Cinerama's. Mitchell, the leading manufacturer of motion picture cameras, was given the contract to build the cameras.

Meanwhile, Joe Schenck told us that there might be some old 70mm cameras for Dr. O'Brien and Todd to work with while Mitchell was completing the first of the new cameras. Schenck said that William Fox, the Fox of 20th Century-Fox, had been impressed with a three-camera Cinerama-like process that had created a sensation in Paris in the mid-twenties. Fox had arrived at the same idea Todd had in trying to perfect Cinerama. He decided to eliminate the seams in the projected picture by using a 70mm camera and projector to obtain a picture that could fill a similarly huge screen. Fox's process, Grandeur Pictures, was first shown in late 1929, and although it was impressive, it was completely overshadowed in the excitement about the new talking pictures. Schenck told Todd that studios kept everything that passed through their hands, and if we looked around we would probably find Fox's old cameras. We did find them, in the old studios in Astoria, Long Island, and after reconditioning they were used to shoot the first tests for the new process.

The Phillips Company of Holland was commissioned to manufacture the 70mm projectors, and Eastman Kodak was hired to manufacture the 65mm and 70mm color film stock needed for the process. The cameras shot 65mm film, and 70mm was used for the projection prints, allowing an extra 5mm of width outside the sprocket holes to carry the six channels of magnetic sound. Four speakers were spaced behind the screen, and there was one sound channel for each side of the theater.

On one of his frequent trips to California during the fall of 1952, Todd came back with a girl friend in tow—the actress Evelyn Keyes. He had met her during one of his conferences on the coast with his friend Eddie Small. Evelyn was starring in one of Small's pictures.

Todd's introductions, without exception, were noninformative. I recognized Evelyn, although Todd never mentioned her first name or mine when he introduced us—just, "Say hello to each other." Then spreading his arms wide so I could see his new getup, he said, "Meet the new Todd."

He had always worn his hair fairly long and combed slickly straight back. It was now a modified crew cut, and instead of his usual custom-made silk shirt and business suit, he was now wearing a cashmere polo shirt and a sports jacket and slacks.

For the next couple of years he labeled all his changed styles and habits part of the new Todd. Besides the new haircut and sportier clothes, there was a shift away from cigars to pipes when he was at home. Allegedly the new Todd did no serious gambling. What this worked out to mean was that he seldom gambled more money than he had. He attributed the stylistic changes to Evelyn, but there was always the hint that the new Todd hadn't just found a new girl and a new style of dress, he was a man of changed habits and perspectives. The new Todd was going to succeed with low-keyed nonchalance, unlike the brash and manic old Todd.

An important part of the new Todd had been created by our dentist, Dr. Samuel Pritz. For years he had been telling Todd that his slightly underslung jaw and resultant bite were going to erode his upper teeth. As Todd's upper front teeth became increasingly worn down, he recognized the truth of Dr. Pritz's diagnosis. Shortly before hooking up with Evelyn, he had Dr. Pritz do a major job of restructuring his bite. The result was that his jaw was pulled back, giving him a less aggressive look. The new Todd was a more relaxed-looking version of the old Todd, but he was still the man who between frenzied spurts of activity would command you to "Hurry up and relax."

The day Evelyn moved into the apartment, Mike pulled me aside and, holding a warning finger to my face, he said, "Evelyn's a real liberal—a little mixed up but very nice. Don't you go picking on her like you did Jack Moss."

In 1947 a New York City bus driver, Bill Cimillo, fed up with complaining passengers and New York City traffic, made front page news by disappearing with his bus. Undetected, he showed up several days later in Florida, where he wired his bus company for money. The bus company had him arrested and returned to New York. All of America was sympathetic and Cimillo was punished with only a reprimand. He was reinstated in his job and put on probation for a year.

Todd felt that a fictionalized version of Cimillo's adventure would make a wonderful movie comedy—a proletarian *Grand Hotel*, with Cimillo's fictional counterpart picking up an assorted group of passengers each of whom would have a reason for wanting to get away from it all. Joan Blondell was to be the female lead, an aging nightclub dancer who joins the excursion in Atlantic City.

Todd reached an understanding with Cimillo on the rights to his story and asked Jack Moss to come east to help him work out a plot outline and select a screenwriter. Jack stayed in our guest cottage during his visit.

One day we all took the train home from New York and Jack and I got into a discussion about communism. Jack's position was that good ends were justified by sometimes questionable means. Jack was a cool and soft-spoken individual. As the discussion continued, I started to get hot under the collar, citing chapter and verse to refute Jack's position. By the time we reached Irvington, I was practically shouting, not understanding how Jack could resist the irrefutable logic of my arguments. Mike sat impassively during the entire forty-five-minute trip, saying nothing except to tell me to lower my voice a few times. The only emotion I could detect on his part was one of slight amusement.

Later that evening after supper, when Jack went down to the guesthouse, Mike turned to me and said, "You were terribly intolerant and impolite to Jack on the train. It's all right to have a political discussion, but you shouldn't violently attack anybody's political or religious beliefs. All that talk about freedom of speech—you hardly gave Jack a chance to get a word in edgewise."

I never did have a heated political discussion with Evelyn, or for that matter any lengthy discussion with her on any subject. Whenever we were in the apartment together, she had little to say to me or Kathryn Baltimore. She was listless when Mike wasn't around, but very lively and amusing when he was. The only thing about her I found slightly annoying was her pretense of having an insatiable appetite for the great books. She had a profusion of heavy tomes scattered about the apartment, but the only time I ever saw her pick up one was right before she anticipated Mike's arrival home. He always phoned as he was leaving the office. On one occasion she fell into the clichéd situation of having so hurriedly picked up her book when she heard him getting off the elevator that she was holding it upside down when he walked in the door. She was a marvelous companion for Mike, though, and I found her pleasant and interesting when he was around. Evelyn and I were in close quarters only a short while, as the Korean War had caught up to me and I went off to Officer Candidate School in Newport, Rhode Island, at the beginning of January 1953. Sarah Weaver and I decided to marry in May, after my graduation from O.C.S.

Dr. O'Brien, with a team of assistants from both the American Optical Company and the University of Rochester, moved rapidly ahead with the lenses for the new system. He supervised the design of the cameras and the projectors. It took over ten years to get Cinerama developed and ready for presentation. Todd's new process was slated to be demonstrated to Rodgers and Hammerstein in less than a year.

The new process needed a name. When the issue was discussed with the Magna and American Optical boards, Mike put forward what he felt was the simplest and most expedient solution to their problem: "Call it the Todd Process." Walter Stewart had the temerity to suggest that the American Optical Company was devoting a great deal of money, time and technical expertise in developing the process and was entitled to gain some degree of public recognition for their efforts. The degree that Mike thought appropriate was to affix their initials with a hyphen to the end of his name. Thus: Todd-AO. Everyone would ask what the *AO* meant, he argued, and the explanation that it represented "American Optical" would call even more attention to their contribution but still keep the name for the process simple.

Magna and Walter Stewart agreed that an executive of the American Optical Company should become the first president of the Todd-AO Corporation, which would hold the patents and license the use of the process. A vice-president, Henry Woodbridge, was selected for this position.

During the four months I was in Officer Candidate School, my father drove up with Sarah for three weekend visits, a ten-hour round-trip drive. The amount of time they spent alone together on these trips would not have been duplicated in the normal course of events in five to ten years' time. The result from Todd's point of view was his appreciation and understanding of what I saw in Sarah, and he told me before our marriage, "Nobody asked me, but you've got a wonderful girl there—for you."

Sarah wasted no time or effort in trying to make any sort of impression on someone she didn't like or find interesting. Todd was impressed with her "tremendous radar"—she could immediately and accurately size up anybody she met. She felt my father was self-centered and egotistical, but she also found him generous, warm and amusing. A vital consideration from her point of view was that he was totally devoted to me. There was a tacit understanding that they were worlds apart in their views, and neither made an effort to be demonstrative with the other. They both had enough self-confidence and self-understanding not to be bothered with the pretense of any real relationship other than through me. They admired and respected each other, but without wasted conversation. It was what my father called a "shorthand relationship."

Sarah and I decided to marry right after the graduation ceremony. I tried unsuccessfully to have the marriage performed by the base chaplain and was unable to get time off to make other arrangements in town. I phoned my father and said that I knew he was busy, but would he try to arrange for Sarah and me to be married in the town of Newport, hopefully someplace a little warmer and more congenial than a clerk's office. He responded immediately, saying he thought the oldest synagogue in the country was in Newport and wouldn't that be nice? I said that Mr. Weaver might think so, but Mrs. Weaver was a practicing Catholic, and our getting married in a synagogue would be pushing things a bit. He said, "Don't worry, I'll fix up something."

What he arranged couldn't have been simpler or nicer. We were married in the lovely Victorian home of Judge Arthur Sullivan, who performed the ceremony, quoted from Shakespeare and provided a bottle of vintage champagne for a good-luck toast. My father was the only member of the wedding party to shed a tear. Embarrassed, he held himself to just a few.

Dr. O'Brien, the American Optical Company, George Skouras and Mike all felt that, from the earliest stage, the development of the Todd-AO process should be guided by experts who had practical Hollywood know-how. Because he was the only active member of the board with extensive production experience, Arthur Hornblow, Jr., was asked to recommend both a camera and a sound expert. Hornblow recommended Schuyler ("Skippy") Sanford, who was working as the camera expert for Hal Wallis at Paramount on a 3-D film. Skippy says that at the end of 1952 he got a phone call early one Sunday morning from Hornblow:

> Hornblow invited me to breakfast, saying that he had someone in from out of town who was interested in what I was doing and wanted to meet me. I went over and was introduced to Mike Todd, who explained that he was building a new film process, and he wanted somebody with Hollywood expertise to come in on the ground floor.
>
> Mike finished, saying, "What makes you think you're the man for the job?"
>
> I said, "Mr. Todd, I didn't ask to be invited here this morning. I already have a job, and I don't know that I want the job you're talking about."
>
> "Good," Mike said, "You're the man. You're hired. I want you to come to New York with me immediately."

He told me he was going to give me so many dollars a week. I told him I was already making more than that. Then he told me he'd pay me twice his first offer. I said that sounded pretty interesting, but I was still working for Hal Wallis. Mike said he'd square that, and he did. Two days later I flew to New York with Mike.

Fred Hynes of Todd-AO recalls his coming to work for the company:

I was interviewed by Arthur Hornblow; by Ampex, who was providing the sound equipment; and by Henry Woodbridge. And after running the gauntlet, being asked what I would do with multitrack sound and some very technical questions, I met Mike Todd, who just asked me one question—"Hynes, can you record a roller coaster?" I said, "Of course, why not?" He said, "You're hired." A short while later I went to New York, and I was staying at the St. Regis. I called the accountant and said, "When do I send in my expense account?" He said, "You don't send in any expense account—you're getting fourteen dollars a day, and that's it." I said, "I can't live on that. I'm paying that much for the room alone. I've got to eat, take taxis, get my laundry done —I'll have to quit." He said, "That's up to you."

The next day Mike came in from the coast and I explained to him that I'd have to go back to California. He told Midori to get the accountant on the phone and tell him to bring five hundred dollars in cash over to the office. When the accountant walked into the office, Mike introduced me and said, "I want Hynes on an expense account from here in, and give him the five hundred dollars as an advance."

That night I put it in the safe at the hotel, because it was a lot of money in those days and I didn't want to be walking around with it. At midnight I got a phone call from Mike. He asked if I still had the five hundred dollars, and I said yes. He said, "I'll meet you in the lobby in twenty minutes. I need two hundred and fifty dollars." The next night he called and said, "I need the other two hundred and fifty dollars."

Dr. O'Brien and his team made incredibly fast progress with the development of the Todd-AO process, as did Mitchell and Phillips with the cameras and projectors. As soon as the lenses and the camera were finished, Todd grabbed them and took Evelyn out to the roller coaster at Far Rockaway. To show

Rodgers and Hammerstein, his board, the security underwriters and the motion picture business that the Todd-AO process would duplicate the effects of Cinerama without the defects, he would open a demo sequence with the same roller coaster ride. The sequence did duplicate the original, "only better—all this and Evelyn Keyes too."

Fred Hynes recalls: "We had quite a crowd when we shot the roller coaster, including Dorothy and Lillian Gish. Why they were there, I don't know. But Mike always made an event out of everything."

From the very beginning some of the camera lenses produced distortions, particularly the most complex and expensive lens, the 128-degree wide-angle lens, which was nicknamed the Bugeye and designed to nearly duplicate the field of vision provided by Cinerama. Dr. O'Brien told everyone not to worry about the distortions produced by some of the lenses; he would design an optical printer that would eliminate the distortions. Skippy Sanford advised Todd that while it was theoretically possible to design lenses for an optical printer that would eliminate the distortions created by the camera lenses, it would be extremely difficult and expensive. Todd insisted that every aspect of Cinerama should be duplicated and perfected, especially the widest possible angle lens. But to avoid getting caught with the bugs from the Bugeye, practically everything he and Skippy filmed was covered by shots with distortion free lenses.

What was needed now was a sequence to prove an intimate scene could be played in the process. Skippy Sanford promoted the use of Elicott Creek Park in Buffalo; he and Mike shot a picnic with some attractive young couples. There were some tight close-ups of the girls and the food. Todd always got his priorities right.

He then took the new Todd-AO camera, Evelyn, Skippy Sanford and a small crew to Europe, where he shot more demonstration footage that would compare favorably with some of the sequences we shot for *This Is Cinerama*. They filmed in the canals of Venice, and in the beautiful opera house there they shot the New York City Ballet Company. In Spain they shot a bullfight, this time with the camera in the ring. Todd had a lot to prove with his short demo film, but he really had to prove his point to only two people—a successful audition for Rodgers and Hammerstein was all he needed to get Todd-AO off the launching pad.

When the big day came in mid-August of 1953, Rodgers and Hammerstein loved the process and were ready to make a deal for *Oklahoma!* The overall terms for such a deal had been discussed, but formalizing the agreement in a contract, with all the *i*'s dotted and *t*'s crossed, was a protracted process. When the contracts were being completed and readied for signature, the last *t* to be crossed was Todd. He had automatically assumed that as the father of the process and the whole deal he would have control of the production of *Oklahoma!*

He wasn't looking for a film credit—his name on the process and his ability to generate personal publicity would sufficiently spell out his association with the project. He was pleased to have Hornblow as the producer. Hornblow was experienced and accomplished and would see to the mechanics of getting the film made and deal with Rodgers and Hammerstein and the director, Fred Zinneman. Todd liked Zinneman and had tried to get him to direct a couple of films during Mike's abortive stay at Universal-International in the mid-forties. Here was a fabulous property and a great team, and with Todd riding herd and providing the overall concepts of how to best marry the picture with the process and then how to market the result, Todd-AO would be the hottest thing in show business.

However, Rodgers and Hammerstein were not going to relinquish artistic control of the movie to Todd. He could make all the suggestions and comments he cared to, but they insisted on having the final say. Todd figured that with his process, his producing company and his board of directors he could either get Rodgers and Hammerstein to back down or they could split, and he would find another property for the first Todd-AO film. Although he had a huge slice of the stock, he did not have the controlling interest. *His* board was thrilled with the process and the prospect of making *Oklahoma!* He was gently and apologetically voted down; Rodgers and Hammerstein would have the final say on the film. It was suggested—unnecessarily, as it was the uppermost thought in his mind—that he should find a property and make the second film in Todd-AO.

Rodgers and Hammerstein's contract gave them the final say on the filming of *Oklahoma!* but this contract, linking their names and their property with Todd-AO, restored Mike's credit and credibility. For the first time since the fall of 1947, he was off the financial hook on which he had impaled himself with his compulsive gambling and his disastrous attempt to conquer

Hollywood. Arnold Grant, the attorney with whom Mike was involved in the purchase and operation of the Del Mar Racetrack, represented Henry Crown in the bankruptcy proceedings and made it an avocation during those six years to keep Todd on that hook, convinced that Mike was the most unprincipled scoundrel he had ever dealt with. Grant was Todd's most devoted enemy and detractor. Todd was oblivious to Grant and his views.

With enough money to go and do what he pleased, Todd made frequent trips to the coast and Europe, looking for a project to make in the Todd-AO process. Evelyn was Mike's companion from the end of 1952 until the early part of 1956. They had the occasional tiff, and Evelyn made a few films and did some stage work, but they were together a lot during that period. Columnists often reported them on the verge of marriage, but until the end of their relationship, my father never hinted at marriage to me, and I never gave it serious consideration. For Todd, Evelyn was lively, attractive and compliant. One of Todd's strongest appeals to both men and women was his total take-charge quality—it's wonderful to have someone managing your life, especially if he is amusing and goes first class all the way.

At the beginning of 1954 the unlikely film Mike decided to present as *his* use of the Todd-AO process was Laurence Olivier's *Richard III*. This was to be a coproduction with Sir Alexander Korda, the Hungarian entrepreneur who had almost single-handedly made the English film industry a factor in the world market. Todd and Korda had come to know and like each other a few years before, when Todd was pushing Cinerama, and Korda, ever alert to new developments in the industry, had evinced a strong interest in the process. Korda was a charming man, brimming with quiet self-confidence.

His brother Vincent, one of the greatest cinema art directors, became a close friend and associate of Mike's. Vincent and I spent over a year together making a film in Spain and kept up a close relationship until his death in 1979. He was devoted to his brother Alex and then to my father. He said that Alex and Todd were similar in many ways. "They were two very exciting creatures and nice men."

Todd and Alexander Korda recognized each other as super salesmen and masters of psychology in promoting their ventures. They were very low keyed with each other, using reverse

English to make their points, knowing that high pressure and hyperbole would be wasted on each other. My father treated Alexander Korda with something approaching the deference he showed Joe Schenck.

Richard III was not the ideal vehicle for incorporating roller coasters—a major use Todd wished to make of his new process. Plans and financing for the film were far along when he and Korda' discussed doing the project together. It soon became clear that Todd would be getting himself into another *Oklahoma!* Between the risks of tampering with Shakespeare and dealing with Laurence Olivier's concepts, Mike would again be bargaining for another seat on the sidelines. Todd dropped out of his coproduction deal with Korda on *Richard III,* but for the next year and a half he made Korda's London Films office his home base when in Europe.

The balance of 1954 was filled with taking on the most ambitious undertaking any showman had ever attempted. He wasn't going to present just an entertainment with his new film process, but through the gargantuan production of one of the great classics of literature, he was going to defrost the cold war and bring the peoples of the world together and into theaters, to see his movie. He decided to go to Moscow and convince the Russians that they should join him on a coproduction of *War and Peace.* No political messages from either side, only the graphic and classic depiction of the futility and waste of war.

First, Todd talked Robert Sherwood into doing the treatment. Sherwood had won the Pulitzer Prize for three of his plays— *There Shall Be No Night, Abe Lincoln in Illinois* and *Idiot's Delight*— as well as for his historical biography, *Roosevelt and Hopkins.* He had received an Academy Award nomination for his screenplay of *Rebecca* and won the Oscar for his script for *The Best Years of Our Lives.*

In 1953 Isaiah Berlin, a philosopher and later a professor of social and political theory at Oxford, published a book entitled *The Hedgehog and the Fox,* an essay on Tolstoy's view of history, concentrating particularly on *War and Peace.* Todd read Berlin's book and found it fascinating. The ideas set forth would, he felt, help him sell the Russians and give an overall concept and point of view to the film, which a story of that length and scope needed. For once Todd didn't order his secretary, "Get me Isaiah Berlin on the phone." He wrote a letter, saying how much he enjoyed and admired *The Hedgehog and the Fox* and that he would like the opportunity to discuss the concepts personally with Berlin on a forthcoming trip to England.

A few weeks later he phoned Isaiah Berlin from London and made a date to meet with him. Over refreshments at All Souls College in Oxford, Todd explained that he was not embarking upon a mere commercial undertaking, but that his production of *War and Peace* could have a transforming spiritual effect on millions of people. Would Berlin act as the story consultant to the production and formulate the thematic thread that would unify the central concept of the film? Berlin said that he thought his advice was not worth having; he knew nothing about filmmaking and he thought that Todd was reading a little more into Tolstoy and into Berlin's essay about Tolstoy's views than were contained in either piece of writing. Todd listened demurely to Berlin, and they ended the interview on the friendliest of terms. Berlin's Tolstoy and Tolstoy's Tolstoy was one thing, but Todd's Tolstoy was going to create a bond of humanity that would help bring the cold war to an end and provide a hell of an entertaining show of epic proportions. He would secure some form of collaboration from Berlin later, when the production got moving. The first meeting was just hello.

Todd went to Moscow and met the minister of culture and many of the leading figures in the Soviet film industry. They got on famously. His sense of humor and lack of concern for protocol and formality struck just the right note with the Russians. They laid on the hospitality and caviar. They showed him *their* Cinerama camera, which of course they had invented several years before Cinerama had opened in New York. They had decided to make no use of it as the necessary installations in the theaters would be too cumbersome and expensive. They showed him a 3-D process they had perfected that did not require glasses. The only problem was that it was effective for an audience of just three people. Seated anywhere else in relation to the screen, one would see only a blurred double image. Todd facetiously asked to see *their* Todd-AO camera. They told him, with straight faces, that this equipment had also been perfected years before, but was now being used in Siberia for a film and was not available to be looked at.

When Todd got down to the main business at hand, he felt a genuine and enthusiastic interest from the Soviet film bosses to proceed on a coproduction of *War and Peace* as he outlined it, but that politically the timing was premature. Malenkov, the Russian premier, did not feel his position secure enough to depart drastically from Stalin's cold war policies. At the end of his visit, Todd was told that the Russians had been long contemplating and preparing their own production of *War and Peace*. Whether or not this was the case, or that Todd's proposal pushed them into action, they eventually came out with their production of *War and Peace* ten years later, in 1964.

Todd left Moscow like Napoleon, without an army. For all his talk about forging a link with the Russians and depicting the waste of war, what he had really been looking for was a free army to film, and of course the tremendous publicity that would accrue to a colossal coproduction with the Russians. Even his preliminary meetings in Moscow had garnered reams of worldwide publicity. Well, if the Russians wouldn't make a deal and provide him with an army, there were other Communists who would, so he set off for Yugoslavia.

Todd got on well or even better with the Yugoslavs than he had with the Russians. The Yugoslavs were more than willing to cooperate and lend him their army, although there would be the slight formality of his picking up their pay. Todd loved exotic datelines, had been phoning his business associates and friends from Moscow and continued his steady stream of calls from Yugoslavia, to keep everybody abreast of developments in his campaign to bring the people of the world together. He was calling Robert Sherwood almost daily, to see how he was progressing, and worked in a few calls to Isaiah Berlin in Oxford to weld their tenuous association.

When Todd returned to the States from his whirlwind tour of Communist Europe, he paused in the West long enough, at the end of 1954, to see the start of the filming of *Oklahoma!* Several months before, forty acres of corn had been planted in Arizona for the opening scene. It was now "as high as an elephant's eye." Mike was going to have his way on at least one aspect of the making of *Oklahoma!* Gordon MacRae, riding through the high corn with the camera following behind, would be the roller coaster at the opening of the movie. During his first discussions with Rodgers and Hammerstein about the new process, he had talked about this shot. There weren't any other shots he was calling, because one of the reasons Hammerstein had insisted on having the final say about the picture was his uneasiness over Todd's talk about roller coasters.

Todd's only other contribution to the film production of *Oklahoma!* was the casting of the leading lady, Shirley Jones. Ten years after the show opened on Broadway, there were still road companies successfully touring the country. Shirley Jones was under consideration for the role of Laurey in the film and was playing this role out of town in one of the road companies. Mike caught a performance and swung the balance in casting her in the part. "She's absolutely it," he said. "She's the perfect Miss Apple Ass."

On the first day of filming, in Arizona, there were mechanical problems with the camera, which Skippy Sanford quickly sorted out. He was, however, still dubious about Dr. O'Brien's unfinished optical printer, so he bought a set of Leica still camera lenses and fixed up a mount so they could be put on the Todd-AO cameras. Unfortunately for the film and the process, a few scenes remained in the finished film that were not covered by shots with distortion-free lenses. Hammerstein, who had the final say, still believed in Dr. O'Brien's optical printer, then referred to by everyone connected with Todd-AO as Dr. O'Brien's Magic Barrel.

In the six months since Todd had signed Robert Sherwood and announced his plans for the production of *War and Peace*, it had suddenly become the world's hottest property. David O. Selznick announced that he was going to make the film. Then Dino di Laurentiis and Carlo Ponti said they were going to make it. Finally, the Russians formally announced they were going ahead with their long-planned production of the Tolstoy masterpiece. The bloom was off the peach. Todd took some time off before he resumed his globe-trotting in search of a property to make in Todd-AO.

While he and Evelyn were staying with Joe Schenck in Florida, he ran into an old friend, John Ringling North, the boss and principal owner of the Ringling Brothers circus. The big show was in the final stages of preparation for its annual tour of the country. Todd ad-libbed a fillip for the New York run in Madison Square Garden.

Late in April, for a charity performance during the 1955 run of the circus in Madison Square Garden, Todd got Marilyn Monroe, costumed in sequins and spangles, to lead the opening parade atop a pink elephant. The picture was on front pages and magazine covers around the world.

Oklahoma! was well along in production. Todd, Skouras and the Magna board wanted to give a private screening to a group of influential exhibitors so that theaters in key cities would be made available to house *Oklahoma!* when it was completed. Todd put together a demonstration film of selected scenes from the picture—omitting, of course, anything containing shots with distortions—as well as the best of the test footage he and Skippy Sanford had shot in the United States and Europe. Skippy was present at this screening:

> It was at MGM, and Mike stood up in front of forty or fifty exhibitors from all over the country. He was proud as a peacock about his new process and was telling them it was Cinerama perfected. This was the first screening for anyone outside the company, and he carried on till finally he said, "Why should I talk about it? You'll see for yourself." The first scene was tailored for Todd-AO, the one Mike had always talked about. The camera dollied, following Curly on horseback, with the corn separating. The exhibitors oohed and aahed. Mike was sitting next to this seventy-year-old big shot, and grabbing his arm and pointing to the screen, Mike yelled, "Look at that! Look at that! How much herring can a Jew eat!" It broke everybody up.

For the second time Todd's extravagant claims were up to the mark. Now all the studio bosses and big producers could see that the Todd-AO process, as Todd was boasting, was Cinerama perfected. And Cinerama was still packing them in.

In response to the spectacular reception Cinerama had received, Spyros Skouras, the president of 20th Century-Fox, consented to use a film process that had been lying around since 1927 on their major production for the year. In 1953 *The Robe* was presented in CinemaScope and made a fortune. Later in the year Paramount followed with its own wide-screen process called VistaVision. CinemaScope and VistaVision, however, were only halfway steps to Cinerama. There were no seams, but the picture quality was mediocre and the images fuzzy at the outside edges of the screen. The biggest complaint was about the aspect ratio of these processes. The elongated screen created the impression that you were looking at the picture through a mailbox slot. Todd-AO was tall, wide and handsome. If Mike didn't get a move on, the boards of Todd-AO and Magna would have no choice but to let someone else make the second picture in the process.

He began searching frantically for a suitable property. On a trip to England, after unsuccessfully attempting to make a co-production deal on John Huston's film of *Moby Dick,* which had already started shooting, Mike returned to his home away from home, London Films. He was pacing back and forth in Alexander Korda's office sounding out ideas. Korda, as much to get Mike out of his hair as to be helpful, got up from behind his desk and walked over to his bookshelves. He pulled out several scripts and said that he had bought the film rights to a musical done by Orson Welles shortly after the war. Todd started to say something, but it was too big a coincidence—he let Korda continue. Alex said that he had had several versions written, but none of the scripts had satisfied him. However, *Around the World in 80 Days* was just the kind of property Mike was looking for and would be perfect for Todd-AO. Todd could barely contain himself. He explained to Korda that he had started to do the show with Welles and had invested $40,000 in it before he had pulled out, since Welles had failed to produce a script. He had loved the idea then, and he loved the idea now. This was it.

CHAPTER *13*

WITH *OKLAHOMA! RICHARD III* AND *WAR AND PEACE,* Todd would have been dealing with heavyweight classics and strong collaborators. One way or another he would have been under constraints and unable to call the shots. *Around the World in 80 Days* was much more his cup of tea—a humorous adventure story within a loose framework, with all the scope he could desire for embellishments. The story had a strong hero whom Mike could not only root for but closely identify with—Phileas Fogg, a man who bets everything he has against heavy odds that he can pull off an improbable feat. In some of the many interviews Todd gave after the opening of *Around the World,* he made the interesting Freudian slip of substituting "I" for "Phileas Fogg," when talking about the adventures of Jules Verne's hero.

As far as he was concerned, the development of Cinerama and Todd-AO were technological advances, and he wouldn't prove himself in his own eyes and in Hollywood's until he had made a film that was a smashing commercial and artistic success.

Todd's reaction to Korda's suggestion was electric and instantaneous. He called me from London that night, and I was mystified by his hello:

"What a schmuck I've been! I've been waltzing around and here's the perfect property—something I've been in love with all my life—the first book I ever read as a kid—I spent forty Gs and three months on it with Welles, and I've got to come to London to have someone sell me my own idea."

Welles was a strong clue, and given a couple of minutes I would have figured it out.

"What idea?" I asked.

"*Around the World in Eighty Days!* You're as big a schmuck as I am."

For the next two years, with just a few days off to court and marry Elizabeth Taylor, he spent every moment planning, producing, financing, reshooting, refinancing, selling and promoting *80 Days*.

He knew *80 Days* would cost millions, and he had nothing to his name but half a million shares of stock with a thin and uncertain over-the-counter market. But now he wanted no partners, not even Korda—he wanted to call all the shots this time. He bought Korda's scripts and rights in the property for $100,000.

Mike was not getting along with Todd-AO's president, Henry Woodbridge, whose ideas on how to present and sell the process conflicted with his own. By 1955 television was providing hours of free entertainment every evening, competing successfully with what could be seen in the neighborhood motion picture house. Some good movies were being shown on television as well. You needed a big show on a big screen to get people into a theater. With the anticipated success of *Oklahoma!* Woodbridge wanted to mass-market Todd-AO.

Todd's theory was to get one installation in each of the major markets, license producers with only the most spectacular and special attractions and make people in small towns or suburbs travel twenty to seventy-five miles to see a show in Todd-AO. Make it an evening when you put on a jacket and tie, go out to supper and make it a special event.

Todd had successfully sold this idea to a friend eleven years earlier. One day at "21" Gradwell Sears, then general sales manager of United Artists, was moaning to Todd:

"I've got this fabulous film and I can't do a goddamn thing with it. I have the American rights to Olivier's *Henry V* and I can't give it away. There's not an exhibitor in the country who wants to put Shakespeare on his screen."

Todd said, "You got no problem, Grad. Four-wall [rent] the Golden or Henry Miller [two of the smallest legitimate theaters in New York] and road-show it at legit prices."

"What do you mean, 'road-show'?"

"Make believe you got round actors and sell hard [reserved] tickets. Only seeing as you got 'em on film and there's no Equity rules, instead of doing eight performances a week, you can work 'em twice on Sunday and maybe even matinees every week-day."

"You're crazy, Mike. How's that going to make it any easier to sell?"

"You surprise me, Grad. I always figured you for an intelligent guy. The average moviegoing stiff wouldn't go to see Shakespeare if you paid him. The carriage trade will swim a river of crocodiles to see it. To show they got class and appreciate the arts, they'd be insulted if you didn't charge premium prices and make it a little hard to see. This way they don't have to rub elbows with the gum chewers. Besides, if you get the reviews and have a hot ticket, the gum chewers will figure out how to get in as well. Once you're a hit in New York, you'll have to fight the out-of-town exhibitors off with a stick."

Sears followed Todd's advice and *Henry V* was a big money-maker where it was road-showed in the largest cities across the United States.

That's why Todd persisted in saying he was interested only in producing "shows." It so happened that these shows were going to be on film, but they would be shows nevertheless. "I'm not interested in making movies. Movies are something you can see in your neighborhood theater and eat popcorn while you're watching them." Todd insisted that popcorn should never be sold in a Todd-AO theater and that this should be part of the contract when an installation was sold to a theater. He knew this was deliberately waving a red flag at the exhibitors, who often made more money selling popcorn than from the receipts of the film they were playing. But this was his way of demonstrating to the exhibitor, symbolically and in fact, that if he made an installation and played a picture in Todd-AO, he was not running just another movie house—he was presenting a show and had to act like a showman to give his theater and the attraction special attention and promotion.

Todd felt that Woodbridge's approach would kill off Todd-AO before it was even launched. He was tired of arguing with Woodbridge and the board of directors, trying to convince them that his way was the right way, when *This Is Cinerama* had proved that his ideas were correct.

In a speech he made at Harvard at the time of the Boston opening of *Around the World in 80 Days,* Todd said that one of the biggest problems he had with people in the movie business and his partners in Todd-AO was "unlearning them things." To illustrate the point, he told the following story—without naming names—about Nicholas Schenck, Joe's brother, who at the time was the president of MGM. At Joe's suggestion, Todd gave a private screening of the Todd-AO test footage for Nick Schenck, who, when it was over, politely said he thought it was beautiful and very impressive. That evening, however, Nick said to Joe, "I'm sorry to tell you this, but you've got yourself involved with an idiot. That film is sixty-five mm. It won't fit in the cans."

Todd's principal investor and equal partner in Todd-AO, George Skouras, believed that Todd's ideas were right, up to a point. But as the head of United Artists Theatres, with a lot of houses to keep busy, Skouras sided with Woodbridge's idea that the Todd-AO process had to be sold widely and quickly.

After a series of futile arguments with Woodbridge and sympathetic conferences with his partners, which left him convinced that he was being listened to but not heard, Todd gave up, kept his mouth shut and went his own way.

Oklahoma! was almost finished. Todd told Woodbridge and his partners that he was going to put together a twenty-five-minute selection for an exclusive industry showing to build Hollywood's anticipation for the film and the process. Word would surely leak out to the public about how great an event the opening of *Oklahoma!* would be in Todd-AO. Rodgers and Hammerstein, Skouras, Schenck and Woodbridge were happy to let Mike play around on a Moviola if it would keep him busy and quiet. If what he put together seemed weak in any way, they would squelch the screening.

They loved what he put together. The twenty-five-minute sampling of scenes from *Oklahoma!* was a knockout. The opening sequence, "Oh, What a Beautiful Mornin'," was a perfect marriage of music, action, story and panoramic scenery. Everyone knew *Oklahoma!* inside out. With a few other high points of the movie touched, any viewer could fill in with his own mind's eye the balance of the story in vivid color and Todd-AO and clearly envision one of the greatest entertainment events in history.

On his forty-eighth birthday—June 22, 1955—Todd held a screening of his trailer for the *crème de la crème* of Hollywood. At least half the audience were cutthroat competitors who found their greatest pleasure in seeing a fellow filmmaker fall on his face. But *Oklahoma!* was an American classic. Disapproval of it would be like burning the flag. Never had so tough an audience responded so enthusiastically. There was tangible evidence the following morning.

The stock, which had been trading in a desultory fashion at around $7.00, skyrocketed the next morning and reached a $22.50 bid. What little float there was had been soaked up in the morning's trading, and there was barely a share on offer. It was all being held by insiders who were waiting for the premiere of *Oklahoma!* certain they would see the stock jump even higher. That is, all but one of the insiders.

Todd spoke to Eddie Small and Joe Schenck, both of whom he had talked into coming in on the venture and sitting on the board. He felt duty-bound to inform them of his intentions of selling out. George Skouras, Rodgers and Hammerstein and the financiers were all big boys and had gone into the deal with their eyes wide open. And, in any event, despite Todd's misgivings about the way the picture and the process were being handled, they probably were still going to supplement their fortunes with *Oklahoma!* and Todd-AO. Although Todd owned over 25 percent of the stock, he had an offer from a large Wall Street firm for the entire lot at fifteen dollars a share. He would realize over seven million dollars from the sale. He could pay off all his debts, make *Around the World in 80 Days* out of his own pocket and probably "still have cab fare left." When Todd explained to Eddie Small his reasons for bailing out, Small said he understood Mike's position and appreciated the call.

But Schenck said no. Schenck pointed out that he would have been perfectly content to live out his life without becoming involved in Todd-AO. This was not a venture he needed or was looking for, but Todd had asked him as a favor to sit on the board. Todd had named the process after himself, and now Todd was going to sell out of Todd-AO and leave Schenck sitting on the board? "No, Mike, you cannot do this." No discussion. No argument. Mike said, "You're right, Joe."

Schenck had bestowed his favor and hospitality on Todd for years. By taking him in and treating him like a son, or at least an errant nephew, Schenck placed a mantle of respectability and importance on Todd that enabled him to circulate freely in the highest echelons of the film industry. Not the least of Schenck's kindnesses had been substantial loans on various occasions when Todd was in trouble. Joe Schenck was one of the genuinely respected and well-liked pioneers of the film business, the most solid stand-up guy in Hollywood, and not just for Todd. He had taken the rap for the whole industry and done a stretch in prison for dealing with Willy Bioff, the labor racketeer, when it was common knowledge that every major studio was bribing Bioff as well. He was now one of the elder statesmen of the business.

Schenck certainly had strong reasons for saying no, but Todd felt Schenck should have understood his position—that he was just looking to get even after ten years of struggle, with the sheriff waiting at the door almost all the way. But if Schenck felt it wrong for Todd to sell out, then he was not going to contest the issue.

My father had told me about his frustrations with Woodbridge and his board several weeks before the industry screening. He was calling me almost daily in Chicago, where I was serving in the Navy. The week before the screening he was confident that his twenty-five-minute trailer would be five times better than the final completed picture, and he was hopeful that within a few days after the screening the stock would double. He told me that if he could get anything more than ten dollars a share he was going to sell out. I had several thousand shares, and I said that I would like to sell a few in order to trade in my old car. Did he mind if I sold some the week following the screening? He said he didn't mind at all, but to make sure that I spoke to him first to get his final okay. He phoned me the night of the screening and told me that the response had far exceeded even his wildest expectations and that he would quit show business if the stock didn't take off right away. There was no need for further calls or explanations; the price tripled within a couple of hours the next morning and then remained steady a point or two above twenty, until the close of the market the next day, Friday.

Todd didn't phone me Thursday or Friday, and there was no word on Monday; the stock stayed above twenty. The top of my convertible was quite frayed, and when I still couldn't reach him that night, I sold a hundred shares the next day, figuring that if a hundred shares was going to depress the price, then everyone connected with the project was in a lot of trouble. Almost as though he had my phone tapped, Mike called me at the office minutes after I had received the confirmation of the sale.

His first words were, "You haven't sold any stock, have you?" I sank into my chair as I admitted I had, waiting for the inevitable tongue-lashing. Barely controlling himself, he asked, "How much?" I told him a hundred shares. His anger dissipated as he warned me not to sell any more. He explained that he could have sold his whole block at six dollars below the bid on Thursday noon, but that Schenck had stopped him. Schenck had told him not to sell, and we were in for the duration. I said that maybe the stock would go even higher after *Oklahoma!* opened.

"The stock will never be higher than it is at this minute," he said. "Your hundred shares will be the top price the stock is ever going to see. Enjoy your new car."

Of course, Todd never breathed a word about his pessimistic view of the future of the stock to anyone else and warned me not to say a thing. He had been preparing the production of *Around the World in 80 Days* for several months—now he would have to produce the film on credit rather than with his own cash.

After volumes of worldwide publicity Todd had been left at the post on *War and Peace,* and as far as producing movies was concerned, going back to his days at Universal-International, he was all talk and no action. No distributor would back Todd on a multimillion dollar picture, especially one that Alexander Korda had kicked around for years.

He was more than square with Lorraine at the moment, or at least it looked that way on paper. He had given her 75,000 shares of stock to cover her investment in *A Night in Venice* and various loans for walk-around money. Even at half the present value of the stock, this would give her all her money back and a tidy profit. He did nothing to disillusion Lorraine and her investment counselors' notion, shared by Wall Street and Hollywood cognoscenti, that the stock was going to be worth even more after *Oklahoma!* opened. Pledging his stock as security, he borrowed two million dollars from her, at a reasonable rate of interest, but gave her no participation in *80 Days*. Their relationship became a great deal more businesslike. Even for Lorraine, two million dollars was not play money.

Todd was hopeful—if not optimistic—that the price of the stock would not slip too much after the opening of *Oklahoma!* in the fall and that he would be able to sell out then, which

273

Schenck had reluctantly okayed. He would then pay off Lorraine and have enough left over to complete all or most of the principal photography. By the time nervous creditors might be closing in he would get all the money he needed from a major distributor by giving them a peek at the highlights of his film.

Todd's shooting script for *80 Days* was a collaborative effort between John Farrow, an Australian writer-director whom he had signed to direct the film, and James Poe, a younger man who had written a few screenplays and later had some excellent credits as screenwriter for *Cat on a Hot Tin Roof, Summer and Smoke, Lilies of the Field, The Bedford Incident* and *They Shoot Horses, Don't They?* Poe was the son-in-law of Bernard Reis, who was Lorraine's accountant and one of her principal business advisors. Todd felt that the script was flat and hired S. J. Perelman to work with him to liven it up. Perelman had worked with the Marx Brothers on several of their biggest movies and was accustomed to improvising. Todd anticipated that there was going to be a lot of on-the-scene and overnight work on dialogue as filming opportunities presented themselves.

Several movies had used a dozen or more stars, but he was intending to use a whole galaxy—some in every sequence, as long as they fit the roles. "I never got them because they were stars. We cast the show as though we had no budget, and we got the best people available for each part." He signed forty-one stars to play the bit and supporting roles, and part of the fun of the picture was identifying them as they flitted in and out of the various sequences. For these guest-star appearances he coined the phrase "cameo roles"—that is, small gemlike portraits.

From the very beginning Todd said he wanted to do a "fairy tale for adults," and in order to achieve this and make the humor of the piece work, all the improbable action and events needed to appear real on the screen. This meant shooting on location, avoiding miniatures as much as possible, with all the stars playing their roles straight and serious. If Buster Keaton and Harold Lloyd had not played their old comedies for real, and if their exploits and misadventures had looked faked, their movies would not have been funny.

The cameo-role casting was a great gimmick, but Todd was sincere about their having to be right for the role and playing it straight. When it became the "in" thing in Hollywood to appear in the picture, Todd was able to get Gregory Peck to play a cameo role. But when he felt that Peck was not taking his bit seriously, he substituted an old-timer from the silent movies who probably had the least recognizable name among the cameo stars. Todd described this incident:

> I had one of the top stars of the whole industry in costume . . . it was a chase and he was at the head of the cavalry who comes to the rescue. But I stopped him. And he said, "What is it?" I said, "You're killing it." He said, "What do you mean?" I said, "You don't get it. This is for real. Don't kid it. The flag is flying and the bugle is blowing and you're rescuing the guy." He said, "Are you serious?" I said, "Yes." Well, we didn't see eye to eye—so, at the heavy expense of the management, I scrapped the shooting and went out and hired a guy named Colonel Tim McCoy. He'd been a real colonel in the U.S. Cavalry, and if you'll forgive me for saying so, he was the real McCoy. He never got over the idea that he was a cavalry officer, even when he was a hero in cowboy movies. He's still riding to the rescue. He so believed the part that I just paid him off with a campaign medal.

The two main characters in the story are Phileas Fogg, a member of London's distinguished Reform Club, described by Jules Verne as "a gentleman of tall figure . . . with noble countenance, magnificent teeth . . . and a zealous interest in whist," and his roguish valet, Passepartout. Fogg wagers his entire fortune that he can go around the world in eighty days—which seemed impossible at the time of the story, 1872.

In terms of his screen image and real personality, which are remarkably similar—that of an extremely likable and attractive person, who possesses humor, charm and imperturbable poise—David Niven was the ideal choice for the leading role.

Mike was in a bathing suit, by the pool when he called Niven on a Sunday afternoon. As Niven reports in his delightful autobiography, *The Moon's a Balloon*, with no introduction or preliminaries a voice on the phone simply announced, "This is Michael Todd. I've got something I want to talk to you about. I'm at Joe Schenck's. Get your ass over here."

When Niven arrived, Mike's hello was "Have you ever read *Around the World in Eighty Days?*" Niven indicated that he had known and loved the book since childhood.

"How would you like to play the part of Phileas Fogg?" Todd asked.

In a burst of enthusiasm Niven replied, "I'd do it for nothing."

"You've got a deal."

Months earlier on a holiday trip to Acapulco with Evelyn, Todd had met Mario Moreno and his business manager-producer-partner, Jacques Gelman. Evelyn knew them from the time she had made films in Mexico. She explained that Mario, who was known in movies as Cantinflas, was the verbose Charlie Chaplin of Latin America and that he and Gelman made and owned their own films. Every film—and they often made two or three a year—netted a million dollars or more. Mario was the biggest box office attraction in Latin America.

Mario privately financed huge housing estates and clinics for the poor. He risked his life repeatedly for charity by annually doing a comic bullfight routine that filled the 70,000 seats of the bullring in Mexico City. Mario said, "The audience knows I'm doing a comic bullfight. I know I'm doing a comic bullfight. But the *bull* doesn't know I'm doing a comic bullfight."

When Todd jumped into *80 Days*, he remembered Mario and wanted him for the role of Passepartout. He was small, athletically comic and very appealing. Mario and Niven would make a hell of a pair to root for. Not only were they a pleasing combination in terms of personality and physical makeup, but it was "good chemistry"—an established star playing with a tremendously talented unknown. Audiences and critics love to discover and make a new star. Cantinflas may have been the biggest movie name in Latin America, but to the rest of the non-Spanish-speaking world he would be a fresh face.

It took a couple of months and several trips to Mexico to land Cantinflas for the role. Gelman was not Mario's partner for nothing. Mario got the highest salary of anyone in the film, plus a hefty percentage of the gross film rental from all the Spanish-speaking territories—and he was worth it, if for no other reason than record-breaking grosses in the so-called Cantinflas territories.

One of the two other leading but subordinate roles in *80 Days* was that of Inspector Fix, who erroneously suspects Phileas Fogg of robbing a bank and follows him around the world, constantly creating difficulties for Fogg and Passepartout. Niven recommended the ideal actor for the role—Robert Newton. Newton could chew a part and fully digest the heaviest set of scenery ever designed, swallow the proscenium arch without belching and, if given the opportunity, devour the entire theater. Here he had the world as his stage, and it was a delight to see him swallow it whole. Newton at this point of his career had a well-deserved reputation as a drinker, and he was hired on condition that he would stay on the wagon while the picture was being made.

The fourth leading role in the picture provided the romantic interest: Princess Aouda, a young Indian girl whom Fogg rescues midway on his journey around the world, as she is about to be burned on her husband's funeral pyre. Much to the consternation of his production team, Todd didn't sign the film's leading lady until two weeks after the shooting schedule had required her presence. Niven and the director questioned Todd's reasoning for casting the blue-eyed, freckle-faced, red-headed, largely unknown Shirley MacLaine in the part of a Hindu princess. She had given a wonderful, offbeat performance as the lead in a whimsical Hitchcock film, *The Trouble with Harry,* which was pleasant enough but not successful at the box office. Todd was taken by her pixie charm, and told the director, "Forget about her looks—just play her zany." However, the performance she gave in *80 Days* was subdued, because she never got the hang of the English accent her role required. Up to a few weeks before the premiere, Todd was still thinking that it would be necessary to get someone else to dub her lines; the intonations of a posh English accent continued to elude her. She was finally able to dub her own dialogue, although she was still a long way from being perfect. Her minor shortcomings were more than overcome by a fabulously funny five-minute interview she did with Steve Allen before the Hollywood opening of the picture, which was telecast nationally. She arrived in what seemed to be a tipsy state. Her husband, Steve Parker, was in Japan and her escort for the evening, Kevin McClory, a production assistant of Todd's, said she hadn't had a single drink before she arrived at the theater. Tipsy or not, she was thoroughly delightful, although what she said did not make a lot of sense. Her humor and charm somehow conveyed the spirit and fun of the picture to millions of viewers across the country. It was worth hundreds of thousands of dollars of paid advertising for *80 Days* and for her.

After engaging S. J. Perelman in New York to work on the script, the first thing Todd did when he got back to Hollywood was to track down and hire a couple of old film production hands. He hired William Cameron Menzies as his associate producer. Menzies had thirty-five years of experience as an art director, director, designer and all-around production expert and had made significant contributions to *The Thief of Bagdhad*, *For Whom the Bell Tolls* and, most notably, *Gone with the Wind*. He had won two Academy Awards for art direction. David Selznick had used him on many of his films and admired, trusted and liked him. Todd got on well with Menzies and relied heavily on his counsel.

Percy Guth also had over thirty years of experience with the production of major films and was hired as a general manager. Shortly after Todd died Guth literally made a federal case of his contribution to the film and claimed that Todd verbally promised to partially compensate him with a piece of the picture. No one behind or in front of the camera, with the exception of Mario, had a piece of the film. The federal judge rejected Guth's claim.

Todd said that all during the production of the picture, Guth kept giving him reasons why he couldn't do things, while Menzies helped him devise ways to get them done.

One of the key people Todd hired in Hollywood, before he left for Europe to start the picture, was the cameraman, who was recommended by Skippy Sanford. Skippy was thoroughly familiar with Mike's "hurry up and grab this" technique of filming and he told Mike that Lionel "Curly" Lindon was the fastest cameraman in Hollywood. Lindon's experience went back to the silent days and he was totally unflappable. He was one of the first cameramen ever to shoot an underwater sequence, and before aerial shots were commonplace in movies he was once strapped on the wing of a plane with his camera. To seal the matter, Farrow, the director, had done a couple of his pictures with Lindon and approved of the choice. Whatever Todd asked of Lindon, which was often improbable or near impossible, Lindon accomplished with barely a twitch of his pencil-line moustache, and only with occasional angry mutterings to his assistants. Sanford warned Todd that Lindon was a dedicated drinker, but he did it all on his own time and it never had the slightest effect on his work. Lindon needed to be well fortified for this job, since much of the picture was shot on the spur of the moment under chaotic conditions. But his tribulations were more than compensated for when he won the Academy Award for *80 Days*.

Kevin McClory first came to work on the picture for two weeks, as a minor production assistant, and soon was put in charge of the second unit. He then became Todd's sidekick-companion and sounding board during the prolonged postproduction period. McClory was a prime example of what Todd called "a Message to Garcia guy."

At the beginning of the Spanish-American War, a general called in one Lieutenant Arthur S. Rowan and told him there was a Cuban revolutionary leader behind the Spanish lines, named Garcia, and that it was urgent that Garcia receive the message that the United States would become his ally and go to war with Spain. Lieutenant Rowan set off from Washington and, with no further directions or instructions, he found Garcia deep in the jungles of Cuba and delivered the message. Elbert Hubbard, a publisher and author who specialized in inspirational literature at the turn of the century, produced a small volume detailing Lieutenant Rowan's exploits, entitled *A Message to Garcia*, emphasizing Rowan's intrepid resourcefulness. During the 1940s, when Todd had a large staff, he had copies of the book bound in leather and gave one to every employee. Later Mike said that this had been a mistake: "If someone had to read the book to get the message, they were never going to be a message-to-Garcia guy anyway."

Mike first met Kevin McClory during the filming of *Moby Dick*. When Todd was hanging around London Films, looking for a property to make in Todd-AO, Vincent Korda suggested that Mike go out to Fishguard on the coast of Wales, where John Huston was shooting *Moby Dick*. "Huston is a difficult but most amusing creature. Perhaps you'll see something there that interests you."

Mike knew Huston—he was Evelyn's former husband. Todd and Evelyn had spent time socially with him.

Todd suddenly had the notion that *Moby Dick* was a suitable classic with tons of action, and would serve wonderfully as his first film in Todd-AO. What difference did it make that the film was already in progress? He would fly to Fishguard with a couple of cases of champagne and a dozen pounds of caviar and convince Huston to suspend shooting and then start all over again with the Todd-AO process.

Amazingly, he was able to seriously interest Huston in his concept, but the Mirisch brothers and Al Crown, who were producing the picture, could not be convinced of the wisdom of abandoning a partially completed production and starting from scratch.

Kevin McClory had worked as one of Huston's assistants on

Moulin Rouge, The African Queen and *Beat the Devil,* but almost lost his life on *Moby Dick.* Kevin attempted to rescue a mock-up whale that was mounted on a submerged barge that had broken loose during a gale. He managed to get aboard the whale and get another line secured, but when this line snapped, Kevin jumped off into an icy sea. He was pulled aboard a tug and further attempts to rescue the whale were abandoned. When the weather cleared, the mock-up whale could not be found. It washed up on the coast of Holland eight months later. This exploit and Kevin's wit and Gaelic charm brought McClory to Todd's attention.

John Huston and Todd got on well together, but on another occasion he ran afoul of Huston's heavy-drinking, macho tendencies. Todd had dined and spent the evening with Huston and his entourage. Huston was drinking steadily and by eleven he was loaded and cantankerous. Spoiling for a fight, he directed some antagonistic remarks towards Todd, who felt that the expedient thing to do was to say good night. Huston was not finished with Todd and stood up to bar his exit. Todd tried to talk and walk his way around Huston, but Huston blocked him and at one point pushed him to keep him in the room. Todd gently pushed Huston back so that he could leave, but even the most gentle push was enough to cause Huston to fall to the floor— Huston had drunk more than even *he* could handle. The shove was the incentive Huston had been looking for to start a fight. Huston struggled valiantly to stand up so that the battle could begin. Realizing he wasn't going to make it, Huston then turned on his side, extended his arms and clenched his fists: "If you had any kind of guts, you son of a bitch, you'd get down here and fight me like a man."

Todd had tremendous admiration for Huston's talents. When he was completing *80 Days* he talked to Huston about making Kipling's *The Man Who Would Be King* in Todd-AO with Gary Cooper and Humphrey Bogart. Twenty years later Huston made a superb job of it with Michael Caine and Sean Connery.

The normal way to shoot a picture like *80 Days* with a gigantic cast, crew and vast logistical problems would have been to start, after some rehearsals with the principals, in a studio under controlled conditions so that the director and stars could get accustomed to working with each other and the tone of the picture could be set without the distractions and complexities of location.

Todd began the filming of *80 Days* by hiring all sixty-five hundred inhabitants of the town of Chinchón, Spain, where the central plaza was traditionally fenced in for an annual bullfighting festival. *80 Days* is set in the year 1872, so a vast number of appropriate costumes, carts, carriages and decorations (to hide anachronistic advertising signs) had to be obtained to dress the town plaza and residents for a sequence that had been written into the story to display Mario's famous comedy bullfighting routine.

It was not sheer perversity that impelled Todd to start the shooting schedule with the largest and trickiest scene in the picture. He didn't know how long the money he had borrowed from Lorraine would last, so he wanted to have the biggest and best parts of *80 Days* in the can before he ran out of cash. He could then put them together—as he had the *Oklahoma!* highlights—in order to raise the balance of the money he would need to finish.

Mario's fame and reputation in the Spanish-speaking world was a key factor in obtaining the services of the first cameo star to be filmed in the picture. The story twist required Mario as Passepartout to match his "amateur" bullfighting skills against those of the greatest bullfighter of the time. Todd asked Mario who was the world's greatest bullfighter. Mario told him Luis Miguel Dominguín, who had retired two years before. Dominguín knew and admired Mario, and like all retired champions was itching to have another go. Dominguín had made a fortune in the bullring and was now one of the leading breeders of fighting bulls. When Todd went to talk to him about money, Dominguín asked him, "How much do you want?"

On the first day's shooting, John Farrow, the director, started to place the sixty-five hundred residents of Chinchón in natural-looking groups around the plaza to create the appearance of an appreciative and festive *feria* crowd. He gave the occasional well-costumed individual a bit of business, such as drinking wine from a goatskin.

Todd started to go crazy. He turned to Curly Lindon and said, "For chrissakes, is this guy going to teach Spaniards how to watch a bullfight and drink wine?" It was August, and Todd figured that by the time Farrow had set and placed the crowd to his satisfaction, they would have to break for Christmas without the first frame of the film being shot. Speaking later at Harvard, Todd described this scene:

> I had this director. We started in Spain, it was nine o'clock—and nothing happened. So I said a few words to him, and this guy said, "I've been making pictures for so and so many years." And one word led to another, and he said the one thing nobody should ever say to me—"Why don't you do it yourself?" I did!

It was Todd and Harry Squires in Vienna all over again, but this time the troops were under Todd's command, not a Russian general's. Todd turned to Lindon, started the action and began screaming, "Get this! Get that!" And in two days they had about ten minutes of some of the most exciting and colorful action footage in the whole picture.

Farrow and his agent had, however, outsmarted Todd. Farrow had received $50,000 in advance. Todd grumbled for the next year about Farrow being paid for an hour and a half of not working. But the Farrow and Poe script was a solid foundation on which the rest of the picture was built and improvised, and with Perelman they won the Academy Award for the Best Screenplay (Adapted).

From Spain the production moved to England, where several major problems were confronting Todd.

Michael Anderson, a young English director, was on holiday with his family in Torquay, having completed his work on a film only three days before. He got a call from his agent, asking him to come to London for a meeting with "an American guy who's looking for a director to take over *Around the World in 80 Days*":

> I arrived at the Dorchester and was sent up to the Oliver Messel Suite. There were dozens of people there. I was sitting there about a half an hour when a figure in a zebra-striped dressing gown came into the room and said, "Is Michael Anderson here?" I held up my hand, and he told everyone else to clear out—which was done in seconds. He took the cigar out of his mouth and asked, "If you were on a penny farthing bicycle, traveling through the streets of Chelsea, where would you put the camera?" I said, "On the handlebars." He said, "You're hired."

In England, not only were stars needed to get the cameo concept rolling, but Todd needed the best actors possible to liven up the opening expository portion of the picture.

In 1954, Noel Coward, in a pinch for money, had consented to the unlikely proposition of headlining a show in Las Vegas. Much to his pleasant surprise, he was a tremendous success. Shortly before he started his stint in Vegas, he signed a lucrative contract to do three television specials on CBS. Todd went to see Coward in June 1955, when he was appearing at the Desert Inn, and began to romance him. With his financial worries resolved, Coward was riding high on his personal triumph. Todd told him about his plans to make *Around the World in 80 Days* and said that if Coward was going to be in London at the end of the summer—which he was—he might find a small but juicy role for him. Coward, who was in a genial mood, nodded pleasantly but noncommittally, little knowing that he was going to be cornered by Todd two months later in London. Coward said, "I was bullied into playing the role over an inferior lunch." However, Coward's long friendship with David Niven surely helped. Todd described his next move:

> In the case of Sir John Gielgud, he asked me, "Why do you want me to play a sacked butler? I am a Shakespearean actor." I said, "Because I know you could do it so well and I know it's right for you." He said, "Let me read it." I gave him the pages and he read it. Then he said, "My dear Mr. Todd, you really want me to play this? Why?" I said, "Because I'm so sure you're right for the role." He said, "Who is playing the other part?" I said, "Noel Coward." He said, "I've *got* to see *that.*" I said, "One way for you to see it— be on the set tomorrow." And he was on the set.

Compensation for many of the cameo stars was the basic Actors Guild minimum, but with little honorariums thrown in— a Thunderbird here, a bit of jewelry there. For older and fading stars who could use the cash, Todd gave them *very* healthy salaries for a day or two of their time. Noel Coward got the minimum, but in appreciation for being the first in setting the precedent, Todd sent him a Bonnard as a Christmas present. In return, Coward sent his own painting of a colorful Jamaican market.

When you're beginning a film in England and trying to establish the concept of cameo roles, landing Noel Coward and John Gielgud is a pretty good start, but there was more work to be done.

Michael Anderson recalls:

> I was going to bed the night before we shot the Reform Club scene and no one had been set to play the Governor of the Bank of England role. I was naturally concerned, but Mike called me up just before midnight and said, "I'm trying all sorts of people, but you forget it, get a good night's sleep, and I promise you there'll be someone there when you come in in the morning." So I go in at six-thirty and an ashen-faced Robert Morley was sitting there, and he said, "I have no idea what I'm doing here." Mike had talked him into playing the role at one in the morning.

What could have been the dull exposition scenes at the Reform Club were made marvelously entertaining by Sid Perelman's witty dialogue and masterful performances by Finlay Currie, Basil Sydney, Trevor Howard, Ronald Squire and Robert Morley, and finally Niven's own performance as the intrepid Phileas Fogg.

At first, the performances of these great English actors almost overwhelmed Niven. I saw all the out-takes of the crucial scene when they are playing whist and Fogg's twenty-thousand-pound wager is made with his fellow club members that he can circle the globe in eighty days. Niven made a minor fumble of a line on the first take. Things got worse, and at some point during the next several takes Niven either blew up or stumbled over a line. All the while Morley, Currie, Sydney, Squire and Howard were building and embellishing their brief bits of dialogue and business, superbly orchestrating the scene among themselves. At last Niven caught up with them and delivered his lines perfectly. The result was a brilliantly polished scene that undoubtedly would not have been achieved if Niven had been letter perfect on the first take. Right at the start of the story and at the beginning of the production, Niven got into high gear and maintained his superb characterization throughout the long and arduous shooting schedule.

Vignettes that made use of John Mills, Bea Lillie, Hermione

Gingold and Glynis Johns were written in the evenings by Perelman and Todd and shot a day or two later. This was not improvisation but facile opportunism.

A problem in England that was to recur with regularity throughout the course of the production was the need for ready cash. Skippy Sanford recalls:

> I was at my tailor's, Sy DeVore, getting a jacket fitted, when this call came through. It was Mike. He said, "Goddamnit! Why aren't you here? I need you." I said, "Are you at the studio?" He said, "No, I'm in London. Get your ass over here. I've got a room for you in the Savoy." I said, "Now?" He said, "Yeah. Get the first plane out." Well, I went, and I always carried a batch of traveler's checks with me, and they wound up being used to get us out of Paris. When I arrived in London the American crew was ready to quit, as they weren't getting paid. Mike said, "Talk to them. See what you can do. It's just a temporary mix-up."
>
> That first night I called a meeting at my suite at the Savoy. I ordered bottles of the most expensive booze, and after they had had a few drinks I explained that I had been with the company several years and that Mike Todd was a responsible person and I would give them my personal guarantee that they would get paid. "Go back to work tomorrow and everything will be fine." They did.
>
> The next night, at the end of the day's shooting, Mike said, "Come with me. We're going out to dinner." I said, "Okay, fine." And we got in a limousine. When I noticed we were driving away from London, I said, "Where are we going?" And Mike said, "To Paris." We go out to the airport and get in this charter plane, arrive in Paris and go to this French restaurant—well, naturally it was a French restaurant, it was France. Mike introduces me to this attractive middle-aged woman, Lorraine Manville, and suggests that I go into the bar and have a drink. I did, and they're busy talking, and then we all had a lovely dinner together. Mike was talking about all the exciting footage we were getting in London. We finished dinner and flew back to London. And that was that . . . except two days later, everyone was paid in full.

Todd's use of cameo stars was making news. Eddie Gilmore, the Associated Press bureau chief in London, knew Todd and invited him to his flat one night for a drink. Kevin McClory had been in Italy since completing his stint on *Moby Dick* and dropped in that evening to say hello to Gilmore. Todd remembered Kevin:

"You're Klevin McClory! Where've you been—are you working?" (Kevin was never sure if Mike's mispronunciation of his first name was deliberate.)

Kevin explained that he had been on holiday and was now, in fact, looking for a job. He was told to report to the production office and start work the next day. Kevin was put to work with the second unit. Kevin's "Message to Garcia" came a few days later while Todd was with the second unit.

The Household Cavalry Band was scheduled to march in front of the palace and out through the gates at eleven A.M. The camera was set up at the entrance, and you could see down the road, with the cars and all going by—which couldn't be 1872. There wasn't time to change the setup—the band wasn't under Mike's control—and the shot they wanted was the band coming right into and past the camera. The second-unit cameraman suddenly said, "We can't shoot." Mike blew his nut. "What do you mean, we can't shoot?" The cameraman explained about seeing the cars and there not being time to move. The first unit was over on Victoria Square, shooting in front of Ian Fleming's house, funnily enough. [Years later, Kevin successfully sued Ian Fleming for plagiarism of a script that Kevin had written and shown to Fleming. Kevin's script was the basis for *Thunderball*, and Kevin became a coproducer of the James Bond film, which grossed over fifty million dollars.] So I went to Victoria Square. I grabbed a half a dozen of the extras who were in costume and pushed them into one of the unit's cars and we drove back to the palace. I placed the extras so that they hid the road and the cars and said, "Now you can shoot." And at that instant, the band appeared and we got the shot—it's in the picture.

When my two weeks were up—I'd only been taken on for two weeks—I went to the studio to collect my money. I went over to the stage where the first unit was shooting, and Mike came up to me and said, "Klevin, how good is your French?"

You know, I have a speech im-p-p-pediment, and Mike so took me by surprise I couldn't get a word out. He said, "Great. We're going to France in an hour." I said, "I'd better go and get some clothes." He said, "No, you won't need any. We're coming back tonight."

We went to Croydon airfield, and Mike and his secretary, Midori Tsuji, and I flew to Paris in a private plane. We had a meeting at the Meurice Hotel, where he had a suite, and there was a French producer, a friend of his, Georges Lourau, and a group of Lourau's assistants. I had no idea what I was doing there. Mike said he wanted so many horse-drawn carriages, and he wanted three hundred extras in period costumes, and then he said, "I want the girl with the boobs." They said, "You mean Martine Carol?" He said, "Yes, that's the dame." Mike asked "How did you make out with Maurice Chevalier?" Lourau said, "Fine, but there are a few things to work out." And for several minutes they discussed what Chevalier wanted.

It turned out that Chevalier wanted an exorbitant sum for half a day's work. This time, however, unlike the fall of 1939 when Todd tried to sign him for the New York World's Fair, he was willing to pay Chevalier's price. But nothing was that simple with Chevalier. He wanted special billing, either above or below all the rest of the cameo stars. Kevin continues:

Mike said that the special billing Chevalier wanted was ridiculous, and they suggested Fernandel. Mike said, "Perfect. Get Fernandel. But I'll use him for a different bit." They said, "He's working now." Mike said, "That's okay, we're shooting on Sunday." They all sat there, and they kept saying, "Ah, oui, monsieur," and they were taking notes. So I took a notebook out, just to keep a record of what Mike said. He wanted the television aerials off, and he wanted the rue Castiglione cleared, which leads up to the place Vendôme, and the Hotel Meurice sign and other signs taken down. And he said, "Right. So we'll do it on Sunday." And they said, "Oui, monsieur." Lourau said, "Which Sunday?" Mike said, "You didn't hear me good. I said Sunday. You understand? Thursday, Friday, Saturday, Sunday. This Sunday." "But, monsieur," they said, "ce n'est pas possible. This is in four days. This is not possible." Mike whispered, "Klevin, come here." And he pulled me into the bedroom. He said, "These pricks. They're not going to do it. You're going to stay here and you're going to do it." I said, "I am?" He said, "Yes, you are." I said, "Okay. I'll do my best." He said, "You'll do it."

So we went back into the sitting room and he said, "Georges, this is Klevin McClory, he's in charge. I've got to go to the airport. I can't spend any more time here. He'll come to the airport with me and I'll tell him everything he needs to know and he'll get in touch with you. Good-bye." And we left.

Fortunately, I had written it all down—so many carriages, so many horses, so many extras. And in the car on the way to the airport he said, "I want lots of parasols and poodles." I said, "What about Fernandel and Martine Carol?" He said, "I'll take care of them." So I wrote it down: *"Fernandel, M. Carol—M. Todd."* Mike said, "We'll shoot Sunday." And I said, "All we've got to do is hope for good weather." He flew off to London, and I arranged everything on the list.

When Mike came back on Saturday, I went out to the airport to meet him. First thing he said was, "Where are we doing the makeup?" He always came out with these catch questions. He'd never mentioned it before. I said, "I've got the barber shop in the Meurice Hotel."

He had left me with a wad of money because I'd said I was going to need it to get rid of the cars parked on the street. So I had taken care of the police. They had said, "No problem, there'd be no parking."

Then Mike said, "What about Fernandel and the dame?" I said, "No, you're doing that." He said, "No, I'm not. You were to do that." I had my notebook there, and I showed it to him. "I'm sorry, Mr. Todd, but you see that? *Fernandel, M. Carol—M. Todd.*" He never wasted time arguing. "Well, how do we get them? I haven't done anything." I said, "Lourau is waiting for us at the hotel. He can reach them." When we arrived, Mike said, "Get Fernandel and tell him I want to see him at eight o'clock." It was late afternoon, and they said, "But, *monsieur . . .*"

That evening we went around to Fernandel's flat, and he was standing by the fireplace. Mike walked straight up to him with his arms outstretched and said, "Ah, the face of France. The face of France. Just imagine that face sixty feet wide, thirty feet high on the Todd-AO screen. Most people who come to shoot film in Paris, you know what they put on the screen? They put on the Eiffel Tower, that pile of iron, everybody's seen it. We're going to put it on the screen— sixty feet wide, thirty feet high—the map of France, your face, Fernandel!"

Fernandel's agent was there, and he started to say something. "But, *monsieur—*" And Mike took a cigar and shoved it in his mouth. Mike carried on, saying how gigantic Fernandel's face was going to be on the Todd-AO screen, and the agent finally got the cigar out of his mouth and said, *"Ce n'est pas possible . . ."* Mike turns on him and shouts, *"Pas possible! Pas possible!* That's all I ever hear around here! We have Noel Coward, John Gielgud, Robert Morley, Trevor Howard, Finlay Currie and David Niven representing England. Who better to represent France"—and spreading his arms again to indicate the size of the face on the screen—"than the great Fernandel?"

Fernandel spoke up:

"Monsieur, this is Jules Verne, *Voyage au Tour du monde?"*

"That's right. That's right," Mike said, "the great French writer."

"Monsieur, it is in period. I would have to have a wig."

"Right."

"You say I am a coachman. I would need a costume."

"That's right. That's right."

"Monsieur, it's tomorrow. *Ce n'est pas possible."*

"You said that word again! Don't use that word!" Mike kept talking: "If I had the wig and if I had the costume would you play the part?"

"But *oui, monsieur.* Of course. But you haven't." And Fernandel started to laugh.

"But you *would?"*

"Oui."

"Shake."

And Mike shook his hand. He had him. "Klevin, go down to the car and bring up the wigs and costumes." At the Meurice he had told me to find out who made Fernandel's costumes and to get a set of costumes and wigs for Fernandel to choose from. The car was loaded with them.

When we got back to the Meurice, Mike turned to one of Lourau's production men and asked, "Where does this dame Martine Carol live?" [Martine Carol was the most popular French film actress of the time—a sophisticated Brigitte Bardot.] Mike phoned and said he was coming over to talk to her. We went downstairs, and we were getting in the car when Mike turned to me and said, "Klevin, I don't need you for this one." And he left me standing there in the street. She was on the set seven o'clock the next morning, eyes beaming, in love with Mike.

At dawn, Sunday, I met Mike at the entrance to the Meurice on the rue Castiglione, and he was in an absolute rage. I have never seen anyone so mad in all my life. There were cars parked all over the place, right where we were going to shoot. *"Klevin!"* he screamed. "I thought you took care of the cops." I had, but they'd just put up No Parking signs late

Saturday night and people had parked and locked their cars for the weekend, starting Friday noon. Altogether there were fifty-seven cars in our way, Mike was jumping up and down, chewing on his cigar. "Get them out of here! Get them out of here!" I called three garages, and while we were standing there arguing, the tow trucks started to arrive. There were three or four policemen standing around and I took them away and gave them some money and told them to go to a cafe. The cars that weren't left in gear, or that didn't have their handbrakes on, could simply be towed away. But there were only a few of them. So we had to jimmy open the doors and windows on a lot of the cars. On the cover of *Paris-Match* that week was a picture of the windows being jimmied open. All fifty-seven cars were gone in time to shoot. Mike had production assistants ready with money to pay off everyone who came back to collect their cars. But unfortunately, one belonged to Robert Schuman, the former foreign minister, and where his car was parked for the night was not near his home, and it was, I think, a source of embarrassment to him.

The sun came out like a miracle, and we shot everything. We went to the Gare du Nord, where we did the scene with Fernandel. Mike wrote the dialogue for the scene in the barber shop of the Meurice Hotel that morning. Fernandel arrived and asked for the script. Mike said: "There is no script; here are the lines. Niven gets into your carriage and says, 'Thomas Cook's.' You turn around, and we have that giant close-up of Fernandel's face—the face of France. You shrug, '*Où?*' Niven says, 'Cooks.' You repeat your line: '*Où?*' Then Cantinflas says, 'C-o-o-o-o-o-ok's.' And you say, 'Aaaaaaaah, C-o-o-o-k's,' and turn around and drive off." And that was the immortal dialogue that Mike ad-libbed.

Evelyn Keyes did a brief walk-on, and Martine Carol slaps Mario's face when he propositions her. Mike flew in on Saturday and flew out Sunday night, but after he left all hell broke loose. Schuman exploded when he found out his car had been towed away. The chief of police came over and was going to arrest everybody in sight and tried to get the film, but Mike had flown off with all the footage. On the way to the airport he described several scenes he wanted me to shoot with the miniature balloons. [Todd's most inspired alteration of the original Jules Verne novel was to add the balloon sequence, which, among a whole series of pluses, provided the logo, the introduction of the theme music and one of the comedy and scenic highlights of the film.] Fortunately, there were *two* miniature balloons, each about eight feet in diameter. Monday morning it was in all the newspapers about the cars being towed away, and all the permits to shoot on location in Paris—no, in all of France—were cancelled. Leland Hayward was doing *The Spirit of Saint Louis* —they stopped him shooting. Carol Reed was doing *Trapeze* —they shut him down totally. Then Mike called, and I told him no filming could be done anywhere in France, by any foreign company.

"In the car—" he began.

I interrupted: "That's what it's all about—the cars being towed away."

"Shut up and listen," Mike said. "In the car on the way to the airport I told you I wanted you to get a shot of the balloon going in the background past the column in the place Vendôme."

"I just told you, Mike, that *no one* can shoot on location anywhere in all of France, let alone Paris."

"You didn't hear me good. I'm going to repeat it. I want you to shoot that today and then call me."

Kevin was a day late getting this shot completed. He had run into the maharajah of Cooch Behar, whom he had met while working with John Huston. He brought him along when he went into a bank in the place Vendôme. Kevin told the manager he was a tourist from Ireland and would like very much to take some pictures from the roof of the bank very early the following morning. The bank manager was most cordial and impressed by the presence of the maharajah and gave his permission. Kevin rented a huge truck in which his assistants had inflated the miniature balloon. Kevin had them park the truck on the sidewalk, facing the traffic, just past the entrance to the Ritz. He knew that once the balloon went up, all the traffic would stop and, as is the Parisian custom, the horns would start honking and the gendarmes would immediately appear. The wind was blowing from the direction of the Ritz, and Kevin told the two men who were to hold the cables attached to the helium-filled balloon that when the camera was in place and he blew his whistle, they were to take the balloon out of the truck and run it across the square through traffic—or, if necessary, "over the bonnets of the stopped cars."

All the equipment was on the roof of the bank except the camera, which was being brought up when the manager arrived. Staring at the huge Todd-AO camera, the manager asked, "What is that?" "My camera," Kevin replied. The manager was irritated that he had been tricked, but again the presence of the maharajah was Kevin's passport. When the camera was ready Kevin blew his whistle, the balloon went up, the traffic stopped, the stalled French motorists honked and the gendarmes arrived in the middle of the second take and arrested Kevin's crew and confiscated the balloon. From the street the police could not see the camera or Kevin, who exited with the film under his arm.

The next day Kevin extricated his crew from jail and the camera from the bank roof. He then went to the Loire Valley to get some footage of the second miniature balloon passing some imposing châteaux. He hired a crop-dusting plane to shoot the footage representing the point of view from the balloon. The police kept getting reports of balloon sightings, but Kevin remained one jump ahead of them until he went to take the final shots of the balloon passing the gargoyles and spires of Notre Dame. The second miniature was confiscated, but by then Todd and Kevin had all the footage they needed in France.

Todd then sent Kevin from Paris with his crew of three, 50,000 feet of film, a script and some money and an air travel card—with instructions to "shoot some *dhows*"—he wasn't sure where. Todd went back to Hollywood to film all the interiors and the American western sequences and to cast the female lead.

Mike described how he sold Marlene Dietrich on playing one of the cameo roles:

> I suggested something very unorthodox to her. I said we would shoot the scene and show it to her and if she didn't like it, I would burn it. It was quite a chance to take considering there was David Niven, Cantinflas, Frank Sinatra, Red Skelton and George Raft in the same sequence. It would have been a very expensive bonfire. I knew that she would have to look stunning. It would be hard, I suppose, to make her look bad, but I took no chances. I got my costume designer, Miles White, to work up something really special. We went out and killed a gold lamé to make her gown. Well, we went to shoot the scene, and something happened which I think convinced her that we knew what we were doing. There was a girl that had a costume that was similar in color, so I made like a big cheese and I walked over to the assistant director and said, "Please have that young lady stay out of

the shots that have Miss Dietrich in them." She watched and heard this and you could almost feel the lump in her throat. Well, she loved the sequence, and she said, "I think there should be another shot of the legs." And, of course, she was right. My motto has always been "Stay with the money," and with Dietrich the legs are her hallmark, and we didn't have enough of them. Well, she became my friend. And a few weeks later we were shooting outdoors at night—the burning of the suttee—and she brings me out boiled beef to the location. She's not only gorgeous and a hell of an actress, but a fabulous cook.

There was a little more to this story than Mike was giving in interviews. I was out on the coast and on leave when the suttee sequence—when Niven and Cantinflas rescue the princess— was being filmed. My father said that it was quite probable that Dietrich might show up. "I've never taken advantage of you in this way before, but you're old enough and married and I hope you won't mind, but I'm going to make you the heavy. I've never been able to get involved with older women, and while she's very nice and very attractive, I just can't get interested in her. I've told her that there's no serious romances in my life without your approval. Now, when you meet her, be pleasant and courteous, but very reserved and cool. Later I'm going to tell her that my hands are tied because you disapprove. Now don't cross me up and fawn all over her."

I'm not a great actor under any circumstances, but Dietrich made my assignment extremely difficult to carry out. The three of us drove home that evening, all in the front seat of my father's car. For a good part of the ride, Dietrich was stroking my left leg while she was talking to me. I know that's what makes horse racing, but no matter what her age, I found Dietrich most attractive.

That same night, while Mike had me cast as the heavy, he was again making like a big cheese with Dietrich. Michael Anderson says:

Mike and I had a wonderful working relationship. Word got back to me early on that Mike had told everyone to leave me alone—so long as the stuff is coming out, not to go near me. And as a matter of fact, I rarely saw Mike during the filming. There was only this one time that Mike came on the set and wanted to take over from me. It was during the funeral pyre scene. He was very nervous that night, and he climbed up this very high tower we were shooting from. He said, "Do you mind if I do this scene? I have a certain idea in mind, and it would be easier for me to do it than to explain it to you." Well, I was quite upset. He had never done anything like this before, and I thought, Is he going to take over the whole picture? I climbed down and Niven came over to me and whispered, "Just sit down, Michael. He's the producer, and it's his money." So I quietly took a seat. Looking around, I saw that Dietrich was on the set watching and perhaps he was trying to show off for her. Anyway, it all started to fall apart. Mike's up on the tower, and Shirley shouts up to him in front of a tremendous crowd of extras, "How do you want me to play the scene?" He shouts back, "You read the script, didn't you? Do whatever it says in the script." She yells back, "Yeah, but do you want me to faint or swoon or cry, or what?" Mike says, "You're an actress, for godsakes. Do whatever seems right." Well, it was a total mess, and everything went wrong. So Mike climbs down, turns to me and says, "I think I've got it under control now, Michael. You can finish it up." Mike strode away, taking Dietrich by the arm. After the next take, Niven came up to me and said, "See, it didn't take long for Mike to realize it's not as easy as it looks."

On October 10, 1955, *Oklahoma!* opened at the Rivoli Theatre in New York. Both the movie and the Todd-AO process were a hit—but there was much more praise for the production than for the process. By a stroke of bad luck or sloppiness, a section of the premiere print was severely scratched, probably by a bit of dirt in one of the projectors, and some of the reviewers mistakenly attributed this to some shortcoming in the process. But the critics correctly had reservations about distortions they noticed in some scenes. Probably only Skippy Sanford and the *Oklahoma!* cameraman, Robert Surtees, were aware that the distortions were caused by some of the lenses and the inability of the American Optical Company to come up with an optical printer that would correct these distortions. Sanford had warned Todd, but the point didn't really sink in until he saw some of the early shots of *80 Days*, which had to be discarded because they were so distorted. The shortcomings of the process, which could be and eventually were inexpensively corrected by the use of distortion-free lenses, prevented the process and consequently *Oklahoma!* itself from having the gigantic impact that was expected by the industry. When Todd opened *80 Days* a year later at the same theater on the same screen, the critics wrote that the Todd-AO process was largely if not completely perfected. But of course by then the ship had sailed, and any chance the process had of eclipsing Cinerama, CinemaScope and the other new wide screen processes had disappeared.

From Todd's preview screening until the opening, the stock had edged downwards from over twenty dollars to just over ten. The day after the opening the stock was bid at eight and a fraction. Todd and Lorraine sold their entire block, which then constituted almost 25 percent of the entire issue, for four and a half dollars a share. On June 23 they could have sold their stock for over seven million dollars. At the end of October they got two million and change. Almost all this money went to Lorraine to repay her investment in *A Night in Venice* and her loans to Mike. She was just about even on her financial dealings with him.

He had been so busy making *80 Days* that he had little time to keep Lorraine involved and amused other than to give her the courtesy of the occasional phone call by way of a progress report. It was no longer fun-and-games time. He was, however, able to stretch his relationship with her to the absolute limit. Giving her a first lien on the picture, plus a reasonable rate of interest, he turned around and got a fresh loan from her. His indebtedness to Lorraine went back up to two million dollars. This gave him the room to get more of the film in the can so that he could make an advantageous deal with a distributor to finish *80 Days*.

Of the twenty-four stars in Hollywood who did cameo roles, Ronald Colman was the most firmly retired, and Todd was particularly pleased to enlist his services. Buster Keaton was the sole cameo role I cast. I had become a tremendous fan of Keaton's after a festival of his films, all of them produced by Joe Schenck, had been shown at Amherst.

When Keaton arrived on location in Colorado, he was somewhat taken aback when he noticed that his trailer was larger and more luxurious than Niven's, Mario's or anyone else's. The first opportunity that Keaton could catch Todd alone, he quietly said, "Mr. Todd, I think there's been some mistake. I've been assigned the biggest trailer." "There's no mistake," Todd replied. "You're the biggest star in the picture."

During the filming of some of the western location material, Skippy Sanford says that Todd called him one afternoon and said, "I want you to go with me to New Mexico."

He had a chartered plane waiting to take us there and suddenly Mike had an important dinner date he had to keep—which probably meant he was talking to someone about money. So we didn't take off till very late. When we got there, there were no landing lights, but there was a bright moon and we could see a little field below, and we landed. It was three or four o'clock in the morning, and there was nothing there but the wind sock to greet us. Everyone must have given up on us and gone back to town, which was twenty or thirty miles away. There were no phone booths and the little shack of an office was dark and locked. Mike kicked in the door and telephoned production to come get us. After a while a limousine came out to pick us up, but it was after five o'clock in the morning when we arrived in town and the company was getting ready to go out to the location. Mike said, "We'll catch a couple of hours before we go out." I was just falling asleep when the chauffeur came and started beating on the door, saying, "Mr. Todd's waiting for you—he wants you to get some clothes." I said, "I'd rather get some sleep." But the chauffeur insisted, and we drove to this store where I found Mike being outfitted. He said, "You can't go around like that, Skippy. You gotta have a western outfit." I said, "But we're only going to be here for a few hours. You said we were going on to meet somebody in Vegas later." He said, "We'll hang around a while. I think I want to shoot some stuff." He bought me a day outfit with some boots, an afternoon outfit with some more boots and then he said, "In case we go out tonight, you need some fancy duds." So he got me a dressy shirt and one of those string ties with the silver and turquoise thing to hold it. We piled all the clothes in the car and drove out to the location, which was about forty miles away. We got there late, and they were in the middle of shooting the scene where Cantinflas is being burned at the stake. We watched a while, and then Mike says to an assistant director, "You got an extra camera?" Well, nobody was paying any attention to him—everybody was busy, and where we were standing nobody knew who he was. Finally, we got a camera and a second-unit crew together and went out on this flat car and shot all these different kinds of animals next to the railroad track. A calf, some skunks, buffalo roaming and all. He wanted it for the point of view for the sailmobile sequence. I think this footage was the end of Weatherwax [the original editor on the picture]. He didn't know that Mike had shot it and he kept cutting it all out, and of course Mike wanted it in.

At the end of a week's shooting in Hollywood, Michael Anderson and Todd were leaving the studio together when Todd took a detour to corner a propman. Anderson remembers this little exchange:

"How many monkeys you got?" Todd asked. Monday morning they were going to shoot a scene of Mario escaping a crowd by running into a sacred Hindu monkey temple. The propman said, "About a hundred and twenty." Todd said, "That's not enough—you're going to lose about half of them in the rafters. Get me another hundred monkeys." The propman said, "It's Friday night, Mike. I can't get another hundred monkeys by Monday." Mike slowly took the cigar out of his mouth and said, "Then I'll *find someone who can.*" The guy was completely taken aback: "Does that mean I'm fired?" Mike said, "Not if you get me the monkeys." So the propman says, "I'll get you the monkeys somehow, Mr. Todd." Mike walked away, but he turned back and said, "I'll give you a hint. Call the place where they make the Salk vaccine and tell them to stop grinding."

In the Far East Kevin was shooting the second-unit shots of the rail journey through India. Kevin was running out of money and started cabling and phoning Todd for more. The cables went unanswered, Kevin was not able to reach Todd on the phone and he was not returning Kevin's calls.

I was dealing with the number-two railway official in Dacca. I promised him more than I had given the other fellow in Karachi, so he was most helpful. We started to shoot and had things so well organized that when the eight o'clock express was coming through from Calcutta he'd say to me, "Can it come ahead? They just called up now. The passengers are getting restless." And I'd say, "No. Just let me get this shot. Then it can go." We really had a superb situation. I had promised him so many thousands of rupees. So you can imagine my distress when after working almost a week in the countryside, we got back to the hotel in Dacca and there was still no reply from Mike. I didn't have a rupee left. The hotel bill hadn't been paid. The crew's mail arrived, and they hadn't been paid from day one. I had been giving them out-of-pocket expense money, but their families back home had nothing for food or rent. I was a bachelor, so it didn't matter that much to me, but I was furious about my crew not being paid. The railway official was saying, "Mr. McClory, you come from Karachi and promise me everything and you do nothing about it. Who do you think I am? No more help till you do what you promise."

The hotel manager came to me and said, "I have your account here. You pay it up now or you are having nothing. *Nothing*, you hear me." I told them, "I work for a man, Mr. Todd, and he is unable to get through to me." The manager said, "That is not my problem. You must pay up now." So I had my crew bring up our truck and I showed it to the hotel manager and told him: "Here is all our equipment. The camera is the newest and finest in the world. You keep it all under lock and key. You give my crew anything and everything they want. I will go to America and see my boss and bring back money. I will be back in ten days. I will pay the bill in full and give you a present, a very handsome present."

So I got on a plane. I still had my air travel card. I was furious. We had been working day and night, and the heat and the dirt—it was intolerable. I was flying halfway around the world—no jets then—it was a very long trip, and I had a beard and a filthy bush jacket on.

I arrived in Los Angeles in the evening and was met by the press agent Mike had hired in England, Ernie Anderson.

"Mike told me to tell you the footage is absolutely fabulous—it's perfect," Ernie said.

"I know all the words," I said. "Where is he?" Ernie went on and on and I stopped him: "WHERE IS MIKE?"

"He's got you a marvelous room in the Beverly Hills Hotel."

"Ernie, where is he?"

"He'll see you in the morning."

"No, Ernie. I've come eight thousand miles and I'm going to see him tonight."

"I don't think you ought to."

"WHERE IS MICHAEL TODD?"

"He's at Chasen's."

"Right. We're going there now."

I walked into Chasen's, all rumpled and dirty, with clothes

I'd been wearing for about three weeks, and there was Mike sitting with his secretary, Midori Tsuji, and Marlene Dietrich. They had just started dinner. I walked over. Mike looked up and said:

"Klevin! Your stuff's great. Have Ernie take you to the hotel. I'll see you in the morning."

"I want to talk to you."

"I'll see you in the *morning*."

"Mike. I've come eight thousand miles to talk to you, and I'm going to talk to you *now*." And I stood right where I was. He didn't introduce me, but of course I knew Midori. He looked at me, then he stood up and took me by the arm out to the entrance hall.

"Who do you think you are coming in here like this and talking to me like that?" He was in a terrible temper.

"The crew has not been paid. There's a huge hotel bill, and you've not answered my cables or calls."

He was furious. The hatcheck girl and the maître d' were listening to what I was saying, so Mike pushed me out the front door. He clenched his fists and I thought we were going to have a fist fight. I said, "They must be paid."

"It's that Percy Guth," Mike said. We exchanged a few more words, and then Mike shouted, "You're fired!"

"I'm what?" And I took my jacket off, ready to have at it. "You can't fire me; I haven't been paid. Tomorrow you're going to pay me and my crew, and then I quit."

Mike had motioned the attendant for his car, which was brought around. And without a word he jumped in and slammed the door and, glaring at me, drove away like a madman. I put on my jacket and went in and sat down with Midori and Miss Dietrich. Midori asked, "What happened?" I said, "He just fired me." Midori said, "Oh no. He's going to double your salary." I laughed and ate the dinner Mike had ordered for himself. I had a very pleasant evening.

I decided: Mike Todd is always one step ahead of me, but this time he won't be. I went back to the hotel right after dinner. I was very tired after my journey, but I left a call for five o'clock. I had a shower and my tea in the morning, and I got to the studio just after six-thirty so I would be there waiting for him. I got to the man at the gate and said, "I am Mr. McClory—" "Oh, yes, Mr. Todd told me you'd be coming about this time. He's in his office waiting for you." I couldn't believe it. Every time, he always outsmarted you. So I went around, and there he was, all clean-shaven and right on the ball. He wouldn't let me say a word. "You know,

Klevin, you were right. That goddamned Guth—I'm going to fire him. Do you know your crew wasn't paid? And you know, Klevin, *you* weren't paid?" I said, "I suspected that." And those were the last words I got to say. He said, "I've been on to New York, and it's all been taken care of. The money is on its way. Meet me here at ten o'clock." And he shot out the door.

He had me waiting around for weeks. I went with him almost everywhere. We watched the first unit shoot. He showed me the footage I had shot and then told me what else he wanted me to get when I got back. I showed him pictures I had picked up, when my plane had stopped at Bangkok, of the Royal Barge and the palaces. He said the King of Siam was a great friend of his and that he had hired him to write some songs for a show he had produced. He told me to just call the king and say that I was working for Michael Todd and the king would give me anything I wanted. Meanwhile I had this marvelous room at the Beverly Hills Hotel, but I'm sure the delay was because he was having difficulties raising more money.

Towards the end of the shooting schedule, late on a Friday afternoon, Michael Anderson got a call from Todd in New York:

I was just finishing the sequence where Mario makes some passes with his jacket at a Brahma bull and he's chased by a crowd of Hindus through the streets for having teased a sacred animal. Mike asked, "How's it going?" I told him, "We're nearly through." He said, "Oh, oh. Get a hold of Ivan (he was my assistant) and send for suppers." I said, "There's an awful lot of people here." He said, "That's the problem— I don't have the money to pay them. And send for lights and keep shooting." I said, "There isn't anything to shoot." He said, "You'll think of something." I said, "How long do I keep going?" He said, "Until you see the white Cadillac convertible with the black guy holding the red bag." I kept shooting close-ups, and the crowd's milling around, staring at me, and all the while I've got one eye on the gate. Finally, it's almost ten o'clock when the car comes rolling in, tooting its horn, and we paid everyone off. If they had known what was going on, I would have had a *really* angry crowd chasing Mario.

When Todd sent Kevin back to East Pakistan, he gave him $50,000 and the following instructions: "Tip lavishly . . . and as soon as you get to Siam, call the king. He's a friend of mine. He'll give you anything you want." His first night in Bangkok, Kevin went into the bar in his hotel, where he met the son of General Kharb, the minister of tourism. Kevin said, "What a wonderful coincidence," and explained that he was in Thailand to film the Royal Barge and scenic backgrounds. Kevin told General Kharb's son that he would be working with his father after he called the king in the morning and told him that he was working for Michael Todd. His drinking companion threw his hands in the air and said, *"Do not mention that name in this country."* And he went on to explain that Todd had used three of the king's songs in one of his shows and had widely publicized and made use of the king's name, but had never paid a cent of the royalties due the king, et cetera, et cetera, et cetera.

Kevin cultivated General Kharb and got fabulous footage. "If I hadn't met the general's son in the hotel bar my first night, I'd still be languishing in a jail in Bangkok."

When Kevin finally finished the second-unit work, Mike kept him on the picture through the completion of principal photography and during the entire postproduction phase. Todd had created the world's most gigantic jigsaw puzzle; there were thousands of feet of amusing, scenic and great action footage, but no continuity sheets or a cogent script to put the pieces together. Kevin, as much as anyone, helped solve the puzzle.

Another tireless worker was an editing assistant, Don Tomlinson, who did a yeoman's job in the cutting room from the time Mike returned to Hollywood. Don says:

> At the time it didn't strike me that the picture was being made in a crazy-quilt fashion because I was so enamored of the way Mike operated. There was no indecision—there wasn't a group of people or chain of command coming down from a black tower. Mike was it—he made all the decisions himself. The only thing that seemed unusual at the time was his constantly going off to New York. He never came out and said he was short. He'd just say, "I've gotta go to New York." And we all knew what that meant.

The only private individual who had a piece of the profits of *80 Days* was Al Strelsin, a construction and real estate entrepreneur whom Todd had known since the 1930s. Mike could always count on a quick, no-questions-asked $100,000 loan from Strelsin. It was understood, however, that Todd had to get refinanced and repay Strelsin before he could go back for another $100,000 loan.

Jule Styne tells about one occasion when Todd needed more than the usual quick $100,000 fix from Strelsin:

> Years after Mike died Strelsin was bragging about how much he made from his piece of *80 Days*. He said that three months into the production of the picture, Mike couldn't meet a payroll. The western sequence was being filmed in Durango, Colorado, and he had all the principals, several cameo stars and a huge company out on location. There weren't many people he could call for a big overnight loan. Strelsin was a wheeler-dealer, but a solid wheeler-dealer. Mike goes looking for Strelsin and he calls him in New York, Chicago and Dallas. All they'll tell him is that Strelsin is out on a project and can't be reached. Other guys take no for an answer, but not Mike. One of the secretaries lets slip that Strelsin's out on the Mississippi River project. That's a clue. Mike now becomes a Scotland Yard detective. He knows that Al Strelsin loves to eat at Antoine's in New Orleans. Mike phones the maître d' and asks him if he's seen Mr. Strelsin recently. The maître d' says, "See him? I send him his food every day." Mike flies to New Orleans and, dropping a double sawbuck here and there, finds out that Strelsin is getting his food delivered to a huge barge that's dredging a section of the Mississippi. Strelsin is on his barge, and lo and behold a helicopter comes out of nowhere and lands right on the deck and out steps Mike Todd. Mike says, "I'm gonna cut it short because I haven't got much time. Al, I need two hundred and twenty thousand dollars right away or I've gotta close the picture down. And I'm not gonna give you any more percentage of the picture than you've already got because now we have all these stars playing cameos and the picture's almost finished and it's fabulous." Mike pulls out clipped frames from the picture and still shots of the setups. Strelsin gave him $250,000 and told him to keep the extra $30,000. He said he'd pretend he lost it to Mike in gin. Mike didn't argue.

For providing this ready emergency source of financing, Strelsin received 1.8 percent of the profits of the picture. To make his "fairy tale for adults" look convincing, Todd reshot a handful of sequences during the course of production. The most expensive and important substitution of the real thing for a miniature and studio work was the final shipboard sequence, in which Andy Devine, Edmund Lowe, Jack Oakie and Victor McLaglen played the cameo roles. As Todd explained:

> When I saw the first rough cut of the picture, I looked at the sequence where Phileas Fogg dismantles the ship, going from New York to Liverpool. He charters the ship from Oakie when he misses his connection. And when they run out of fuel, he buys the ship and dismantles it, chopping it to bits for fuel. It was shot in the studio, and I didn't like it. Everybody said it was marvelous, it was great, and to do it the Hollywood way, it was okay. But it's late in the picture, and everything else we've done is for real. When I say late in the picture, it's the last big production number before we wind up the story. It cost about two hundred and sixty thousand dollars, and I scrapped it. I bought a schooner from the Scripps Institute, and I made a side-wheeler out of it—took it out in the ocean, chopped it to bits and we burned it. And it's for real. That sequence, with the retake, will cost about five hundred and fifty to six hundred thousand dollars . . . unless you know somebody who wants to buy a slightly burned, used boat.

When Todd sold his stock after the *Oklahoma!* opening, he resigned from the boards of Magna and Todd-AO. Nevertheless, he was intensely interested in seeing Todd-AO enhance its reputation and prosper. Despite their mutual interest, Woodbridge and Todd were both determined to prove the other wrong about how to best use and sell the process. Todd-AO had opened up facilities in Hollywood for recording, mixing and editing Todd-AO as well as conventional films. After a halfhearted attempt to get along, they found themselves at each other's throats, and Mike moved out to do what postproduction work he could elsewhere.

On an extended weekend shortly before I had got out of the navy, Mike told me to come out to the coast to see how great the picture was shaping up. Sarah was about seven months' pregnant and didn't feel like making the long, round-trip airplane flight for a two-and-a-half-day visit.

Evelyn was in Europe at the time, but Mike was not lonely.

Several months later I found out that during his frequent trips to New York he was seeing a famous model and television personality, Nancy Berg, as covertly as it was possible for him to escort a gorgeous girl around town. He was busy in California after work as well.

Saturday morning of my weekend trip to the coast, we were finishing breakfast at my father's rented house in the Hollywood Hills, prior to going to the editing room to look at more footage, when Mike received a phone call. He was abrupt with the caller and said, "Look, I don't have time to talk. I was due at the cutting room twenty minutes ago." More conversation from the caller, and then, really curt now, he said, "Look, I've got to run. Good-bye." His uncharacteristic sharpness caused me to ask who had phoned.

In a tone of voice and with a look of irritation that told me it was not a joke, he answered: "Grace Kelly. She's been chasing me for weeks."

I was stunned. "And you don't want to get caught? Are you out of your mind?"

"Look, I'm a big boy now—I can pick my own playmates."

About ten-thirty Sunday morning an attractive young woman appeared at the house and Mike's embarrassed, mumbled nonintroduction indicated he had forgotten to cancel his date with her. The three of us spent the day together at the house. The girl was in her mid-twenties. She was quiet, intelligent and good-looking, but not flashy. The first time Mike left the pool for what proved to be a long telephone conversation, I introduced myself to the girl. Being a little pushy and very curious, I asked if she had a job. She said she was a secretary at Metro.

The day was relaxing for me, but Todd was on edge the entire time. He was clearly signaling that this was not a serious romance. Whenever I tried to loosen things up a bit, he became even more ill at ease. She seemed slightly apologetic, although I felt she was too sensible to feel a part of the Hollywood caste system. She apparently knew Mike well enough to understand and share his embarrassment. I thought, Here's a wonderful young civilian girl, and why couldn't it be? But they both seemed to take it for granted that their friendship was not going to lead anywhere and that this was merely a pleasant interlude for both of them.

Several months later, I asked my father, "Whatever became of that girl who worked for Metro?" He brushed the question aside as if that Sunday had never happened and she didn't exist.

A month or so later Mike woke up one morning with Esther Williams in his bed. He was quite surprised, as he hadn't gone to bed with her the night before. After she gave him a coy good-morning over a barely suppressed giggle, her husband Ben Gage burst into the room, laughing so hard he was unable to act out the enraged-husband routine he and Esther Williams had planned. As a rule my father hated practical jokes, but he did find this one amusing, especially as it enabled him to get off the topper: "Go ahead and laugh your head off, Ben, but if you had waited another two minutes to open that door, the joke would have been on you."

On a few occasions long after my father's death, the question of the women in his life came up with Elizabeth Taylor. She said that Mike had a strong interest in Jean Simmons during the final production period of *80 Days*, and then she asked with interest if I thought my father had slept with Marlene Dietrich; he had specifically told her he hadn't. Elizabeth said that when she was married to Eddie Fisher, Eddie had said that Mike had of course been lying to her—it would have been impossible for him not to have succumbed to Dietrich's appeal. I reassured Elizabeth that Mike's interest in Dietrich was confined to her boiled beef. While we were on this subject, I asked if my father had included in the list of the women in his life the secretary at MGM. No, this was news to Elizabeth, but she seemed completely uninterested and obviously shared my father's feeling that secretaries at MGM didn't count . . . and moved on to another subject.

A few days after I got out of the navy Mike was in New York on a quick business trip. I went up to the apartment early one evening after work. I was on the second floor, where my bedroom had been, rummaging through the closet to see if I had left any clothes behind when I went off to the service. My father came upstairs. He looked serious and slightly wary, waiting for me to give him my full attention. When I looked up, he said in a low voice, "I'm going to marry Evelyn." I was amazed and without thinking said, "You're crazy." He bowed his head, waiting for me to continue. "You're only marrying her out of a sense of obligation for her hanging around for three years. It would be a terrible mistake for you . . . and for her. Look, you're always saying 'spread a little sunshine'—just take good care of her. Get rid of your guilt that way. Don't marry her." He turned and walked back downstairs without saying a word.

My reaction to his announcement was instinctive and reflected his apparent lack of conviction. He had never said a word to me about the causes of his and Evelyn's minor but frequent arguments and the resultant separations. I knew, however, that he was very uneasy about Evelyn's going to a psychoanalyst. He had briefly seen one at Joan's request at the end of his marriage to her. He had felt silly then, and I know he felt that Evelyn's seeing an analyst was a vote of no confidence in him. In any event, I never heard anything further about his plan to marry Evelyn.

The time had now come when Todd had to show his almost-finished picture to a distributor. He had spent the last of Lorraine's loan several months before, and his creditors were hounding him. He would be unable to do the last bits of photography and the vast amount of postproduction work unless he came up with fresh money. Out of deference to Mario's relationship with Columbia, he screened the picture first for them. I was on the coast and present at the screening for Mr. and Mrs. Harry Cohn. Almost all the postsync dialogue had been completed and there were some wild track sound effects, but there was no musical scoring or opticals. The final editing had not been completed on some sections of the film, and Todd intended to do a prologue, but no work had even begun on this. Film executives are, of course, thoroughly familiar with looking at a film in this unfinished state, and there was no need for him to make excuses or apologies—nor did he. It was clearly a marvelous piece of entertainment. Mrs. Cohn seemed to love it, but she kept looking at her husband for confirmation that she was right. Cohn smiled occasionally but gave no evidence of any great enthusiasm—except that his magic ass never stirred from his seat. (Cohn claimed that his bottom was the world's best box office barometer—that it became twitchy during an inferior film.) Todd was almost as cool as Cohn. He not only expected to get a great deal of money from a distributor, on very favorable terms, but he wanted hats-in-the-air enthusiasm to go with it. At the end of the screening Cohn said that the picture needed some work but was pretty good. Todd should go in and see his boys in the morning. Cohn's first lieutenants were Abe Schneider and Leo Jaffe, who ran Columbia very capably with, or perhaps despite, Harry Cohn's supervision. Todd had previously described to Columbia the kind of deal he was looking for —which was basically a four million dollar loan against a low distribution fee and 10 percent of the profits of the film.

The next morning Todd went to Columbia and met with Schneider and Jaffe. They indicated that they and Cohn liked the picture, but there would have to be some slight modifications of the deal he proposed, which they spelled out. Todd accepted their revised deal, but there was one minor problem to be dealt with before signing.

"What's that?" Schneider asked.

"I like you and Leo and I'm ready to make the deal. All you've got to do is get rid of Harry Cohn as president and I'll sign."

Todd knew from the screening that in one way or another Harry Cohn would insist on fiddling with *80 Days*, if not to put his mark of genius on it, just to show he was and always would be the boss.

This was the period when the majors were beginning to give way and make room within their own organizations for independent producers. United Artists for many years had worked only with independent producers. They had no studio facilities and no production personnel on their payroll.

Todd next invited Arthur Krim and Bob Benjamin, who ran United Artists, to see the picture. They were enthusiastic about what they saw. They had only two decisions to make. Was the picture good enough to get their four million dollars back? They felt confident about this. Their second decision was a tougher proposition. Would the unusually low distribution terms Todd was insisting on set a precedent for them with other producers that they would not be able to live with? Todd maintained he was going to road-show the picture in all the major cities of the world—arbitrarily between themselves, they had limited this number to 125 engagements before the picture went into general distribution. Todd told them up front—but confidentially—that he wanted to do only ten performances a week with his road-show engagements and that he or his organization would be selecting and making most of the deals for the road-show theaters; he wanted the usual 30 percent distribution fee cut to 10 percent for these 125 engagements. The rest of the distribution would be at the normal fees. He figured, going back to *Henry V* and Cinerama, that at least half, if not more, of the film's earnings would come out of the road-show engagements. This was a tough proposition for Krim and Benjamin, but they decided that if any producer came to them with an almost completed picture, without a cent of United Artists money at risk, they would be willing to make a similar deal if it was anything like *80 Days*. Besides, only a handful of films had been road-showed in the history of the movies at that point. Todd's was an exceptional proposition in many regards, and they would not be setting themselves an unlivable precedent. The deal was verbally agreed to, and while the contract was being prepared by their lawyers in New York, the money was advanced to Todd so that he could finish the picture and pay off Lorraine's loan.

CHAPTER *14*

WITH THE FRESH money, Todd started to explore a novel idea he had about doing the credits in animation at the end of the picture. In effect, it would be a fanciful, chronological cartoon flashback of the whole picture, principally to highlight the names of all the cameo stars. The technical credits would be thrown away as quickly and humorously as possible. Saul Bass executed the ideas so effectively that the credits themselves drew applause.

Meanwhile the film had to get down to a final edit before the scoring and mix (combining all the sound elements) could start. Paul Weatherwax, the original editor engaged, was meticulous about the way he worked. The jigsaw puzzle presented to him was like no other job he had ever had. It was going to be a gigantic task to get the film smoothed out, and eight grueling hours a day were as much as Weatherwax could handle. Gene Ruggiero, who was a great deal younger and had done a good job on *Oklahoma!* which made him the only film editor with Todd-AO experience, was doing a film at Metro during the day but was willing to work at night with Kevin to speed up the editing.

Kevin tells about an important incident that occurred during this stage of the editing:

> Ruggiero and I would work till one or two in the morning, or until we were too tired to continue. Then I'd meet Mike at the studio very early in the morning, or else I'd go and pick him up at his house. I'd get there at seven A.M., and Mike would be floating in the swimming pool with a cigar in

his mouth. We'd talk about what Gene and I had done the night before. On this occasion, as we were driving down to the studio, he turned to me and said:

"Everybody knows who you're seeing, and I don't think it's right."

"What do you mean?" I asked.

"You and Elizabeth Taylor," he said.

Elizabeth's marriage with Michael Wilding was on the rocks by then and she and I were seeing quite a lot of each other. Very, very quietly. The only people who really knew about us were Shirley [MacLaine] and Steve [Steve Parker, Shirley's husband] because we used to go out to their place in Malibu. Elizabeth phoned me at the studio, and Mike somehow got wind of it. I was in love with Elizabeth, and I think she was in love with me. Anyway, we were planning to get married.

Mike continued his lecture, and I told him: "I will work day and night, as many hours as I am able, but my personal life is my own."

Mike said, "Okay, but I don't think it's right that you're going out with a married woman."

From that point on he called me Kevin. There was no more Klevin. It was strictly business.

A few days after the lecture, while they were changing reels in the cutting room, Mike turned to me and said, "You know, I'd like to meet them." I didn't know what he was talking about, and I asked him, "Who do you mean?" He mumbled, "You know, the Wildings." Well, this took me completely by surprise, but I thought, Sure, why not, and I said that I would fix it up when the next suitable occasion arose.

Just a few days later, we saw a picture in the Los Angeles *Times* of the Japanese training schooner that had arrived in San Francisco on a courtesy visit and was heading for Los Angeles. Mike said, "Let's grab some shots of it in full sail and kick out that other goddamned miniature."

We hired a big yacht called *The Hyding* to film the Japanese training vessel, and I said to Mike, "I've got a couple of friends you said you'd like to meet—the Wildings." He said, "Fine, bring them along." Evelyn was there. Mike's secretary, Dick Hanley. Kurt and Ketti Frings. Art Cohn and his wife, Marta. And it got to be a whole weekend party. After the filming was completed—and it went quite well—there was a lot of champagne flowing. Mike hardly ever drank at all, but this evening he had a few, and he got very argumentative with me. I had no idea what it was about. I figured he had just had one too many, and I forgot about it.

Right at that time it was settled that Elizabeth and Wilding were going to split up. I was in love with Elizabeth—she was a very difficult person not to be in love with. We had been talking about marriage, but I told her I couldn't afford to keep her in a big house with a pool in the Beverly Hills area, and she said she'd be happy to live with me in a small place like Shirley and Steve had at Malibu. At that time I was having a real struggle visualizing myself getting married to a star like Elizabeth on my meager finances.

One evening we went out to dinner with Shirley and Steve. I usually had along a friend of mine from England, a priest, George Long, who was in Los Angeles at the time, to cover our being together. Most of my conversation with Elizabeth had been along the lines of "You mean you'd do my shirts and all?" Shirley and Steve had a boxer, a marvelous animal—but this night, we got back to the house and the dog had been sick and messed all over the floor. Without any hesitation, Elizabeth, who was wearing a lovely frock, got down and scrubbed up the mess. Right then and there, I said "This is the woman for me," and that we were going to get married.

Don Tomlinson, who put in long hours with Kevin in the editing room, tells about his brief involvement with Kevin's romance:

Kevin came in and told us he had met Elizabeth Taylor out in Malibu and that he had fallen for her in a big way. He'd come in and talk about her, but it was no news to me. My future wife was the telephone operator at the studio, and if you're going with Elizabeth Taylor there's no way it's going to be kept a secret. One day he came in with a little gold locket—it must have set him back twenty dollars—and he said, "I'm going to get engaged to her." I said, "With *that?* That's not enough." He said, "What do you mean, that's not enough?" He got all upset, so I kept quiet and went back to work.

Kevin relates:

Soon after *The Hyding*, Mike threw a big party for Edward R. Murrow and his wife after we had filmed the prologue with him. Evelyn was there and dozens of prominent Hollywood people, including the Wildings, but I didn't think anything about Mike's possible interest in Elizabeth.

The only significant occurrence for me at the party involved Ernie Anderson. Ernie had gotten reams of publicity for the picture, but Mike wanted to be in *Time* magazine. He wanted his image changed—I think he felt he was still being portrayed as a Broadway mug. Ernie was a real go-getter, and if Mike wanted to be in *Time,* he'd get him in, no matter how. From somewhere he found a picture of Mike sitting in a bathtub smoking a cigar. He got the picture and a piece on Mike in *Time.* Mike absolutely blew his stack and said it was the most terrible thing that had ever been done to him. Ernie said, "You wanted to get in *Time* magazine—I got you in. They wouldn't have been interested in a picture of you sitting in a restaurant smoking a pipe." Mike and Ernie had long and bitter fights about this, mainly because Ernie was a very stubborn man. Ernie kept bringing the matter up, saying he had done the right thing, and Mike, who was trying to forget it, became furious every time Ernie reminded him of it—until eventually Mike told me one morning when we were driving to the studio, "If Ernie brings up that damn *Time* magazine picture one more time, I'm going to fire him." That same week he threw the elaborate party for Murrow, and he asked me to come up early and bring Ernie with me. I collected Ernie and warned him that he was on very thin ice, and to talk about anything else but never to bring up the picture in *Time*—ever again. We got to the house and there was a very lavish spread. Mike was working up his adrenaline, fussing about. He was a perfectionist. He wanted everything just right for Murrow and his guests. I went over to the piano, where there were pounds of fresh beluga caviar laid out. I'm rather partial to caviar, so I started to help myself. Mike saw me and shouted, "That's for the guests!" I said, "But aren't I one of the guests?" He said, "Yes, but the party hasn't started yet, and the way you're going, there won't be any left." Just then Ernie came over to the piano and said to Mike, "You know I'm right about that photo in *Time,* and I want you to admit it." Well, Mike went through the roof and fired him on the spot.

On the next trip to New York, Todd put Bill Doll and his company to work on all the U.S. publicity and promotion for the picture. But when *80 Days* opened in London, Anderson was rehired to handle the English and European publicity. Between

Todd and Anderson, the London opening was on the front page of practically every newspaper and was the best-publicized picture opening in English film history.

On the night of the Murrow party, Todd was undoubtedly edgy for a reason other than Kevin's denting the caviar supply and Ernie Anderson's stubbornness. A short while later, Todd again invited the Wildings to his house, this time without Kevin, for a much smaller gathering, a barbecue where he did the cooking.

Elizabeth describes a surprise meeting she had with Mike soon after the barbecue:

> I'd seen Mike at several parties and knew him. It was fun being with him. I was attracted to him but not overly. He called me and said he had to see me right away. He just told me! So I met him at MGM. I was sitting there with my feet on the table, and he came in and picked me up by the arm and without a word dragged me out of the office, down the corridor, shoved me into an elevator, still not speaking, just marching along breaking my arm, and took me into a deserted office. He sort of plunked me on the couch, and he pulled a chair around and started in on a spiel that lasted about a half an hour without a stop, saying that he loved me and that there was no question about it, we were going to be married. I looked at him the same way I imagine a rabbit looks at a mongoose. All kinds of things went through my mind. I thought, Oh well, he's stark, raving mad. I've got to get away from this man!

Kevin describes his next discussion with Elizabeth, which took place that evening:

> Elizabeth called, very upset about something, saying that she had to talk to me. I went to see her, and she told me Mike had seen her that afternoon and told her that she was going to marry him—he had made up his mind and that was it. She said, "I told him about us and that I was going to marry you, and Mike went absolutely berserk." Mike said to her, "You are never going to see me again," and slammed the door. She was in tears, and the rejection was hitting her, and she said to me, "I've lost a friend." I said, "You've only just met him." The weekend on *The Hyding* had been only a short while ago. "He's not a friend, you don't know him. He's just someone I work for. That's who he is. And he's a marvelous man.

A great man. But *you've not lost a friend.*" For me, the whole thing was her being dramatic. I told her to forget it. I didn't take it seriously at all. I must have been a right muggins, but of course I was young.

I had been after Mike for weeks to let me shoot an ending with Mario for the bullfighting scene. Ruggiero and I had run the footage backwards and forwards and upside down. I knew every inch of it, but there was no way to end the scene. I kept saying to Mike, "Let me go to Mexico, and I'll shoot a scene with Mario and a bull so we'll have an ending," and Mike said, "We can't afford it." So I kept on about it. And I said, "We don't even have to have a crowd. I'll shoot the scene from above, and all we'll see is Mario and the bull." He said, "No, we'll have to find some other way to do it." Ruggiero and I went crazy, and I told Mike we had to do something. But Mike kept saying no.

One day we were walking to the delicatessen on the corner of Sunset, and Mike turned to me and said, "Kevin, I think you're right. We've got to go and do that thing in Mexico. How long do you think it will take you to set it up?" I said, "No time at all." Mike said, "Can we go this weekend?" I told him I thought so, and when we got back I made a few calls. Mario said he could get the bull and Gelman would lay on the crew.

Evelyn, Mike and I flew down and we stayed at Mario's house in Mexico City. Mario agreed to kneel down and turn his back on the bull, but Gelman wouldn't allow it, as it was too dangerous. Just to get Gelman out of the way, we told him we were just going to do a couple of simple shots. But I built a cage for the camera, the crew and myself—I'm crazy, but I was not going to be in there with a bull unprotected. Mike suddenly said to me, "You don't need me around here anymore. You handle it. I've got to get back to Los Angeles." That seemed strange, because Mike always wanted to be in on everything. He said, "Evelyn's going to Caracas from here, and I want you to put her on the plane for me." I said, "Oh, is she going on a holiday?" "No," Mike said, "I'm having her look at some theaters to select one for Todd-AO." I said, "She doesn't know anything about Todd-AO." Mike said, "She'll figure it out when she gets there. You see her off and call me when she's gone." I thought that was odd. So then Mike went, and the next day I saw Evelyn off. I called him, and he said, "Are you sure she's in the air?" I said, "She's on her way." He said, "Good. I'll call her tonight to make sure everything's all right." It took me another three or four days to get the sequence in the can. Mike had told me that this was very important and to make sure I got it right and to take my time. And actually we got one thing wrong. The sequence was marvelous. The bull's horns were just inches away from Mario's back. He could have been killed in an instant, but he kneeled there for what seemed like hours. But this bull had a white cock, and the one in Chinchón had a black one. There was no way of avoiding it. Ruggiero and I tried everything not to show the bull sideways, but there was no way of doing it properly. It was, you might say, a proper cock-up.

But I was very pleased with the way it had all gone. We had gotten Gelman out of the way and the sequence was in the can. On the flight back to Los Angeles, there were newspapers on the plane, and I picked one up and read about the girl that I was going to marry. . . . Mike left us in Mexico City; he chartered a plane and went to Danville, Kentucky, where Elizabeth was on location making *Raintree County*, and picked her up and took her to New York, where they had disappeared. I'm reading this, and my whole world fell apart—I was in love.

Elizabeth says:

Mike's courtship was like being hit by a tornado. It swept you up and carried you away. I was on location in Kentucky, making *Raintree County*, and somehow he found out where I'd be almost every minute of the day. He'd phone at all hours, and at night we had long conversations. Then presents would arrive, and huge bundles of flowers. I like presents, I like pleasant surprises—we have our share of unpleasant surprises. But with Mike it was one pleasant surprise after another. His tenderness, his consideration, his enormous sensitivity—that came as a surprise. The little I had known about him made him seem like a Damon Runyon character, but he wasn't that way at all. He was full of energy and vitality and at the same time was a gentle man.

I had two weeks off from *Raintree County*, and Mike sent a charter plane to pick me up to bring me to New York. He met me at the airport and that was that. From that moment on we were getting married.

Kevin continues:

Mike didn't show up in the cutting room for some time. I finished my work on the picture, but we didn't talk about anything but business. At the New York opening, where he appeared publicly and prominently for the first time with Elizabeth, he and I sat together in the last row, fighting over the knob that controlled the sound level. He kept turning it up, with the six channels blaring full force, and I kept turning it down so the audience wouldn't be deafened. But he did a wonderful thing on the platform in front of the theater before the show started. While he was on television he pointed down to me and said, "Without that man this film would never have been made."

After every film I always took a trip. This time I sold the Ford Motor Company on my producing a commercial about one of their cars making a trip around the world in eighty days. But when I scouted and planned the whole expedition, I told them it would take one hundred and four days. They were to give me a bonus of a black Thunderbird if I did it in that time, and, like Phileas Fogg, I just made it—I had two minutes to spare . . .

But Mike's maneuvering in Mexico City was a logistical masterpiece. And I gave him the scenario by saying, "Please let me go to Mexico." I was just going to shoot bulls, but he always took everything a step further. That gave him the opportunity to put it together—unscrupulously, ruthlessly and with purpose. And it worked, which is most important. It could have gone wrong so many ways, but he had supreme confidence. It was a hell of a challenge. He was a winner. He was never a loser. I have the greatest admiration for any man who could do what he did. That I became another example of his ability to get what he wanted is beside the point. Sure, I was brokenhearted, but by the time I had driven around the world . . .

We arrived in Saigon just before twelve noon on the hundred and fourth day. Then the cars were going to be shipped to San Francisco and driven to Detroit to complete the trip. I was too exhausted. So I wanted to go back via Hawaii. I was going to take a couple of days off—not see or talk to anyone. I arrived very early in the morning.

I walked into the hotel—"Hello, Kevin." It was Mike. I couldn't believe it. The sun had just come up. We exchanged greetings.

"You probably know why I'm here," he said.

"No, I don't know why you're here."

"We're on our way to Australia. We're on sort of a honeymoon."

"Congratulations."

"Come and have breakfast with us," he said.

"No, I'm really tired. I'm just going to my room and have a rest."

"First come up and have breakfast—Elizabeth would love to see you."

"Possibly . . . but at this hour?"

"Sure, we'll wake her up."

I still couldn't figure out what Mike was doing there in the lobby at seven o'clock in the morning. I went straight to my room, and I'll never forget this: I picked up the phone, rang the front desk and said, "Look, is there a nice hotel two or three miles from here that you can recommend?" And Mike's voice said, "*Kevin*, we're having breakfast together!" You could never get ahead of that man. It was uncanny. He had gone to the hotel switchboard and told them, "As soon as he makes a call, put him through to me."

So we all had breakfast together and he said he was going to do *Don Quixote* next, and would I come back and work with him again. "What happened has happened, and it would be very good to have you with us on the picture." I told him I was going to make pictures on my own now, and he asked, "What are you going to make?" I explained I had picked up a *Reader's Digest* in Phnom Penh that had a story in it called "The Boy and the Bridge," and I was thinking of making that picture, or I was going to make an underwater film in Todd-AO. He said, "Do you have a story for that?" I told him no. On a visit to the Bahamas it struck me that an underwater picture on a wide screen *must* be a huge success —I'd write that story . . . or I'd make the other picture. Mike said, "Kevin, make the underwater picture." I said, "Why do you say that?" And it was curious, over this breakfast we had actually picked up our old friendship. Even while I was talking to him and Elizabeth, I didn't really know what I was going to do. And if he had started his picture first, I probably would have gone back to work for him. He said, "I know you, Kevin. You make this story you just told me about, the boy on the bridge, and it's going to go to film festivals, and win awards. But remember this—*you can't eat awards*." Those were the most prophetic words. I raised the money privately and made *The Boy and the Bridge*. It represented Britain at the Venice Film Festival, then went to the festival at San

Sebastian and other festivals. And it made no money. Afterwards, I went back to the Bahamas and started writing the underwater picture, which became *Thunderball*. Mike was always one jump ahead of everyone.

Todd had always been breezy, self-confident to the point of being cocky, smoking dollar cigars when he had a bankruptcy hanging over his head, but he was now over the moon with what he knew would be a smash hit, and with the world's most beautiful girl on his arm. This was the state he was in when he drove from New York to Croton-on-Hudson to introduce my future stepmother to me in September 1956. As he quipped later, "I'm married to a girl who is a few years my junior. As a matter of fact, she's a few years my Junior's junior. There were no ifs, ands, buts or questions asked this time. He was going to get married. And his bride was a fun-loving, free-spending young beauty who could enjoy herself and him. Elizabeth recalls:

> I was petrified on the drive to Michael junior's house. Mike said the marriage would be off if Mike junior didn't approve of me. Then he told me I was going to meet my grandson and that he wasn't sure if he wanted to marry such an old broad—a grandmother. [Todd junior's child, Cyrus, had been born four months earlier.] I knew he was kidding, of course, but the whole business terrified me. How was I supposed to behave? Mike was no help at all. He kept trying to scare me, and I was scared. Even after we arrived, Mike continued making jokes about my being a grandmother, and the first half hour is a complete blur. But when I saw that Sarah and Michael junior were paying no attention to him, I relaxed and we all got on fine.

When Todd arrived with Elizabeth, she was frozen and speechless. To break the ice, my opening sally was "What was Glenn Davis really like?" In her state, she could barely remember the name, and Mike was totally confused, not having a clue as to who Glenn Davis was (the famous Army football star). Even Sarah, who knew my fanatic interest in football, wasn't sure if I was serious. Elizabeth mumbled something about her really having had only one date with Davis, and that it had all been arranged by Metro for publicity purposes. Mike was off-balance for only a minute, and then he took charge, supervised the preparation of the meal and painted pictures of the glorious times ahead for all of us.

The four million dollars from United Artists went fast, paying off all the old obligations and paying for the final pickup shots and the animated credits, plus three separate prologues—the first two of which were costly but inferior and were quickly discarded.

All of this, plus the use of a large symphony orchestra to record Victor Young's score, the completion of the rest of the postproduction work and the purchase of the odd trinket during the courtship of Elizabeth, exhausted the United Artists advance and put us back in the red. Todd quickly and easily picked up an additional $750,000—a loan from Bob O'Donnell, the proprietor of Texas Interstate Theatres, against the receipts of the picture, plus generous terms for the engagements of the film in his theaters. If I hadn't been a nervous Nellie, O'Donnell's loan would have seen us through the opening. But I was having a near nervous breakdown, holding off creditors owed about half a million dollars on the East Coast. Todd borrowed an additional $750,000 from his friend William Paley, giving CBS a 10 percent interest in the film. He made this deal just to ease the pressure on me, because in his own mind he was millions to the good with *80 Days*. Stalling the payment of $500,-000 for a few months would have required only a couple of jovial phone calls in his present frame of mind, and he would have wound up with 88.2 percent ownership of a film that finally came in at $6.3 million and netted over $25 million in film rental. All this would have been accomplished without his putting a cent of his own in the picture. Of course, he didn't *have* a cent of his own, but that was no bother to Todd. Two weeks before the picture opened he turned down an offer of $10 million from industrialist Roy Little for his 78.2 percent of the picture, which would have netted him almost $4 million dollars, without gambling on its success.

One of the last steps in the postproduction work on a film is the scoring. Todd hired Victor Young, one of the most prolific and talented of Hollywood's composers, to write the music. Todd viewed *80 Days* as a show—and a musical show at that. Part of his deal with Young was to buy the publishing rights to his score. The sound track album for *80 Days* was the first nonmusical movie album to rack up gigantic sales.

He listened critically and attentively to every theme and piece of music and liked almost everything but thought the underscoring for the train sequence in India was not simple enough. Young protested, wanting to know exactly what it was Todd was looking for. "Look, just write me Victor Young's 'Song of India.'" Young's new train theme came across exactly that way.

Todd was enchanted by the music Young wrote for the balloon sequence. He felt it was the most melodic piece in the picture—and the most important. He had always visualized the balloon as the logo for the advertising and this sequence the one most likely to be associated with the picture. He and Young agreed it should be the main theme music. Mike commissioned Harold Adamson to write lyrics for this melody.

Never before or since has an independent motion picture producer dealing with a major distributor assembled a complete organization to oversee every aspect of the distribution, exploitation and promotion of a motion picture. Krim and Benjamin were not all that delighted to see Todd put together his own minidistribution setup that worked within and sometimes against their own organization. However, Todd got on well with Krim and Benjamin, and whatever distress he caused them by his stretching his distribution agreement to the limit and controlling every last detail of the handling of his picture was more than overcome by the outstanding success of *80 Days* and the resultant prestige and revenue garnered by United Artists.

The premiere of *80 Days* on October 17, 1956, exceeded even Todd's highest expectations. There was a standing ovation during and after the credits. All of the reviews were raves.

> Michael Todd, who had already shaken the foundations of the legitimate theatre with an onslaught of highly heterogeneous and untraditional musical shows, is apparently out to shatter the fundamental formation of the screen. . . . This mammoth and mad pictorial rendering of the famous old novel of Jules Verne . . . is a conglomeration of refined English comedy, giant-screen travel panoramics and slam-bang Keystone burlesque. . . . Spectacular entertainment—Mr. Todd outdoes the movies with *Around the World in 80 Days*.
>
> —BOSLEY CROWTHER, New York *Times*

Phileas Fogg, Michael Todd—the names somehow seem to go together . . . Michael Todd may be neither proper nor English, but he shares Phileas' intrepidity and purposefulness. He has made a movie version of *Around the World in 80 Days* which in its fantasy, freshness and fun leaves poor old Jules Verne far behind. . . . Mr. Todd's mighty spectacle is far-ranging, imaginative, fanciful entertainment.

> —HERBERT KUPFERBERG, New York
> *Herald Tribune*

You can roll out every glowing adjective in the book for Michael Todd's production of *Around the World in 80 Days.* . . . For Todd's come up with a fabulous entertainment that'll have you laughing and gasping and applauding. . . . It's big. It's beautiful. It's hugely amusing.

> —ROSE PELWICK, New York
> *Journal-American*

What a dazzling frolic Mike Todd is conducting on the Rivoli screen these days! *Around the World in 80 Days* is a huge spectacle, a romping farce, a mischievous prank and a solid delight. . . . Infectious laughter never ceases. There is only one proper summary of *Around the World in 80 Days.* Just one long loud Wheee-ee-ee!"

> —ALTON COOK, New York *World*
> *Telegram & Sun*

Four stars—A smash hit.

> —KATE CAMERON, New York *Daily*
> *News*

Titanic, titillating and thrilling.

> —LOUIS GILBERT, New York *Daily*
> *Mirror*

Breathtaking superspectacle.

> —ARCHER WINSTON, New York *Post*

Michael Todd's show makes this a better world.

> —MARK BARRON, Associated Press

Smasheroo! Sure fire hit of the year.

> —*Daily Variety*

321

> The greatest show ever seen on stage or screen.
> —*Hollywood Reporter*

> Extravagant! . . . funny! . . . spectacular!
> —*Time*

On the opening night Todd not only unveiled the masterwork of his theatrical career, but on national television introduced the love of his life: "I see you're curious about my friend. Meet Miss Lizzie Schwartzkopf."

The next day, pictures of Todd and Elizabeth appeared in newspapers around the world. Todd had more than pulled off his gigantic three-horse parlay. "All this and Elizabeth Taylor too. How's that for lucky?" For the remainder of his life, he enjoyed Elizabeth and his success to the utmost.

CHAPTER 15

DESPITE THE FABULOUS notices, Todd saw several spots in the picture that he thought needed tightening. Standing partially hidden at the side of the screen in a fire exit, he watched the audience and saw their attention wane momentarily at several places, particularly during the western sequence—material that he had originated and shot. Pride of authorship ended when the patrons began to look at their programs. He went back to Hollywood and cut over six minutes out of the picture. This added another quarter of a million to the cost of *80 Days*.

At the end of the first week of the run, Inez Robb, a columnist on the New York *World Telegram*, wrote: "Whoever thought we'd live to see the day when tickets to a movie would be as difficult to scrounge as those to *My Fair Lady*?"

I was in charge of the New York office, and Mike went back to Hollywood to make the needed cuts and trims. Among other responsibilities I was in control of the tickets. About ten days after the opening, Cecil B. DeMille called me about noon and asked if he could buy a dozen seats for that evening's performance. Although there was a tremendous demand for tickets, it would have been no problem for me to get two dozen seats, but they wouldn't be all together. Knowing Mike's theories about making a hot ticket even hotter and thinking that nothing would get the word of the success of *80 Days* back to Hollywood quicker than DeMille's inability to get the tickets he wanted, I called back in an hour and said I could dig up only four tickets. DeMille said, "Thank you, but I need a dozen and will have to try the brokers or see it at a later date." Two days later I remembered the incident when speaking to my father on the phone and proudly told him how I had handled DeMille's request. Mike groaned and said, "Oh, what a terrible thing to do . . . if just as a professional courtesy, you should have given him anything he asked for . . . with our compliments." Well, as Mike always said, "There are no rules in show business."

At the end of December the now completed and trimmed *80 Days* was received in Los Angeles as well, if not even more enthusiastically, by the press and public as it had been in New York. Todd's entry into the motion picture business and reception in Hollywood was everything he had visualized for the past ten years. In the first week of January 1957, the New York film critics voted *80 Days* the best picture of the year.

He felt that producing a motion picture was easy compared to producing a legit show, where everything had to be done in about five weeks—from the time the show opened out of town until it opened in New York—with the whole show riding on opening night. You could go on fixing a motion picture forever—if you didn't run out of money; and you'd have a hit—if your original concept was correct. So as not to be disagreeably cocky and tempt fate, like Jed Harris, who stated that he would never produce a flop (Harris made this statement after a string of hits and then produced a steady stream of failures), Mike always said in interviews, "It's much better to be lucky than smart—and I've been lucky."

At the height of his Broadway success, Mike was sitting one day in Lindy's, which was opposite the Winter Garden, where *Mexican Hayride* was playing to standing room only. Irving Berlin came over to his table and said:

"You know, that show, *Mexican Hayride*, across the street, isn't bad. If you were smart, Mike, you'd quit now. You caught lightning in a bottle."

Mike replied: "Irving, remember years ago they used to say that you had a little colored boy in your closet who wrote all the Irving Berlin songs? Well, Irving, that little colored boy that used to write your songs is now working for me."

At the time of the premiere Todd bought Elizabeth a twenty-nine-carat, emerald-cut diamond engagement ring—"Thirty carats would have been vulgar," he said. To mark their formal engagement and get a breather after he had recut *80 Days*, Todd took Elizabeth on a quick trip to the Bahamas. On Lord Beaverbrook's boat there, she fell down a few steps and injured her back. She had had a series of minor back problems for a number of years but nothing that ever required serious medical attention. This time, however, she was really in pain. Todd, who always enjoyed excellent health, nevertheless was never one to put off seeing a doctor. For the past several years he had been getting an annual checkup with Dr. Dana Atchley, one of the most highly regarded internists on the East Coast. With his bride-to-be in pain he rushed her off to see Dr. Atchley, who had her examined by a top orthopedic specialist, Dr. John Lattimer. Dr. Lattimer reported that the lower part of Elizabeth's spine was in dreadful shape. Three of her discs were shattered and without corrective surgery she would not only live in constant pain but risk the imminent probability of becoming crippled for life. Todd wouldn't permit Elizabeth to leave the hospital and insisted that she have the necessary surgery immediately. The three shattered discs had to be reconstructed and fused. Mike was in constant attendance before the operation and during the long recuperative period. To brighten up her hospital room, he bought her a van Gogh (a small one), a Pissarro, a Mary Cassatt, a Monet and a Renoir, all through Elizabeth's great-uncle, Howard Young, a prominent art dealer. Todd paid only 50 percent of the purchase price for these paintings, figuring that a future in-law wouldn't be a pesky creditor and that he could pay the balance when the big money started to roll in from *80 Days*. Also, if Elizabeth didn't like his selections, he could trade it against something she preferred. Elizabeth liked the paintings. On the way to the hospital, Todd, gesticulating with a pencil, punched a hole in the van Gogh. He took an adjoining room in the hospital to keep Elizabeth company and for the same nickel got his own annual checkup. He was in perfect shape, unlike the van Gogh.

About seven months later, when Mike had his semiannual dental checkup, Dr. Pritz told him he had a precancerous condition on the inside of his mouth called leukoplakia and that he ought to cut down severely or give up smoking entirely. He was then smoking fifteen big cigars as well as several pipes a day. He left Dr. Pritz's office and never had another smoke the rest of his life. At the time, between humidors at Dunhill's in New York and Beverly Hills, he had three or four thousand expensive Havana cigars, which he gave to me. Not knowing that Todd had given up smoking, the Upmann people gave him a gorgeous inlaid humidor the size of a suitcase, containing five hundred cigars, for the first-anniversary party of *80 Days* at Madison Square Garden. He gave me these as well. One of my functions as vice-president of the Michael Todd Company was to sit in an upwind seat when dining out so that I could blow smoke from his cigars at him after a meal.

As pushy as Todd was, it might seem a little strange that he became engaged to a married woman. But for over a year Elizabeth and Wilding had both understood their marriage was over, lacking only the formality of a divorce. Wilding was most accommodating and ready to give Elizabeth a divorce whenever she and Mike set the date. When I met Wilding a year later at a house Todd had rented in Palm Springs, Wilding was as friendly and genial to Elizabeth, my father and me as any close relative would have been. He seemed genuinely pleased to see Todd and Elizabeth getting on so happily together.

At the beginning of 1957, when Elizabeth was again fully mobile, although still heavily corseted and occasionally in pain with her backbone still knitting, Todd began to make plans for his wedding. Inasmuch as the quickest divorce could be obtained in Mexico, he decided the wedding should take place there as well. Mario was a friend of two wealthy and influential brothers, Ferdinand and Enrique Parra, who had homes a few miles south of Acapulco in a large compound that also contained a vacation home of the ex-president of Mexico, Miguel Alemán. The houses were on a hill overlooking a beautiful bay, which was enclosed by a totally undeveloped peninsula. By this time, Todd and Elizabeth's doings were not just the lead items for columnists but were prominent wire service news stories. Mario had his own gorgeous holiday home in Acapulco, but the big advantage of getting married at the Alemán-Parra compound was that it was completely ringed in by a high barbed wire fence and vigilantly patrolled by a large contingent of Mexican troops. No one was permitted past the guards without the approval of Alemán or the Parras. There would be no possibility of Todd's marriage to Elizabeth being swamped by journalists; despite their absence the wedding was front-page news around the world.

The Parras, one of whom was a prominent attorney and the other a leading architect, attended the ceremony but did not stay overnight; they gave Todd and Elizabeth and the wedding party the use of their homes. The ceremony and party were held at the architect's house, which provided ample evidence of his talent and took full advantage of the beautiful setting.

I flew to Mexico City without Sarah, who didn't want to leave the baby, and stayed overnight with Mario. Many people have tennis courts, but this was too tame a sport for Mario, who had his own jai alai court. Mario and I flew to Acapulco in his private plane.

Elizabeth's parents, Sara and Francis Taylor, her brother, Howard, and sister-in-law, Mara, were already at the Parras' house when Mario and I arrived.

Both my first wife, Sarah, who died in 1972, and my second wife, Susan, have stated that Elizabeth's brother, who is two years older than she, is the handsomest man they've ever seen. Handsome is as handsome does, and Howard Taylor has a character, a lifestyle and a wife that I admire tremendously. Howard has happily done what he has wanted to do during his lifetime. He married a delightful girl whose personality almost perfectly counterbalances his own. He and his wife, Mara, have devoted unusual time and attention to raising their five children. Howard successfully combined his major interests in art and oceanography in his professional career as an illustrator for the Scripps-Howard Institute in LaJolla, California and later at the University of Hawaii. He accomplished one of my life-long ambitions, spending several years with his family sailing the South Pacific. He has lived in two of the most scenic and peaceful places in the world—the northern, scarcely populated side of the Island of Kauai, and in Taos, New Mexico. Mara has a puckish sense of humor and is the only person I know who can keep Elizabeth totally off balance. She uses a subtle blend of teasing and near blatant put-on—and still never offends Elizabeth. Mara was able to keep even Mike off balance for short periods of time—a feat that Don Rickles and Jack E. Leonard were never able to accomplish.

Debbie and Eddie Fisher were principal members of the wedding party. Debbie had grown up with Elizabeth at MGM and Eddie, by the time of the wedding, had become Todd's surrogate show business son. I was a great companion for my father at home or work, and you could take me anywhere for a meal. But between college, the navy and getting married to a girl who, like me, preferred staying home to going out, I was not the companion eager to do the town with him at night.

Eddie filled this role neatly and nicely, especially as he was a celebrity in his own right. My father appreciated and even encouraged the fact that I had a totally different personality and set of interests from him. But Todd needed young people like Eddie, Kevin and for that matter Elizabeth to keep up with him and share his zest for fun and games.

An added starter for the festivities was Lorraine Manville, Jr., who was in Mexico on holiday.

The ceremony was a simple civil one, conducted in broken English by a local official, a friend of Mario's and the Parras'. It was held in the late afternoon. There were bushels of flowers everywhere, champagne and caviar, margaritas and a mixed Mexican buffet. There was no formal dress; the men wore summer suits and the women cotton or silk dresses. Elizabeth wore a short blue chiffon dress. It was the kind of occasion Todd always referred to as "just cold cuts and young people." When he was at Universal, he had been invited to a party at Leo Spitz's house. He phoned Mrs. Spitz and asked, "Frankie, that party you're throwing Sunday—what should I wear?" "Nothing fancy," she replied. "It's just cold cuts and young people."

Todd and Mother Nature provided a lovely and dramatic conclusion to the party. As the last of the wedding supper was being consumed, there was one of the most glorious sunsets I've ever seen. We all stood out on the terrace sipping champagne as the sun disappeared across the bay. Then Todd took over. Fifteen minutes after dark he trooped us back on the terrace, and on his signal a barge, which must have been towed into the bay after sunset, provided us with a spectacular fireworks display, the finale of which was a fiery six-foot-high legend reading MIKE—LIZ. When we started to return to the house, Todd corralled us out into the driveway. That morning Howard and Mara Taylor, Debbie and Eddie Fisher and I had gone for a cruise and a picnic lunch on Alemán's yacht. When we returned in midafternoon, four workmen were putting up a miniature grandstand in the driveway, facing the hills behind the house. When I asked the purpose for the grandstand, Mike replied, "None of your business."

After the fireworks, we were told to sit in the grandstand facing the empty pitch black hills behind the house. He then gave a shout, and suddenly a dozen torches were lit high in the hills. They flitted in, around and behind the vegetation in graceful and interesting spirals. After a minute or two, we began to see the figures bearing the torches—a group of beautifully costumed native dancers. They placed their torches in stands to provide the lighting and then proceeded to do a ferociously erotic fertility rite ballet. The torches and the figures coming out of the jungle and the dance performed on the hillside were masterpieces of showmanship, ideally suited to the occasion and the setting. Todd had been in too high a gear for the past year to permit anyone else to cater and stage his own wedding. He put on a hell of a show. It was a spectacularly original wedding, and everyone enjoyed it immensely. Elizabeth says:

> Our wedding was perfect—well, almost perfect. Mike was in control and took total charge of everything. He planned and attended to every detail of the arrangements. The ceremony was dignified but simple—the food and flowers were marvelous. And the fireworks and the native dancing Mike staged were fabulous. There was only one problem—my back, my aching back. It was killing me the whole day. Every step I took was pure torture. I tried to keep smiling through, but Mike kept looking at me and caught me wincing. I just had to lie down as soon as the show was over. Mike was worried, but I assured him I was all right. Anyway, he brought things to a sort of an abrupt close and corralled everyone out of there. But it's a shame, it was such a gorgeous location and a perfect party, it could have gone on all night. Instead, poor Mike had to cater to his crippled old lady.

As the last guests were departing, Lorraine junior asked me if I wanted to go to Acapulco with her to have a few more drinks. I started to get into her convertible when suddenly Todd came running out of the house. I was astounded to see him reappear, as he had made his apologies to everyone and retired at least twenty minutes earlier. He asked me where I was going. I said I was going into Acapulco with Lorraine to have a few nightcaps. He said, "I don't want you to go. Stay here." I said, "Don't be silly. It's been a wonderful day and a marvelous evening, and I feel like carrying on with it—besides, I'd like to see more of Acapulco." He said, "I'm asking you as a favor. *Please do not go.*" I said, "That's crazy. What difference does it make to you? I'm going. Congratulations and good night." All the while Lorraine was sitting in her convertible with a bemused expression on her face. He pulled me away, saying he wanted to talk to me alone for a minute. If I went into Acapulco with Lorraine, he said, he was going to leave instructions at the security gate not to allow me back into the compound. I was staying in one of the guesthouses, not far from the main house. I said I didn't know what this was all about, but if it meant so much to him, I certainly wasn't going to ruin his wedding day and would stay put. I went back to the car and told Lorraine that for some reason my father didn't want me to go into town, and in order not to upset him I would stay behind. I thanked her and said good night.

My father's mysterious behavior was inadvertently cleared up a year later over a dinner that Elizabeth, Mike and I had in Palm Springs. We all had had a few drinks before and during the meal and were in a bit of a silly, slightly intoxicated state. In some connection, but not in relation to her being at the wedding, Lorraine Junior's name came up in the conversation. Giggling, Elizabeth turned to me and in a stage whisper announced, "You know, your father slept with her once." Mike seldom was flustered or embarrassed, but on this occasion he turned scarlet and quickly changed the subject, after giving Elizabeth a stiletto glance.

Another fact Mike was trying to hide from me was that he was occasionally doing some hefty gambling again. Lenny Gaines, who is now a film producer and actor, was a road manager and majordomo with Eddie Fisher for years. He remembers:

> I was staying with Eddie at the Beverly Hills Hotel, and one morning I met Mike, who was playing gin with Duke Manacher, who owned Blue Coal. Manacher was worth millions. Duke was a very sharp gin player, and Victor Potamkin, the top Cadillac guy in New York City, and Arthur Rosenberg, who owned the Food Fair chain, each had a piece of Duke's action with Mike. I hate to think how big that game was—big, important money. They really had Mike over a barrel, but still he noticed me and liked me hanging around. I know he liked me, because before the start of a session I heard him tell the lifeguard, "Every time you see that kid, bring him an ice cream soda." So while Mike was playing gin I'd be floating in the middle of the pool and the lifeguard was bringing me ice cream sodas. Later, I was with him on a trip to Vegas when I think he lost all the preopening money for *80 Days*. He dropped a bundle. He called me and said, "Are you ready? C'mon, we're going to Vegas in

fifteen minutes. Be outside your joint. I'll pick you up." On a trip to Vegas he'd have a guy he was playing gin with, and they'd play on the plane and then it would be the same thing on the way back, and I wouldn't be able to keep my eyes open. On the first trip, we landed and he went right to the tables. We were staying at the Sands. He had the Presidential Suite. He always had the Presidential Suite, but I don't think he ever saw the inside of it. He wasn't there to see the shows, to eat or sit in the sun—just gamble. He'd be moving around, and wherever you heard the noise and saw the crowd, that was the table Mike was at. I'd go up and rub his back for luck. "Hey, hey, the man with the golden arm." But he'd just grab some silver dollars out of the rack and hand them to me. "Here, you look like a dollar bettor to me. Go do yourself some good." I was twenty years younger than him, but I'd get exhausted. I'd go up and get some sleep. I'd come down in the morning and there'd be one table with a crowd, and he's still shooting craps. Some dame would have a hot hand and he'd throw one-hundred-dollar chips at her. "Atta go. You know how to shoot, darling." But I'd walk up, and he'd just hand me the silver dollars. Two, three days, and he'd get it out of his system and go right back to work like it never happened. I'd have to rest up for a day when we got back.

I remember one time Eddie and I spent a week with Mike and Evelyn Keyes at Joe Schenck's house in Miami Beach. Schenck loved Mike. We had the run of the house. But whenever Mike wanted to play gin, he'd tell Eddie, "Take Evelyn out for a drink or go and grab some groceries. Go ahead, enjoy yourselves." But later, with Elizabeth, forget it. He told me and Eddie and everybody—and he was kidding, but kidding on the square—"When I'm out of town *you* stay away from the house." And he meant it. He didn't even like anyone looking at Elizabeth . . . Boy that was some place Schenck had in Miami.

Todd's marriage to Elizabeth changed his attitude about a number of things. Arnold Grant finally got to him. Friends on both coasts told Mike that Grant was continuing—as he had for the previous ten years—to warn anyone, when the subject of Mike Todd came up, which it now did with regular monotony, that Todd was the biggest and most treacherous swindler on the loose in the country. Todd now decided to get Grant, since he didn't want his bride to hear this kind of talk.

In the spring of 1957, he decided we needed our own in-house counsel and general business manager. He hired Herman Odell, who had been a partner in the law firm of Berman, Becker and Odell. Colonel Sam Becker had originally handled the beginnings of Mike's bankruptcy proceedings, and Emile Zola Berman dealt with even more desperate cases—among others, successfully defending Sergeant Matthew McKeon, who had marched six recruits to their death in the swamps of the Parris Island Marine Corps camp. Todd had never paid the fees he owed Berman, Becker and Odell, and Herman chased him for a couple of years and finally instituted court proceedings. Todd grudgingly paid up. When he hired Herman he said, "Any son of a bitch who can successfully collect money from me I want on my side."

Soon after Herman came to work for us, Todd repeatedly asked him to make an appointment with Berman to start a suit against Grant for libel. Odell finally took him to see Berman. In a fury, Todd outlined the way Grant was assassinating his character and slandering him and demanded that Berman take immediate action. Berman replied, "No, Mike, just consider. We're going to have an impossible time proving that what he says is a lie. You and I both know there's at least a grain of truth in some of it. Why do you want to give Grant the chance to rake up all this old muck? Forget it. Quit while you're ahead."

I am quite superstitious and accordingly did not make the trip to California to attend the Academy Award ceremonies. I felt that making a special trip across the continent would somehow put a hex on my father's chances of winning any Oscars.

There were shots on television of Todd sitting with Elizabeth and smiling appreciatively, if somewhat nervously, when each of the lesser four Academy Awards won by *80 Days* were announced for Best Film Editing, Best Color Photography, Best Musical Score and Best Adapted Screenplay. The Academy Award ceremonies then were not as carefully programmed and timed as they are today. There were a lot of long acceptance speeches that evening, and it was well after midnight in New York when they got around to the final award for the Best Picture of the Year.

Several strong factors weighed against Todd winning the big

award. Aside from the other outstanding pictures in contention—including *Giant*, in which Elizabeth had starred—few voting members of the Academy worked with United Artists and, understandably, the major studios exerted subtle pressure on their employees to vote for their pictures. Also, Todd's arrogance and anti-Hollywood attitude was likely to cost the picture many votes. He was genuinely surprised when *80 Days* and his name were announced for the Best Picture of the Year award, and he instinctively leaped out of his seat and ran up the aisle, but after a few steps turned back to plant a quick, joyful kiss on Elizabeth. Then he went full tilt up to the stage. For the viewers in the eastern half of the country, his abbreviated acceptance speech—"Thanks. I'm gonna grab this before you change your minds."—and his equally rapid return to his seat were a refreshingly fast curtain for the evening.

The third opening of the picture, in Chicago, came shortly after the Academy Awards. It was a total triumph of the hometown boy making good and not only bringing in the prize picture of the year, but the most gorgeous girl of the decade. Guy Biondi, who had been hired prior to the New York opening to control the paid advertising and help Bill Doll with publicity, tells about an incident that occurred at this opening:

> Mike had a habit of calling a meeting every time he left New York. At the end of it, as he was going out the door, he'd turn and say, "And fellows, remember, leave a little for me." That was Mike's getaway line until *Eighty Days* opened in Chicago.
>
> Mike came out a few days early, because it was not just the opening of the picture, but the opening of his Cinestage Theatre as well—which represented a gigantic investment. Mike and Elizabeth were on the front pages of all the Chicago papers for three days in a row. We made a one-hundred-and-fifty-thousand-dollar ticket sale to an appliance dealer, no discount on the tickets—he took huge ads and gave the tickets away if you bought a washing machine, or whatever. On the opening night there was a huge crowd filling the whole block, trying to get a glimpse of the Chicago bigwigs, and Mike and Elizabeth. We had arranged for the premiere festivities to be on local television. We had a local deejay act as the master of ceremonies. We paid him only seventy-five dollars, as every deejay in town was fighting for the prestige of doing the job. Paul Montague was our Chi-

cago press agent. He had selected the deejay and instructed him somewhere during the course of the proceedings to plug an Italian restaurant Paul was handling on the side and the restaurant's month-long Saint Patrick's Day special of green noodles, which it was still featuring. With the crowd and the traffic, everything was going slowly, and Mike was the last of the celebrities to appear on camera. Paul had to lead him away, as the film had to start. Mike was saying good night to the crowd and to the M.C. and the television camera, and as he crossed past Paul to go into the theater, he overheard Paul turn to the M.C. and *sotto voce* say, "Don't forget the green noodles." Mike stopped dead in his tracks, turned to Paul and said, "What's with the green noodles?" Paul was so flustered that he came straight out with it, "Well, I've got this little Italian restaurant . . ." Mike fired him on the spot. Bill Doll got Paul reinstated the next day, but from that time on Mike's exit line at all his staff meetings was, "And don't forget, no green noodles."

Guy talks about Todd at the staff meetings:

Early on, we had a meeting about the selection of key cities and when we would open in them. Of course, the size of the market was a major factor. Someone would ask what the population was, and without a second's hesitation Mike would rattle off a figure. Later in the meeting he saw me checking his figures against a little pocket reference book I had. He interrupted himself and asked, "Well, Guy, was I right?" He was so right on all the figures it was spooky. He had a total command of every aspect of what went into his business.

Much later he persisted in trying to pull off an unprecedented feat. One of the least successful, and practically the only mediocre, first-run engagement the picture had was in Buffalo at a big downtown Skouras theater. Mike was bound and determined to show up Skouras and the U.A. salespeople, who had forced the deal through by reopening the picture in Buffalo for a second first-run engagement. After the first one had played about six months, Mike junior got the Schine organization to put in a Todd-AO installation in a new shopping center house and reopen the picture. The problem was to regenerate interest. We needed a big premiere to kick it off. None of us could come up with an idea. Mike said, "Wait a minute, Buffalo has a big Catholic population. We'll do a benefit opening for a Catholic charity. What's the name of the bishop there?" Nobody said a word. Mike said, "Who's the Catholic here in the office?" I said, "I am, Mike." And he said, "Well, what's his name?" I said, "I don't know the name of the bishop in Buffalo." He said, "Find out." So I called the chancellery office and told Mike the man's name—Joseph Aloysius Burke—and Mike immediately said, "Oh my God. I must be getting old. How could I forget Joe Burke." And he told his secretary to get him on the phone. The bishop immediately took Mike's call, and after a few reminiscences they fixed up the charity opening together.

For several reasons Todd wanted to make his home base in the New York area. Although he intended to continue producing motion pictures—first, *Don Quixote* and then, possibly, *The Man Who Would Be King*—they would be shot almost entirely on location; so he would have to be in California for only a few months at a time. He could feel at home almost anywhere, but he thought of himself as a New Yorker.

There were two personal idiosyncrasies that made him want to move back East. He thought that Los Angeles was an awful place to bring up a family. There were the two boys from Elizabeth's marriage to Wilding, and now she was expecting his child. Todd's secretary on the West Coast was a closet homosexual. He had been Louis B. Mayer's private secretary, and he was efficient, loyal and resourceful. He worked at Todd's side sixteen to eighteen hours a day, seven days a week, without a grumble, and had proved invaluable. There was no question, in Todd's or in anybody else's mind, of his ever committing any impropriety. Nevertheless, Todd felt that his continual presence around the Wilding boys and the new baby would be an unhealthy influence. He wanted and could afford to keep him on the payroll in California, although he was planning to spend most of his time in the East.

On his next trip to New York with Elizabeth, he decided to take her house hunting. He liked suburban Connecticut, and the idea of a longish drive to the city was never an obstacle, since he enjoyed driving. David Stillman, his attorney for motion picture matters, had a house in Westport and Mike had been there on many visits. Westport is a pleasant area and its proximity to Long Island Sound was appealing. Living there would have another advantage. Stillman and a large circle of his friends in the area were avid gin players. Stillman always had all the current film business gossip, and Todd would never be at a loss to fill his leisure time.

Stillman recommended a real estate agent, and Todd and Elizabeth spent a full day looking at all the available homes in the area. Elizabeth saw nothing she liked. The agent invited them back to his house for a drink before they returned to the city. Elizabeth immediately fell in love with the real estate agent's house and grounds. Todd said, "We'll buy your home." The agent said, "It's not for sale." Todd said, "How about renting it to us for a year until you find us another?" The agent said he had several children in school and just couldn't uproot them at a moment's notice. Todd said, "How would you and your family like to spend a year in Europe?" The agent said that might be interesting but he would have to discuss it with his wife. Todd had Midori phone some exclusive schools in Switzerland, and arrangements were made to accommodate the agent's children. He closed the deal by paying the school tuition fees.

The U.S. openings came fast and furious after Chicago, and Todd decided it would be convenient to have his own plane to attend these, and for his other frequent business trips. He named it the "Lucky Liz." He left it in the States when he and Liz went off to launch the picture in Europe. At the Cannes Film Festival *80 Days* played out of competition, and the picture and Todd and Elizabeth made a big splash. Elizabeth recalls:

> Traveling with Mike was a delight. He'd do things and go places on an impulse. And there was lots of lovely shopping. He'd want to buy something in every place we'd go. On our first trip to Europe Mike rented a villa in St.-Jean-Cap-Ferrat, owned by Lady Kenmare. I went shopping in Cannes and took some things on approval to make sure Mike liked them. His secretary, Midori, was staying with us and I picked out something special for her. When I was showing Mike some of the things I had selected, Midori came in the room. I pulled out the green silk Lanvin evening coat I had bought for her and told her to try it on. Mike stopped me and said, "That's not a very practical gift. If you want to give her something, get her a suede coat or something else she can use." I told Mike, "I wanted to give her an evening coat—

you can buy her something practical." It looked stunning on Midori.

Mike was meticulous about his own clothes. No matter how rushed we were, he always took the time to carefully pack his shirts and even his shorts—each shirt had its own plastic case—so that they'd come out of the suitcase without a wrinkle. His wardrobe was as big as mine, but he knew every piece of clothing he owned and remembered where it was. He might appear to be careless about money, but he was careful about clothes.

The principal purpose of the trip to Europe was to publicize the first foreign engagement—the opening in London. The film got rave notices, with the *Daily Mirror* going so far as to suggest on its front page that Todd should be knighted. An even greater success was the party he threw afterwards for the entire opening-night audience. Kevin's brother, Desmond, who is a producer for the BBC, had briefly met Todd two years earlier at the start of the production. Todd had asked him to do some research on the Middle East, to give Kevin an idea of what the second unit should film. Desmond had a huge briefcase filled with research material and chased around Paris trying to locate Todd, but was never able to find him or Kevin. Desmond describes his rather mystifying evening at the premiere. Kevin was not around at the time.

When the film opened in London, Mike went to great lengths to see that I was there, considering that I had met the man only once. I was directing a film for the BBC. I had been in the Seychelles, and when I got back, there were all these messages from Mike Todd. Everybody wanted to go to the opening and the party. It was the greatest party ever thrown in this country. To this day, people still talk about it, and to be invited . . . I think I was the only person there from the BBC. The director general couldn't get a ticket. We went to the Astoria Theater, and there was Mike, furious, standing in front of the theater. He was shaking his fist at the sky—the audacity of it daring to rain when he was going to throw a party afterwards—outdoors. He greeted me, and we saw the magnificent film—it really was. The thunderous applause it received—not only at the end, but punctuating the highlights of it. When we came out, there were buses to transport us all down to the Embankment. And then I found

I was on the number-one boat, with Olivier and all. I thought I'd have rated the number-ten boat, but there I was, and there were bands playing on every one and a bar serving champagne—the very best champagne—or anything else you wanted. And so the flotilla arrived at the South Bank [at the Battersea amusement park] and we were all handed plastic macs, as it was a rainy night. Somehow during the course of the film he had managed to purchase and get delivered fifteen hundred plastic mackintoshes. Everyone was given a great bag of coins to operate the slot machines. Mike had taken over the whole Fun Fair. It was very new at that time. He had set up fourteen different restaurants in the food concessions to serve all the different foods from all the countries visited in *Around the World in 80 Days*. It was the grandest party in London since the days of the Vauxhall Gardens. [Famous for the lavish outdoor parties held there in the days of the Prince Regent at the end of the eighteenth century.]

At the time, I was totally mystified by the great lengths Mike had gone to have me present and make me welcome. A long time previous I had seen one or two items about Kevin and Elizabeth, but you know how unreliable Hollywood gossip is. Kevin was very discreet—he never said anything to me. Subsequently, I realized that the star treatment Mike gave me was all because of Kevin. It must have been. There could have been no other reason.

Sarah was pregnant and we had decided to name our second child Liza if it was a girl. I had mentioned this to my father on several occasions. When Mike and Elizabeth's baby was born in August, I was quite put out when they called her Liza. (Her legal name is Elizabeth Frances Todd.) Four years later Sarah and I named our third daughter Eliza. I had never seen Todd more excited or proud than he was at Liza's birth.

Before Todd and Elizabeth returned to New York for Liza's birth, he reached an agreement with Vincent Korda to work with him on *Don Quixote*. His happy and productive collaboration with William Cameron Menzies (who had died a few months before) fixed the idea in his mind that working with an accomplished art director would enable him to capture the spirit of the kind of picture he wished to produce and enable him to have it all before him on a drawing pad.

Vincent was fluent in half a dozen languages, all spoken with a strong Hungarian accent. He was eloquent with his misuse of English, squeezing the most wonderful new meanings and shadings out of colorless words and phrases. His visual imagination was even more inspiring. By his own candid appraisal, he was a mediocre artist in Paris when his brother Alex summoned him to London to assist full time in the production of films. Earlier Vincent had established his talent as an art director by his excellent work on a number of Ernst Lubitsch films in the 1920s, but in London Vincent proved to be brilliant, not only as an art director but in his ability to deal with difficult people and situations.

Vincent's long list of distinguished credits included *Lady Windermere's Fan, Things to Come, Four Feathers, The Thief of Bagdhad, To Be or Not to Be* (Carole Lombard's last picture), *Miracle in Milan* and *That Hamilton Woman.* However, three of his films—*Summertime, The Fallen Idol* and especially *The Third Man*—illustrate most vividly how the sets and locales can provide an all-pervading atmosphere that gives a film a distinctive mood, which in some instances is the key to its success. Todd had tremendous respect for Vincent's imagination, his talents as an art director and as someone who got things done with a minimum of fuss.

There were four men in Todd's life whom he loved—his father, me, Joe Schenck and finally Vincent. Vincent felt just as strongly about my father. Many years later I found out that he had flown four thousand miles to be a distant and silent observer at my father's funeral.

During the summer of 1957, it was agreed that Vincent would go to Spain with his still camera and sketchbook to scout locations and put together a storyboard.

To get around English tax regulations, the print used for the London engagement of *80 Days* was on 34mm film. Both *Oklahoma!* and *80 Days* were shot with two sets of cameras—65mm Todd-AO for the road-show engagements and 35mm for regular release. Todd felt he had to do everything possible to preserve the quality of the picture for the London engagement, which he considered to be the most important one in the world outside of New York, Los Angeles and Chicago. Although it was then a very new and expensive process, he had the picture printed down from the 65mm negative to 35mm and then had 1 mm trimmed off one edge of the film to beat the British taxes. With new but inexpensive lenses, the picture was projected on a screen the same size and shape as that used in the Todd-AO theaters in the States. No one could tell the difference. The "print-down version" on 35mm, of course, had the same amount of information on it as the 65mm Todd-AO version and so did not look grainy or washed out on the large screens. The roller coasters played as well. There was, in fact, no discernible difference between the print-down version and Todd-AO, and as a result Todd reached some startling and important conclusions about the process. Seven years after the first Cinerama test film in Oyster Bay, and millions of research dollars later, he realized that to achieve Cinerama out of one hole with no seams or other distortions he needed only to adequately fill, with a good quality picture, the same size screen. In other words, the size and shape of the screen were almost everything.

Vincent Korda introduced Todd to Ned Mann, a muleheaded and inventive technical expert from Missouri who had been head of the optical and special effects departments for London Films. In five weeks, for less than two thousand dollars, Ned purchased a set of lenses used on various still cameras that could be adapted to fit a 65mm motion picture camera; these would be the equivalent of the Todd-AO set of lenses that cost well into seven figures to design and construct. Todd then ordered three 65mm cameras from Mitchell to film *Don Quixote*. He told Ned to design and construct an optical printer that could be used for special effects and, most important, that could do a 35mm print-down version of the 65mm *Don Quixote* negative he was going to shoot.

Todd made no public announcements or disclosures—even to his associates, especially in the press and publicity department— that would remove all the hocus-pocus from Cinerama and Todd-AO. He was now, on the quiet, going to put together an improved version of both film techniques with the loose change in his pocket. Several years later, Bobby Gottchalk, with the help of some experts from MGM, did just what Todd was intending to do and established his Panavision company as a leading supplier of camera and other film equipment to independent producers.

Todd came back from Europe thrilled about the 35mm print-down version. Its development came at the most opportune time. Although not all of the first thirty Todd-AO engagements in the major domestic markets had opened, they had been booked, and the time had now come to make bookings for the second wave of distribution for the next hundred or so cities in the United States. The film could make a lot more money if it didn't have to help amortize the cost of a Todd-AO installation for the second-wave road-show engagements. They were all done with a print-down version on Todd-AO-sized screens, and critics and audiences alike never knew the difference.

While Mike and Elizabeth were doing Cannes, London and Paris, Sarah and I did the civilian tour, attending the openings of the picture in Toronto, Ottawa, Winnipeg, Saskatoon, Calgary, Edmonton and Vancouver.

The next order of business when Todd came back from Europe was how to commemorate the first anniversary of the opening of *80 Days*. By the time most movies are a year old, they have practically completed their theatrical distribution, but we were just starting. Mike wanted to do something for the first anniversary of *80 Days* that would attract nationwide, if not worldwide, attention. Guy Biondi relates:

> We all knew that Mike was working on some big idea for the first anniversary. Soon the word got out that his plan was to throw a gigantic block party in front of the Rivoli. He called a meeting and announced that some high city officials were about to give him permission for closing off Broadway, but we probably wouldn't get their full cooperation and he wanted to have an alternate idea. I suggested that we have a party at the Palisades Amusement Park. "It was a great thing you had in England, Mike—the party at Battersea Park got big space everywhere." He just jumped all over me— how could I be such a stupid so-and-so, you never go back, you can't do it again—he just laid me out. "No, we've got to have another idea."
>
> There were several suggestions that Mike quickly dismissed and suddenly he pointed to me and said, "Guy's wrong . . . but he's right. We've got to have a party, and we've got to have a big place for the party. Look . . . it's simple, we've used the expression all our lives: 'We had so many people show up that we could have filled . . .'" We all turned and looked at each other, and then Mike said it . . . "Madison Square Garden!"

Mike told everyone: "It's just a little private affair. I'm only going to invite eighteen thousand of my closest and most intimate friends." Word about the party quickly circulated—it was an event that captured people's imagination.

Our offices were in the United Artists Building at Forty-ninth Street and Seventh Avenue. We installed a dozen additional telephone lines, and from Labor Day on, from eight in the morning until nine or ten at night, it could take two or three hours, if you were lucky, to get a call into our office. For the two weeks prior to the party, the lobby and the street in front of the building were so jammed with people wanting tickets that the building had to put on extra guards to get the people who worked there through the crowds and into an elevator. Bill Doll received a wire the day of the party that read: BILL WHY HAVE YOU FORSAKEN ME. I MUST GET TWO TICKETS. HARRY. Bill never did figure out who the forsaken Harry was and had the telegram framed and hung in his office.

Todd was paid $175,000 by CBS for the rights to televise the party, preempting their top-rated drama series, "Playhouse 90." Walter Cronkite narrated the event, backed up by a team of assistants that made it seem like a national political convention. Vincent Korda temporarily put aside his work on *Don Quixote* to decorate the Garden and add a few sage comments to the management of the affair.

Lenny Gaines had been released by Eddie Fisher for temporary emergency duty to assist Todd with the staging of the party. He describes his participation in the event:

At the end of August in New York, Mike said, "All right, you go to work for me here." I promoted the dancers. I got fifty Willys Jeeps. We painted them white to carry in all the food. We had chocolate-covered ants, grasshoppers, everything. We had the Dancing Waters on the floor. It got to be the hottest ticket there ever was. This was the old Garden, and guys in the street were offering me five hundred dollars for a pair of good seats. Mike would phone in to see how things were going. I went out and hired five hundred people to ride on horses—kids from Greenwich Village, friends of mine. Most of them had never seen a horse before. I got the costumes for them. Mike said, "That's great, you're a genius." The next time I'd tell him something else on the phone, and he'd say, "Forget it, you're an idiot." Nobody knew what was happening. Mike didn't show up until three days before. It was a complete shambles. First thing, when Mike walks in, Art Cohn, the writer, says, "I don't want my name on it." I held up my hand and said, "Put my name on it." Everything was up in the air. We're in the offices in the U.A. Building, and in comes Cronkite and Byron Palmer, the director, and all the crew from CBS. They all want out. Nobody knows what the show is. Mike rolls up his sleeves and says, "Here's what happens. The Mummers come in first. Bam! Then the Danbury State Fair comes in. Boom! We got the folk dancers and Humphrey. Then the elephants there, and other parade here. We got this! We got that! And then Elizabeth cuts the cake." Everyone got excited. "It's terrific!" "Wow!" "It's sensational!" "There's never been anything like it!" I didn't think that Mike remembered or knew anything, and he lays it all out like we've been preparing it for a year. Everyone could see the whole thing. When they left, Mike turns to me and says, "What is it we got, Lenny?"

Chaotic situations and near panic on the part of collaborators had always been Todd's ideal set of working conditions. But catering and entertaining a party for eighteen thousand people on national prime-time television—with over a thousand entertainers, dozens of animals, three orchestras and numerous marching bands, and with only a tentative running order set the day before and a partial rehearsal on the afternoon of the event—was a bit much, even for him.

One of Todd's ideas in line with the *Around the World* theme was to assemble a floorful of amateur folk dancers. To lend a touch of class and significance to the gathering, he had asked his friend Senator Hubert Humphrey to come up from Washington to make a few brief remarks on the America-as-the-melting-pot theme at the conclusion of the folk dancing.

Senator Humphrey showed up at the Garden in the middle of what approximated the only rehearsal—five hours before the start of the party. Todd was besieged on all sides by people wanting to know what, when and how to do their part of the show and especially by the television production team, who were threatening to quit unless they were given some vague notion as to what specifically was to happen that evening. Elizabeth was watching Todd, supremely confident that he would be able to assemble a three-hour spectacle in the course of one brief afternoon. I was at his side, trying to be of some help but doubtful that he was going to pull this one off. Someone in the press department recognized Humphrey and brought him over to my father. They greeted each other jovially. Before Humphrey could really absorb the full state of panic surrounding us and think of some pressing legislative duties that would require his presence back in Washington, Todd put his arm around him and headed for the Forty-eighth Street exit, motioning Elizabeth and me to follow. He steered us across the street to a seedy little hotel that catered to the lesser circus and rodeo performers. I knew Senator Humphrey and had said hello to him. Todd did one of his usual one-way introductions, saying to Humphrey, "You know my bride, Elizabeth, don't you?" In the coffee shop he briefly indicated the staging of the folk dancing that would precede the senator's speech.

To get a temperature reading, Humphrey started to try out his speech on us. Elizabeth was totally confused as to what was going on and wondering why Mike had left the arena, where his presence was urgently required. In the middle of Humphrey's proposed speech, Elizabeth looked up from her coffee with dismay. I could see she didn't think much of it. I gave her ankle a gentle rap with my shoe. She gave me a confused look, and then interrupted Senator Humphrey. "You can't say anything like that—it's too corny." I gave Elizabeth a sharp kick in the shin. Mike somehow turned Elizabeth's remark into what he made out to be a running family joke. Largely reassured, Humphrey finished his speech. The hasty cover-up and my kick kept Elizabeth silent, although perplexed, for the remainder of the meeting. We said good-bye to Senator Humphrey on Forty-eighth Street, where a limousine was waiting to take him back to his hotel, and Mike rushed back into the Garden. Following behind, Elizabeth asked, "What was the kick for?" I explained who Humphrey was and said that you couldn't tell a leading member of the Senate Foreign Relations Committee what kind of a speech he should make about international understanding and goodwill.

"Well, nobody told me who he was, and besides, it *is* a corny speech." Guy Biondi recalls:

> I'll never forget walking into the Garden the night of the party. Anybody who had ever been to a fight or a basketball game was just stunned. It looked like a magic wonderland. The money Vincent Korda had spent was all hanging in the

air. The whole arena was transformed overnight. It was fantastic. And nine thousand men in tuxedos. Formal dress was required, and no one got in without a dinner jacket. There wasn't a tuxedo left to rent in all of New York City.

Todd correctly surmised that the program would require a great deal of improvisation and instant decision making and that he should remain on the floor and act as his own ringmaster. His adrenaline was really flowing as we entered the Eighth Avenue entrance of the Garden, with photographers' flashing bulbs popping all around us. The marquee carried the legend CLOSED FOR A LITTLE PRIVATE PARTY TONIGHT. Todd escorted Elizabeth to her seat and I trailed behind. Unfortunately, not far enough behind; Elizabeth was wearing an off-the-shoulder velvet evening gown with a short train, which, in my nervous anxiety, I carelessly stepped on, partially severing the gown at the waist. Showing the strain of the pressure he was under, Mike snapped at me, unnecessarily pointing out how clumsy I had been. Much to my relief, Elizabeth found the incident amusing. Midori fortunately had a sufficient supply of safety pins in her purse to repair the damage. With a scowl of nervous apprehension, Mike set off for the floor of the Garden to take up his managerial tasks. There was still a tranquil scene inside, but outside a couple of thousand would-be gate-crashers in tuxedos were trying to slip past the gate attendants.

The first ominous sign of trouble was when we discovered that the five thousand bottles of champagne we had promoted were being peddled by the waiters at five dollars a pop, instead of being distributed gratis. When the lights dimmed and the show began, on time, surprisingly, things went relatively smoothly. Early in the program, though, was the Mummers Parade. The sound of scores of banjos, their outrageously flamboyant outfits and strutting style were a spectacle that captured everyone's attention and provided entertainment of a sort, but enough is enough. Their lead group started to head around for a second tour of the Garden. Todd, who was trying to direct the show and traffic from near the Forty-ninth Street exit, started jumping up and down, screaming, "Off! Off! Get those Mummers off!" Lenny Gaines, who was acting as the assistant on the floor, reported later that one of the lead Mummers shouted: "Screw you, sweetie, we dragged our asses all the way in from Philadelphia, and we're going around twice." Strumming their banjos and flouncing their ostrich feathers, they made their second circuit of the arena.

Fortunately for CBS and thirty-five million television viewers, most of the marchers, dancers and other elements of the parades and pageants had done their individual bits many times before. So with cutaways for commercials, commentary and interviews with guests, it seemed to be a hell of a party, or at least a fascinating disaster. The CBS-TV special got one of the highest Nielsen ratings of the year. In the Garden the proceedings seemed more ponderous and disjointed. At the conclusion of the "entertainment" Elizabeth was supposed to draw the winners of the dozen top door prizes—a Cessna airplane, a trip to Europe for two, a motorboat and trailer. This was to be followed by a buffet and dancing on the floor of the Garden. As the food was being driven in and Duke Ellington was beginning his dance music, some of Todd's "intimate and closest friends" leaped onto the arena floor and fought each other to carry off any of the prizes that they could grab. I escorted Elizabeth down to Todd, where she was supposed to make the prize draw. However, a brouhaha of epic proportions was in progress. Mike turned away from a stunned Lenny Gaines, who was standing at his side, and motioned Elizabeth and me to follow him. Lenny says:

> Mike starts walking away and all hell's breaking loose, and he turns and throws some keys up to me and says, "Here, kid, lock up." I am standing there with these keys, watching him disappear into the crowd, and I shout, "Lock *what* up?"
>
> I was begging Ellington to play the "Star Spangled Banner," but he said, "The man is paying me for the gig and I'm gonna play." When the mob got right up to the bandstand, he started to get frightened and quit. It looked like all these guys wearing tuxedos were gonna rip the Garden apart. They almost did. Big-time agents were carrying motorcycles out. I had these two detectives with me and without them I'd have never gotten out of there alive.

When we got back to the apartment, there was a continual stream of telephone calls from friends reporting their impressions of the party. While the returns were coming in, Elizabeth, Mike and I had a couple of stiff drinks. For those in the Garden the party was a flop and for those watching it on TV it was a qualified success. It turned out that Todd was the unexpected star and comic relief of the show; the TV director had used zoom close-ups of him shouting, jumping up and down and waving his fists trying to keep the show moving. He gulped down two more drinks and cheerfully reached the conclusion, "So I threw a lousy party. If they didn't like it, they don't have to come to my next one." Later, he blamed the failure of the party on Art Buchwald:

> Art was coming over from Paris, and a few of us boys decided to get together and throw him a party. Well, Jack Harris called up and said, "Do you mind if I bring so-and-so." And then Irving Hoffman said, "Gee, I've got to bring these guys that are in from Hollywood." And before you know it we had thirty or forty people. So we decided to make a guest list. With Elizabeth's relatives alone, I figured we were going to have quite a few added starters. So then Buchwald called up and said, "Gee whiz, Mike, that's Thursday night, the seventeenth, can't you change it? My aunt from Brooklyn has already bought a chicken and she doesn't have a deep freeze." Well, the next thing you know, we wound up with eighteen thousand and I had to hire the Garden. And it taught me a lesson—seventeen thousand five hundred okay, but eighteen thousand gets unwieldy.

Todd had been sending Art friendly insults by telegram for years. Buchwald saved money by returning the insults in his column in the Paris *Herald Tribune.* Or if Todd was not too far away he would return a wire and charge it to the paper:

> MIKE TODD
> VILLA FLORENTINA
> CAP FERRAT
> LEAVING FOR TWO WEEK TRIP. IN MY ABSENCE PLEASE SEND ALL TELEGRAMS TO MY SON JOEL.
> REGARDS.
> ART BUCHWALD
> NYHT 21 RUE DE BERRI
> PARIS 8

A week later, Todd sent a letter with a package to all the newspaper people and friends who had gone to the party. "It has come to my attention that not everybody I invited to that little party I had last week had an enjoyable evening. Just in case you are one of those that didn't, I enclose the following Do-It-Yourself Party Kit. Have fun." The package contained a bottle of vintage French champagne, swizzle sticks, party hats, noise-makers, confetti and so forth.

The film was still playing to near capacity in the largest cities in the country. After the party, however, business shot up 15 to 25 percent in the smaller cities, so that practically all the engagements were selling out again. Business was booming and stayed at this boosted level throughout the balance of the year.

With his continuing avalanche of prosperity, Mike put off getting down to serious work on *Don Quixote*. Jule Styne describes a dinner party that took place at this time:

> It started out with me inviting Frank Sinatra, who was going with Betty Bacall at the time, out for a nice, quiet dinner. Frank said, "Well . . . you know . . . going with Betty . . . I'd like to make it more than a quiet dinner . . . I'd like to have someone else talking or else it gets too serious between her and me." Well, Mike was in town with Liz, so I called him and said, "Do you want to have dinner tonight?" He said, "Oh, terrific." All right, so now the cast is Sinatra and Bacall and Mike and Liz. Mike called back an hour later and said, "Do me a favor, Jule. Eddie's having trouble with Debbie. I'd like to take the kids along—maybe it'll help a little bit." So I tell Frank, and he says, "Oh Jeesus, Eddie Fisher." I said, "Look, do it for Mike." Frank says, "Okay, but sit Fisher on the other side." So there we were at the Beach-comber's. . . . First there was a great confrontation between Sinatra and Bacall. In the middle of it, my girl turns to Frank and says, "You'd be lucky to marry her." Well, that's the last thing Frank wants to hear, and I give my girl a nudge, but immediately Frank hates me and my date. Next thing there's a big hassle between Eddie and Debbie, and they're carrying on across the table from each other. And Mike, trying to settle it down, says, "Come on, Debbie, Eddie's a nice kid." In the meanwhile, Liz is irritated because she's being ignored and sitting in the middle of this battlefield, and she tells Mike to mix out. Mike turns to me in a stage whisper and says, "Thanks, Jule, this is a wonderful idea. We ought to make it a regular weekly event."

Todd and Elizabeth took two extended trips during the winter of 1957–58, first to the Far East, returning in December to spend the holidays with the family, and then a leisurely trip to Europe, with the main stop Moscow. They attended the openings of *80 Days* in Hawaii, Australia, Hong Kong and Tokyo on the first trip. Ostensibly, the main purpose of the second trip was to sell the picture to the Russians.

When Mike and Elizabeth flew to the Far East, Vincent Korda went back to Spain to continue reconnoitering for *Don Quixote*. Todd had made an arrangement with Benny Thau, a senior Metro executive and old poker buddy and friend of his, for Elizabeth to wind up her contractual obligations to MGM by doing *Cat on a Hot Tin Roof* when they returned from Europe in March. When Elizabeth started work, he intended to begin in earnest on the preproduction work on *Don Quixote*. He had announced that he was going to start shooting the picture in the late spring or early summer, by any reckoning an impossible date. Other than Fernandel playing the title role and Elizabeth playing the small part of Sancho Panza's slatternly, shrewish wife, his casting ideas changed from day to day. There was some thought of Mario playing Sancho Panza, but then he switched, and I was not alone in strongly opposing his idea of casting Mickey Rooney as Sancho Panza, which only reinforced his feeling that Rooney in this role would arouse interest and prove to be a disarmingly apt choice. Even the logical selection of Gary Cooper in the title role was talked about. Pursuant to his "superstition" that you shouldn't get too far along on a project without a script, he put Art Cohn and me to work preparing a comprehensive treatment of *Don Quixote*.

Art had been a sports writer, editor and columnist for various California newspapers. He became a screenwriter with over a dozen credits and wrote the best-selling Joe E. Lewis biography *The Joker Is Wild,* for which he also wrote the screenplay. Frank Sinatra played the lead in the successful movie. Todd so enjoyed the book that he gave Art a call to tell him so. They met a few times subsequently and became friends, so they decided it might not be a bad idea if Art wrote a biography of Todd. It was almost finished when Todd went to the Far East with Elizabeth.

Mike decided that it would be better for the children, and for Elizabeth, who was still recovering from Liza's birth and the previous year's back operation, not to spend the winter in the cold and snowy East. He rented a large house in Palm Springs and had me, Sarah and our two kids come West, where I could start the *Don Quixote* treatment with Art. The Cohns, my family, Liza and the Wilding boys all settled into the house in Palm Springs.

In Cincinnati, Syracuse and several other cities, we had opened our first-run road-show engagements of *80 Days* in new shopping center theaters, the first film to play a major first-run engagement a considerable distance from the downtown theater district. Todd was impressed that these engagements were doing as well or better than those in downtown houses, which had much higher overhead costs. He decided that we should try to make more shopping center deals. Guy Biondi says:

> Bill Doll showed Mike a *Time* magazine cover story about Henry J. Kaiser, one of the nation's leading industrialists, who had just built a Buckminster Fuller–designed geodesic dome to demonstrate the versatility of aluminum, of which he was a major manufacturer. The cover had a picture of the dome, and Bill brought it in to Mike and asked, "What do you think of that?" Mike said, "Hey, that's something," and shouted out to Midori to get Henry Kaiser on the phone. It took a few minutes, but Mike was still keyed up when the call came through. I could hear him saying, Henry, we can do this and we can do that. It'll revolutionize the theater business. Next thing I hear Mike say: "No, no. I'm not in Hawaii—I'm in New York." And then he made a date to see Kaiser. Mike hangs up and says, "I'll get twenty of them. Twenty of them around the world. My own domes."

Todd's friend, Pat Weaver, the former president of NBC, was a consultant to Kaiser. Todd got in touch with Weaver and together they ad-libbed dozens of ways to book a shopping center dome in between road-show performances of a film.

Although Buckminster Fuller is a respected, even revered, name in architecture, he didn't mean a lot to the general public. Frank Lloyd Wright was flamboyant and always attracted attention. Arrangements were made for Wright to join the meeting in New York with Kaiser, Weaver and Todd.

Herman Odell went to the meeting as Todd's attorney:

> It was held in a suite at the Plaza Hotel, and from the start Wright held center stage. He demanded total autonomy in designing the settings and decor for the geodesic domes. Mike could see that Kaiser wasn't reacting favorably, but

Mike was confident he could handle both Kaiser and Wright once he got them in bed together. He interrupted Wright in the middle of one of his flowing descriptions of what he would create by saying, "Frank, you're the biggest ham actor in the world. We'll work this all out when we get the basis for a deal set." After the meeting a phone conversation indicated that Kaiser wasn't buying Wright's ideas, but he did buy *80 Days* to launch the geodesic dome he had built next to a new hotel he had constructed in Hawaii.

The Todds' first stop on their way to the Far East was Honolulu. The visit was to publicize the opening of *80 Days* and the new dome's use as a theater, and for Todd it was going to be the linchpin in a deal with Kaiser to set up a worldwide network of Kaiser-Todd dome theaters. Kaiser personally escorted Elizabeth and Todd to the Presidential Suite in his new hotel. Todd was a little put out that his potential partner insisted that all the press parties and opening-night celebrations be held at the hotel. It was his first trip to Hawaii, and he would have liked to have had one of the bashes at a top Polynesian restaurant. Todd expected Kaiser to pick up part of the tab for these events, as they wound up providing more publicity for the hotel and theater than for the premiere of *80 Days,* and at the very least he expected some sort of favorable rate for the suite. When presented with a full tab for everything except the complimentary basket of fruit, he decided that Kaiser was not a kindred spirit. Todd forgot about owning twenty geodesic domes.

In Palm Springs Art and I were turning out about five pages of the treatment a day. I was eager to bowl my father over with the completed outline by the time he returned. With two weeks' notice I had somehow plowed through four English translations of the lengthy Cervantes classic. The book is episodic and has little narrative flow, but I had formulated a rough continuity of what I thought were the key episodes.

Art was friendly and cooperative but experienced enough to realize that at the very best we were creating only a basic framework. At my insistence we included some sizable portions of dialogue, along with a scene-by-scene description of the story and characterizations as we saw them—or rather, largely as I thought they should be. At the time, I thought Art was dragging his feet, even though he conscientiously put in about six hours with me every day. In retrospect, I can see that we were working in a vacuum until the Master delineated the lines along which he saw the property being developed. Art indicated we were getting into too much detail but that possibly there was a bright spot here and there that might prove useful later. I felt we were putting together an orderly synthesis of Cervantes's sprawling novel; Art did not seem to share my illusion.

Todd and Elizabeth made big news every stop on their trip, not all of it complimentary. The Australian press was offended when at a banquet Mike leaned across in front of the prime minister, Robert Menzies, to kiss Elizabeth. Tokyo was one of the few places in the world where *80 Days* was not a gigantic success. Either the humor escaped the Japanese or, more likely, as United Artists explained, Japan was the one place where traditions counted in all areas of life, even moviegoing. Roadshowing a motion picture was a new idea and obviously not understood or accepted. It was the one place where old customs did not bow to Todd's concepts.

During their European trip Todd made his third trip to Moscow in four years. Elizabeth says:

> It was the first time in my life I'd been completely anonymous, although people were staring at me, but it was because of my mink coat and my knee-high, fur-lined red leather boots—which you'd think wouldn't be a novelty in Russia. But I must have had the only pair in the country, from the way they all stared. When people came over to our interpreter, they asked if I was a ballerina—the height of Russian glamour. They stared at my hairdo, which had just been done in Paris, and my jewels, but otherwise I was ignored and Mike was the center of attention. He was on some "secret mission" for the State Department that he could never tell me about. He was always going for walks with our ambassador, because the U.S. Embassy was bugged. Mike met with the minister of culture and other big-shot Russian officials. I rarely got a chance to say anything anywhere we traveled, but in Russia the only chance I had to talk was in our hotel room, where we made up long, silly conversations to amuse ourselves and befuddle the eavesdroppers on the other end of the bugs.

Todd never gave me any details about his "secret mission" either, but it may not have been a coincidence that their interpreter was the translator who accompanied Khrushchev on his trips to the United States and to the meeting in Vienna with President Kennedy. In 1956, on his previous trip to Moscow, he had had a top-level meeting that the State Department was most interested in. This was during one of his final kiss-and-make-up flings with Evelyn. Because of visa problems Evelyn had arrived late and missed the May Day parade and Mike's big meeting a few days earlier with B & K—Bulganin, then premier, and Khrushchev, then first secretary of the Communist Party. The minister of culture must have found Todd extremely interesting and amusing—Todd had no idea why he was invited to the Kremlin to meet the bosses of the Soviet Union. It turned out B & K's interest in Todd was political. They were curious to hear from an ordinary United States citizen whether Stevenson had a chance of being renominated and defeating Eisenhower. Todd told them he knew and liked Stevenson, but that the American public distrusted anyone who was too intellectual and sophisticated. This meeting took place two days before May Day. When the interview was ending, he spoke up and said that he didn't want to "stage-manage" Russian affairs, but they had a worldwide peace campaign going on, with Picasso doves and gigantic amounts of money and effort being spent trying to convince the world that the Russians were interested in peace, while the biggest show they put on annually, their May Day parade, destroyed their whole sales pitch with an endless line of weapons and soldiers. The translator fearfully repeated Todd's criticism and was not reassured by the stunned silence from B & K that followed his translation. Mike wasn't too sure himself whether he was about to be unceremoniously booted out of Russia after an icy good-bye from B & K. However, he was given a V.I.P. seat on the reviewing stand, and to the surprise of commentators around the world, that year's parade had the most abbreviated display of military hardware of any May Day celebration. No new weapons were revealed, and in a five-hour-long parade with several hundred thousand marchers, only a small percentage were in military uniform and the display of old weapons lasted only thirty-five minutes. That May Day parade featured dancing peasants and children with flowers instead of guns, soldiers and missiles.

On the trip to Moscow with Elizabeth, Todd was indignant about the trifling sum offered for *80 Days* to play in the Soviet Union. He stuffed himself with their caviar and rejected the offer.

On their Far Eastern tour, he and Elizabeth had gone on a buying spree in Hong Kong and returned bearing huge bundles of gifts. The next day he showed me half a dozen elegant Swiss watches he had bought for the men at the top of his Christmas list. He spread them out and told me to take my pick. I selected an ultra thin, very plain Audemars, Piguet. He asked me if I was sure that was the one I wanted. I said it was positively my first choice. He demurred, saying that he had it really in mind for Eddie Fisher, but if I was sure, it was mine.

I never saw Mike happier or more content than when he and Elizabeth returned to Palm Springs. She was on top of the world as well. Whatever period of adjustment every marriage requires had already passed by this time. They were relaxed and delighted with each other and themselves. There had been frequent stories and pictures of their spats, but he often said, "Liz and I have more fun fighting than most people have making love." In my view their fights—and they did have them—were a form of game playing that, among other things, was an expression of their supreme confidence in themselves and their relationship. It has been said before, but I think it was true, that Elizabeth often provoked him for the pleasure of seeing him exert his dominance over her. His attitude was, "If that's what you want, that's what I'll give you." But by the time they had returned to Palm Springs the game was largely over, except for the occasional reprieve, when things got a little dull. And being a father again was his greatest pleasure. He reveled in holding and playing with Liza.

Elizabeth did not have a great education and is not analytical. She reacts quickly and instinctively to the people she meets and the situations she finds herself in. Having been an actress almost all her life, she unconsciously plays roles off screen. These roles complement the personalities and attitudes of the people with whom she is most deeply involved. Basically, she was and is a warmhearted, thoughtful and loving person, but because of her background she also can be spoiled and self-centered. For the more than twenty-five years I have known her, she has always had a lively sense of humor and a high-spirited sense of fun. She has the courage, nerve and ability to get what she wants and sooner or later to overcome any obstacles to her happiness. These attributes are a constant in her personality, and they matched and complemented my father's similar traits. By the time she and Mike had completed their long trips, he had already largely cajoled, reasoned and shouted away the negative aspects of her personality. I believe their marriage would have improved with age, barring a sustained period of failure in Todd's business career. If my father decided to make something work and put his belief in a person, he was a limitless source of strength and love. He and Elizabeth made each other tremendously happy and comfortable. If any couple ever had the ability to spread a lot of sunshine for themselves and others, it was Todd and Elizabeth. He once said, "You know, a lot of boys grow up and they want to become President of the United States. With me, I just wanted to grow up and marry Elizabeth Taylor, and I did." It was one of his better jokes, but in a very real sense it was true.

Several days after his return to the States, my father gave me a nasty shock, which at the time I couldn't help but take personally. Art and I had almost finished our outline for *Don Quixote*, which ran to about 160 pages. I thought it was a considerable accomplishment, since we had had only five weeks to work on it. His first day back I mentioned the outline in passing, giving him the chance to get at least one good night's rest before tackling it. The next day I presented it to him and pressed him to start reading it that night. The following morning I eagerly awaited his reaction. He was evasive at breakfast, but I was too pleased with the job we had done to settle for anything less than a detailed critique. He ducked my questions, but I insisted on getting a clear-cut opinion from him. Finally, after I cornered him that afternoon, he said, "I don't want to hurt your feelings, but I only read the first three pages, and it's all wrong." I was outraged. "How can you judge one hundred sixty pages by just the first three . . . what's wrong with it?" He said, "Excuse me for a minute."

He went into his bedroom and brought out a large package that contained the first set of sketches Vincent Korda had sent him from Spain. On top was a rough watercolor of Don Quixote on horseback, lance lowered, approaching a hill with several windmills on it, behind which the sun was setting. It was possible to see how, in the fast-falling dusk, Quixote could mistake the windmills, as Vincent had depicted them, as menacing knights in armor. Trailing behind Quixote on his donkey was Sancho Panza, and with a few simple brush strokes, Vincent had portrayed Sancho Panza's state of resigned apprehension. My father showed me a few more of the sketches, illustrating how

Vincent saw some other major incidents in the story being filmed. The sketches conveyed a feeling of humor and warmth. Mike said, "Here is my script. This is the picture I want to make."

While I admired Vincent's sketches, I was still deeply offended and couldn't grasp how Mike intended to proceed without some words on paper. I said, "The least you can do, after all the work Art and I have put in, is read through the entire outline before dismissing it." I had really dragged Art in by the heels, both in my argument with Todd and on the entire endeavor. Art had correctly anticipated that it was premature to start work on a comprehensive outline before Todd had refined his own concepts.

I went back to New York a few days later with Sarah and the children, confused and a bit put out with my father. He was the boss, and *Don Quixote* was his project, but at the time I couldn't understand his approach to getting it going.

While I was in New York minding the store, Mike and Art had some discussions on the coast about a script for *Don Quixote*— without, I am sure, any further reference to the treatment.

A year earlier my father had taken a long-term lease on a Lockheed Lodestar, the same type of aircraft that Howard Hughes had flown around the world on a record-breaking trip in 1939. Herman Odell and I tried then to talk him out of it as a needless extravagance.

Herman and I unsuccessfully prodded him to get rid of the plane in late 1957, when a survey indicated that because of its age—even with the thorough maintenance it received that kept it up to F.A.A. standards—its safety was questionable. It was very expensive to maintain, and while it was still only in the offing, the imminent use of jet aircraft for commercial travel would soon make the Lodestar obsolete for anything but a short hop.

The Friars Club was staging a testimonial dinner on Sunday night, March 23, in Todd's honor, and there was an accumulation of business matters that needed his attention in New York. Elizabeth had a heavy cold, and while she very much wanted to make the trip and attend the banquet, she had started work on *Cat on a Hot Tin Roof* and couldn't hang around New York while her husband was working. She also needed to recuperate from her cold so that she could resume work during the week.

They both reluctantly agreed that Elizabeth should remain in California.

Ostensibly to talk about *Don Quixote*, but undoubtedly mostly for his company, Todd asked Art Cohn to fly to New York with him. Art agreed.

Herman Odell phoned me early Sunday morning at my home in Croton to tell me that my father, Art Cohn and the crew had all been killed a few hours earlier in New Mexico, where the plane had crashed, trying to fly through a storm.

Final Words

There was a heavy snowfall in New York the weekend my father died. The hilly long road I lived on was impassable. Being snowbound gave me the isolation I needed to try to pull myself together. I decided my father would have most liked to be buried next to his father and asked my Uncle Dave and Herman Odell to arrange for the funeral to be held in Chicago. Sarah took all the other phone calls, but I spoke to Elizabeth to tell her about the funeral arrangements and to say what I could to her. She was in a largely incoherent state.

Howard Hughes provided Elizabeth with a TWA Constellation to fly to Chicago. Sarah and I met her at the airport. She was in a state of shock that approached paralysis. After a few minutes of tearful embraces, I tried to talk to her in a controlled manner about mundane matters. At first she registered disbelief that I could start an ordinary conversation at such a time, but then she made an attempt to respond.

The funeral was an agonizing ordeal, and only Colonel Gottlieb's help in obtaining the cooperation of the local police forces prevented us from being totally swamped by thousands of curiosity seekers and hundreds of journalists. Elizabeth's brother Howard and her doctor, Rex Kennamer, felt that she could identify more closely with me than with anyone else; the nearest she had come to facing the reality of death had been in my presence. They asked me if I would go back to California with Elizabeth. I told Sarah and Herman Odell that I would be back in New York in a week.

Elizabeth was in a totally uncontrollable state for all but the briefest periods during the first days after my father's death. She asked me if Kathryn Baltimore, who she felt would be of some comfort to her, could come to California for a while, Kathryn flew out the next day. One morning Kathryn confided to me that every night she dreamed that my father returned to the apartment at 715 Park Avenue and when she met him with surprise at the door he would tell her, "You silly nigger. You thought I was dead, didn't you? I was just lying low till I got a few things straightened out." Several years later she told me that she continued to have the same dream. I had the same kind of dream regularly for fifteen years. After a week Kathryn said she was not doing all that much in California, she had a family to care for and wanted to go back to New York. I explained the situation to Elizabeth, and Kathryn went home.

Elizabeth and I never left the house for ten days. Howard and Mara decided a change of scene might be beneficial, so we all went to visit a longtime friend of theirs, Arthur Loew, Jr., at a ranch he had in Arizona. Arthur has a great sense of humor, and Elizabeth on occasion was able to laugh at some of his jokes. The total change of atmosphere in Arizona was a first big step for Elizabeth in coming to grips with the fact that she had a life to lead without my father. It was obvious to me that Arthur was more than just fond of her. On a couple of occasions, in an effort to get Elizabeth to relax, Arthur massaged her feet. Although she made no comment, I felt that Elizabeth interpreted these foot massages as subtle sexual advances, and she became rather uneasy about our stay in Arizona. We returned to the house in Beverly Hills.

It was a step backwards. Elizabeth relapsed into a state of near hysteria. Several times every night she called out to me. When I came into her room she would be crying and fighting against the fact of his death—just as Kathryn and I were doing in our dreams. But awake Elizabeth would say: "Mike can't be dead. I don't believe it."

I was very uncomfortable and thought my presence was no longer helping her to reconcile herself to my father's death, nor was it improving my state of mind. Several weeks had gone by since the funeral. I phoned Sarah and asked her to come out and join me for a few days before we returned to New York together. It was my way of telling Elizabeth that I had to get back to picking up my life. Elizabeth resumed the filming of *Cat on a Hot Tin Roof* shortly after Sarah and I left.

I kept in close touch with Elizabeth, who made a very slow

but steady recovery. One weekend in September she phoned me at home. She told me she was at Grossinger's with Eddie Fisher and that she had something important to talk to me about, and would I come up and have dinner with her. The three of us had a pleasant evening and towards the end of the meal Eddie excused himself from the table. When we were alone, Elizabeth looked at me with a fearful expression and said, "I have to tell you about Eddie." Totally misreading her, I said, "Is he being a nuisance and making passes at you?" "No! No!" she gasped in horror. Taking a deep breath, she said, "You don't understand. We're in love and we want to get married. We'd like your approval." Embarrassed, but pleased to have a chance to recover, I said, "Of course. I'm delighted." I liked Eddie, although I didn't think he had a lot upstairs, and I was best man at their wedding eight months later.

Others who know Elizabeth well feel, as I do, that she is able to immerse herself in any role, on screen or off. She can adapt to any situation and follows through with conviction and authority. During her marriage to Richard Burton she found herself surrounded by a group of hard-drinking yarn spinners. With liquor, Elizabeth is more than a match for anybody. I have never known anyone who can better hold their drink, and I've never seen her drunk. After a full day and night of drinking with Richard, and after only three hours of sleep, she would look as fresh and glamorous as ever, while Richard, I and the rest of the group looked bedraggled and wrung out. Richard is extremely competitive and something of a male chauvinist to boot. Having started the ball rolling, Richard almost drank himself into oblivion, in a futile attempt to keep up with Elizabeth. She became more than he was able to cope with. When Richard puts his mind—which is a good one—and his personality—which can be strong and fascinating—to work, he can accomplish almost anything. He can excel in any game he chooses to play, but often comes to realize he would rather be playing a different game.

Elizabeth has matured but not mellowed. She is her own woman, and she too can accomplish anything she sets her mind to, and there are always laughs and excitement along the way.

My father did an interview with Robert J. Levin for *Redbook* magazine the day before he died. Recently I came across a transcript of the tape of the complete interview, from which selections were taken for the published article. Well aware that he wasn't Plato, my father always called this kind of chatter "thoughts while thinking," saying that it was nothing to be "carved on Mount Rushmore." Nevertheless, he was in a rather reflective mood and expressed his views on some matters that were important to him.

On his childhood:

> We had a happy life, but our family wasn't closely knit. I could be away for three days at a time and they didn't know I was gone. . . . We lived in a small town in Minnesota where we were the only Jewish family—they'd never seen a Jew. There wasn't anything different about us, except that my father had a beard. There was never any anti-Semitism because they never had any contact with Jews, the same way there wasn't any anti-Indian feeling. . . . I use a lot of Jewish expressions, and in all my interviews I make a point of my real name. There are people who analyze that and think I am self-conscious about being Jewish. Nothing is further from the truth. It's like with the two headshrinkers—one of them says hello, and the other says, "Wonder what he means by that?"
>
> When we lived in Bloomington, my father became a member of the community in no time. And they accepted him, beard and all. He was a great citizen, and he was a *tsadek*—a scholar. My father wanted me to go to *cheder*—Hebrew school—but he knew it would go in one ear and right out the other. He was very catholic, in the Jewish sense—*beshert*. You know what that means? Ordained. He was a poetic guy, a man with great taste. I had a great affection for my father. I had a very special relationship with him. . . . He was a mild man, not particularly meek, but mild. He was a failure in business and he had a sense of resignation about this. Which wasn't too good, you know . . . I wouldn't accept being a shoe clerk. But I do accept my origins. . . ."

On Elizabeth:

> Everyone says I spoil Liz. But the first Saturday she says, "Where's my present?"—that's when she stops getting them. [Mike made a game out of giving Elizabeth a surprise gift every Saturday during their marriage. Often something beautiful and expensive, sometimes just hokey and inexpensive.] . . . Now Liz is a girl who is unusually bright; but when

it comes to the children, she can make mistakes like everybody else. For instance, she has let it become a contest between herself and the nurse. I can't tell her this. I can tell her about her acting—I can say, "You stink." And I can tell her, "When a guy's talking, pretend you're interested—listen!" But I can't say, "Don't compete with the nurse. You're the mother. Let the children know you're the mother."

I have real patience on important things. Because she'll get around to it and see it. But she's got to be the one that discovers it, and she will. I've seen it work out that way . . . I've got confidence in Liz. This is one of the things that make our relationship so solid and secure. . . .

On his favorite son:

My son is one of the most unusual guys. He lives quietly in Croton, and he doesn't live the way he lives as a rebellion against me—don't let anyone kid you, he's got a great appreciation for our relationship, and he likes me. He'd worry if he had houses he didn't need, but he doesn't resent it in me. And me, I don't worry about it. . . .

Michael is serious about responsibilities. He could never do *Around the World* without having that week's payroll. If he didn't have the last dollar in a bank, he could never start. That is good—for him. . . .

I think that Michael's marriage is good for him. I never once said, "Michael, if I were casting for a daughter-in-law—" which I have absolutely no right to do—"it wouldn't be Sarah." Now, Sarah is all right with me, because he loves her. But I never go overboard with Sarah, because then he'd know I was a phoney. . . . Now, Michael is one of the nicest guys I've ever known. But then, I didn't spoil my son. I gave him a very modest allowance, and even then he insisted on taking less. A friend of mine gave his kid a huge allowance, and when I said something about it, he got mad and said I spent fifty times that amount in five minutes. And it's true. I could piss away a *hundred* times the amount in five minutes. But that's got nothing to do with a kid sitting in a candy store, buying everyone sodas. . . .

When Michael was at Lawrenceville, I never missed a Father's Weekend, never once. Now, this friend of mine whose boy was at Lawrenceville didn't go to Father's Day. He had good business reasons for it, but he'd have been better off at the school. Now that sounds corny, real corny. But what's more important, your business or your son? . . .

I always wanted to write, but because of my father I never had to. Over the last several years, when circumstances dictated that I start this book with Joe McCarthy, my late father-in-law, and then to really work on it and rework it and finish it, I found myself achieving my ambition to write, mostly because I had a subject that I was familiar with and enthusiastic about—my father. He was right—as he usually was: his life story was a valuable property.

INDEX